NEWSHAWKS
IN BERLIN

NEWSHAWKS IN BERLIN

THE ASSOCIATED PRESS AND
NAZI GERMANY

LARRY HEINZERLING
AND RANDY HERSCHAFT
WITH ANN COOPER

Columbia University Press *New York*

Columbia University Press
Publishers Since 1893
New York   Chichester, West Sussex
cup.columbia.edu

Copyright © 2024 Ann Cooper and Randy Herschaft
All rights reserved

Library of Congress Cataloging-in-Publication Data

Names: Heinzerling, Larry, 1945–2021, author. | Herschaft, Randy, author.
Title: Newshawks in Berlin : the Associated Press and Nazi Germany / Larry Heinzerling and Randy Herschaft.
Description: New York : Columbia University Press, 2024. | Includes bibliographical references and index.
Identifiers: LCCN 2023032984 (print) | ISBN 9780231217170 (paperback) | LCCN 2023032985 (ebook) | ISBN 9780231210188 (hardback) | ISBN 9780231558310 (ebook)
Subjects: LCSH: Associated Press—History. | AP German Picture Service—History. | Foreign correspondents—Germany—Berlin—History—20th century. | National Socialism—Press coverage. | Germany—Politics and government—1918–1933—Press coverage. | Press and politics—Germany—History—20th century. | Press and politics—United States—History—20th century. | Holocaust, Jewish (1939–1945)—Press coverage—United States. | Associated Press GmbH
Classification: LCC PN4841.A85 H45 2024 (print) | LCC PN4841.A85 (ebook) | DDC 070.4/35—dc23/eng/20230907
LC record available at https://lccn.loc.gov/2023032984
LC ebook record available at https://lccn.loc.gov/2023032985

Cover design: Noah Arlow
Cover images: Wisconsin Historical Society, WHI-(157925) (*top*), Alamy Photo (*bottom*)

To all who seek to bring truth out of dark places

And to Larry (1945–2021)

In war, truth is the first casualty.

—variously attributed to many, from ancient Greek dramatist Aeschylus to Senator Hiram Johnson

War is hell and the reporting of this war is growing tougher and tougher. We have had to do a great many things that we didn't like to do. I don't think any responsible reporter or editor is going to come through all of it without something on his conscience.

—AP executive editor Byron Price, July 17, 1941

CONTENTS

Foreword xi
ANN COOPER

Introduction 1

I LONG SHADOWS

1 Kristallnacht 11
2 "It Is More Important for Us to Remain in the Field" 25
3 The News Bureau 41
4 The GmbH 53
5 First They Came for the Jews 63

II AT WAR

6 Poland 81
7 Blitzkrieg 101
8 Lochner Under Fire 113
9 Photo Blitz 129

10 The Nazi Photographer 139
11 Operation Barbarossa 155
12 Berlin at War 167
13 "We Leave for the Jug" 175

III THE PHOTO DEAL

14 "Close Your Juice Shop" 197
15 Büro Laux 209

IV RECKONINGS

16 Unveiling the Holocaust 219
17 The Collapse 243
Epilogue 263

Acknowledgments 275
Notes 279
Bibliography 325
Index 331

FOREWORD

ANN COOPER

In March 2022 Russia decreed that anyone using the word "war" to describe its so-called special military operation in Ukraine would be fined or imprisoned. Similar punishment awaited those who "discredited" the Russian military. Censorship was nothing new in Vladimir Putin's Russia, but now it had become so draconian that hundreds of local and foreign journalists fled the country, including Moscow-based correspondents for the Associated Press (AP), the *New York Times*, and other Western news organizations that had maintained bureaus in the Russian capital for decades.

Russia in 2022 was but the latest example of foreign correspondents in an authoritarian regime forced to grapple with the choice: Do I stay and report what I can within the government's restrictions, or do I leave, conscience clear but no longer able to report on the ground? It's a debate that went on for years among the Berlin "newshawks," correspondents for AP and other foreign media who were the world's eyes and ears in Nazi Germany. It was no secret that those who stayed practiced self-censorship. Those who were pushed out or left to write books could describe what they'd seen, free of censorship, but once they departed, further reporting was virtually impossible; in that pre-internet age, there were no citizen videos flooding social media accounts or YouTube commentators making instant revelations of new Nazi atrocities.

By the time the United States and Germany declared war on each other in December 1941, the reporters at the Associated Press and its wire service rivals, United Press and International News Service, were among the few American journalists left in Berlin. This book describes the internal AP debates that led the company to maintain a presence there until its reporters were rounded up with other Americans and eventually exchanged for Axis journalists and diplomats detained in the United States. Staying in Nazi Germany led to accusations that AP's venerable Berlin bureau chief, Louis Lochner, was a Nazi sympathizer. The charge reached a crescendo in 1940, when editors at a group of newspapers that subscribed to AP took the extraordinary step of censuring AP's reporting; one of them charged that Lochner "has swallowed Hitler's propaganda 'hook, line and sinker.'" Lochner's defender-in-chief, AP general manager Kent Cooper, noting that the censure vote came in the wake of the AP Berlin bureau's reporting on Germany's successful military Blitzkrieg, dismissed the criticism. The American editors were unhappy with his reporters, he said, "because they had told the truth" about the Nazi victories in Europe.

Cooper and Lochner are key characters in this book's other tale of AP and Nazi Germany, one that came to light only decades later. In 1931, as part of Cooper's ambitious plans to make AP the world's dominant agency for news text and photos, the company registered a photo agency in Germany, known as the AP GmbH. Though supervised by AP executives in London and, somewhat reluctantly, by Lochner in Berlin, the GmbH had a staff of local hires: Germans and other Europeans living in Berlin, including some of Jewish heritage. Two years after the GmbH was founded, the Nazis came to power. German media became servants of the Nazi state, and some of them twisted news photos from AP into anti-Semitic propaganda messages. Nazi laws forced the dismissal of the AP photo agency's Jewish employees, and wartime edicts put the GmbH's German photographers into service with Wehrmacht or Waffen-SS propaganda companies—while they remained on the AP payroll. The work of propaganda company photographers was distributed to AP subscribers before the war, and later through a little-known exchange run with the blessing (and using the German diplomatic pouches) of the Nazi Foreign Office.

That story, revealed by a German historian in 2016 and later detailed in an AP report by the authors of this book, is reported in greater depth here. The authors explore how Cooper's business ambitions and Lochner's devotion to remaining "in the field" shaped the choice to keep AP in Nazi Germany. It's a choice that meant the agency's reporters remained in the news bureau through 1941, even as growing censorship eventually limited their ability to report little beyond official statements. And that choice kept the photo operation, the AP GmbH, doing business with the Nazi government throughout the war, when other international photo agencies chose to leave. At war's end, a U.S. counterintelligence investigation concluded AP's wartime photo exchange may have violated the Trading with the Enemy Act. The same investigation questioned Lochner's loyalty as an American citizen. Like so much of the history of the GmbH, that investigation disappeared for several decades into archival files—first with the U.S. military and later with the U.S. National Archives and Records Administration.

Earlier books examining media coverage of Nazi Germany have focused on how the press reported on the mass of Nazi decrees, laws, and policies used to repress, expel, and finally attempt to exterminate the entire Jewish population of Europe. Some argue that more prescient coverage and more prominent display of stories could have galvanized American public opinion to support greater government action to save Jewish lives. Similar arguments are made in contemporary media criticism: if journalists did a better job reporting on climate change, for instance, world leaders might do more to save the planet. Or if reporting resources were more evenly distributed, journalists would continue deep coverage of the war in Ukraine without letting Taliban abuses in Afghanistan fall off the news—and policy—agendas.

These are important discussions that always need a caveat: journalists can inform and expose, but they do not make public policy and cannot force governments to act. And in the case of AP and Nazi Germany, it's essential to note that the coverage—whether complete or self-censored—went through additional filters before reaching the public and policy makers.

The initial gatekeepers who oversaw the coverage of Nazi Germany were AP editors and managers in New York and London. AP is a member-driven not-for-profit, created more than 175 years ago by five American newspapers, which banded together to pool resources for reporting the Mexican-American war. As AP grew under the ownership of its newspaper members, new members agreed to share news (and thus save reporting costs) with others in the cooperative. And all, in turn, shared the costs of AP bureaus—like the one in Berlin—that would supply the entire cooperative with news from around the globe.

AP's influence in the Nazi era cannot be overestimated. The stories and photos AP's gatekeepers approved went to its members: more than 1,200 in the United States during most of that era. Collectively, those papers reached tens of millions of newspaper subscribers. By comparison, a single big city paper like the *Chicago Tribune* might reach no more than one million. In that pre-internet, pre-TV time, with news radio in its early years, the print papers delivered to doorsteps or sold at newsstands were America's most important source of news, and the Associated Press was the papers' most important source of foreign news.

But AP itself did not publish anything directly to the public, and not every AP member paper treated stories in the same way. Once stories and photos left the hands of AP gatekeepers, they were scrutinized by editors at AP subscriber newspapers in cities large and small across America. These local gatekeepers decided what (or whether) to publish, and where each story and photo received from AP would appear. They also could cut or rewrite stories and change AP's suggested headlines and photo captions. They were men (very few women held any newsroom jobs in that era) with personal biases and different views on news, on local interests, and on just how threatening Nazi Germany was to the United States and the rest of the world.

AP differed from its newspaper members in other ways, too. Though American journalism widely espoused objectivity, AP tended to embrace that notion of impartiality more firmly than most. And while a correspondent for a daily paper generally had just one deadline to meet each day, AP and other wire services faced "a deadline every minute," referring to the differing deadlines, in different time zones, of the many different members who depended on AP coverage. Accuracy and objectivity were paramount, but so was speed.

Correspondents covering today's dictatorships and conflicts, or seeking to verify war crimes and other atrocities, have far more sophisticated tools than those available to the newshawks in Berlin. While the newshawks dictated war reports from the field over bad phone lines that could be cut by censors, wifi and satellite phones now make it feasible for a journalist to file text, photos, and videos from even the most remote front lines. And crucially, those reporting today on war crimes in Ukraine, or protests in inaccessible places like Iran, can use digital techniques to verify videos on social media posted by citizens on the ground. For the newshawks, stories of atrocities were not only often beyond belief, they were largely beyond their means to independently verify until Allied forces liberated Nazi massacre sites, death camps, and concentration camps.

The newshawks also lacked the decades of hindsight through which we now view the Nazi era. This book describes the journalists and their work through a real-time prism: diary entries, letters, memos, the stories they filed, and the photos they took all put into context what they reported, how they reported it, what they left out, and why. Issues they faced—how to report in a dictatorship, whether to embed with military forces, how to report on accounts of atrocities that cannot be independently verified—all remain dilemmas for today's journalists covering war in Ukraine, protests in Iran, dictatorship in Myanmar, or human rights violations in every region of the world.

Authors Larry Heinzerling and Randy Herschaft had finished a lengthy first draft of this book in the summer of 2021 when Larry was diagnosed with cancer that took his life just a few weeks later. I'm Larry's wife, a lifelong journalist, a former foreign correspondent (for National Public Radio in Moscow and Johannesburg), a press freedom advocate (former executive director of the Committee to Protect Journalists), and a journalism instructor (professor emerita at Columbia Journalism School), who read and commented on all the book as the authors put together their manuscript. I have continued working with Randy to refine the story he and Larry set out to tell: how America's most important news organization in the 1930s and 1940s dealt with censorship, criticism, propaganda, the dangers of war correspondence, and so much more in covering Nazi Germany.

This is an independent history and reflects the views of the authors. It does not reflect the views of the Associated Press. Between them, Larry and Randy have over seventy-five years of work experience with AP (I also spent about six months working in AP's Moscow bureau in 1987 before the Soviet Foreign Ministry approved my application to open a bureau for NPR). Some may read those many years of experience as a disadvantage, clouding their ability to be objective. The depth of the research here belies that notion, as do the understanding and insights Randy and Larry have brought to this narrative about a crucial era in the life of one of America's most important, and least understood, news organizations.

INTRODUCTION

My father worked with or knew most of the protagonists in this tale of intrigue. It involves the Berlin bureau of the Associated Press and its struggles to cover the Nazi dictatorship before, during, and after World War II. Yet, whether out of his lifelong modesty or the sheer horror of it all, Lynn Heinzerling rarely spoke about Berlin or the war.

He was thirty-two in 1938 when he was plucked from AP's Cleveland, Ohio, bureau for his first foreign assignment to help cover the most important story in Europe. Aside from a summer escapade to La Baule, France, paying his way by playing trombone for an Ohio Wesleyan University student band, he had never been abroad.

After a transatlantic crossing aboard the SS *Bremen*, he, my mother, Agnes, and their first son, Lynn, Jr., a toddler, boarded a train at Bremerhaven for the German capital. Louis Lochner, the AP's longtime Berlin bureau chief, greeted their train at the Friedrichstrasse Bahnhof the evening of October 20, 1938.

My father joined Lochner's bustling bureau of "newshawks," as *Time* magazine in those days insisted on calling reporters. There, he met Wilhelm "Willy" Brandt (not the future chancellor), the young German who later was put in charge of the AP GmbH, the German subsidiary established by AP in 1931 to collect and distribute photos in Germany.

Brandt was to become a legendary but controversial figure in AP's history, a man who tried to save much of AP's vast German photo archive during the Allied bombing of Berlin, harboring rare photos dating back to the 1910s. He plays a major role in this account of an American news agency at work and its extraordinary, little-known relationship with a wartime enemy.

An out-of-focus photo found in my father's files many decades later shows him with Brandt in the AP Berlin office on Zimmerstrasse. It was taken somewhere between 1938 and 1940. Both men are smartly dressed in suits, vests, and ties, the attire of news professionals at the time, their feet indecorously perched, respectively, on a desk and a chair. Another photograph, published in AP's house organ, shows the two of them in 1945 in Berlin talking about equipping a new AP bureau, the prewar office having been reduced to rubble in the wartime bombing of the German capital.

After his death in 1983, I learned more about my father from his own files and those of AP—and from my mother. For example, it wasn't until my parents retired in Elyria, Ohio, that my mother revealed the story behind the silver-plated tray on a tripod that had served for years as a small side table in their various living rooms. It was, she told me, the gift of a terrified Jewish family my parents had sheltered during Kristallnacht less than three weeks after their arrival in Berlin.

Nor did I learn until years later, leafing through his papers, that my father witnessed the historic first shots of World War II on September 1, 1939, in the Free City of Danzig, a semiautonomous state primarily populated by Germans, though the League of Nations gave Poland certain rights there after World War I. My father and the other correspondents in Danzig that day had all suddenly become what AP general manager Kent Cooper called "soldiers of the press."[1] A total of 175 men and 5 women would end up serving AP as war correspondents in U.S. military uniforms during the war. Seven won Pulitzer Prizes for their reporting. Four were killed in action, a fifth executed by the Nazis.[2]

My father also never mentioned his coverage of the Russian invasion of Finland in 1939, the beginning of the so-called Winter War, nor what happened while he was dictating the story to AP's office in Copenhagen from a telephone booth in Helsinki's Torni Hotel just as Soviet war planes struck. The phone booth shook, he heard screams in the street, and sirens howled. A huge skylight fell into the floor above him.

"When I walked out of the hotel, the whole section of the city in which the Torni was located was blotted out by smoke," he wrote later. "Some 250 men, women and children lay dead on the streets under piles of brick and stone. The reverberations of the raid, the deadliest of the war, had been heard on the telephone as far as Copenhagen."[3]

In reporting the Soviet-Finnish armistice reached after Finland's defeat in March 1940, he quoted Finland's foreign minister Väinö Tanner telling his people by radio they had lost against Moscow. "All that can be said against us," he said sadly, "is that as a nation we are too small."[4]

Nor did my father ever tell me about his eyewitness coverage of what the Nazis had done that spring to Rotterdam, home of the Dutch merchant fleet, leaving it only a scar of a city, "its main business and financial district a pile of bricks and mortar serving as headstones for hundreds of dead."[5] There was also no mention of his coverage of the takeover of Denmark, where a German machine gunner in a Copenhagen street "kept telling the sad and bewildered Danes around him to go home and enjoy the German occupation of Denmark like any other Danish holiday. 'Heute ist Feiertag' (Today is a holiday), he kept saying."[6]

It was my mother who told me a German sniper had wounded my father while he was with the British Eighth Army at Ortona, Italy, in December 1943, a shot that caught him under his left arm. He dismissed the injury as an insignificant flesh wound and therefore declined an offered Purple Heart.[7]

From Ortona, with the U.S. Fifth Army, he proceeded to cover the destruction of the historic abbey, founded by St. Benedict in A.D. 529 at Monte Cassino, that dominates the Liri Valley and the road to Rome. Scores of U.S. Flying Fortresses bombed the hilltop monastery, which the Germans had converted into a fortress. "Nazi troops have taken up positions there, Allied headquarters declared, to send murderous fire against U.S. troops assaulting the hill overlooking the town of Cassino," he reported.[8] That was one event he shared with me, producing a large poster he had found of St. Benedict, the back of which had been used by the occupying Germans to draw a map of the passageways inside the monastery. I have since returned the poster to the monastery.

At war's end, he took on an assignment that he called "the crowning sadness."[9] In October 1944 fellow AP war correspondent Joe Morton had joined a daring, top-secret, but doomed military mission deep in the heart of Adolf Hitler's occupied Europe. When the mission went awry, Nazis captured Morton and those he was traveling with. They were taken to the Mauthausen concentration camp in Austria and executed in January 1945.[10] Months later my father's reporting unraveled the story, confirming that Morton was the only American correspondent known to have been executed by the enemy during the war.

After visiting Mauthausen for his reporting, my father wrote to my mother: "If I had my way there wouldn't be any pictures shown in German theaters for a year except pictures of concentration camps and extermination chambers. The whole Austrian countryside is befouled every few miles with these camps. And yet the Germans try to say they didn't know what was going on."[11]

Perhaps the accidental death in Berlin of my ten-year-old brother Lynn, Jr., in June 1947 was the final horror that led my parents—my father in particular—to bottle up the German nightmare. He spent his remaining years in silence, as many war veterans do, moving on to serve AP elsewhere, in Geneva, Johannesburg, Columbus (Ohio), and London.

I was almost two when Lynn, Jr., died from gas fumes released after a U.S. Army demolition squad destroyed a residential air raid shelter. He had been playing around the excavation and fell into a gas-filled hole. Rescue workers had difficulty reaching him through the narrow opening, and he was overcome by the fumes almost immediately.[12] I learned many years later, from AP files, that my parents had witnessed Lynn's death, standing helplessly by as the rescuers fought to revive him.

My own involvement in the Nazi saga came several years after I had retired from a forty-one-year career with AP. I had worked almost a decade as a foreign correspondent, reporting from West Africa and South Africa in the 1970s, before taking on management roles, first in Germany and later in New York, where I served as director of World Services. There, I worked on behalf of securing the freedom of Terry Anderson, our Middle East correspondent held captive for almost seven years in Lebanon. My final posting was as deputy international editor for World Services.

Despite my many years at AP, including several in the top editorial job in Germany, I had never heard the story that German historian Harriet Scharnberg revealed in 2016. In an academic paper Scharnberg asserted that AP ceded influence to Nazi propagandists over the production of its German photo service, which distributed photographs both inside and outside Germany from 1933 to 1941 and continued a photo exchange even after the United States and Germany declared war on each other. Scharnberg also reported instances of AP photos being used in anti-Semitic Nazi publications and said that some German AP photographers served in Wehrmacht and Waffen-SS propaganda companies while also drawing AP salaries as staff or freelancers.[13]

All this was news to the current generation of AP managers and staff, including coauthor Randy Herschaft and me. The news cooperative, owned by its newspaper members in the United States, had no formal corporate archives until the appointment of archivist Valerie Komor in 2003, when AP was still headquartered at 50 Rockefeller Plaza in New York. The basement levels there contained hundreds of boxes and filing cabinets, eventually brought into order by Komor and enabling researchers to explore the company's rich history—including the long-lost story of the wartime photo exchange with Nazi Germany.

Startled by Scharnberg's claims and uncertain of their accuracy, AP's John Daniszewski, vice president for standards and editor at large, asked me to take on a project to comb those archives and produce an official AP history of the period, "warts and all." In other words, report on AP with the same rigor and honesty as the news service strives for in covering national and world events. Daniszewski assigned Herschaft, investigative researcher in AP's News Research Center, to contribute to what became a yearlong study of AP activities in Nazi Germany from 1933 to 1945. A highly skilled investigator and news staff veteran of thirty-six years, Herschaft helped AP win the Pulitzer Prize in 2000 for documenting atrocities in the Korean War by American soldiers who fired on hundreds of civilians with machine guns under a bridge at No Gun Ri. He has also partnered with AP Berlin correspondent David Rising to report on ex-Nazis.

Herschaft's roots in journalism and his abiding interest in Germany and the Holocaust run deep. His parents, Jacques and Jean Herschaft, raised him in a conservative Jewish household in Brooklyn, New York. His mother worked for almost fifty years as a reporter and columnist for the *National Jewish Post & Opinion*, an independent weekly published in Indianapolis. From an early age, Herschaft knew the story of Solomon Sachs, brother of his maternal grandmother, who disappeared in France during World War II. The family never learned details of his fate until 1983, when Herschaft and his mother attended the American Gathering of Jewish Holocaust Survivors conference in Washington, D.C.

There, on page 524 of "Memorial to the Jews Deported from France 1942–44," a book listing train convoys that transported Jews to their death, they found: "Solomon Sachs, born 3/8/1900 Jerusalem." They learned that on March 7, 1944, their relative was sent by train convoy #69 with 1,500 other souls to the death camp at Auschwitz and never heard from again.

Two decades later, Herschaft took on an assignment for AP that enabled him to help others uncover the fate of family members who went missing in the chaos of the Holocaust. His reporting involved pushing for public access to closed Nazi records in the archive of the International Tracing Service, administered by the International Committee of the Red Cross in Bad Arolsen, Germany. The archive held some fifty million documents—including transport lists, registration books, medical records, and death records—on more than seventeen million people. Among them was the original file on Herschaft's relative, Solomon Sachs.

The resulting AP series, "The Holocaust Papers," was published between 2006 and 2008. It detailed the long struggle to open the files and also brought to light revelations of how Nazi war criminals lied about their past to gain entrance to the United States.

A decade later, Herschaft joined me in search of details about the Associated Press itself and its actions in Germany as it reported on the war and the Holocaust. We looked at previously unexamined AP archives, including the extensive AP photo libraries in New York and London; corporate records; oral histories; letters of American and German employees; and the private papers of Louis Lochner and other AP reporters in Berlin.

Then we searched U.S. military and other government records and made dozens of Freedom of Information Act requests to declassify still-secret documents. In researching the report, Herschaft took special interest in the fate of AP's Jewish employees in Germany who left the country under Nazi diktat but survived the war. He also provided an accounting of other Jewish employees not immediately identified in AP records, keeping memory of them alive.

The essential findings, which confirmed Scharnberg's research and went into deeper detail, were published by AP in 2017, in "Covering Tyranny: The AP and Nazi Germany: 1933–1945."[14]

"Covering Tyranny" focused on the AP photo operation and its relationship with the Nazi government. In the years since, we have broadened our research, bringing to light a far more detailed picture of the entire AP news operation that covered Nazi Germany from its earliest days, through the war it waged in Europe and the accounting that came after—especially for the atrocities that came to be known as the Holocaust. The result is this book, an account of AP's "newshawks," their war coverage, their battles with the Nazi hierarchy, their professional rivalries, their self-censorship, their life in wartime Berlin, and an account of AP's coverage of the Holocaust as it unfolded.

It is the story of American journalists who survived bombings, dueled with the Ministry of Propaganda, stayed until war was declared on their country, and spent months in internment to cover a brutal regime as best they could.

It is also an account of the fortunes of AP's German photo service, the AP GmbH, especially its leadership under Willy Brandt, and of its most controversial figure: Franz Roth, a Nazi, an adventurer, and a Waffen-SS frontline war photographer who, out on the German frontlines, was simultaneously an asset to both the Associated Press and Joseph Goebbels's Ministry of Public Enlightenment and Propaganda.

Larry Heinzerling
New York, 2021

I

LONG SHADOWS

1

KRISTALLNACHT

Guenther Beukert, chief photo editor of the Associated Press in Germany, said he left a birthday party in Berlin around 11 p.m. that Wednesday night in a friend's car. As they reached the intersection of Leipzigerstrasse and Friedrichstrasse at the center of the German capital, they saw mobs of people, shattered store windows, glass on the sidewalk, and fur coats being thrown out of a shop located under the Café Steinmeyer. They stopped the car. Members of the Sturmabteilung (SA), the Nazi party's paramilitary known as Storm Troopers or Brownshirts, were roaming the sidewalks and streets. They wore "high boots, black pants but otherwise civilian jackets, not distinguishable as SA members," Beukert recalled later.[1]

When his companion, Kurt "Kutti" Boecker, a photographer who freelanced for AP, got out of his Opel P4 and approached men on the street, he was told to leave or face arrest (Boecker himself was an SA member but apparently documented, rather than participated in, the Kristallnacht violence). The two photographers then rushed to the AP bureau at 68 Zimmerstrasse. Beukert immediately phoned the Ministry of Public Enlightenment and Propaganda from the fourth-floor office that the AP's German photo subsidiary shared with AP's American news staff. The call was "to cover my back," as Beukert put it in an interview in 1983.

Usually, when Beukert phoned the propaganda ministry he had to deal with Heiner Kurzbein, the cocky Nazi overlord of the ministry's photo department. The hour was late, though, and he ended up speaking with Kurzbein's assistant, a man named Henke. "Henke, what can I do?" Beukert asked. "A couple of shops are smashed to pieces. I want to take photos. Even if we only use the pictures for nothing but the archive. But it has to be done." Henke apparently consulted Kurzbein and called back. "You may have photos taken," Henke said. "But not a single picture goes abroad. And we want to see all the pictures." So shortly after midnight, in the early hours of Thursday, November 10, 1938, Beukert rousted other photographers and ordered them onto the streets to cover one of the biggest prewar stories out of Nazi Germany, the night we now know as Kristallnacht, the Night of Broken Glass.

Headlines out of Europe had grown increasingly ominous throughout 1938. The AP Berlin news bureau and its German photo subsidiary were on front pages across America in March that year, with vivid eyewitness accounts of Hitler's takeover of Austria and details of assaults on the country's Jews, who now came under the anti-Semitic Nürnberg Laws promulgated in 1935, which had already stripped Germany's Jews of citizenship, banned intermarriage on the basis of a new racial definition of the Jews, and foreshadowed ever-growing persecution. Months later, the September agreement that allowed Hitler to partition Czechoslovakia became a huge story, viewed initially as a diplomatic victory that would halt further German territorial claims and prevent war in Europe. Only after Hitler broke the Munich Pact in March 1939, by invading the rump Czechoslovak state and wiping it off the map, did European statesmen understand it was a colossal failure.

Austria and Czechoslovakia both presented reporting challenges: a strict censorship regime was imposed shortly after the Austria takeover, and AP's Melvin Whiteleather was arrested twice while covering the conflict that led to Hitler's annexation of Czechoslovakia's Sudetenland.

But perhaps no major event better illustrates the difficulties of reporting on the Nazi dictatorship in prewar Germany than Kristallnacht. As four AP photographers—Boecker, Franz Roth, Eric Borchert, and Gerhard Baatz—fanned out through the city, each with film for about three dozen photos, they collected more than a hundred images, according to Beukert, their editor. All worked for AP's German subsidiary, the Associated Press Gesellschaft mit beschränkter Haftung, or AP GmbH. The GmbH sold photos to the German media and sent photos from Germany to AP's offices in London and New York for worldwide distribution to newspapers and other publications. But most of the photos they took of Kristallnacht would never be published.

Beukert complained that every quarter hour that night, one of the photographers got arrested and he would have to call the authorities to get them released. When they gathered in the AP darkroom to process their work, the photographers "carefully picked out only the pictures that had a chance to be released," Beukert said. The thirty-four photos he submitted to the propaganda office showed smashed windows, destroyed shops, and "Jews who already had to sweep up the shards of glass, things like that. I gave some of those too. I had to give them something to ban," Beukert said. "On one picture there was a quarrel between a Jewish shopkeeper and the SA people," he said. When the shopkeeper tried to protest, "they struck back. I did not send those worst scenes."

To transmit a photo out of Germany under Nazi control required a blue release stamp from Kurzbein's propaganda ministry office. A red stamp indicated a photo had been banned. Kurzbein, a cofounder of Berlin's Hitler Youth movement and a member of the Nazi Party and the Schutzstaffel (the General SS), was appointed head of the Ministry of Propaganda's photo department in 1933 when he was just twenty-three years old.[2] Beady-eyed and sporting a tightly cropped moustache, he was described by those who knew him as a pugnacious, unpleasant hardliner who rarely missed an opportunity to wear his black SS uniform with three stars.[3]

Only Kurzbein, Henke, and an assistant identified by Beukert as Mrs. Ernst were authorized to clear photos for distribution. It's unknown whether Kurzbein and Henke were unavailable when Beukert took his photos to the ministry or whether he was deliberately avoiding them. Whatever the case, the AP photo editor told Ernst she simply had to release some photos. The AP news reporters and their competitors at Reuters, United Press, and International News Service, he explained, had been writing and sending stories of the carnage overnight and throughout the day to newspapers around the globe. "The whole world knows about it," Beukert pointed out. "Why don't you release a few pictures for me now already, some which are not that great and tell me which ones?" he asked. "Then I can already start printing and have copies made."

Beukert said the assistant agreed and selected a few photos, signaling that those might get eventual approval. But they were not yet stamped for official release. Despite that, Beukert said he rushed the first print copies by air freight to an AP representative in Copenhagen—perhaps an effort to make sure that something got out of the country in case the ministry eventually tried to block all the photos.

Beukert's account apparently is the only detailed telling of the AP Kristallnacht photo story. It was not recorded by AP itself, but by interviewers for a German book on the Nazification of press photography, who spoke with Beukert in 1983, when he was seventy-six.[4] Beukert recalled fielding hours of frantic phone calls from AP's

European headquarters in London, demanding to know when they would receive photos to go with the dramatic text stories that AP's Berlin reporters had already filed about the anti-Jewish rampage.

"I said: 'Guys, I cannot talk further here,' etc. No one could imagine that such a thing was happening all over Germany and there were no pictures, we couldn't send a picture," Beukert recalled.

In those tense hours, AP's German photo competitors and the propaganda ministry apparently learned that some AP photos had left the country. Kurzbein was furious. The ministry "gave me an earful," said Beukert, enumerating the threats hurled at him. "Yeah, professional ban, to say the least. He offered to send me to a concentration camp, and I don't know what else, a court case, but nothing came of it."

Despite the threats, some of the AP photos were approved for release the night of November 10. AP photo archives indicate that Berlin transmitted them to London, which sent them to New York via radio transmission for distribution to AP clients throughout the United States. Beukert's otherwise detailed account offers no explanation of how he eventually got blue stamps on a few photos. In the interview in 1983, he said photos that didn't get the ministry's stamp of approval were kept under lock and key, with some eventually sent to AP in New York labeled "do not publish." It's not known what became of those images.

Records in the AP archives indicate Beukert managed to quickly get at least six photos out of the country. One of the first two images distributed was of a smoldering Berlin synagogue with a fire truck parked next to it (firefighters let synagogues burn that night but were on hand to protect nearby buildings).[5] The other image showed broken storefront windows.[6] Both were widely displayed in U.S. newspapers on November 11 and 12, 1938. The other four photos sent by Beukert include another synagogue scene—a burned-out structure on Berlin's Fasanenstrasse—as well as more images of the aftermath of looting and destruction. In one, a man with a broom prepares to sweep up glass on the sidewalk from the smashed windows of the Kaliski bedding firm.

Life magazine splashed AP's Kristallnacht photos across the top of pages 14 and 15 in its November 28, 1938, edition under the headline: "Brutal Nazi Wrecking Gangs Leave Path of Destruction." "Nazi censorship clamped down at once on pictures of the Nazi Terror against Jews," *Life* reported. "The best of the few pictures that seeped through the censorship are shown on these pages." *Life's* readers would be unlikely to know AP was the source of those photos unless they carefully scrutinized the picture credits back on page 68, squeezed between ads for electric shavers, a Florida resort hotel, and neckties that don't wrinkle.[7]

The photos gave crucial visual reinforcement to the front-page stories written by AP's Berlin news staff, such as one of bureau chief Louis P. Lochner's early accounts:

> BERLIN, November 10 (AP)—The greatest wave of anti-Jewish violence since Adolf Hitler came to power in 1933 swept Nazi Germany today and Jews were threatened with new official measures against them.
>
> Millions of dollars' worth of Jewish property was destroyed by angry crowds. Jewish stores were looted. Synagogues were burned, dynamited or damaged in a dozen cities.[8]

Lochner, reporting the government's official position, said the violence was a nationwide day of vengeance for the murder of Ernst vom Rath, secretary of the German Embassy in Paris. The diplomat was shot by Herschel Grynszpan, a seventeen-year-old born in Germany to Jewish immigrants from Poland, who confessed to killing vom Rath as a protest against the deportation of some twelve thousand Polish Jews from Germany, including his parents.

Bands of youths roved the streets of Berlin and other cities from early morning on, [Lochner reported,] smashing windows of Jewish shops. In many places crowds which gathered after daybreak pushed into the establishments and came out with loot. Most of Berlin's 1,000 Jewish stores were plundered.

Sounds of breaking glass and shouts of looters died away only near midnight. Hundreds of Jews voluntarily spent the night in jails fearing worse violence as reports of burning and looting continued to come in from many cities.

After hours of violence, the virulently anti-Semitic Propaganda Minister Joseph Goebbels made a radio address calling for a halt to the destruction he had helped instigate. Goebbels declared "the final answer to Jewry will be given in the form of laws or decrees," which would deprive Jews of their property and jobs.[9] The following day AP reported a new round of restrictions: Jews would be barred from owning businesses, they would not be allowed into public events such as theater and concerts, and they would be forced, collectively, to pay Germany $400 million as a penalty for the killing of vom Rath.

In his vivid interview about Kristallnacht, Beukert portrays himself and his colleagues as dedicated journalists, risking violent assault to get the story and then cleverly maneuvering to slip some of their work past the censors. The photos that did get out depict destruction of Jewish property, but none showed the violent assaults on Jews, such as the Brownshirt attack on a shop owner that Beukert said he held back from the censor. As Beukert explained in the interview, he did not send "those worst scenes" because the propaganda ministry would surely have nixed them. But his interview sheds no light on a mystery surrounding a photo he did send out—a mystery discovered decades later in AP's London photo files.

The photo in question shows the man about to sweep up broken glass in front of the Kaliski bedding store. The version in the AP

New York photo library—distributed in the wake of Kristallnacht and published widely in the United States—shows the storefront, the sweeper, and a few passersby. A different version, stored in the AP London photo library and only uncovered in 2018 during research for this book, shows a slightly enlarged scene, with three police or other officials standing to the side while looking toward the photographer. Their presence—there, but taking no action either to help the shop owner or stop the photographer—can be seen as contradicting the government's attempt to portray the Kristallnacht pogrom as a spontaneous uprising. It's not known who cropped them out, when, or why. But the image that includes them was only sent to AP's London offices sometime later, possibly not until the end of 1945, which suggests Beukert or his staff cropped the men out of the version they sent from Berlin just after Kristallnacht.

The AP photos gave Americans their first look at the Kristallnacht aftermath, but they did not give newspaper readers a full picture. "This focus on property has at times obscured the massive terror against *people* that was unleashed during the pogrom," according to *Kristallnacht 1938*, a detailed examination of the violence published in 2009.[10]

Like the photos, AP's print stories described widespread property damage, but the text accounts also included reports of assaults, arrests, and deportations. Lochner's early story included fragmentary accounts of arrests and other actions: Munich's Jews were ordered to leave the country within forty-eight hours; Jewish men aged eighteen to sixty were arrested in Frankfurt; and Salzburg, Austria, declared itself "Jew-free" after deporting three hundred families to a concentration camp. Lochner's story also cast doubt on the government's "spontaneous" description of the violence, noting that it was "conducted with a thoroughness and precision that left little to chance." Still, in a November 28 letter to his children, less than three weeks after the pogrom, Lochner acknowledged that foreign correspondents, including himself, had not reported every detail of Kristallnacht, lest they endanger their sources. "All the foreign correspondents lied—lied in the sense that they understated many times rather than even approach the truth for fear that their authentic sources might be led to new torture if they were revealed," he wrote.[11]

The name *Kristallnacht* (literally, crystal night) comes from the shards of broken glass from smashed store windows that littered the sidewalks of German cities. Accounts of the violence from AP and its news agency competitors prompted condemnation from newspapers across the United States.

"In the weeks following Kristallnacht, close to 1,000 different editorials were published on the topic," wrote historian Deborah E. Lipstadt in *Beyond Belief: The American Press & the Coming of the Holocaust 1933–1945*. Eyewitness reports from Germany ran on the front pages of many newspapers for more than three weeks, and "practically no American newspaper, irrespective of size, circulation, location or political inclination failed to condemn Germany."[12] An opinion poll taken two weeks after the pogrom showed Americans overwhelmingly disapproved of Nazi treatment of Jews.[13] At the same time, less than a quarter of those polled said the United States should allow more German Jews to enter the country. Anti-immigration sentiments were strong in parts of America, as was anti-Semitism. So while public opinion was appalled by the Nazi action, the public did not support a strong American response to rescue Germany's Jews; the most high-profile action taken was the recall of the American ambassador in Berlin.

Still, the widespread media coverage in America made a strong impression on Hans-Heinrich Dieckhoff, Germany's ambassador in Washington, according to Jacob D. Beam, third secretary at the U.S. Embassy in Berlin at the time of Kristallnacht. Beam himself wrote that he was impressed by "the scope and vivid detail of

American press reporting from Germany. It was credible in every respect, and was deeply moving." And, according to Beam, it prompted Dieckhoff to write his superiors at the Foreign Office in Berlin, warning that "the respectable patriotic circles (in the USA), which are thoroughly anti-communist and, for the greater part, anti-Semitic in their outlook, also begin to turn away from us." Even such figures as Thomas Dewey, Herbert Hoover, and William Randolph Hearst—all previously somewhat sympathetic—were adopting a violent and bitter attitude toward Germany, which Dieckhoff warned "is a serious matter."[14]

Lochner, the Berlin bureau chief who had covered Germany for AP since 1924, described the violence and its aftermath as "the most terrible experience in all my life."

"I never dreamed that human nature could descend to such depravity and to such sadism and cruelty as I was witness to these last weeks," he wrote in the letter to his children. Lochner said he and "hundreds" of other foreigners had sheltered Jews during the pogrom. "Haunted and hunted creatures pitifully begged for a night's lodging, and no Christian that I know said no: we left it to the heathens to take upon themselves the odium of perpetrating crimes that will some day cost the country dearly."[15]

Recalling Lochner's reaction to the carnage, Wallace "Wally" R. Deuel of the *Chicago Daily News* reported that for two hours straight on the night of the rioting, Lochner, a lifelong pacifist, raked an unidentified but high-ranking propaganda ministry official "over the coals," following the ministry's complaints about AP's reporting. "Lochner lectured him on how in First World War days he, Lochner, was head of an organization in the U.S. that was fighting for a written declaration of the United States' war aims," Deuel wrote. "As a consequence, he got his house painted yellow [a color associated with cowardice] and very nearly got strung up . . . he, personally, knew what it was like to be persecuted, and he certainly had the right to tell off the German government."¹⁶

Lochner was also upset at the treatment of one of his reporters covering the story. "One of our men who had been present at a wrecking scene went into a public phone booth to telephone me what he had seen," Lochner wrote later. "He was nearly mobbed on the grounds that he was spreading false reports."¹⁷ The Germans had shouted "You atrocity monger!" at the unidentified reporter but let him go unharmed.¹⁸

Kristallnacht brought into focus how the German photographers, editors, and other staff members of AP's photo subsidiary had been forced to become licensed functionaries of the Third Reich after Hitler took power in January 1933.

The Schriftleitergesetz, or Editor's Law, that went into effect a year later defined journalism as a public task regulated by the state. It banned non-Aryans from working in journalism, required media workers to avoid publishing anything "calculated to weaken the strength of the Reich," and required some thirteen thousand German journalists to register for a permit to work with Der Reichsverband der Deutschen Presse (the Reich Association of the German Press), subordinated to the propaganda ministry.¹⁹

The ministry supervised German and foreign correspondents and set the rules and punished violators of what it dictated could and could not be published, when and where. While foreign correspondents, operating under a system of self-censorship and the ever-present possibility of expulsion, could joust with Nazi authorities up to a point, the plight of AP's German employees was another matter entirely. For German journalists, serious transgressions could result in banishment from the profession, losing the right to write, edit, or photograph for a living, and possible time in a concentration camp—or worse. Under the strict Nazi rules, Goebbels conceded privately that "any person with the slightest spark of honor left in him will take good care in the future not to become a journalist."[20]

Goebbels, portrayed by *Time* magazine as a "barking, brawling, screaming propaganda maniac," was also, *Time* said, "one of the great political orators of this century."[21] "It is impossible not to be stirred by Goebbels' speeches, even if you hate everything he says," wrote Deuel, the *Chicago Daily News* correspondent who had witnessed Lochner's Kristallnacht confrontation with a propaganda ministry official.[22] Lochner, forever concerned about AP's German operations being shuttered, had another perspective. "Any man who dared violate the instructions of the Propaganda Ministry soon was given an opportunity to think things over in a concentration camp," he noted.[23]

Thirty-one-year-old Beukert seemed particularly at risk. He joined AP's Berlin news bureau as a reporter in 1934 and transferred to the photo subsidiary, where he was appointed chief editor, in 1937. Before taking the position, Beukert wrote to Gideon Seymour, then managing director of the Associated Press of Great Britain (to which the AP GmbH reported), saying he was prepared to "pilot a smooth course in Germany without harming AP principles, and American interests or the business."

Beukert was concerned, however, about the future and whether AP would be forced to stop selling photos in Germany and simply become a conduit through which the propaganda ministry could distribute German photos abroad. "Should circumstances, which can never be foreseen in a dictatorship country like Germany, ever force us to shut down the picture department to a mere picture service for abroad—which I neither believe or hope—I wish to be given the chance to return to the news side," he wrote. [24]

That opportunity never arose. AP dismissed Beukert in April 1939, charging him with managerial incompetence; he was careless about responding to AP correspondence and keeping his superiors informed, one supervisor wrote. Beukert, who had survived Kurzbein's wrath over the Kristallnacht photos, was soon at work at Presse-Hoffmann, a rival photo agency headed by Heinrich Hoffmann, Hitler's personal photographer.[25] He also worked as a wartime censor, but at war's end, a U.S. Army report on German journalists listed him as sympathetic to "democratic ideals."[26]

Of the four photographers on the streets of Berlin that night covering Kristallnacht, one, Franz Roth, was a committed Nazi who became an official photographer for the Waffen-SS while also working for AP. Another, Eric Borchert, also became a military photographer; Roth and Borchert both died on German battlefields. Gerhard Baatz, twenty-four, began his career as a darkroom apprentice at age sixteen. He would later play a role in an astonishing wartime photo liaison between AP and Nazi Germany whose details only came to light more than seventy-five years later.[27]

When Kristallnacht occurred, the Nazis' Final Solution had not yet been conceived. The nationwide pogroms, which continued over two days throughout Germany and Nazi-occupied Austria and Sudetenland, were designed "to compel the Jews to leave Germany, preferably with as little of their wealth as possible."[28] Official German figures put the death toll at 91 Jews, but later scholarship has suggested hundreds died from Kristallnacht violence. The Nazi government reported 191 synagogues destroyed; later estimates said hundreds had been burned or destroyed, and an estimated 7,500 Jewish businesses were trashed and looted in Germany.[29] Some 30,000 Jews were detained and taken to Dachau, Buchenwald, Sachsenhausen, and other concentration camps. Anti-Semitic violence was not at all new in Nazi Germany, but it had reached a new level, challenging journalists already worn down by six years of ever-tightening censorship.

2

"IT IS MORE IMPORTANT FOR US TO REMAIN IN THE FIELD"

On March 10, 1933, just weeks after Adolf Hitler was named chancellor of Germany, Jewish attorney Michael Siegel marched into Munich police headquarters to file a complaint on behalf of his client, Max Uhlfelder, whose department store windows had been smashed by Storm Troopers the day before. The police, now under the leadership of longtime Hitler confidant Hermann Göring, took Siegel to a basement room where a number of Brownshirts, some deputized as police, were waiting. There, Siegel was beaten and suffered several lost teeth and a perforated eardrum. He was then marched back onto the streets of Munich with his pants cut off at the knees and a placard hung from his neck.[1]

An unemployed Munich photographer named Heinrich Sanden captured the cruel public display with his Nettel 9X12 camera, first at Stachus, the city's large central square, and then when Siegel and his escorts reached Prielmayerstrasse.[2] The photos did not clearly show what was written on the placard, but Sanden recalled years later the message was, "Ich werde mich nie mehr bei der Polizei beschweren" (I will never again complain to the police).[3]

When Sanden offered his photos to Munich newspapers, they rejected them, fearful of official disapproval. Anxious to dispose of his explosive material, he shopped for other buyers, suffered more rejections, but eventually sold the negatives to George Pahl, the Berlin agent for William Randolph Hearst's International News Photo service. The shocking images created a sensation when they appeared in the *Washington Times* and other U.S. newspapers, some of which doctored the photo to make the message on the placard legible.[4]

Hearst's photographic scoop gave the photo desk at AP headquarters in New York heartburn. New York cabled the Berlin bureau with a "rocket"—an urgent message, in news agency parlance—demanding to know why AP was "licked" on the photo scoop. "Nazi attacks on Jews played big," the cable noted.[5]

In Berlin, Nazi authorities searching for the source of the photos staged a nighttime raid on the office of the AP GmbH, the company's photo subsidiary, but found no evidence that it was involved. Official apologies followed.

There was no evidence of Sanden's photos because AP Berlin chief of bureau Louis Lochner, who had also been offered the photos, decided to reject them. When New York reproached him for that call, Lochner responded with what was to become a common refrain throughout his remaining years in Germany: "It is more important for us to remain in the field here, even if occasionally we are licked, than to risk having our whole organization destroyed by publishing a picture to which the regime in power objects," he wrote to AP general manager Kent Cooper two weeks after the police assault on Siegel. "In this case, New York, instead of complaining of not having the Nazi attack pictures, can be darned glad we did NOT send them, for if we had, we'd today be out of business in Berlin," Lochner added.

Sanden's images of the humiliated attorney were an early, dramatic harbinger of the official anti-Semitic savagery that would engulf Germany, and Lochner's decision not to buy them for AP was a highly controversial call. But Lochner made clear to Cooper that his higher priority was to avoid expulsion and closure of the AP news bureau and photo service. To ensure that, Lochner believed fiercely that AP needed to self-censor, a practice familiar to journalists who work in authoritarian regimes all over the world. Forced to balance the imperative of reporting the news against the possible consequences from vengeful authorities, journalists make educated guesses on where the invisible red line lies, the one that, if crossed, can mean expulsion or worse. In the process, they open themselves to charges of hiding the truth.

Lochner's action in declining the Sanden images shows that self-censorship was in practice even before the new government had formally established the Reich Ministry of Public Enlightenment and Propaganda, the agency that came to govern the flow of information in and out of Nazi Germany. To avoid the mouthful of a title, the agency was usually referred to as the propaganda ministry or, in a somewhat pejorative nickname used by correspondents, "the promi." Once it was established, by a decree issued just days after the Siegel incident, the new ministry began to develop strict censorship regimes for broadcast and photography. Radio correspondents were required to submit their scripts in advance and to accept changes made by censors before they broadcast. Photos also required ministry signoff—like the approval Guenther Beukert sought for the Kristallnacht images—before they could be transmitted.

Print media were kept in check with a more ambiguous, but no less insidious, system that came to be known as "responsibility censorship." On the surface, it sounded fairly benign: foreign correspondents in the German capital were free to send dispatches to their newspapers with no prior review by the government. But woe to the correspondent who stepped across an unstated, ill-defined boundary or wrote about an explicitly banned subject.

Particularly sensitive, Lochner told an interviewer years later, were stories showing the shortcomings or harshness of Hitler's Germany. "Thus, he and his staff used their combined judgment to revise those stories unfavorable to the regime, until they could see no factual ground for challenge," wrote Joy Schaleben in 1967 in a thesis on Lochner.[6] Nazi leaders were less concerned about stories revealing their anti-Semitism than, say, a report on internal party politics, according to Lochner. "So blind were the Nazis in their hatred of the Jews that they had less objection to truthful reporting on anti-semitic measures and actions than on almost any other manifestation of Nazi-regimented German life," he wrote.[7] Military issues were always sensitive, but after the invasion of Poland in 1939, more red lines appeared. Even reports on the weather were forbidden, Lochner told the American Women's Club of Berlin in January 1940, "lest they reveal military information" useful for Allied strikes.[8]

Depending on how seriously Nazi authorities judged a transgression, sanctions ranged from a verbal warning to a public dressing down at a news conference or, in the worst case, to expulsion or other pressure to leave the country.

To avoid the more serious consequences, most correspondents in Berlin practiced at least some degree of self-censorship. For maximum safety, they might confine much of their reporting to official announcements. Or they could bury unsavory elements of a story far down in the text, or fail to aggressively pursue sensitive subjects, such as rumors of a Nazi euthanasia program (when the first articles about the Nazis' euthanasia of mental patients and others appeared in American media in 1941, their authors were outside Berlin and thus beyond the reach of Nazi censors).

AP's Melvin Whiteleather described working in such conditions as having "a sort of Damocles sword eternally hanging overhead."[9] Enforcement relied on sharp-eyed German press attachés, working in America and elsewhere, who "watched every newspaper and read carefully the stories which appeared under a Berlin dateline," AP's Ernest Fischer wrote in an unpublished manuscript. "Any displeasing part was cabled back to Berlin where the Foreign Office kept a record called a 'blue sheet,' a dossier on each correspondent," said Fischer. "When an offensive story appeared abroad, the correspondent was called onto the carpet and reprimanded. It was understood that about three reprimands meant expulsion."[10]

Despite Lochner's rejection of the Siegel photos, his bureau's coverage regularly focused on Germany's increasingly virulent, officially sanctioned persecution of Jews, both before and after the Nazis took power. In July 1932, a few months before Hitler became German chancellor, a Lochner story had warned that hatred of Jews was a cardinal Nazi doctrine and Germany's Jews were "doomed to a period of social ostracism and treatment as second-class citizens" under Hitler.[11] The following spring, after Lochner turned down the photos of Michael Siegel, the bureau reported the early wave of official Nazi anti-Semitic actions: Jews were banned from the civil service and several professions; public book burnings targeted Jewish authors, among others; and on April 1, 1933, Storm Troopers launched a nationwide "Judenboykott" of Jewish businesses and professionals. AP described the boycott as "the greatest organized antisemitic movement of modern times" and distributed photos showing police harassing an elderly Jew and Nazis driving through Berlin in open-air trucks, urging Germans to join the boycott.[12] When the Nürnberg Laws were adopted in 1935, Lochner wrote that they "relegated Jews in the Germany of the future to their position during the Middle Ages." Jews could not be German citizens, "intermarry with Aryans, have intimate relations with gentiles nor even employ Aryan servant girls under 45 years of age."[13]

From the early days of Nazi rule, Lochner's bureau reported on the creation of concentration camps that would eventually play a horrific role in the Nazi drive to eliminate Jews. In March 1933 AP reported the planned opening of the first camp at Dachau and distributed a photo of its buildings awaiting prisoners.[14] Two months later, photos of inmates at the Oranienburg camp near Berlin were distributed, as was an AP story that put the number of concentration camp prisoners at eighteen thousand. Most were socialists or communists who would remain incarcerated until they became "fit citizens," according to the interior minister.[15]

A year later, in 1934, AP reported a new arrest campaign that would swell concentration camp populations: those targeted were so-called fault finders (critics of the Nazis), nearly all of them German Jews.[16] Early stories about the camps were often brief. Some relied mainly on government statements, and on the rare occasion when a foreign correspondent was allowed to see camp conditions, they were sanitized. A journalist for the Newspaper Enterprise Association, which sold feature news to hundreds of American papers, was escorted by Nazis through the Dachau camp in 1935. In his story about the tour, reporter Frazier Hunt said he didn't doubt inmates suffered brutality. "Maybe there are torture chambers and secret execution grounds, but I did not see them," he wrote.[17]

But by June 1938, still several months before Kristallnacht, it was abundantly clear, AP reported, that a "merciless official campaign against Jews, reinforced by mob action, was extended to all Germany today by secret police orders."[18] The campaign included shipping thousands of Jews to concentration camps; sixty-five busloads of Berlin Jews were arriving every night at Buchenwald concentration camp, AP wrote.

In addition to reporting specific actions to persecute, push out, or imprison Jews, the Berlin bureau filed stories on public threats by Hitler and other Nazi officials to annihilate the Jewish population. In November 1938, in an AP story reporting the collective "fine" the Nazis imposed on Jews after Kristallnacht, Propaganda Minister Joseph Goebbels vowed the Nazis would persevere "until the Jewish problem is solved—until the Hebrew is driven from German life."[19] The same story reported that *Das Schwarze Korps*, the official publication of the Schutzstaffel (SS), had warned that unless a new state were created to which Germany's Jews could be deported, they faced "inevitable extinction." Just a few weeks later, in January 1939, Lochner reported Hitler's warning that a new world war would lead to "the annihilation of the Jewish race in Europe."[20]

The message from the highest levels of Nazi officialdom was clear, and it was widely disseminated by AP's news feed to its newspaper subscribers, who served tens of millions of American readers. At the same time, Lochner continued taking a cautious approach to the bureau's reporting, particularly on stories where sources could not be named or would be endangered if they were. Other U.S. correspondents also reported treading carefully, lest a story put a source in danger. But in his letter to Cooper in 1933 about turning down the photos of the humiliated Jewish lawyer, Lochner also presented another argument. Distributing the pictures, he said, would have given German photo agencies the ammunition they badly wanted for their argument that the Nazi government should shut down the AP GmbH, their business rival.

"Believing as I do that you want us to try in every way to keep our hold in Germany, rather than risk being expelled, we have passed up things that have come to us from trustworthy sources which, however, refuse to be quoted because they are afraid [for] their lives," Lochner wrote. "Some of these things are hair-raising. But unless I am authorized to cite chapter and verse, in other words, to name either my informant or the victim of a Storm Troop excess, I don't feel I can afford to send the story."[21]

AP needed to exercise extra caution not only to protect sources, Lochner argued, but also because of its unique position in American journalism. The "specials," meaning correspondents for individual newspapers, such as Edgar Mowrer of the *Chicago Daily News*, could take more risks, Lochner said, because if they were thrown out, their editors—whose papers subscribed to wire services as well—would still receive reporting from Berlin. Besides, he noted, some saw expulsion as a way of burnishing their careers. "Several of the 'specials' have told me that the best thing that could happen to them would be to be ejected, as they could then be martyrs in the eyes of their papers and their countrymen," Lochner wrote.[22]

The "martyrs" piled up in the prewar Nazi era. Lochner, who served for years as president of the Foreign Press Association in Berlin, counted forty foreign journalists formally expelled or forced out of Germany between 1933 and 1937.[23] Radio correspondents, such as William Shirer of CBS, were generally safe. Unlike the news agency and newspaper reporters, their broadcast texts were vetted ahead of time, so the correspondents could always simply blame the censor if there were objections later. Newspaper correspondents could take more chances, since their papers would still have reporting from AP and the other news agencies if they were expelled. But if the wire service reporters at AP, United Press, and International News Service were forced out and could not be replaced, their hundreds of newspaper clients, most of whom had no reporters of their own in Germany, would suffer.

AP's Ernest Fischer took a decidedly cynical view of some who were expelled. "Sometimes the motive was to gain personal publicity and make capital of it by writing a book or a series of articles 'burning up' the Nazis," he wrote. "From some of these writings one gets the impression that the entire conflict revolved around 'me and Hitler.'"[24]

This was a possible dig at Mowrer, the *Chicago Daily News* correspondent and the first American reporter forced to leave Nazi Germany. Mowrer won the Pulitzer Prize as a foreign correspondent in 1933 for his coverage of Hitler's rise to power. While in Germany, he produced several books, including *Germany Puts the Clock Back*, which so enraged the Nazis that the German ambassador in Washington told the State Department his government could no longer guarantee Mowrer's safety. Mowrer left Berlin in late 1933.

He was transferred to Tokyo and later returned to Europe to take over the *Daily News* Paris bureau.

American correspondent Dorothy Thompson's exit in 1934 was perhaps the most high-profile expulsion. Three years earlier, when Hitler was still largely unknown, Thompson had been granted a personal interview with him. While on the mark in most respects, her account of their conversation, titled *I Saw Hitler!*, included one of the more embarrassing journalistic misjudgments of the times. In describing what she called the "startling insignificance of this man who has set the world agog," she wrote: "He is formless, almost faceless, a man whose countenance is a caricature, a man whose framework seems cartilaginous, without bones. He is inconsequent and voluble, ill poised and insecure. He is the very prototype of the Little Man."[25] When Thompson returned in 1934, the year after Hitler took power, she was officially ordered out of the country. Berlin-based correspondents gathered at the train station to see her off, *Time* magazine reported: "There they filled her arms with great sheaves of American Beauty roses."[26]

Arrests of foreign correspondents were rare but frightening, particularly after war began. In 1941 the Gestapo detained United Press correspondent Richard Hottelet in Germany, while Jay Allen of the North American Newspaper Alliance was detained in Paris for allegedly entering occupied France from Vichy France without authority. In Berlin, Hottelet was convicted of currency violations, "a charge of which every foreign correspondent was guilty," wryly noted a U.S. diplomat involved with his case.[27] Ultimately, the two were exchanged for a pair of managers from Germany's Transocean news service, who had been arrested in New York and convicted for failing to register as foreign agents.

Another notable departure was Beach Conger of the *New York Herald Tribune*. Though not formally expelled, Conger left after he was denied cable, telephone, and mail privileges and barred from all press conferences in 1939, apparently in reprisal for reports of discontent among submarine crews in Hamburg and his (accurate) prediction of the Nazi invasion of the Low Countries.[28]

Threats of access denial must have thrown a scare at Lochner in 1935 when he and his staff became the focus of just the kind of Nazi wrath he had sought so hard to avoid. Bernhard Rust, minister of science, education, and national culture, issued an order in August to boycott AP. Rust instructed government officials to withhold all interviews and information from its journalists because of "particularly spiteful reportage."[29]

The order did not identify what triggered the ban, but Lochner said it likely was one of three recent stories from the bureau. One was a graphic, eyewitness account quoting Varian Fry, a New York editor who led rescue efforts for Jews and other Nazi targets in wartime France. Fry described how Jews had gathered at Berlin's fashionable Kurfürstendamm to protest the arrests of Jews and Aryans for having sexual relationships. He said crowds of Germans had lined the protest site, forcing all cars to run a gauntlet. Any Jewish-looking men and women were dragged from their vehicles and beaten.[30]

AP reports about Nazi persecution of Catholic and Protestant churches also might have prompted Rust's ban. But perhaps the most sensitive (in the Nazis' view) story the bureau had filed in that period described a catastrophe at an explosives factory outside Wittenberg. An estimated one hundred to one thousand people died in the explosions, and local German newspapers were ordered to publish nothing until they received sanitized reports from DNB, the official German news agency. AP, ignoring the instructions, published a dramatic account based on information from the town's mayor. Its story was published widely in the United States.[31]

Minister Rust's ban on contact with AP was cause for alarm, Lochner wrote to Cooper. "It seems to have dawned upon the powers that be that the news agencies in merely reporting facts are far more dangerous to the regime than the individual correspondent who writes a single story for his paper only, and who advises his home office to pick up the spot news from the AP," he wrote.[32] Lochner also noted that the ban was probably a sign of heightened government sensitivity to any negative news in the months leading up to the 1936 summer Olympics, viewed by the Nazis as an opportunity to showcase Teutonic efficiency and sporting prowess.

The motive for the ban was never clear, but it was lifted in February 1936. Battles over censorship continued for years, though, a constant source of tension for Lochner with the Nazi government, as well as with his AP editors in New York, who were frequently frustrated by what they viewed as his overly cautious approach to reporting the world's biggest news story.

The tensions between Lochner and New York affected what newspaper readers saw all across America. By the eve of World War II, AP was sending its daily harvest of news to more than 1,200 U.S. newspapers.[33] More than half also took AP's photo service. In 1941 AP's member newspapers had a total circulation of over thirty-four million, or 83 percent of the entire U.S. audience reached by the three main wire services.[34] By comparison, the *Chicago Tribune* had just over a million daily subscribers that year, while the *New York Times*'s daily circulation was less than half that.[35] (Both papers had their own Berlin correspondents, and distribution on syndicated services boosted readership of their stories somewhat.)

Despite its vast daily reach, AP's reporting was seldom recognized as having the cachet of the prestigious, metropolitan *Times*. Lochner's name became a familiar byline, and many stories by the other Berlin newshawks were identified by author when AP distributed them. But AP journalists generally were far less likely to become household names than, say, Edward R. Murrow did with his wartime broadcasts for CBS radio, and newspapers often identified the news agency's stories simply as (AP) or By Associated Press, with no author name given. Scoops were encouraged more than graceful writing style. Speed was paramount for text stories, and especially for AP's photo service. In his drive to make AP the leading global news service, Cooper pushed the company to embrace new technologies that could speed delivery of photos, enhancing their newsworthiness. AP promoted the service heavily with newspaper ads extolling "WORLD PICTURES WITH THE SPEED OF LIGHT," leaving space where members could insert the name of their publication. One ad, published on February 12, 1939, by the *Daily Oklahoman*, boasted that "only eight hours and thirteen minutes after Adolf Hitler finished his historic speech to the German Reichstag, this dramatic picture was printed in THE DAILY OKLAHOMAN and was being rushed to readers throughout Oklahoma."[36]

If AP lacked cachet, though, no other media outlet could match its broad reach to American audiences. "AP is a vast, intricately reticulated, organization, the largest of its kind, gathering news from all over the world, the chief single source of news for the American press, universally agreed to be of prime consequence," wrote a panel of three judges appointed by a U.S. District Court to hear an antitrust case brought by the federal government in 1943 against AP.[37] That theme, "chief single source of news for the American press," was one Lochner returned to again and again in his frequent tangles with AP editors and executives over the Berlin bureau's coverage.

In 1938 those editors had moved from crowded offices on New York's Madison Avenue to the new AP headquarters at "50 Rock," in Rockefeller Center, surrounded by the giant skyscrapers of midtown Manhattan. Its entrance was decorated with a massive bas relief sculpture representing five reporters at work and titled "News." Inside, soundproofing only partially muffled the twenty-four-hour clackety-clack of teleprinters, the beeping of radiophoto transmitters, and the whoosh of the overhead pneumatic tube system delivering copy and messages from one desk to another. The occasional ding-ding-ding from the teleprinters signaled transmission of the most important stories, each designated as a "flash," a "bulletin," or an "urgent."

The newsroom was where stories arrived from Berlin, ready for scrutiny by editors seated at a U-shaped desk, staffed round the clock, at what was then known as the cable desk. Cable desk editors processed more than a million words a month, fixing spelling and grammar, rewriting, asking questions, and sometimes demanding more reporting before a story from abroad was released to AP members for publication.

The cable desk editors were the first line of "gatekeepers," shaping the news report from around the world. Once AP members received stories from the cable desk, another set of gatekeepers—the editors at each newspaper—chose which stories and photos to share with their audiences and where to place them: front page, deep inside the paper, or bumped from publication altogether by other news of the day. They also could cut or rewrite stories and change AP's suggested headlines and photo captions.

A story from 1942 offers a clear illustration of how one AP report could play very differently in newspapers across the country. In November that year, Rabbi Stephen Wise, chairman of the World Jewish Congress, told AP the U.S. State Department had confirmed to him that the Nazis had murdered two million Jews and that Hitler had ordered the extermination of all Jews in Nazi-ruled Europe before the end of the year. Earlier stories reporting on the Nazi slaughter had often been downplayed or even dismissed as unverified and too horrific to be true. But the Wise-State Department story was considered solid confirmation of the Nazi extermination program, and AP's story ran on front pages in cities across the country—among them, Des Moines, Iowa; Huntsville, Alabama; Hartford, Connecticut—and in the *New York Herald Tribune*. The same story was reduced to two paragraphs on page 6 in the *Washington Post*, and the *New York Times* ran a version on page 10 that did not mention the Nazi goal of exterminating all Jews in German-held Europe.[38]

AP's cable desk editors were the first to react if a rival agency got a story Berlin didn't have or if a report from Berlin seemed to bury the news. They could challenge Lochner's news judgment. But they were also aware that he could—and often did—appeal to his ultimate boss: Kent Cooper, AP's number one "gatekeeper" and Lochner's staunchest defender in the agency.

Cooper ran AP as its top executive from 1925 to 1948. His corner suite at 50 Rock, a few floors above the newsroom, had its own shower. Cooper worked from an easy chair, keeping papers spread on a nearby table as a secretary took his dictation for memos and letters on everything from broad ethical questions to minute staffing issues. "Cooper was outgoing, impulsive, seat-of-the-pants creative, and a man about town" was the assessment of an unpublished history of the AP that described his twenty-three-year tenure as "a one-man show," often operating "without regard for the feelings of his executives."[39] One of those executives, Alan Jenks Gould, joined AP in 1922, rose through the ranks to executive editor in 1941, and "clashed frequently with Cooper, who had second-guessed the editor's news judgement at every turn. Cooper was once heard to say, 'Gould sticks that square chin out and I love to hit it,'" according to the unpublished history.

AP had long been essentially a domestic U.S. news service, restricted from seeking global subscribers by a business alliance with Reuters and other European news agencies (UP, its main U.S. rival, had no such restrictions, so while UP was smaller than AP in America, it had a larger global reach). Cooper longed to break free of the restrictive alliance and make AP the world's premier source of news and photos. The photo service he created in Germany was a key part of that vision, and Lochner, knowing his boss's devotion to it, would cite the photo agency's survival as a justification for being cautious with the news.

Cooper was also very much AP's chief gatekeeper for news and how it should be reported. In a memo circulated to staff in 1936—which all were required to read and initial—he defined the agency's reporting standards. True, unbiased news, he wrote, rather hyperbolically, was "the highest original moral concept ever developed in America and given to the world." He called absolute impartiality "the fundamental creed of the Associated Press" and said AP stories needed to be so balanced that they "can be read unchallenged by hostile critics in the United States or any other country." Facts must be facts, Cooper wrote, "but frequently they alone are not enough. Sometimes there must be background to make those facts appear in their true light. Often one set of facts tells one side of a story and other facts are needed to balance them."[40]

After war began in Europe, Cooper used far less lofty language to make the same point in a June 3, 1940, memo to editors and bureau chiefs: "Let facts continue to tell what is happening. This country is not at war. Let's not get off-side ourselves by whooping it up for either belligerent on any idea it is our duty to whoop it up for either."[41]

For all his emphasis on objectivity, Cooper himself held fierce political views. In an oral history interview in the 1980s, Alan Gould described his boss as "a strong Republican, a qualified, card-carrying Roosevelt-hater and he detested the British and the French." Gould said he did not think Cooper was pro-German but added that in private conversations, he "would indicate he was happy to see France collapse early on and thought the Germans would finish the job with England if they invaded across the channel." In a private meeting with Cooper and another AP executive, Byron Price, Gould said Cooper offered some "pretty hot" views about the war in Europe.

After Gould and Price left the room, they turned to each other (according to Gould) to share the thought: "For crissakes, let's hope that what we have just been listening to is confined to the corner [office]."[42]

As gatekeeper-in-chief, Cooper's views mattered above all others. And on the question of reporting from Berlin under censorship rules, his view was very clear. In a letter to a Pennsylvania publisher just weeks after the Nazi invasion of Poland in 1939, he wrote that "the Associated Press has very much at stake in the matter of keeping its staff abroad in good standing with the respective governments of the countries in which they are assigned."[43] AP correspondents, in Cooper's view, were "guests of the countries in which they are accredited," and therefore "they should not abuse their hospitality." Cooper noted no exceptions, even for AP's Berlin journalists, who were working in decidedly inhospitable conditions.

3

THE NEWS BUREAU

In the summer of 1933, several months after Adolf Hitler came to power, Louis Lochner fielded an unusual query from Wilson Hicks, then head of features news for AP in New York. Would Hitler be willing to write some columns for AP, Hicks wondered. "We are led to hope," he wrote, "that he might consider such an undertaking because of the violent reactions which have greeted some of his measures in this and other countries."[1]

As outlandish as that proposal sounds today, what Hicks suggested was not an original idea. Even before the Nazis took office, American publisher William Randolph Hearst had commissioned columns from Hitler and top aide Hermann Göring, offering a platform in Hearst's more than two dozen daily newspapers for "Hitler's talking points," according to historian Kathryn S. Olmsted.[2] Chief among those talking points was Hitler's warning that the Treaty of Versailles ending World War I required such onerous reparations to be paid to the war's victors that Germans were being forced to transfuse "their own lifeblood from Germany to France, England, and America." In his belligerent column published by Hearst September 28, 1930, Hitler warned the Versailles agreement would drive Germany "into the beckoning arms of Bolshevism."[3]

Several years later, Kristallnacht would turn publisher Hearst passionately anti-Nazi, but in the early 1930s he was attracted to the party by its fierce antipathy to Soviet communism. Hearst and a few other prominent Americans, including Charles Lindbergh and former president Herbert Hoover, paid high-profile, largely sympathetic visits to Berlin after Hitler took office. Lindbergh stirred controversy in 1938 by accepting a Nazi medal, ostensibly honoring his contributions to aviation but also putting a veneer of acceptability on the increasingly brutal dictatorship—or so Nazi propagandists hoped. News organizations, including AP, covered the visits, convincing some Nazi leaders that there was value in having foreign correspondents in Berlin.

The idea for a Hitler column to be distributed on the AP newswire appeared to die quickly, though. "That is a big order indeed which you gave me," Lochner responded when Hicks proposed it. "You may rest assured," he added, "that I will do everything possible to secure such a series."[4] No series ever appeared, and there is no evidence that Lochner actually made any effort to take the idea to Hitler. Had he done so and succeeded, he no doubt would have given added ammunition to critics who, a few years later, accused Lochner of Nazi sympathies.

Lochner, dean of AP's correspondents in Europe, who chronicled the rise of fascism and frenzied anti-Semitism in Germany, headed both the agency's news bureau in Berlin and its photo arm, the AP GmbH, though he regarded his role as manager of the photo agency as something of a nuisance. His heart was in the reporting done by the news bureau, which had two German reporters and a staff of six Americans, most of whom had joined AP after reporting local news for papers in the Midwest.

Lochner had by far the strongest credentials in the bureau. Fluent in German and a veteran of the AP Berlin bureau since 1924, he had a rich network of news sources, particularly in political and cultural circles: socialists as well as industrialists; the military and the intelligentsia; rabbis, Lutheran ministers, Catholic priests; and Germany's old aristocracy—including Crown Prince Louis Ferdinand of Hohenzollern, whom Lochner counted as a close friend. Over the years, he met and interviewed many of the most noteworthy personalities of Germany's Weimar Republic as well as the Nazi regime, including Hitler, both before and after he came to power.[5]

Lochner played Berlin's social game with energy and style. He served terms as president of the Foreign Press Association and as head of the American Chamber of Commerce in Germany. "There was hardly an official or unofficial function at which Louis was not present, circulating among friends, listening to bits of news and giving his own, talking seriously with diplomats and Germans," wrote Martha Dodd, daughter of William E. Dodd, then the U.S. ambassador in Berlin.[6]

In photos, Lochner looks like a college professor: slightly built, eyes peering through tiny, rimless spectacles, always smartly attired in a suit with vest and tie. Martha Dodd saw him more scathingly, though, describing him as a "short bald-headed bulbous-looking man resembling a gnome, somewhat officious and patronizing towards some people."

Lochner was born in Springfield, Illinois, in 1887, the son of a Lutheran minister, the Reverend Frederick Lochner, and Maria von Haugwitz. Both parents were born in Germany, and Lochner was raised bilingually. Notes for an unwritten memoir show he was believed to be related to Katharina von Bora, the wife of Martin Luther, on his mother's side. He graduated from the University of Wisconsin in 1909 with Phi Beta Kappa honors and worked as a reporter for the *Milwaukee Free Press* and the *Madison Democrat*. Lochner and Emmy Hoyer, his first wife, who died in an influenza epidemic in 1920, had a son, Robert, and a daughter, Elsbeth, who remained with their maternal grandparents in the United States when Lochner went abroad.

Journalism and pacifism led him to Germany. He served as press spokesman for a quixotic mission, headed by Henry Ford, that sailed to Europe in 1915 to call for a peace conference to end World War I. He also helped establish the Milwaukee-based Federated Press news service, which was sympathetic to the peace movement, supported by organized labor, and often accused of Communist leanings.[7] When the news service offered him an opportunity to report from Europe, he moved to Berlin in 1921 and freelanced for labor publications until AP hired him in 1924. Four years later, Lochner was appointed Berlin bureau chief.

In 1922 he married Hilde Steinberger De Terra, a German divorcee with a four-year-old daughter, Rosemarie. Hilde's parents were Christian Hugo Steinberger, judge of the Supreme Military Court, and his wife Emma, who had strong connections to Germany's conservative and monarchist elements. The Steinbergers invited the newlyweds to move into their spacious home, where they lived until December 1941, when the United States and Germany declared war on each other, and Americans were rounded up and eventually expelled.

When writing to his family in America in the 1930s, Lochner often shared unvarnished views of the Nazi leaders that he didn't put in his wire service stories. In July 1934, shortly after Hitler's Reichstag speech justifying the Night of the Long Knives purge of political enemies, Lochner wrote to his daughter about the Nazi leader's "gangster methods" and described the speech as "the ranting of a man who is not normal." That September, after he covered the annual party rally at Nürnberg, attended by hundreds of thousands of fervent Nazis, he wrote home that the account he filed for AP had been genuine, "BUT IT REPRESENTS ONLY ONE SIDE OF THE

SITUATION." Away from the rally, he said, it was easy to hear grumbling about the Nazis. "It would be a mistake, however, to think that this regime is cracking and will be gone shortly," he wrote. "All elements of force are in its hands, so no counter-movement has any chance presently."[8]

He also told his children about internal AP machinations, including how he was nearly removed as bureau chief in early 1939. Lochner had announced to the Berlin staff that he would step down as chief to become a roving European correspondent based in Berlin, a change proposed by a London AP executive, Milo Thompson. At the time, Thompson oversaw the Berlin bureau, and Lochner was frequently irritated by his supervision. Thompson, in turn, once described Lochner's bureau as "the worst in Europe," and the "roving correspondent" offer was a ruse to depose its chief. It nearly worked—until Lochner learned that his replacement was to be AP Moscow bureau chief Wade Werner, who had filled in as head of the Berlin bureau during a Lochner visit to the United States. "I had no sooner turned my back on the Berlin office, than Werner began to write unfair, nasty letters about me to the home office, all in hope of putting himself in my place here," Lochner fumed in a letter to his children.[9]

In May 1939 Lochner was able to scuttle the plan, after Columbia University announced he had won the Pulitzer Prize for his "dispatches from Berlin" the previous year. He was fifty-two, at the pinnacle of his career, and talk of replacing him with Werner was stifled. "The AP home office seemed very happy, for usually the prize goes to the Primadonnas of our profession, the special correspondents, and not to wood-sawing agency representatives," Lochner told his children.[10]

The practical side of Lochner's victory, though, was that as bureau chief he continued to be burdened with the administrative duties with which he'd told his children he was "fed up." As chief administrator for AP Berlin, he dueled constantly with the propaganda ministry over photos and dispatches to which the regime objected, jousted with AP editors in London and New York over the handling of stories, and lived with the nagging fear of expulsion for transmitting something the Nazis would deem a violation of their censorious dictates.

All of that left Lochner with relatively little time to put his broad grasp of German affairs to use as a news analyst. Increasingly, the breaking news from Germany was handled by his reporters, several of whom had minimal practical preparation for dealing with German censorship or the pressures of covering a huge international story. All learned on the job as they reported the growing Nazi menace and later became war correspondents and documentarians of the aftermath of Nazi atrocities.

Next to Lochner, reporter Melvin Whiteleather had the most experience in Europe. He began his newspaper career in France in 1927 at the Paris *Times* and joined AP there in 1929. In 1934 Whiteleather, then thirty-one, transferred to the Berlin bureau. When his name turned up on a guest list for a Nazi film premiere, Ernst Hanfstaengl, the party's liaison to foreign correspondents, quickly called Lochner.

"Louis, why are you sending me a Jew?" Hanfstaengl demanded of the bureau chief. Hanfstaengl apparently was alarmed by the first part of Whiteleather's name in German: Weiss, a common Jewish surname. "My dear Putzi," Lochner replied, using Hanfstaengl's nickname, "it so happens that Whiteleather is not Jewish."

"That was my first personal contact with Nazi anti-semitism, and it came in the very first week of my assignment to Berlin," Whiteleather wrote in an unpublished memoir.[11]

During his years in Berlin, Whiteleather wrote occasional articles for a U.S. journalism review, noting in June 1939 that "no newspaper man can know how difficult news gathering can be until he has tried it in a dictatorship."[12] The same year, he wrote for AP about the more than two million party loyalists who formed a "vast army of ears" spying on neighbors and preparing reports for the propaganda ministry. "That their work is well done would seem to be indicated by the almost perfect scores registered in national elections," noted Whiteleather; the Nazis, for example, claimed to have swept 99.028 percent of the votes in balloting that followed the annexation of Austria in 1938.[13]

Alvin Steinkopf, a Minnesotan who arrived in Berlin in late 1939, was the only reporter in Lochner's bureau with any war experience: he had served as an ambulance driver with the Allied Expeditionary Force in World War I. Later he worked at the *St. Paul Pioneer Press* and the *Milwaukee Sentinel* before joining AP in Milwaukee in 1931. That year, he wrote a lengthy autobiographical letter to Kent Cooper, saying he had been encouraged to think about a career abroad but concluding, "I am ready to go anywhere, but just as ready to stay [in Wisconsin] in any job that makes a challenge for distinctive service." Within three years AP had sent him to Vienna. He was forty-two when he joined the Berlin bureau in 1939. Steinkopf was a prolific correspondent and an elegant writer with occasional flashes of humor, once describing the overweight Hermann Göring as "one of the best nourished men in Germany."[14]

The other Americans in the bureau had skimpier resumes. Lynn Heinzerling was thirty-two when he arrived in Berlin from Ohio with no foreign reporting experience. He had dropped out of Ohio Wesleyan University in 1928 to become a reporter in Cleveland for the *Plain Dealer*. He joined AP's Cleveland bureau in 1933, moved to the New York cable desk five years later, and took up a Berlin assignment in 1938 just weeks before Kristallnacht. In the days following the pogrom, he reported ongoing waves of anti-Semitism and police roundups of Jews.[15] Then, in early 1939, he described a new Nazi blueprint for getting rid of Jews: shipping up to fifteen million of them to "reservations" in British Guiana or French-owned

Madagascar. All could be financed, said Alfred Rosenberg, Hitler's top theorist and ideologue, by "Jewish millionaires and billionaires from all the world."[16]

Wisconsin native Edwin "Eddie" Shanke attended the journalism school at Marquette University in Milwaukee. He joined the AP bureau in Milwaukee in 1935 and two years later, at age twenty-seven, arrived in Berlin. He landed the posting, he told a company newsletter years later, "because AP found out I spoke a little German." Like all the correspondents, Shanke covered a gamut of news, writing about an "underground railway" that smuggled Austrian Jews into Switzerland; about strident German propaganda designed to justify a Nazi takeover of the Sudetenland in Czechoslovakia; or about the bizarre scene in a busy Berlin restaurant run by Hitler's half-brother, Alois Matzelsberger Hitler Jr. "As each customer enters the doorway, a hearty 'Heil Hitler' rings in his ears from the first waiter to spot him," reported Shanke. "He's due for another 'Heil Hitler' when the menu is presented and again when he leaves. Each greeting is accompanied by the Nazi salute."[17]

Novice Angus Thuermer, of Quincy, Illinois, had by far the least experience but was perhaps the most excited about his job in the AP bureau. A recent graduate of the University of Illinois, Thuermer, twenty-one, had come to Berlin to study German. When Lochner hired him in early 1939, Thuermer wrote his parents that it was a "dream come true." A blue-eyed blond with a neatly trimmed mustache, he was six foot three inches tall and towered over everyone else in the office. He was a precocious adventurer and a wit, who once described Julius Streicher, notorious as a sadistic Jew-baiter and publisher of the virulently anti-Semitic *Der Stürmer*, as "an earthworm among men."[18]

As the low man on the totem pole, Thuermer was initially given the overnight "graveyard" shift at the office, though he seemed not to mind the schedule. "The AP is a real he-man, dirty, noisy, cluttered news office where real news happens and typewriters click and there are no dames underfoot with the exception of the telephone girl," he wrote.

As in most wire service foreign bureaus, the American correspondents worked side by side with "local hires"—German reporters. Rudolf "Rudi" Josten joined the AP as a messenger and editorial assistant in 1925 when he was just eighteen. By the time Hitler came to power, he was helping Lochner cover breaking news, like the Night of the Long Knives in 1934 when Hitler purged political enemies, including leaders of the Sturmabteilung. The following year Josten was reporting on the sobbing German mother of Bruno Richard Hauptmann, who appealed unsuccessfully to President Franklin Roosevelt to save her son from the electric chair. Hauptmann had been found guilty and sentenced to death in the sensational Lindbergh kidnapping and murder case.[19]

Robert Schildbach, AP's other German reporter, was a longtime veteran of both the Berlin and Vienna bureaus. In 1939 he detailed how the Nazis had devastated Germany's publishing world. "Since 1933 more than 6,000 publications—books, periodicals, and newspapers—have passed out of existence," he wrote, and Propaganda Minister Joseph Goebbels had ousted more than 1,500 journalists from the profession for representing "unqualified elements." The moves eliminated all opposition press, leaving Germany served only by media completely controlled by the Nazi Party.[20] Schildbach's byline was withheld from the story, presumably to protect him from the wrath of propaganda ministry officials.[21]

In August 1934 a news exchange agreement was signed under which AP's Berlin bureau received German news from the Deutsches Nachrichtenbüro (DNB), and DNB's office in New York received AP's U.S. news.[22] The DNB was a Nazi creation that took over Germany's two biggest news agencies: the Telegraphen-Union, owned by Hitler supporter and anti-Semite entrepreneur Alfred Hugenberg, and the Wolff Telegraphic Bureau, founded in the nineteenth century by Bernhard Wolff, the son of a Jewish banker. The DNB's output was edited and censored by Goebbels's underlings before being sent to virtually every media outlet in the Third Reich—and to most of the foreign news agencies with offices in Berlin. Its reports came clattering into AP's offices via teleprinter.

Photos of the Berlin bureau, on the fourth floor at 68 Zimmerstrasse, show overhead lamps on long cords, dangling over a cluster of writing tables in the center of the newsroom. The tables were covered with typewriters, ashtrays, and disheveled stacks of newspapers and magazines. Two soundproof phone booths stood on the far side of the bureau so that it was possible for someone to take dictation from a reporter in the field in one booth while someone else dictated an urgent news story from Berlin to London in the other. Overcoats and the fedora hats that were in vogue at the time were draped over a wooden coat rack at the newsroom entrance.

Pinned to the walls were maps, calendars, and, on one, a list of AP European stringers and various German contacts, "everyone from the foreign office and von Ribbentrop to Jo's, the joint downstairs who bring us weenies," as Angus Thuermer put it.[23] The bureau radio behind the news desk was usually tuned to Reichssender Berlin, the official German station, to assure no government announcements were missed, but the reporters would also tune in to British broadcasts. While any German listening to foreign radio stations faced a potential death sentence, foreign journalists were allowed to tune in to international broadcasts, and they monitored the BBC regularly. "There was the hilarious day in Berlin," Lynn Heinzerling recalled, "when Winston Churchill's voice came growling over the radio calling Hitler 'that guttersnipe.'"[24]

In letters home to his parents, Ed Shanke painted a picture of the Berlin bureau as chronically understaffed—"We are just as shorthanded as ever," he lamented in the summer of 1938—as reporters rotated in and out or jumped on trains and planes to cover breaking news events in Vienna, Prague, Warsaw, Budapest, and other places.[25] The bureau had lost two veterans in recent transfers, and Lochner lamented having only a single replacement, Shanke, "who is promising enough and a nice lad to work with, but who neither knows German nor has yet learned his way around Europe. So I've got to watch the news desk pretty closely."[26]

One Saturday, however, Lochner, attending the opera, was not on watch when Shanke was thrown into a big story. Shanke described in vivid detail how the bureau scrambled to write about Hitler's February 5, 1938, shakeup of his cabinet, in which the Nazi leader took direct command of all armed forces and weeded out his conservative critics in what amounted to an internal coup d'état. It was huge news, delivered in a dizzying blitz of urgent communiques on what had up to then been a slow Saturday shift. The official announcements also revealed that Hitler had elevated Göring to the highest military rank of field marshal general and appointed the zealous Joachim von Ribbentrop, the Champagne salesman then serving as ambassador to the Court of St. James, as foreign minister.

In the office with Shanke were Wade Werner, the reporter who later nearly replaced Lochner as bureau chief, and an AP German staffer. They first flashed the news by cable and telephone to London. "Then rapidly about 10 communiques came, one after another," Shanke wrote later, "leaving us plenty bewildered. So many things were done in one full-swoop, that it kind of left us gasping. We worked like troopers keeping the news running by telephone to London which called us every 10 minutes. Mr. Werner wrote the leads, trying to get organization into the story, and to put across the significance of what it meant."

Shanke's account, written to his parents, continued:

It was an awful story to handle because Hitler did so many important things at once in liquidating the "crisis." By this time, Mr. Lochner, who had gone to the opera, called. When he found out what had happened, he hurried to the office and wrote a wonderful interpretive story which only an old hand like himself could write. Then we began to pick up a few loose ends and the story was cleaned up for the morning newspapers. Our first bulletins caught many afternoon papers [in the United States] because of the great difference in time. While Mr. Lochner was writing that last lead, Mr. Werner and I went out and enjoyed a good dinner and a glass of champagne.[27]

Lochner likely wrote his "wonderful interpretive story" from his corner office, pecking away at the typewriter on his large desk. Next to him on the wall hung photos of the bureau chief at various social occasions and, more ominously, a large map that marked the ever-expanding prewar boundaries of the Third Reich.

Years later, Morrell Heald, who edited a volume of Lochner's letters, offered a blunt assessment of the bureau chief. "By no means a daring adventurer, a sparkling stylist or a brilliant analyst of the sweep of events," wrote Heald, "he was instead a sturdy, conscientious, hardworking, patient and relentless gatherer of contacts and information."[28] But when the Pulitzer Prize elevated his journalistic standing, Lochner's sometimes contentious relations with the home office "were suddenly reversed. New York now seemed almost to hang on his every word and to bend over backwards to meet, if not anticipate, his needs."

That meant funding and staffing requests were no longer issues, "nor were inclinations to second-guess his news judgments," wrote Heald. From Lochner's "position of galling subjection to the demands of the home office and criticisms of his nominal regional chief, [Milo] Thompson in London, Adolf Hitler had quite inadvertently and incidentally exalted Lochner to the upper reaches of the AP's reportorial hierarchy."[29]

4

THE GMBH

As AP's staff of reporters and photographers in Berlin covered the Nazis and wrestled with censorship, the company's relationship with the German government began to intertwine, often in troubling ways, through its photo subsidiary, the AP GmbH. The details of that relationship were largely buried in AP corporate files and U.S. government records after World War II, until 2016, when German historian Harriet Scharnberg revealed that AP, through its photo subsidiary, had been a major conduit for sending thousands of Nazi-made, propaganda ministry–approved photos to its newspaper clients outside Germany.[1] These included photos from German photographers employed by the AP GmbH who were simultaneously working for the Nazi propaganda ministry—or, during the war years, serving in Wehrmacht or Waffen-SS propaganda companies.

Scharnberg's study said that Germany also had used photos it received from AP in the United States in its anti-Semitic propaganda: images of Jews appeared in Nazi publications that denigrated and ridiculed them.

For AP's twenty-first-century managers, these revelations from more than seven decades earlier were news, part of a long-forgotten history about a German company, incorporated by AP, answering to

AP management, but also very vulnerable to Nazi edicts—far more so than the news service's own correspondents in the news bureau. While the news bureau's reports were subject to "responsibility censorship," meaning no advance clearance was required to file a story though there could be consequences later, prior censorship became the rule for photos. Photos could not be distributed from Germany without advance review and approval from the propaganda ministry. The ministry also applied a heavy hand in censoring the captions on AP photos distributed inside Germany. And as a German company, the GmbH was subject to racist rules that eventually required AP either to dismiss its Jewish employees or to close down the photo operation altogether.

The AP GmbH was officially registered in Berlin in 1931 as a subsidiary of the Associated Press of Great Britain, Ltd., which in turn was a subsidiary of the Associated Press of New York. Both the German and British companies were part of an effort by Kent Cooper, the ambitious general manager, to expand what was essentially a domestic American news agency into a global player. The new enterprise in Berlin then acquired the German subsidiary of Pacific and Atlantic, Ltd., the European branch of Pacific and Atlantic News Photo Service.

For Cooper, this expansion was a crusade, one he sometimes couched in grand and noble terms. In his autobiography, published after retirement, he said his goal had been to make AP "the world's greatest news and newsphoto agency," one no longer serving just an American audience, but "as many in every country in the whole world as could be reached, hopefully that the truth would contribute to mutual international understanding."[2]

That was the dream. The hard reality was that, to accomplish it, Cooper would need to break up a four-member news agency cartel composed of Reuters of Great Britain, Havas of France, the Wolff Telegraphic Bureau of Germany, and AP. The cartel agreement bound each company to share its news reporting with the others, while limiting where each could sell those reports. At the beginning of the twentieth century, AP was prohibited from selling its news outside North America; South America was added to its marketing sphere in 1918.[3] But the long-standing agreement that set these restrictions "was so antiquated that it never included reference to news in picture form," Cooper wrote in a memoir. Thus, by forming the AP GmbH—a new service, just for photos—Cooper could sell an AP product globally and begin to break down the cartel's geographic barriers.[4]

At its founding in 1931, the GmbH and its photographers faced few restrictions on their work. The images they took were distributed widely, inside and outside of Germany. But trouble began soon after the Nazis came to power in 1933. An early Nazi edict imposed prior censorship of photos, requiring the AP GmbH and others to submit every image they wanted to distribute to the increasingly hostile bureaucrats at the propaganda ministry. Rejection by the censors meant an image could not be sent to clients.

The Editor's Law enacted in January 1934 gave the ministry extraordinary powers over all German media. Foreign photo agencies registered as German companies were singled out for particular attention in a legal commentary issued by the ministry.[5] Even if an agency's owners were not German, it said, they were subject to the Editor's Law, requiring them to employ as photojournalists only German citizens "of Aryan descent and not married to a person of non-Aryan descent." Photographers also had to have "the qualifications necessary for the task of spiritually influencing the public."[6] After the Editor's Law took effect, AP bureau chief Louis Lochner wrote: "Many naive souls evidently thought that outward conformity would suffice to save their jobs. They soon learned that their records were carefully examined, their political past searched, their blood tested as to its freedom from Jewish taint."[7]

The ministry required Lochner himself, as manager of AP's German-registered photo agency, to produce evidence of Aryan descent back to his great-grandparents. He was furious about the demand and asked for guidance from New York, which responded that "so long as the antisemitic decrees of the present German government were the law of the land, and since our picture section was a German company, I must comply."[8] That view, from AP corporate executives in New York, suggested that they did not see the GmbH as an integral part of AP, bound by the same standards and ethics that guided the company's operations in the United States. It's a view some New York executives appeared to hold throughout the Nazi era.

Further restrictions came in Nazi changes to labor law, which called for a new Council of Confidence (Vertrauensrat) to replace the work council (Betriebsrat) that traditionally dealt with employee-management relations in German businesses. Under the law, the employee representative was no longer elected by workers but was approved by the Nazi Party. Lochner laid out the details in a letter to AP headquarters in New York: "I, as Geschäftsfuehrer [managing director of the photo subsidiary], must call together the entire staff of the AP GmbH and in their presence pledge [to] the Nazi representative on the Council of Confidence to live up to all the principles of this organization, and I in turn must pledge that our GmbH will obey the rules and regulations of the Nazi state." As a foreigner, said Lochner, he was not required to say "Heil Hitler" after taking the pledge, "but in spirit I must accept the regulations or else our company is threatened with dissolution." Lochner told New York he had discussed the new demands with various American legal and business representatives, "and all have agreed that there is nothing that we can do except bow to these regulations."[9]

By the mid-1930s the AP GmbH had become a miniature battleground. As its top manager, Lochner grappled with Germany's anti-Semitic edicts, restrictive press laws, and the formidable Nazi propaganda apparatus of Joseph Goebbels. The yearslong battle—with the GmbH in the middle between AP London and the propaganda ministry—often revolved around captions on photos distributed in Germany. Fiery ethical debates ensued. The German photo staff, treading carefully to avoid the wrath of the propaganda ministry, was also under the watch of AP supervisors in London who were determined to hold the line on truth.

One photo in particular, an image from the Spanish Civil War, set off such a fierce debate that at least one London manager strongly suggested AP should consider closing the German photo service in order to preserve its journalistic integrity. The photo arrived in Berlin November 6, 1936, in the package of images from around the world that London sent each day to the German photo subsidiary. GmbH employees made copies of the images and wrote new captions in German to deliver to some ninety newspapers and magazines in Germany, Switzerland, Italy, and Scandinavia.[10]

The photo from Spain showed a Madrid morgue after an air raid carried out by forces loyal to Generalissimo Francisco Franco and his fascist rebels. London's caption on the photo said that "insurgent bombers" had carried out the worst air raid on Madrid since the start of the civil war, killing ninety-five people: "Bombs fell in busy streets and one wrecked a school killing 70 children. Associated Press photo shows a view of the Madrid morgue on Oct. 31, after an air raid the previous day. This picture was issued by the Madrid ministry of state to show the results of the rebel [Franco forces] air raid on Madrid."[11]

The AP GmbH photo desk replaced the London caption with its own version for German clients: "Horrors of the civil war—Thousands of innocent victims have already been claimed by the frightful Spanish Civil War, into which the irresponsible Communistic wire-pullers have plunged the country." Gone was mention of the "rebel air raid" by Franco's forces, who were backed by Nazi Germany. Instead, the caption's message was one more palatable to the Nazis: that Spain's leftist, democratically elected government— the "irresponsible Communistic wire-pullers"—was to blame for the civil war.

When Munich's *Münchner Neueste Nachrichten* ran the photo, the caption had morphed even more in the direction of Nazi propaganda, implying (falsely) the morgue image showed victims of the government—even though the government itself had released the photo. "Mercilessly killed by the Reds—This frightful picture presented itself to the national [fascist] troops advancing on Madrid in a suburb of the Spanish capital. The Reds had previously killed all the hostages who were in their power."

AP in London eventually saw both the GmbH and Munich captions, prompting a sharp rebuke from Gideon Seymour, managing director of the Associated Press of Great Britain and supervisor of the German photo operation. Seymour wrote to Rudolf Josten, the German journalist who had been transferred to the AP GmbH photo desk from the news bureau that year, despite having no photo experience. Seymour said he understood the GmbH could not be held responsible for the caption written by staff of the Munich paper. But "the AP GmbH itself is much more gravely at fault," he wrote, for omitting the truth in its version—the caption attributing the civil war to "irresponsible Communistic wire-pullers."

"If you cannot issue pictures with honest captions do not issue them at all," Seymour instructed Josten. "Remember that your honor and integrity as a newspaperman are something never to be exchanged for sales, and that the honor and integrity of the organization you work for is worth more to it and to you than all the money the GmbH will earn for the rest of eternity." Seymour also asked Josten to respond with assurances that the AP GmbH would never again engage in "this despicable sort of propaganda."[12]

Lochner, in his role as director of the photo subsidiary, replied to Seymour, saying that "the Propaganda Ministry simply ordered [Josten] to write such a caption." In similar future situations, Lochner said, the GmbH would "withdraw the picture and not permit its use in Germany." But Lochner added that he himself would need to take responsibility for such a decision, to shield Josten, a German citizen, from possible ministry retaliation.

As German citizens, Josten and other GmbH employees were subject to Nazi edicts, set forth at daily propaganda ministry press conferences, in Foreign Office "commentaries," and through instructions received from the official DNB news agency.[13] They were also subject to the Editor's Law, which meant "their loyalty to nation, government and Führer had to exceed their loyalty to their employer," according to one German historian of Nazi photography. Perceived violations could lead to "occupational bans, honor trials and imprisonment should they fall in disgrace at the Propaganda Ministry."[14]

If Lochner thought his response would reassure Seymour, he was wrong. More letters flew back and forth between Berlin and London. Seymour sought details about how the propaganda ministry exercised control, warning that if the Nazi government could dictate which photos could be put out and what their captions could say, "we cannot tolerate it for a minute." Seymour even suggested that AP consider closing the German photo service. "If there is no alternative to toleration but closure, I fear the answer must be closure," he wrote.[15]

Seymour's strong anticensorship position was a marked contrast with Lochner's commitment to working within German restrictions in order to "remain in the field." German journalists, Lochner told Seymour, could not ignore the dictates of the propaganda ministry. "They are often instructed even how the headlines must read, so that every paper in Germany carries the same monotonous headline," he wrote. "Were Josten on a German newspaper he would probably find himself out of a job the next day if he did not yield to such a 'request.'"

The controversy over the Madrid morgue photo eventually died away (though not until Seymour had suggested to AP management in New York that Lochner should be replaced as GmbH managing director but remain chief of the news bureau—a change that was never made). But a few weeks later the larger battle over captions erupted again—this time after New York mayor Fiorello La Guardia referred to Hitler as "that brown shirted fanatic who is menacing the peace of the world."[16]

La Guardia's March 1937 speech was immediately denounced in Germany. *Der Angriff* (The Attack), a Nazi propaganda sheet, displayed the mayor's picture under the headline "Scoundrel La Guardia." The caption called him a "lout" and an "impudent Jew." Two days later (after the United States offered a sort-of apology to "a government with which we have official relations") the GmbH photo service issued a stock photo of La Guardia to the German press.[17] Its caption described the mayor as "unruehmlich" (shameful) and his speech as "Hetzrede" (a diatribe). When Seymour in London saw it, he shot off an angry note to Josten about the "biased and poisoned" caption. "Are you unable to avoid scurrilous captions, or are you unwilling?" he asked. Josten, who had distributed the photo at the insistence of the propaganda ministry, replied: "The caption was biased, yes," but it had been sent only to German clients. "They [the German media] had similar but stronger orders," he told Seymour. "Believe me, it's not fun to be under two fires, but don't you think I should also try to please the authorities occasionally?"[18]

The sparring over captions—and the ministry's pressure on Josten—continued until, a month after the La Guardia photo controversy, Josten returned to the AP's news bureau. His position at the AP GmbH was filled by another German reporter from the news bureau, Guenther Beukert, who took over in May 1937 and would direct the critical photo coverage of Kristallnacht the following year.

Seymour resigned from AP in August 1937. He went on to work for *Look* magazine and later served as vice president and executive editor of the *Minneapolis Star Tribune*. No explanation for his departure from AP has come to light in the company's archives, but after leaving the company he gave public talks about war coverage, describing AP journalists—including Lochner—as fully capable of distinguishing news from propaganda.[19]

Though he did not criticize his former employer, it's not difficult to imagine Seymour was deeply frustrated with the endless tug-of-war over Nazi meddling with the photo service. It's possible that his view—that AP should consider closing the photo operation if it could not operate up to the company's ethical standards and independence—did not sit well with Kent Cooper. Cooper and other New York executives were keen to make the AP GmbH a successful financial venture, and a steady supply of news photos from Germany would help enhance sales and subsidize the news bureau. Cooper also had made clear his view that journalists should obey the rules of countries where they worked, even when the rules ran against ethical principles.

In scouring AP's surviving records of the period, Seymour emerges as the most vocal champion of journalistic principles, the most ardent AP adversary of the German propaganda ministry, and a major critic of Lochner's management of the AP GmbH. His departure removed an important voice that might have continued to speak out as the GmbH's entanglement with the Nazi government grew ever more compromised.

5

FIRST THEY CAME FOR THE JEWS

As the propaganda ministry tightened its grip on the information seen by German citizens, its anti-Semitic campaigns increasingly forced the GmbH, AP's photo subsidiary, into positions that would later open the company to charges that it cooperated in Nazi vilification of Jews and abandoned its own Jewish employees. The vilification charges were based on the use of AP photos in Nazi propaganda publications. One example was a Nazi pamphlet *Die Juden in USA* (The Jews in the USA), produced in 1939 by Hans Diebow, photo editor of the Nazi Party's publishing house, Franz Eher Nachfolger GmbH. The pamphlet's copyright notice says over half the 105 photos it contains came through the AP's German subsidiary, though the individual photos are not labeled by source.[1]

Most of the *Die Juden in USA* images show prominent American government officials and celebrities, including U.S. Supreme Court justices Louis Brandeis and Felix Frankfurter and journalist Walter Lippmann. On the cover is a photo of Mayor Fiorello La Guardia, whose mother was Italian-Jewish. The unflattering image shows La Guardia, his mouth wide open, about to bite down on a sandwich. The message: he's a glutton, and a Jew. Inside the pamphlet, Secretary of State Cordell Hull is shown next to his wife over a caption saying he had "married Jewish." Film star Claudette Colbert, a Catholic, is captured dining with her husband, physician Joel Pressman, under the line, "Film star's Racial Shame."

The images in *Die Juden in USA* are routine photos, the product of covering the news of the day, and they were widely distributed to AP's U.S. newspaper members. But the same photos, in the hands of the Nazi press, were no longer merely images of newsmakers. German propagandists wrote new captions perverting their meaning and supporting the Nazi denigration of Jews.

Other anti-Jewish captions appeared on photos from Poland, distributed by the GmbH, that had been taken by a photographer working for the German military. The Nazi Party's *Illustrierter Beobachter* published the series of pictures made in occupied Poland in 1939. Three of the photos depicted Jewish men forced to carry bricks for a road repair project. The AP GmbH issued them with a caption: "Following the invasion by German soldiers, Polish Jews must repair roads under the supervision of the Labor Service." But in *Illustrierter Beobachter* the photos appeared with text stating: "The Jews Must Work," "They are clearly unfamiliar with manual labor," and "Polish Jews are learning to work, but so far not very energetically; a German construction worker can carry five times as many stones up a ladder."[2]

The "Jews-learning-to-work" photo series was "intended to support the claim that the Polish Jews had never worked, and reinforced centuries-old anti-Jewish stereotypes that well-off Jews had only lived from the work of others," historian Harriet Scharnberg wrote in 2018 in *Die "Judenfrage" in Bild*, her book on anti-Semitism in Nazi photography. AP credit lines on these photos gave them credibility when they ran in the German press and left the impression that the scurrilous captions originated with AP. A search in AP's corporate archives found no evidence that AP ever protested this practice by Nazi publications. Later, by the 1960s, standard AP news and photo contracts barred subscribers from distorting captions or other content in ways that would impugn AP's integrity.

Though he was legally in charge of the GmbH photo operation, AP Berlin bureau chief Louis Lochner considered dealing with battles over issues like captions a "thankless task."[3] "Technically, I was the manager of this company," he wrote after the war, "although it was understood between our head office in New York and myself that I was to be its top executive in name only, my duties as news correspondent being far more important to AP and me."[4]

As managing director, though, it was Lochner who had to deal with "Gleichschaltung," the process of Nazification and totalitarian control that was gradually imposed on all German society, including the Jewish employees of the AP GmbH. Those on the Nazi target list at the photo subsidiary were chief photo editor Leon Daniel, a Romanian; senior staff photographer Willy Jacobson, a German; sales director Cecile Kutschuk, a Russian who later changed her surname to Kuchuk; librarian Lisa Jordan, a German; and Berthold Leopold Seidenstein, another photo editor, who used the name Harry Jenkins. Seidenstein was born in Poland but held Austrian citizenship. A sixth target was photographer Alfred Eisenstaedt, who had freelanced for AP since 1928.

All the GmbH Jewish employees eventually were transferred to other bureaus in Europe or were dismissed from the photo subsidiary, and when its operations came under scrutiny decades later, some critics charged that AP had made a Faustian bargain—to comply with Nazi anti-Semitic laws in order to remain in business in the country. Research on the Nazi pressures and the ultimate fate of the AP Jewish employees suggest a more complicated picture, though. Lochner did indeed dismiss some of them, after a long-running campaign to keep them on the payroll failed, but AP also helped them leave Germany and, in several cases, emigrate to the United States.

Lochner's campaign began even before passage of the draconian Editor's Law on October 4, 1933, which banned Jews outright from working in media. In an April 1933 letter to his daughter Elsbeth, nicknamed Betty, Lochner wrote that he had successfully refused Nazi efforts to make him fire the GmbH Jewish employees. "They are efficient, they are honest, they are splendid characters, they are well educated and speak three or four languages," he wrote. "There is no reason in the world outside of the accident of their having been born Jews that I should fire them."[5]

But in September that year, Lochner wrote his daughter again about new pressure: the government had ordered the deportation of GmbH employee Seidenstein, an Austrian citizen, in reprisal for Austria's decision to ban the Nazi Party. Lochner indicated he had appealed to multiple officials, and the deportation "was finally rescinded when I stated the man was essential to our picture service."[6] (Seidenstein later was transferred to AP's bureau in Paris and in 1938 moved to the United States, left AP and settled in California.)

In his letters home, Lochner put a humanitarian cast on his efforts, but with the Nazis he used the argument that the Jewish employees were "essential for business," even enlisting help from the U.S. Embassy to press his case. Raymond Geist, the American consul in Berlin, reported that embassy officials negotiated for several months with the propaganda ministry, seeking "special dispensation" for the AP GmbH's Jewish employees. Geist said Lochner argued that losing them would be "tantamount to putting their firm out of business."[7] But ultimately, the "essential for business" argument proved unpersuasive with a Nazi government bent on purging all Jews from German media.

That was clear in August 1935, when *Das Schwarze Korps* (The Black Corps), the weekly magazine of the dreaded Schutzstaffel (SS), launched an incendiary "exposé" titled "Jetzt aber herunter mit der Tarnkappe" (Off with the cloak of invisibility). The magazine listed what it claimed were all the Jewish employees still working at German photo agencies, including the AP GmbH, and in German publishing houses and urged its readers to boycott them.[8]

Stanley Thompson, an American supervising the AP GmbH's photo editors at the time, wrote to New York about the article. His letter, which never addressed the racist assault on his fellow employees, said he had demanded a retraction: the magazine, he said, had mixed up some titles and listed two employees, Daniel and Seidenstein, who had left the country and no longer worked for the GmbH. He also boasted to New York that he had landed a big photo contract with *Das Schwarze Korps*, which would be "printing a two-page series of German pictures from us" in its next edition. The magazine, Thompson told New York, "is a good customer of ours, buying mostly foreign pictures but sometimes German ones."[9]

Thompson had assured his New York superiors that AP could "benefit wonderfully" from the photo spread, but that was far from the case when it actually appeared two weeks later. The photos, credited to Eitel Lange, a German freelancer working temporarily for the AP GmbH,[10] were part of a package in which *Das Schwarze Korps* sought to discredit a Canadian reporter's story about poor conditions in a Nazi labor camp for women. The SS article claimed the Canadian had never visited the camp and that the camp's inmates were angered by her allegedly distorted account. One of several obviously staged photos shows grinning women waving frying pans, hammers, an ax, and other implements to show how they would greet the reporter, should she ever show up.[11]

Then came the hammer blow.

"We had all [the Canadian journalist's] assertions checked out on the spot and photographed," the magazine said. "The pictures were taken by a representative of the American picture firm 'Associated Press'—which by the way informs us that on the basis of our recent publication in *Das Schwarze Korps* of 'Off with the Cloak of Invisibility,' the chief editor, all editors, and the business leadership of the Associated Press GmbH are all Aryan, and the Jewish employees named by us have been dismissed."

Thompson and Lange both left AP shortly after the *Das Schwarze Korps* affair. Lochner reported to New York that Thompson had "proved a failure." Lange went on to serve with the Luftwaffe as a war photographer and for a time as personal photographer for Hermann Göring.[12] There is no known reaction by AP's executives in New York or London to the *Das Schwarze Korps* publication. But Scharnberg points to this article as evidence that "from 1935, the Propaganda Ministry had the Berlin AP [GmbH] photo service under its control just as it did the German picture agencies."[13]

Leon Daniel, the chief photo editor who had been on the early Nazi target list, departed Germany in early 1935 and embarked in June from France for New York. Before he left Berlin, Daniel had been contacted by Heinrich Hoffmann, Hitler's personal photographer. Hoffmann had amassed a considerable fortune as the Reichsbildberichterstatter, the official photographer of the Reich, and ran a highly profitable photo agency. He proposed that Daniel act as his agent in the United States.

"But don't you know I am a Jew?" Daniel asked him. "Oh, that makes no difference," said Hoffmann. "Nobody cares what I do in America, and I want to make money."[14] In the United States, Daniel partnered instead with AP's Jewish freelancer Alfred Eisenstaedt when he came to New York in November 1935. They cofounded the PIX photo agency, which specialized in helping struggling photographers from Europe get a start in the United States. Daniel and Eisenstaedt were later joined by two other AP GmbH Jewish employees from the Nazi target list—librarian Lisa Jordan and

Cecile Kuchuk, the head of sales, who became business manager at PIX.[15]

Daniel, Kuchuk, and Jordan were dismissed by AP; Lochner later wrote that he had had no choice but to let go Jewish employees, as AP's "head office was not ready to renounce its operations in Germany in protest." All he could do for them, he said, "was to help arrange their emigration to the United States, where they have fortunately established themselves well and with our friendship unmarred."[16]

One of the GmbH's Jewish photographers, Willy Jacobson, was still employed by AP when the first *Das Schwarze Korps* article appeared. But soon, the Nazis came for him, too. Jacobson began his career in the early days of the Weimar Republic at the photo agency Internationaler Illustrations-Verlag. Later he worked for Pacific & Atlantic Photos GmbH, which was taken over by the AP GmbH in 1931.[17] For some time after the Nazis came to power, Lochner had been able to rebuff their demands to dismiss Jacobson because he had been decorated "as a brave, front, trench fighter" in World War I.[18] The exception was granted, Lochner explained, under a law that said non-Aryan public officials who fought in the war could remain in their positions. "Analogous to this law governing public officials, Jacobson was to be left in our office in his capacity of senior photographer," Lochner wrote.

But a few days after the SS denunciation in *Das Schwarze Korps*, the police gave Jacobson twenty-four hours to surrender his license to work as a journalist or face arrest. Lochner arranged his swift transfer to AP's Vienna bureau and temporary safety, where he headed AP's main photo office for Austria and the Balkans.[19] Then, on March 12, 1938, the Wehrmacht's Eighth Army marched into Austria, with Hitler announcing the Anschluss, or union, of his native country and the Third Reich. Alvin Steinkopf, then serving as AP bureau chief in the Austrian capital, wrote that Hitler arrived two days later in Vienna, "master of all he surveyed."

> No ancient despot could have exercised more control over a people than did Hitler when he stood on the balcony of the Imperial Hotel and proclaimed of his new Pan-Germany: "No force on earth can shake us!"
>
> His words were a challenge and a warning to the wide world which a fanatically enthusiastic crowd acclaimed with deafening roars.[20]

But away from the cheering crowds, AP reported, Austria's Jews were beaten, wholesale arrests carried out, and a purge launched to get rid of "anti-Nazi forces" and "traitorous elements."[21]

"Hysteria swept Vienna Jewry today as Austria became but a name in history, her land, her people, her Army, and her government now a state of Fuehrer Hitler's Nazi Germany," wrote the Berlin bureau's Melvin Whiteleather, who was on temporary assignment in the Austrian capital. Whiteleather described hundreds of Jews lining up outside foreign consulates, desperate for visas that would enable them to escape Austria.[22]

Among those arrested was Willy Jacobson, who was working in the darkroom of the AP Vienna office when a uniformed Storm Trooper entered on March 16, four days after the takeover. Jacobson was put into custody without charge or explanation.[23]

Some days later, Nazi officials told AP that Jacobson could be released, but only if he was moved somewhere outside "greater Germany." The date when he was freed is not clear, but AP photo records in New York show he was in Prague in late May that year, taking pictures for AP of Czech preparations for a Nazi invasion. Sometime later he returned to Berlin but was unable to go back to work there because of the ban on Jews in media. "The only charge against him," lamented an AP executive in London at the time, "was that he was a Jew."[24]

There is no known account of how Jacobson survived the war, but whether by circumstance or by choice, he appears to have settled behind the Iron Curtain in East Berlin after the war. Postwar photos found in one of Lochner's scrapbooks show Lochner in Berlin with a credit to the Jacobson-Sonnenfeld photo agency, which Willy Jacobson apparently established.[25] And the database of the German Federal Archives contains a digitized photo credited to Jacobson; it is dated August 1945 and shows a bulldozer clearing rubble in the Soviet-occupied zone of Berlin.[26]

Louis Matzhold, an AP correspondent in Vienna, managed to remain in touch with Jacobson. In 1948 Matzhold wrote to Steinkopf that the "Jacobsons are in a pitiful condition in Berlin. Nobody seems to care for them from the old colleagues."[27] Matzhold wrote again in 1950, informing Steinkopf that Jacobson was still in Soviet-controlled East Germany and apparently out of a job, "because he has no camera." But the Jacobsons now had an apartment, he noted, "which seems the first step to a new life—Eastern as it may be."[28]

Jacobson photographs have been found from the 1950s showing commemoration ceremonies at Ravensbrück, a Nazi concentration camp for women north of Berlin, and the German Historical Museum houses images he made of East German leaders.[29] His reflections on photography in Germany, including his arrest in Vienna, were published in 1957 in the East German periodical *Neue Deutsche Presse*. The publication offers only a brief glimpse of his career and makes no mention of his whereabouts during the war.[30]

The forced departure of the AP GmbH's Jewish employees was part of a systematic assault on foreign photo services operating in Germany in 1935. In July that year, Germany expelled Julius Bolgar, manager of the *New York Times* picture service Wide World Photos, which—like the AP GmbH—was incorporated in Germany. DNB, the Nazi news agency, reported that the *Times* manager was a Hungarian national of Jewish descent who "has repeatedly given expression to his spiteful and hostile attitude towards the new state and its leading men, making it completely impossible for Bolgar to remain in Germany."[31]

Bolgar's expulsion prompted Frederick Birchall, chief foreign correspondent for the *Times*, to urge publisher Arthur Hays Sulzberger to close the newspaper's Berlin picture service. Its business had already shrunk because of the newspaper's Jewish ownership and the boycott called for by the SS magazine *Das Schwarze Korps*. To continue doing business in Germany meant being "in accordance with the Nazi rules—that is, as an Aryan outfit," Birchall wrote Sulzberger. The Nazi conditions, he wrote, "are abhorrent to every principle I hold, and I am quite sure how you personally will feel about it."[32]

Five months later, the *Times* closed its Wide World Photos office in Berlin; AP later acquired Wide World in August 1941. The *Times* Berlin news bureau kept operating.

The same year, Bert Garai, another Hungarian who served as European manager for the U.S. photo agency Keystone View Inc., sold Keystone's German subsidiary to the DNB, which renamed it Weltbild GmbH.[33] Garai wrote that he felt it wiser to "get out while the going was good." From the Keystone offices, in the same building as the German agency DNB, "our staff could not help watching the processes of the Nazi propaganda machine, producing calumny and falsehood like sausages—and they were obviously keen to squeeze us out," Garai said.

The DNB absorption of Keystone left the AP GmbH as the sole foreign agency collecting and distributing photos in Germany. It competed against the Nazi-favored national agencies, Presse-Hoffmann, Weltbild, Atlantic, Presse-Bild-Zentrale, and Scherl Bilderdienst. By the end of 1935 the AP GmbH had fully complied with the Nazi edict banning Jewish employees. And despite the onerous conditions under which it operated, AP chose to keep its German photo business open, making money from an exchange that depended on staying in the good graces of the Nazi government.

Even after the dismissal of its Jewish employees, the AP photo subsidiary was still not in compliance with Nazi law, which required that the legal head of the AP GmbH, the Geschäftsführer or managing director, be a German citizen. Louis Lochner was, of course, American, and the Associated Press of Great Britain retained ownership rights, though the law required German ownership. Years of wrangling over these issues ultimately ended with AP handing full control of the company to one of its local employees, Willy Brandt, an idealistic young German whose meteoric rise from entry-level news assistant to managing director of the photo subsidiary was boosted by both Nazi edicts and AP's global business goals.

Born in Berlin in 1910 and raised in a family of Social Democrats, Wilhelm Erwin Brandt was twenty-five when Louis Lochner hired him to work in AP's Berlin bureau to scour Germany's regional newspapers for news. Working for AP in the Hitler era, he would say years later, was a political statement: "Being able to serve the AP meant to me the promotion of democratic thought, meant helping in the battle against the dark forces of the evil spirit which had risen with Hitler."[34]

As a student, Brandt had joined the Social Democratic Party and actively supported the Reichsbanner Schwarz-Rot-Gold, a centrist, Weimar-era paramilitary organization founded to counter the paramilitary wings of the Nazi and Communist parties.[35] In 1928, while studying medicine at the University of Berlin, Brandt became a Reichsbanner block leader. Family financial troubles forced him to drop out of school in 1929, as the world sank into the Great Depression and hyperinflation engulfed Germany. He pursued journalism at the *Anzeiger des Berliner Nordens* in the Pankow district of Berlin. But his hopes for a career as an independent-minded reporter were dashed after Hitler came to power and German newspapers were rapidly Nazified into government mouthpieces.[36]

Brandt's political leanings threatened not only his professional opportunities but his personal safety as well. The Nazi takeover in January 1933 led to a ban on the Reichsbanner and mass arrests of those who opposed the new regime. When Brandt helped a friend escape by emigrating to Czechoslovakia, the Gestapo searched his parents' home. They left without arresting Brandt, warning that he was being given "an opportunity to improve himself politically."[37]

A venture into medical equipment sales ended in failure in late 1934. Then, by chance, the son of a friend working at AP put Brandt in touch with AP's bureau chief.[38] Lochner hired him in February 1935 and the following year transferred Brandt to the AP GmbH to work as the company's bookkeeper and cashier.

Brandt had no experience with news photography, but he was energetic and quickly won the confidence of his American superiors. Gideon Seymour, the AP executive in London to whom the GmbH reported, was impressed with his business sense. Brandt, he said, had successfully steered the company through fiscal problems, and "the 1937 outlook is the best financially since 1933."[39] Lochner appointed Brandt office manager, a new title, in July 1938.[40] He may have thought Brandt's elevation would satisfy the demands of the propaganda ministry for German management, but it did not. Lochner was still managing director of the company, the GmbH was still under the control of its AP bosses in London and New York, and the ministry was still demanding that both things change.

Change did come, under pressure and through a convoluted chain of events triggered by a German proposal to AP in New York in 1938. Although the precise language of the proposal is not known, it apparently included a Nazi ultimatum: AP must finally turn over the GmbH to German management and ownership voluntarily, or else the Nazis would seize the photo operation by force.

Lochner apparently objected to the Nazi proposal, but his boss in New York, Kent Cooper, looked past any ethical issues and sought to preserve what he hoped would be an increasingly lucrative business—one that could help subsidize other AP operations, including the Berlin news bureau. In a December 1938 letter to Lochner, Cooper argued that AP would benefit financially by Germanizing the GmbH's ownership and management. "If that company [the GmbH] complied [with Nazi demands] it might get a great deal of business that it does not now get. It might even get the benediction of German officials. After all, that company in Germany is a German company," Cooper wrote.[41] Cooper even suggested AP's news operation in Berlin could benefit if the Associated Press of New York used its influence "to bring the practices of [the AP GmbH] in harmony with the suggestions of the German government."[42]

What Cooper's letter outlined was an astonishing proposition that would elevate money-making over ethics: the Associated Press, an American news organization that embraced basic principles of balanced reporting and press freedom, might consider bringing the professional practices of one of its subsidiaries "in harmony" with the suggestions of a foreign government. And not just any foreign government, but one that spewed propaganda, practiced ruthless censorship, and cast an increasingly menacing shadow over its Jewish population and much of the rest of Europe.

In the end, AP came up with a compromise of sorts. Willy Brandt was named managing director in June 1939, replacing Lochner, and two months later the company transferred ownership title to him as well (though AP said the New York company still controlled the GmbH stock). Both moves put the GmbH in technical compliance with Nazi law, while also placing the business in the hands of a

German considered by Lochner and AP executives as a trustworthy guardian, one who shared AP's journalistic values. The AP GmbH's lawyer executed the final transfer on September 1, the day the Nazis sent armored columns into Poland, and it was officially registered in a Berlin court three days later.[43]

After the war, Lochner objected when U.S. military investigators suggested he had helped the propaganda ministry achieve its goal of controlling the company. A more accurate account, he wrote, would state that "'the Nazi authorities insisted that Louis P. Lochner, until then manager of the GmbH, relinquish his position since he was a foreigner. Mr. Lochner thereupon recommended Willy Brandt as Geschäftsführer.'"[44]

Though the court registration should have made everything official, the appointment of Brandt as owner of the AP GmbH did not sit well with Heiner Kurzbein at the propaganda ministry or with the Reich Association of the German Press. Both sought to block Brandt's takeover by refusing to issue a permit needed to validate the transfer. Kurzbein's objection likely was based on personal animosity; after the war, Brandt said he'd been warned by a propaganda ministry official that Kurzbein had suggested, more than once, sending Brandt to a concentration camp as punishment for his anti-Nazi views.[45]

While the propaganda ministry succeeded in keeping the photo operation in a kind of legal limbo, it did not prevent Brandt from taking charge of the veteran photographers, photo stringers, darkroom specialists, archivists, and sales staff, whose work was in increasing demand as war broke out in Europe. They included three of the Kristallnacht photographers, Gerhard Baatz, Eric Borchert, and Franz Roth, who, while still on AP's payroll, would serve as photographers with German military units. Roth, the SA member from Austria, joined a Waffen-SS unit and became AP's most controversial German employee. Borchert served with the Wehrmacht in Poland and later battlefronts. Baatz, an AP photographer since 1934, quickly volunteered for the military when Germany invaded Poland. After a month there, he returned to Berlin, to a bizarre arrangement where he worked for AP while the propaganda ministry also gave him assignments throughout Germany's conquered territories. Regardless of who made the assignment, the AP GmbH distributed the photos to German clients and to AP's photo editors in New York and London.[46]

As the war escalated, so did compromising relationships between the Nazis and the GmbH and its employees. AP may have felt it had put the operation in safe hands with Willy Brandt, a loyal employee, but in fact it had thrust Brandt into an untenable role. He was now head of an American-created business, with American values, working in a dictatorship that saw all media as tools for its political ends. Not surprisingly, Brandt faced conflict with Nazi officials throughout the war years. And in the war's aftermath, he came under Allied suspicion for his role in a little-known exchange that kept wartime photos flowing between the United States and Germany even after the demise of the GmbH.

II
AT WAR

6

POLAND

In a Danzig hotel lobby, AP's Lynn Heinzerling heard a German officer request a wakeup call for 3:15 the next morning, Friday, September 1, 1939.

"I realized then it was coming," he wrote.

When gunfire woke Heinzerling a little before 5 a.m., he ran down the hotel stairs several steps at a time.

"The night watchman said: 'Es geht los.' (It's started).

"I ran towards the Vistula River. There I saw what it was—The German cruiser Schleswig-Holstein firing on the Polish munitions depot of Westerplatte."[1]

The German salvos set off deafening explosions that rocked the city and reverberated through the streets.

"It came rolling up from the harbor like the rumble of doom," Heinzerling wrote later. "Men began to die here as Hitler stepped out on the road to ruin."[2]

Overnight, Heinzerling and his colleagues from the AP Berlin news bureau—young or middle-aged men, most of them sent to Europe after a few years covering local news in the United States—were transformed into war correspondents. In Germany, they had learned to work within the limits of "responsibility censorship" and suffer the threats and directives of the Nazi propaganda machinery. Now, they would face new challenges, including the physical threat of working in war zones.

Heinzerling's most immediate obstacle, though, was more prosaic. When the German invasion began, outgoing communications were cut in Danzig (modern day Gdansk). After writing an eyewitness account of the attack on the port city, Heinzerling "found that he was completely cut off from the outside world with only one consolation: George Kidd of the United Press, Walter Dietzel of the International News Service, and other correspondents were in the same fix," *Newsweek* magazine reported later.[3] Heinzerling was finally able to file, free of censorship, after making his way to Riga, capital of the Baltic state of Latvia. On September 6 he wrote that when he had left Danzig the day before, there was "no sign of surrender" by the embattled Poles there, though "artillery echoes through the city, troops roll through on lorries, and Danzigers are sealed up completely by the German army and Gestapo (secret police)."[4]

Heinzerling and reporters from rival services were in place to witness the assault on Danzig because the foreign correspondents based in Berlin had for some time recognized the warning signs. On August 18, nearly two weeks before the Schleswig-Holstein began firing on the Polish munitions depot, AP bureau chief Louis Lochner had reported that diplomatic chatter and a "violent anti-Polish campaign in the Nazi press" made it clear "the Danzig problem between Germany and Poland was nearing a decisive turn."[5] Even before that, on August 15, AP Berlin reporter Angus Thuermer wrote his parents that Lochner was dispatching three bureau reporters to cover the expected assault on Poland. "Well, Angus, I guess we are going to have to make a war correspondent out of you," Lochner told Thuermer, the bureau's junior member. Thuermer was assigned to leave the next day for Upper Silesia, "where [German] troops are expected to move in from the south on Poland."[6]

As they monitored signs of the war to come, the Berlin news bureau's staff focused on the surprise Molotov-Ribbentrop nonaggression pact that August—a secret provision of which dismembered the Polish state—and the late August rush of diplomatic maneuvers among Hitler, France, and Britain, aimed, ostensibly, at heading off war.

Then, on Thursday, August 31, as Heinzerling waited in Danzig, the final signals of imminent invasion were revealed in Berlin. Ed Shanke, on the overnight shift that started at 8 p.m., spent the night cabling New York with running updates of Nazi claims of Polish military aggression. One report from the Nazi news agency DNB alleged Polish forces had attacked the German radio station at Gleiwitz, in Upper Silesia, then German territory. Numerous other claims spoke of scattered fighting between German and Polish troops (all were dismissed years later as fabrications). Perhaps the most audacious Nazi move that night was revealed after the war, at the Nürnberg trials of Nazi leaders: Hitler had demanded that several dozen concentration camp inmates be taken to the German-Polish border dressed in Polish uniforms, given empty guns, photographed, and then shot.[7]

Just after 5 a.m. on Friday, September 1, about the same time that Danzig first came under attack, the DNB Heilschreiber teleprinter in the AP Berlin office again burst into life to deliver the official Nazi report that Hitler had ordered German troops into Poland.[8] Using AP style for filing, Shanke delivered the news in a series of staccato bulletins. Each started with his last name (in the possessive case), followed by a sequence number. Then came the text, which announced the start of momentous events but was written in special "cablese" that read like not-quite-proper-English.

SHANKES 10516 HITLER ORDERS ARMY MEET FORCE WITH FORCE.

SHANKES 20516 QUOTE GERMAN ARMY WILL CONDUCT FIGHT FOR HONOR AND RIGHT OF LIFE OF RESURRECTED GERMAN PEOPLE WITH FIRM DETERMINATION UNQUOTE HIS COMMAND SAID

SHANKES 30516 HIS ORDER OF THE DAY TO ARMY READ COLON QUOTE POLISH STATE HAS REJECTED MY EFFORTS TO ESTABLISH NEIGHBORLY RELATIONS COMMA INSTEAD HAS APPEALED TO WEAPONS

SHANKES 40516 REQUOTE GERMANS IN POLAND ARE VICTIMS OF BLOODY TERROR DRIVEN FROM HOUSE AND HOME

SHANKES 50516 REQUOTE SERIES OF BORDER VIOLATIONS UNBEARABLE FOR GREAT POWER SHOW THAT POLES NO LONGER WILLING TO RESPECT GERMAN BORDER

SHANKES 60516 REQUOTE TO PUT END TO THESE INSANE INCITATIONS NOTHING REMAINS BUT FOR ME TO MEET FORCE WITH FORCE FROM NOW ON.[9]

Later that morning, Hitler spoke to a hurriedly summoned session of the Reichstag at the Kroll Opera House in Berlin and announced that Germany was at war with Poland. A weary Shanke joined Lochner in covering the event, along with photographer Gerhard Baatz, who captured a grim Hitler at the podium with Field Marshal Hermann Göring seated behind him.[10]

Hitler demanded that Poland return "German" Danzig to the Fatherland, just as he had insisted on the return of Czechoslovakia's Sudetenland the year before. He also claimed the Polish Army had invaded Germany. Signaling his determination, Hitler and his entourage appeared at the opera house in field gray army jackets despite the sultry end-of-summer weather. "I am putting on the uniform and I shall take it off only in victory or death," Hitler said to wild cheers of the faithful, including every leading figure of government and the military.

"Hitler was at his oratorical best," AP reported. "He looked worn and harried but his voice was strong, his eyes fiery, and his gestures vigorous."[11]

While the Berlin bureau was reduced to reporting the official German version of events and Heinzerling stewed incommunicado in Danzig, the AP Warsaw bureau was able to file a gripping account of the Luftwaffe's first air raid on the Polish capital, in close to real-time dispatches. The bureau, hastily established that spring in anticipation of war, was staffed by Lloyd Lehrbas and Elmer W. Peterson; the latter served as bureau chief. Scrambling to make a reliable communications connection with the outside world, they managed to establish a phone link with AP's bureau in Budapest in time to file the first eyewitness account:

GERMAN WARPLANES SWOOPED OVER WARSAW THIS AFTERNOON IN AN AIR ATTACK IN ADVANCE OF THREE GERMAN ARMIES INVADING THIS COUNTRY.

I AM TELEPHONING THIS DISPATCH TO BUDAPEST WITH THE PHONE IN ONE HAND AND A GAS MASK IN THE OTHER.

FROM WHERE I AM I CAN HEAR THE WAIL OF POWER-DIVING FIGHTING SHIPS AND CAN SEE 14 GERMAN BOMBERS SLOWLY, STEADILY FOLLOWING THE COURSE OF THE VISTULA RIVER, POLAND'S OUTLET TO THE SEA.[12]

One apparent German goal was to destroy all the city's bridges. The AP story reported that hundreds of Warsaw's inhabitants watched the bombing from rooftops. "Tremendous explosions are shaking the city and rattling windows," the Warsaw bureau reported, as antiaircraft shells burst around the invading bombers.

Peterson and Lehrbas took turns going to the roof to witness the air attack and then dictating what they saw by phone to the

Budapest bureau. AP rules, however, prohibited double bylines, so Budapest bureau chief Robert B. Parker, who wrote the first-person, eyewitness story sent to AP subscribers, based on the accounts dictated from Warsaw, flipped a coin before five witnesses. "Heads it's Peterson; tails it's Lehrbas," he announced.[13] The coin landed tails up, Lehrbas got the byline, and the following year the Pulitzer Prize committee gave him honorable mention for best foreign correspondence of 1939, including his coverage of the first air raid of World War II.[14] Peterson's role went unmentioned.

Sunday, September 3, dawned quietly in Berlin, "with church bells summoning the faithful and families streaming to the parks," wrote AP's Alvin Steinkopf.[15] But peace was soon disrupted, as Hitler rejected ultimatums from London and Paris to withdraw from Poland. In London, AP bureau chief J. C. Stark flashed the British response in a series of cables to New York:

PRESS ASSOCIATED NYK

1116 [AM, LONDON TIME] FLASH CHAMBERLAIN PROCLAIMED BRITAIN AT WAR WITH GERMANY

STARK

PRESS ASSOCIATED NYK

1116 FLASH CHAMBERLAIN REQUOTE YOU CAN IMAGINE WHAT A BITTER BLOW IT IS TO ME UNQUOTE

STARK

PRESS ASSOCIATED NYK

1117 FLASH CHAMBERLAIN REQUOTE THE ACTIONS OF THIS MAN (HITLER) SHOW CONVINCINGLY THAT HE WILL NEVER DO OTHERWISE THAN USE FORCE IN THE ATTAINMENT OF HIS WILL UNQUOTE

STARK

PRESS ASSOCIATED NYK

1118 FLASH REQUOTE CONSEQUENTLY WE ARE AT WAR WITH GER-
MANY UNQUOTE

STARK[16]

Suddenly, Europe had stumbled into war.

Two days later, a caravan of some 1,350 diplomats and civilians from thirty-odd countries, including most of the Americans in Warsaw, fled the Polish capital during a four-hour German-Polish truce. Peterson, the Warsaw AP bureau chief, accompanied them, reporting on their four-hundred-mile trek to the Russian border, his dispatches carried by hand to the Polish border with Romania.

On September 6, with the Germans nearing artillery range of the capital and motorized units spread out to attack from a dozen directions, Lehrbas, who had remained in Warsaw, followed the retreating Polish government and other diplomats out of the city. When the Poles surrendered on September 27, he made his way safely to Bucharest. Meanwhile, Peterson, reporting the same day from "SOMEWHERE IN SOUTHEASTERN POLAND," looked back at "the remarkable efficiency of air attack" staged by the Germans. While he described the Polish resistance as courageous, the "willingness to die or risk death means little when the enemy cannot be reached with rifle, machine gun and hand grenade."[17]

The eyewitness reporting by Lehrbas and Peterson was the exception rather than the rule for foreign correspondents attempting to cover the German invasion. After the initial attacks, correspondents based in Berlin were barred from traveling to Poland. Left corralled and spoon-fed by the extensive Nazi propaganda apparatus, they were limited to official statements and the censored photos and reports sent from front lines by photographers and reporters drafted from German media (including the AP GmbH) into the Propaganda

Kompanien der Wehrmacht, or PKs (Armed Forces Propaganda Companies).

PK photos and news reports were quickly cleared by military and propaganda ministry censors and made available to domestic and foreign news services and photo agencies in Berlin for wider distribution. While foreign news services seldom picked up PK stories, the dramatic, frontline pictures captured by PK photographers got wide distribution by photo agencies, hungry to give their audiences images of the world's hottest story—even when the photos were taken by German photographers in the service of the military and the propaganda ministry.

Aside from reporting by the German PK journalists, the only way the Berlin bureaus could gather news from inside Poland was to go there under German military escort. Traveling with one side in combat, under ground rules set by the military, a form of what's now known as embedding, is a practice that dates back to at least the Crimean War in the 1850s. It has never been without controversy, and embedding under Nazi military rules was no exception.

Germany's early press tours, aimed particularly at American correspondents and reporters from other countries that remained neutral, were organized to impress the world with Nazi military prowess (and discourage the neutral Americans from entering the battle). Another goal was to undermine enemy propaganda claims, and at the end of the daily Berlin press conference on September 4, 1939, the Nazi government spokesman pulled aside Lochner and his counterparts at United Press and International News Service. The invasion of Poland, just four days old, had already yielded a story, the spokesman said, that bore exploring: that the venerated Black Madonna of Częstochowa, Poland's holiest shrine, had been destroyed in a German bombing raid.[18] Polish papers had reported it, and the archbishop of Paris appeared to have confirmed it, in a broadcast where he claimed that "the Virgin's National sanctuary in Poland is aflame."[19]

The German spokesman told the three American news agency chiefs that one of them could travel with German military to Częstochowa on a "mission on behalf of truth" to examine the claims.[20] The bureau chiefs were left to decide which of them would make the trip.

Lochner wrote later that six years of working as correspondents under Nazi rules "made us look at the proposal with jaundiced eyes," meaning, they realized the trip would not have been offered unless the Black Madonna remained unharmed. Still, on offer was the first opportunity for a Berlin-based foreign correspondent to visit Poland since the Nazi assault began. The three journalists decided to draw lots and pledged that all would defend against any charges that the winner had fallen into a Nazi propaganda trap. They also agreed that whoever made the trip would treat the Black Madonna's fate as just part of a broader story and would insist the Ministry of Propaganda relay his story in full (except for possible breaches of military secrecy).[21]

The trip fell to Lochner, who was given a gas mask and first aid kit by the War Office in Berlin, flown to the German-Polish border, and then taken to Częstochowa—southwest of Warsaw—by military escort. His story of September 6, datelined "WITH THE GERMAN ARMY OF THE EAST," focused on the danger of Polish snipers to the German occupation forces and the flood of refugees fleeing the fighting.[22] While noting that he was under military escort, he reported that railway tracks had been torn up, and every bridge from the German border to Częstochowa had been destroyed by the retreating Poles. He described a long German military procession heading one direction, while refugees fled the opposite way. "Barefooted women with babies tied on their backs and one cow walking behind, old men carrying heavy burdens wrapped in bedspreads, boys and girls pushing their bicycles, on which they had fastened their scant belongings, pushcarts bulging with knickknacks while families huddled on horse-drawn vehicles—such was the procession of miserable humanity coming towards us," he wrote.

Lochner's story briefly confirmed that neither the city's monastery nor its cathedral had been harmed, and that he saw, intact, "the famous Black Madonna." As further proof, AP distributed a photo of Lochner, made by a German army photographer, in the United States and Germany. It showed the AP bureau chief observing Poles worshipping at the undamaged shrine.[23] Only later was Lochner able to confirm that the earlier story of the damaged Black Madonna was disinformation deliberately planted by the German propaganda ministry, using a Nazi stooge close to the archbishop in Paris.[24] So, as Lochner and his news agency counterparts had understood, the Nazis intended the trip as a purely propaganda stunt. "Obviously the High Command would authorize trips only if they were likely to result in reports of victories or in findings favorable to Germany," he wrote later.[25] But the trip also afforded Lochner an opportunity to give the world a first, eyewitness account of the devastating aftermath of the German invasion.

Reporting from escorted trips like the one Lochner took did not impress Douglas Freeman, editor of Virginia's *Richmond News-Leader*. In a strongly worded editorial less than two weeks after the attack on Danzig, he wrote, "Newsmen who have been escorted to the zone of action for a few days have been stuffed with predictions of early German conquest. Photographs that helped create an impression of German invincibility have been passed gladly."[26] In a separate letter to Frank Fuller, AP's chief of bureau in Richmond, Freeman was more colorful: "These men [the foreign correspondents in Berlin]," he wrote, "are being stuffed full of prunes."[27]

Freeman was not the only one suggesting American journalists were being duped by the Germans. A German photo distributed by AP and published on September 6, less than a week after the Nazi invasion, prompted a tirade from the New York representative of the state-owned Polish Telegraphic Agency. The photo showed a German soldier, a member of a tank unit, lighting a cigarette for a Polish prisoner.[28] "No Nazi soldier plays the role of a good Samaritan," complained Nawench Morawski in a scathing letter to AP executive editor Byron Price. "He does not offer a smoke to [a] Polish prisoner of war but stabs him with his bayonet."[29]

Morawski suggested AP not only was being duped by propaganda but was ignoring alleged Nazi atrocities that he claimed had been "authoritatively" verified, including throwing gas bombs on Polish towns and villages; making air drops of poisoned candies and cigarettes; bombing Polish Red Cross trains; and firing at peasants and children as they worked in farm fields. He also accused Berlin bureau chief Lochner of being pro-Nazi.

Price wrote back that he was "astonished and disappointed" at Morawski's letter and the "entirely unjustified" accusations against Lochner "without producing the slightest bit of evidence."[30] "As far as the German pictures are concerned, they are the only pictures of actual hostilities which have been made available by anyone and no one who tries to cover the news could possibly refuse them," Price said. "Nor is there anything anomalous about the picture of soldiers in opposing armies fraternizing, as anyone will tell you who has served in battle." Then, in a reminder that AP and the Polish agency had a partnership agreement to exchange news and photos, Price said Morawski could help assure "a fair balance" in the AP report by prodding his headquarters in Warsaw to fulfill the agreement—because, despite repeated requests, "we have been able to get no pictures from Poland."

The Polish stories of poisoned candy and village gas bombings triggered memories for some journalists of the pitfalls of atrocity reporting in World War I, when both sides had peddled gruesome stories about crucifixion, baby mutilation, and other tortures. Media published some of these stories without independent verification, only to learn they were pure fiction, designed by warring parties to stoke support for their military efforts. Now, a new war underway, AP's Melvin Whiteleather noted in a September 5, 1939, diary entry (four days after the Nazi invasion of Poland): "Atrocity stories are pouring in. But I have not used a single one. The last war is still too fresh in memory."[31] Two days after Whiteleather wrote his diary entry, the *Miami Herald* called the poisoned candy stories "sheer poppycock" and warned that they were "the same brand of propaganda" that had "suckered" the United States into World War I.[32]

A few weeks later, as rumors continued to swirl, AP apparently considered a proposal for a new column that would address some of the more outlandish stories. General Manager Kent Cooper opposed the idea, saying: "I personally don't like to see another column started, and I don't like the idea of recounting in a column rumors that we have heard or carried."[33]

Two years later, though, on August 7, 1941, AP initiated a feature called "Today's Rumor Deflator," to explode rumors "of the type not carried by the Associated Press, which flood the world daily."[34] One month after it began, Rumor Deflator disappeared from the AP news report. No public explanation appears to have been offered, though in remarks he wrote for a publishers' group in September 1941, Cooper suggested he had killed the feature. "Today any individual, openly or secretly, can broadcast from a recognized or a secret [radio] station any statement whatsoever," he wrote. "Newspapers can point out each time that a statement that is made is merely a rumor, but the public will be talking about that rumor as a fact," he added. "That's why I regret that newspapers demand we give them all of these rumors."[35]

In addition to relaying officially produced images of the German offensive, AP also had exclusive rights to distribute still photos taken from the newsreel films of Paramount News. Most of Paramount's material came from the same official source everyone else relied on—the PK journalists. But the company managed to smuggle out some early, independently made images of Nazi bomb destruction in Warsaw. AP distributed at least nine photos from that material, which were published in various newspapers, including the *Tampa Sunday Tribune* on September 17, 1939.[36]

The PK photo monopoly was breached again briefly in late September, when an American photographer who had remained in Warsaw, working independently, returned to the United States. "There were more dead by far than during the most hectic days of Verdun [the longest battle of World War I], when I served with the French ambulance corps," said photographer Julien Bryan. "Civilians were much harder hit than Polish military forces."[37] Bryan said he had been trapped in Warsaw until a two-hour truce, called on September 21, allowed him to make his way to Sweden. There, he boarded a ship to the United States carrying five hundred photos and six thousand feet of film showing the destruction of the Polish capital. AP and rival photo agencies distributed a series of his photos, including chilling images of a boy squatting amid the ruins of his home and a girl imploring her dead sister, machine-gunned while picking potatoes in a field, "Tell me what's the matter."[38]

AP offered an uncensored, non-PK, eyewitness text report when correspondent Daniel De Luce, based in Hungary, managed to slip into Poland and report from Lwow (modern-day Lviv in Ukraine). De Luce reported that the city of more than 300,000, bombed by the Germans for two weeks, was doomed. "An acute food shortage, the danger of plague and the horror of bombing attacks have reduced the remaining residents to a state of panic," he wrote in a dispatch couriered to Budapest. Panic was particularly acute among the city's

100,000 Jews, De Luce reported. "In shell-scarred synagogues, the Jews began their new year celebration by offering up prayers for rain which they hoped might halt the march of the German army," he wrote.[39]

On September 19, 1939, less than three weeks after the invasion began, the Germans flew some sixty foreign correspondents from Berlin, Lochner among them, to witness a triumphant Hitler reclaim Danzig as part of the German Reich. On the same excursion, Lochner also reported on the sad plight of several thousand Polish troops, still fighting against great odds up the Baltic Sea coastline at Gydnia because—as one prisoner held by the Germans there told him—"We are waiting for the British to arrive."[40]

Then, on Saturday, September 30, the denouement.

"Warsaw is in ruins," reported Whiteleather, the first American correspondent to enter the city, albeit under German escort. From the Luftwaffe plane that took him there, Whiteleather described a heavily bombed city "lying under piles of bricks, plaster and charred debris," a city "whose roof was ripped open to the sky during the 20-day siege by German armies."[41] On the ground, he found the first of thousands of Polish prisoners being marched out of Warsaw, the streets all but deserted, a few hundred people milling about Pilsudski Square.

Whiteleather also visited Brest-Litovsk, in Soviet-occupied Poland, where he spent two and a half days under escort of the Soviet Army, an unexpected journalistic bonus. The Soviet Union had seized its share of Poland from the east on September 17, under the secret clauses of the Molotov-Ribbentrop Pact signed by Germany and the Soviet Union less than a month earlier. Whiteleather reported that the Soviets appeared to have poured in well over one million fully equipped men in dust-colored uniforms, "marching day and night, division after division, from the interior of Russia."[42]

"Soldiers gnawing hard black bread and drinking tea around campfires at night with guns stacked nearby and supply trains resting and feeding horses gave a picture similar to descriptions of American Civil War armies," Whiteleather wrote. He noted that much of the Soviet military equipment was in poor condition and that truckloads of Communist literature and Stalin portraits had been brought to eastern Poland, apparently to preach the Bolshevist gospel in towns and villages.[43]

The outbreak of war forced the Berlin news bureau and the AP photo subsidiary to seek new routes for sending German news and photos out of the country. With Berlin and London now enemies, telex, cable, and phone links to AP's European headquarters in Britain were cut off, so the news bureau sent routine stories via telex machine to AP in Amsterdam (which then relayed them to London) and sent more urgent material by more costly cable or phone directly to New York. On the photo side, editors radioed the most urgent images to New York and rushed duplicate daily photo shipments on flights to Berne and Moscow, which shipped them forward to London.

These routes would change again as the war progressed. When the Nazis swept into Holland the following year, for example, Berne, capital of neutral Switzerland, became the news bureau's new telex destination. And the routes were almost always busy, as Berlin reporter Angus Thuermer wrote to his parents. "When World War Two broke out in September 1939, the AP bureau filed every shred of copy we could. We crowded the wires. This was a great big war. This was history," said Thuermer. But there were occasional breaks—such as the time a month into the war when the New York news desk cabled the instruction: DOWNHOLD WORLD SERIES. The message meant bureaus should limit the number of stories during Major League Baseball's annual championship games because extensive coverage of the World Series between the New York Yankees and the Cincinnati Reds would limit the space available for other stories on AP's news wires.

"That was the leading wire service's appraisal of the interests of American newspaper editors and readers with a big war going on," Thuermer concluded.[44] The Yankees swept the series in four games.

Adolf Hitler celebrated the surrender of Poland with a triumphant visit to Warsaw on October 5, 1939, reviewing fifteen thousand goose-stepping troops in a victory parade through city streets surrounded by rubble. Following the parade, Hitler walked over to reporters covering the event, among them Lochner, shook hands all round, and smiled. "You see for yourselves what criminal folly it was to try to defend this city," Lochner reported him as saying. "The defense of this town collapsed after only two days. I wish certain statesmen who are trying to turn all Europe into another Warsaw might have seen what you saw today."[45]

The following day, in an eighty-minute speech before the Reichstag, Hitler proposed a "laying down of arms" and a European peace conference "on a comprehensive basis." If the allies rejected this offer, he added, it would be his last.[46] Ignoring the belligerent warning, on October 12 Britain and France spurned Hitler's proposals. The months to follow saw a kind of uncertain truce. There was virtually no ground war, but nor was there peace, and this period of stalemate was termed a "phony war," the so-called Sitzkrieg.

Lochner, traveling with several journalists under German Army escort in late September 1939, had captured this interlude as he viewed the western front along the border with France. "This afternoon I stood only 250 yards away from a French bunker yet no French soldier made the slightest move to shoot at me," Lochner wrote of his time visiting troops at a German bunker.[47] "What is more, no French soldier shot at the generals with broad red coat lapels and red trouser stripes standing next to me," he added. "Such is the war in this sector of the West Wall."

Melvin Whiteleather, who had written the eyewitness account of Warsaw's destruction for AP, returned to the United States in early 1940, possibly suffering what today would be called posttraumatic stress syndrome. In an article for *Journalism Quarterly*, published shortly before his departure, he described the professional frustration for Berlin-based correspondents. Now identified as war correspondents, they found few opportunities to actually witness the war's soldiers or their battles. In fact, without the handful of German-escorted trips to Poland and the west wall, he wrote, "there would have been several cases of suicide from ennui among my colleagues."

"I don't believe there is a correspondent in Germany who has seen a dead soldier," Whiteleather said. "Graves he has seen, many of them, and dead civilians, but no soldiers."[48]

After the initial escorted tours, Poland was sealed off, leaving the fate of its three million Jews to play out beyond the world's eyes and ears. By late 1940, though, official German statements made clear Poland's Jewish population—Europe's largest—was being herded into ghettos, as the Nazis would do in Lithuania, Czechoslovakia, and other states conquered in its eastward drive.[49]

Estimates at the time said that as many as five hundred thousand Jews were crammed into the Warsaw ghetto, Poland's largest (later estimates put the number at four hundred thousand). Independent journalists had no access to Warsaw, or to any of Nazi-occupied Poland, with a single exception: in October 1940 the Germans approved a thousand-mile journey by car for AP's Alvin Steinkopf, who was escorted by two German doctors.[50]

Steinkopf visited Krakow, Lublin, Radom, Szydlowiec, and Warsaw. Of the Polish capital, he wrote: "There is ruin everywhere; houses without roofs, houses without windows, houses that now are but a few blackened walls." Warsaw's Jews were forced to wear blue and white arm bands on their right sleeves, and their forced labor had been used to build a wall "eight feet high and so tight a cat couldn't get through it" that enclosed the Jewish ghetto. Jews were not yet permanently sealed in, and eighteen streets remained open, Steinkopf reported. "But at a moment's notice the authorities, by posting eighteen policemen at the points of entry, can close off the entire district." Steinkopf's minders apparently did not permit him inside the ghetto, which consisted of "a hundred or more city blocks into which the population is crowded with astonishing density." The wall, he said, blocked streetcar lines: "it is built right over the rails."[51]

"It is not a wall against Jews," insisted Dr. Jost Wallbaum, one of Steinkopf's escorts. "It is a wall against typhus." Wallbaum, a Berlin physician who wore military uniform while escorting Steinkopf, was serving as the minister of health for the Nazi-occupied zone that included Warsaw. "When it comes to communicable disease, I'll lock up any possible spreader of contagion, be he Jew, gentile, prince or pauper," Wallbaum told Steinkopf, insisting again that such action should not be construed as "persecution of the Jews."[52]

On November 25, 1940, shortly after Steinkopf's return to Germany, AP reported from Berlin that "dispatches from the former Polish capital" confirmed a new German decree would seal off the ghetto and its Jewish residents from the rest of Warsaw. The decree "brought about a wave of frantic purchases outside the ghetto in an effort to stock up on things that might not be obtainable within," AP reported.[53]

In early 1941 a series of exclusive AP pictures depicting Polish life under the swastika made a splash in U.S. newspapers. Poland, the accompanying AP photo caption said with serious understatement, was "an area from which pictures have become increasingly rare."[54] One showed the huge ghetto wall Steinkopf had seen in Warsaw; the *New York Times* published the dramatic image across four columns atop page 3 on January 3, 1941.⁵⁵ Other photos in the series showed children being lectured by a German officer to wash their faces every day; a streetcar in Krakow where Jews were separated from non-Jews; and an image of men of the Lublin ghetto, with armbands marking them as Jews, deferentially doffing their caps to a German officer. The camera lens was slyly aimed at five little ghetto boys in the foreground smiling for the camera.⁵⁶

The photographer was not named, but it was Steinkopf. The pictures were considered sensitive enough that, while they were distributed to newspaper clients, AP did not share them with PIX, the New York–based photo agency founded by Alfred Eisenstaedt and other Jewish former employees of AP's German photo service. "I was fearful some publication of the 'advocate' character might get them and do a splurge—harmful not only to the source that distributed the pictures [AP] but to the person that took them [Steinkopf]," wrote Lloyd Stratton.⁵⁷

Most of the inhabitants of the Warsaw ghetto were eventually sent to die in gas chambers at the Treblinka death camps in a forest northeast of Warsaw.

7

BLITZKRIEG

BERLIN, May 10—(AP)—The thunderous impact of German total war descended upon Western Europe today.

So began Louis Lochner's May 1940 Berlin dispatch introducing Germany's "Blitzkrieg" style of warfare to millions of newspaper readers across America.

Adolf Hitler, proclaiming the start of a fight to "decide the fate of the German nation for the next 1,000 years," pushed his tremendous armies by land and air across the frontiers of Holland and Belgium, through the tiny grand duchy of Luxembourg and gave these countries and his great enemies, France and England, their first real taste of hell from the air.

Lochner's dramatic narrative cited Germany's land, air, and sea attacks by "superbly equipped platoons" and "swarms of bombers," the latter destroying airports in Belgium, Holland, and France, while "other planes darted straight for the heart of England, to drop bombs and engage defense fighters."[1]

Such descriptions served as warnings of the German military might about to sweep much of the continent, but they also fed the growing complaints—some from American editors whose papers subscribed to AP—that Lochner's effusive language reflected Nazi sympathies.

As with the invasion of Poland, the far-reaching attack was not a total surprise for Lochner. Rumors had swirled for some time, and on the eve of the offensive, at a Berlin social occasion, he and others heard worried talk about imminent attacks on Holland and Belgium. The Germans in the room who overheard the remarks rejected the idea in disbelief, said Lochner. "That was one of the strange things about the war against Holland and Belgium: practically every foreign correspondent in Germany knew it was coming, yet very few Germans had any inkling of it," he wrote later.[2]

The blitz spelled the end to the "Sitzkrieg," the eight months of relative quiet in Europe after Poland was dismembered. Even without active warfare, though, the Sitzkrieg period provided ample evidence of the hot war to come. "More than a million German soldiers, including all their active divisions and armoured divisions, are drawn up ready to attack, at a few hours' notice, all along the frontiers of Luxembourg, of Belgium and of Holland," Winston Churchill, then Britain's First Lord of the Admiralty, warned in a March 30, 1940, broadcast.[3]

The Sitzkrieg came to an end days later. On April 9 Lochner reported from Berlin that the Germans had invaded Norway and Denmark to provide what the Nazi news agency DNB described as "armed protection" to "counteract British aggression against their neutrality."[4] The Norwegians resisted; the Danes did not.

The Berlin bureau's Lynn Heinzerling, in Copenhagen on temporary assignment, witnessed the Nazi takeover there with fellow AP correspondent Wes Gallagher.[5] Heinzerling recalled hearing the roar of airplanes early that April day, looking out his hotel window and seeing "a squadron of German bombers, the swastikas on their tails easily visible."[6] A dispatch was phoned to Berlin but delayed by

German censors. As published in the United States, the story offered an early description of the same military might that Lochner would report a few weeks later, when the assaults began on Belgium, Holland, and Luxembourg.

> Copenhagen, 7.50 a.m. April 9 (By way of Berlin). (Delayed). With minute Teutonic efficiency, Germany today took control of the affairs of the entire kingdom of Denmark after a swift, relentless, two-hour military coup which left the nation stunned but resigned to German rule.
>
> By land, sea and air the Reich's green-clad legions swept into the little kingdom crushing slight opposition in Jutland and at an airport just outside Copenhagen.[7]

The same day, AP distributed an official photo received from the AP GmbH in Berlin showing German troops on the move somewhere in Denmark.[8] Then, two days later, Louis Lochner and seven other foreign correspondents in Berlin—including AP's chief American rivals from United Press and International News Service—boarded Foreign Minister Joachim von Ribbentrop's private plane bound for Copenhagen.[9] There, they interviewed the German commander of the army of occupation, who offered scant news other than that speed, surprise, and secrecy had enabled the Germans to seize Denmark with little bloodshed—only ten Danes and one German were killed, according to the German estimate.[10] The Danes later put the Danish casualty figures at sixteen dead and twenty-nine wounded.[11]

The story was different in Norway, where fierce resistance initially denied the Germans a similarly swift takeover. But despite British support, the Norwegians ultimately succumbed. Photos quickly produced by the Germans in late April and relayed to the United States via the AP GmbH reinforced Nazi claims of victory, showing British prisoners of war being marched through the streets of Trondheim.[12] With no AP reporter in Oslo, Wes Gallagher, now in neighboring Sweden, reported on May 4 that, less than a month after the invasion began, the end was near as Allies retreated and Norwegian resistance collapsed. "Alone and encircled, with only enough ammunition for one day," Norway asked Germany for an armistice, while "acknowledging the Nazis as masters of Norway" and denouncing the Allied retreat as an "incomprehensible action," Gallagher wrote.[13]

Six days later, when the Blitz attack began at sunrise on Luxembourg, Holland, and Belgium, French and British forces initially came to their rescue. But German firepower quickly gained ground, and by May 26 Dunkirk was the only French port left from which the retreating British, French, and Belgian troops could escape.

The lightning German thrust marked a humiliating defeat that led to the largest evacuation in military history, as hundreds of naval vessels and civilian boats, threatened by German war planes, ferried over 330,000 Allied soldiers from the beaches of Dunkirk to British shores. France surrendered on June 22, 1940. In less than three months, Germany had overrun the Netherlands, Luxembourg, Belgium, Denmark, Norway, and France, expanding the Reich's reach to nearly sixty-five million more people.

While the offensive on the western front was still underway, Hitler and his generals were so pleased with their progress that the heads of all three American news agencies in Berlin, equipped with steel helmets and gas masks, were shuttled across the German border in army staff cars to give accounts of Germany's prowess—this time, as eyewitnesses to live warfare.[14] As with Poland, such escorted tours offered foreign correspondents a rare option to visit battlegrounds but also opened them to criticism of succumbing to Nazi propaganda. It didn't help that Lochner and the other news agency bureau chiefs all made a point in their dispatches of noting that their travels were at the "personal invitation" of Adolf Hitler, as if that offered them added cachet.

"It has been the dream of every newspaperman in Berlin, ever since May 10 when the Reich's gigantic offensive by way of Holland and Belgium began, to see Hitler's amazing and awe-inspiring armed forces in action," gushed Lochner in his report dated May 20.[15]

Lochner's admiring accounts of the German offensive would soon earn him sharp criticism in both journalism and diplomatic circles at home. His critics deemed stories like the May 20 one to be pro-Nazi, with graphic accounts of what Lochner described as "terrorizing" German bombers smashing towns, destroying railway tracks and telephone lines, and annihilating columns of soldiers on the march. German military superiority was evident throughout his descriptions: "Regiment after regiment of infantry, detachment after detachment of well-nourished cavalry and seeming inexhaustible reserves of air force and artillery poured into the operational areas."[16]

And there was more to come, he said. "Hitler is not nearly as much interested in Paris as in London," Lochner reported after a meeting with General Walter von Reichenau, commander in France of the German Sixth Army, a tall Prussian who spoke perfect English and wore a monocle over his right eye. Hitler, Lochner wrote after the meeting, "regards the present war primarily as a fight with the British Empire." Lochner noted that "every radio announcement concerning events in the west ends with the stereotyped playing of the song, 'We Are Sailing Against England.'"[17]

On May 23, still on their German-led tour of the western front, the American news agency correspondents reached the English Channel. "It seems almost unbelievable that I should find Germany at this Channel," Lochner wrote. "But the Nazi Swastika waving from the local commander's headquarters leaves no doubt about it.

Crews of U-boats and speedboats are champing to be sent on their errands of destruction."[18]

Lochner reported seeing roads jammed with infantry and formidable artillery, "backed by an air force equipped to the last fine detail." All, he said, awaited Hitler's final command to go to England. Lochner was also impressed that the Germans were "so cocksure of victory" that at one headquarters a general had left in plain sight an enormous map with details of what appeared to be Nazi military plans. "Nobody seems to care any longer whether the enemy knows the German plans," Lochner concluded.[19]

A critical study of Lochner's reporting published in 1942 suggested he had left his journalistic skepticism far behind as he traveled with his German escorts. "It is difficult to envision High Command officers leaving 'highly significant' maps around to be 'discovered' by the foreign press," the study said. "Might it not have been reasonable to assume that these maps were deliberately left lying about in a not-too-subtle campaign of press agentry?"[20] Such an assumption is highly reasonable, given the enormous propaganda efforts of the Nazi regime.

Further evidence of German military superiority, Lochner suggested, could be seen in the claims of Britain's Air Ministry, which said that 1,500 German planes had been destroyed in the two weeks since the invasion of the Low Countries. Lochner, however, reported that he and the other American correspondents, traveling 1,200 miles in six days, "kept straining our eyes for Allied planes and saw none."[21]

On May 30 Lochner reported the Germans had reversed course. "Talk in army circles," he wrote, was that instead of going for England next, Germany planned to attack Paris, with the Italians providing support from the south.[22] "Now one hears artillery shooting across the narrow channel and the Stuka bombers are to keep England in a state of jitters while France is being finished," wrote Lochner.

For AP editors in New York, it must have seemed a journalistic coup to be able to distribute reports from Lochner, visiting battle areas in France with the German Army, alongside eyewitness accounts from his AP colleagues describing how the German onslaught looked from the other side. On June 3, as Lochner prepared to head for Calais and Boulogne with the German Army, waves of Luftwaffe war planes raided Paris just as AP bureau chief John Lloyd lunched with several U.S. Embassy officials at the Hotel Crillon in the French capital. Lloyd and his lunch companions rushed across the street to the roof of the embassy, where they saw planes circling slowly overhead, dropping bombs as they proceeded over the Church of the Madeleine, the Bourse, and other targets.

"In great waves they roared out of the misty blue north shortly after noon, flying high and moving perilously over a curtain of bursting shells sent up by anti-aircraft defenses and the bullets of numerous machine guns mounted on rooftops," the Paris bureau reported. "They flew in steady procession over the very heart of the city, and, as the air raid sirens shrieked and the hundreds of guns fired away, they sent down their incendiary bombs in screaming clusters."[23]

With the fall of Paris imminent, Lloyd covered the story of the flight of the French government en route to Vichy. From Bordeaux, on June 17, he reported the armies of France continued to fight even though their government had asked Hitler for terms of peace. After twelve days of retreat, the exhausted French, Lloyd reported, nevertheless demanded an "honorable peace" as the condition of surrender.[24] Hitler himself set out the German terms at Compiègne Forest, where he personally received the French envoys on June 21.

Meanwhile, Lochner, on another escorted trip to the front, reached Paris with other foreign correspondents ahead of the main German occupation force. He described Paris as a "ghost city," generally undamaged by war but abandoned by most of its people, with swastika flags flying from its most famous sites, including the Arc de Triomphe, the Hotel de Ville (city hall) and the Eiffel Tower.[25] Just two days later, though, he reported the city "shows signs of returning to normal," with street cleaners and garbage collectors at work and some cafes reopening.[26]

To publicize AP's on-the-spot coverage, photo editors in New York distributed an official German photo of the agency journalists walking with their Nazi escorts down the Avenue des Champs-Élysées, the Arc de Triomphe looming in the background. Lochner is not the only newsman in the photo, but the image of him flanked by uniformed press and propaganda officials makes him look part of an official Nazi entourage, no doubt adding ammunition to the arsenal of those who already viewed him as pro-Nazi.[27]

CBS correspondent William Shirer, no fan of either Lochner or his INS rival, Pierre Huss (also in the photo), wrote that the Germans made Lochner, Huss, and the third American news agency chief on the trip, Frederick Oechsner, promise not to speak to U.S. ambassador William C. Bullitt, Jr., or visit the American Embassy while in Paris, "a pledge they scrupulously kept though Fred Oechsner [of United Press] had the courage to phone the embassy and pay his respects." Shirer himself made a point of visiting Bullitt when he reached Paris a few days after the agency journalists. "I feel under no obligation not to act as a free American citizen here," he wrote in his best-selling *Berlin Diary*.[28]

Lochner's early entry into Paris meant AP was among the first American news organizations on the scene, but it fell to other AP reporters to give readers more perspective on the defeat of France.

"France went to war against Germany last September without adequate equipment, without adequate manpower and—it can now be said frankly—without adequate enthusiasm," wrote Taylor Henry of the AP Paris bureau. "Result: utter defeat in a month-long blitzkrieg, casualties estimated at 1,500,000 killed, wounded or missing;

a stunned nation only now beginning to realize what happened, a stunned leadership grimly groping toward the future."[29]

Henry's analysis, dated July 1, 1940, was filed from San Sebastian, Spain, beyond the reach of censors. He had followed the fugitive French government when it fled Paris to Bordeaux. When the French accepted defeat, he then crossed into Spain, finally free of French censorship to report his views on the catastrophe that had befallen the land of Napoleon and William the Conqueror.

Later that July, Henry C. Cassidy, another AP Paris correspondent who was headed to a new assignment in Moscow, filed poignant portraits of France's fate. Cassidy did some of his reporting from an unusual vantage point: a German troop train that he managed to ride from Paris to Berlin, passing through France, Belgium, and the Netherlands.

"Judging from scenes along our route there won't be many battlefield tours after this war—so swiftly did the blitzkrieg pass," Cassidy wrote. "While fields and forests were left intact, most towns were standing, and even in those where the Allies offered resistance, only a few quarters were smashed. Everywhere there were signs of quick reconstruction and compared to the devastation of the World War trench fighting this war generally left only slight traces."[30]

France, a country Cassidy had called home for four years, had "fallen back almost a century" under German occupation, he wrote from Berlin. The French republic had disappeared, "just as the empire did in the last century. With it have gone the power, finances, industries, pleasures—even the automobiles—which made Paris the capital of Western Europe in the 20th Century."[31]

Hitler's carefully choreographed postarmistice homecoming on July 6, 1940, was a tumultuous affair. Lochner's story on the return was accompanied by an overhead photo by Franz Roth, which captured Hitler's cavalcade, the Berlin sidewalks teeming with ecstatic crowds giving the Nazi salute as the dictator's black limousine glided by. While some observers, safely out of Germany, later described the scene as staged spectacle, Lochner seemed convinced he was witnessing a genuine nationalist frenzy. "BERLIN—(AP)—Adolf Hitler came back from his conquests yesterday to ride across a vast carpet of flowers and hear the tumult of a welcome such as Berlin never had seen before. The proportions of this homecoming were Napoleonic—the press, in fact, in an article written by Hitler's own press chief, Dr. Otto Dietrich, compared the Fuehrer to both Napoleon and Caesar."[32]

Lochner wrote that he had seen enthusiastic Hitler parades at Nazi Party conventions, in Danzig, and when Hitler returned from the Austrian Anschluss, "but yesterday it was different. The distinguishing feature was the complete abandon with which the population cheered, waved flags and cried 'Heil!'"

Lochner wrote a number of dispatches in this period that fed his critics. In a fawning July feature, he praised the Nazi logistical planning for the carefully staged armistice signing with France three weeks earlier. The surrender ceremony in Compiègne, he wrote, "graphically demonstrated Adolf Hitler's sense for the dramatic, the Fuehrer's proverbial luck where weather is concerned, the German army's famed efficiency and the Teuton capacity for detail." The trip, arranged by Karl Boehmer, director of the foreign press section of the propaganda ministry and longtime trusted deputy to ministry chief Joseph Goebbels, "went according to schedule, with clocklike precision," Lochner reported. Correspondents were assigned to an army transport plane with a crew of three "tanned, blue-eyed, tawny haired young men" who made an overnight stop "in charming, medieval Goslar, just as the last rays of the sun gilded the clouds in the west and a full moon rose above the eastern horizon," Lochner wrote.[33]

One can only wonder whether Lochner's intended readers were American newspaper subscribers or Boehmer at the propaganda ministry, on whom Lochner relied for access to news.

While Lochner was reporting from the front under German escort, the AP news bureau in Berlin was juggling the day-to-day news gleaned from German High Command communiques, reports from Propaganda Company war correspondents, German newspaper stories, and the DNB national news agency. The correspondents wrote spot news and explanatory background stories and, when permitted, traveled to war zones. Stories from Berlin might describe German military might and innovative tactics—how the German speedboat "mosquito fleet" harassed Allied shipping with hand-guided torpedoes, or how parachute troopers got secret training "for special operations far beyond normal infantry practice."[34]

But stories from the field, even reported under German escort, focused on the tragedy left in the wake of all that military power. Reporter Lynn Heinzerling traveled to the Netherlands to provide an eyewitness account of what the Nazis had done to Rotterdam, home of the Dutch merchant fleet. What was left, he wrote, was only a scar of a city, "its main business and financial district a pile of bricks and mortar serving as headstones for hundreds of dead."[35] Heinzerling quoted "authoritative German sources" as saying there were only 354 casualties, while unofficial estimates, he wrote, "have ranged as high as 10,000." Significantly higher casualty estimates were reported later.

Even Lochner's tone, full of excitement in describing battle scenes, turned somber after traveling on roads choked by advancing Nazi columns in France and Belgium. "There is nothing more pitiable than these endless streams of human misery that I have encountered again and again in Northern France and Belgium," he wrote in a lengthy piece describing "one of the most tragic migrations in history."³⁶

In another account, Lochner reported how people in the town of Aerschot, Belgium, reacted when they saw him. "I travel every day in a (German) First Lieutenant's car. I suppose the population takes me for German. If looks could have killed, I would have been a corpse in Aerschot, which was the scene of the most violent tank fights."³⁷

But often details like the hatred he saw in Aerschot came many paragraphs into his story—buried, perhaps, in hopes of avoiding German reprisals. Lochner had done the same thing when he covered the Nazi takeover of Poland, displaying a seemingly contradictory nature that could sound almost exultant in the heat of war and yet took the strong tone of a pacifist—as he'd been in World War I—when it came to the civilian impact of battle.

8

LOCHNER UNDER FIRE

AP's reporting on the military victories of Hitler's legions thundering across Europe in 1940 brought little joy to American newspaper editors or Washington policy makers. Some believed fervently that AP was exaggerating the Nazi successes, and they blamed AP's main messenger in Berlin: Bureau Chief Louis Lochner.

At a September meeting, editors of the Chesapeake Association of the Associated Press, representing area newspapers receiving the news service, cast a startling, unanimous vote censuring AP's reporting from Berlin. Those attending included representatives of the *Annapolis Capital*, the *Baltimore Sun*, the *Hagerstown (Md.) Herald*, and the *Hanover (Pa.) Evening Sun*. The editors' comments were blunt, their judgments harsh: "Lochner's reports are biased," "Lochner is spreading Hitler's views," and "With due allowance for censorship, I have the impression that Lochner has swallowed Hitler's propaganda 'hook, line and sinker.'"[1]

AP general manager Kent Cooper presented critiques of the Berlin bureau's reporting three weeks later at a meeting of AP's board of directors. Jumping to the defense of his men in Berlin, Cooper told the board that some newspaper members "condemned and demanded removal of members of the foreign staff because they had told the truth."[2]

Cooper's case was a sound one: the Blitzkrieg had stunned much of Europe into submitting to the Nazis, and that was the story reflected in AP Berlin's reports. The board brushed aside the criticism from the Chesapeake editors and voted unanimous approval of Cooper's confidence in Lochner. The board also endorsed a message of "affectionate regards" to be sent to all AP correspondents working in war zones. "Proud of the work of the entire foreign staff in these stressful times," it said.

The board vote fended off critics for the moment, but as the war progressed, AP's staunch defense of Lochner's work did not prevent fresh complaints from newspaper editors and others. Nor did Cooper's defense waver. In June 1941 he penned a lengthy response to a reader of the *New York Times* who complained about a "blatantly pro-Nazi" Lochner story appearing in that newspaper. "I have confidence that he is honest in reporting what he sees," Cooper wrote, describing Lochner as a loyal American and a reliable reporter whose dispatches passed through the hands of editors "who are as zealous of The Associated Press avoiding bias as you would have them be."[3]

The following year, concerns about Lochner's reporting—and about AP's photo subsidiary in Germany—rose to a higher level when U.S. secretary of the interior Harold L. Ickes forwarded a copy of a blistering critique to Frank Noyes, the former president of the news agency's board of directors. The text—taken from a report titled "American News Sources in Nazi Germany"—had no author's name attached to it, and though Ickes told Noyes he could not vouch for the facts as presented, he clearly supported its theme: that U.S. media were passing on Nazi propaganda to their audiences.

The report praised some correspondents, including Beach Conger of the *New York Herald Tribune* and Otto Tolischus of the *New York Times*, both of whom were forced to leave Germany because of their reporting. But it also complained that "the practice of *The New York Times* to print Hitler's speeches in full is clearly recognized [by the Nazis] as an immense asset—obtained entirely free of charge."[4] In one speech, Hitler had struck out against Ickes as one of several "agitators" who were fomenting anti-German sentiments in the U.S.[5] Ickes had criticized Henry Ford, Charles Lindbergh, and other Americans for accepting German medals "at the hand of a brutal dictator who, with the same hand, is robbing and torturing thousands of fellow human beings."[6]

Much of the report forwarded by Ickes was devoted to AP and both its news and photo coverage, and the language was scathing. Although Lochner "honestly strives at impeccable neutrality and is loyally serving American interests," the report said, he was also "an easy victim for many a Nazi trap." The report said Lochner appeared to have been misled by the Nazis when he assured readers that "Hitler is not nearly so much interested in Paris as in London," but then "the Germans turned against France and vanquished it in 43 days."[7]

The report also took aim at photo coverage, in particular AP's distribution of German-supplied pictures of U-boats at a naval base on the French coast. At least one such photo, published in August 1940, confirmed how far Nazi Germany had advanced and how much of a threat it now posed to transatlantic shipping. But the author of the Ickes report saw something more ominous in AP's distribution of the U-boat photos: pictorial support of "the implied Hitlerian threat against the United States."[8]

In his cover letter to Noyes, Ickes said he understood "what difficulties the American newspaper correspondents must necessarily work in Germany at this time." But, he added, "I sometimes wonder whether we would not be better off without dispatches from that country if the alternative is to be fed daily doses of arsenical propaganda."[9]

While the identity of the author remains unknown, a copy of the report archived in the Library of Congress reveals that Ickes had received it from Arthur Upham Pope, a curator of Persian art, who founded the Committee for National Morale in 1940. The committee favored aggressive U.S. government–sponsored use of propaganda to counter German propaganda. In his letter to Ickes, Pope noted that the section of the report he was forwarding was particularly explosive about AP and showed "how Louis P. Lochner is really used as a stooge by Germany's propaganda."[10]

The unsigned report also targeted Germans employed by AP's photo subsidiary, the AP GmbH. Photo salesman Gerhard Meixner was "known to be an ardent Nazi," it said. Eric Borchert worked as an AP GmbH photographer at the same time that he took war photos for the Wehrmacht, and the report also raised concerns about the Nazi ties of Austrian-born photographer Franz Roth. Did it serve American interests, the report author wondered, to have "an allegedly American news agency in Berlin which employs predominantly German staff both in its news and news picture departments and thus exposing itself to the direct influence of the Propaganda Ministry."[11] The claim that Germans made up a majority of AP's Berlin news staff is in error; most were Americans. But it correctly reflected the makeup of the AP GmbH photographer staff.

When Noyes received the report from Ickes, he forwarded it to Kent Cooper. He also replied to Ickes with a robust defense of AP's Berlin bureau, suggesting that the report's anonymous author (or authors) "fundamentally misunderstood the mission of the Associated Press and its correspondents, including Lochner," whose "dispatches during the invasion of Holland, Belgium and France seem to me to have been tragically and prophetically true." The report's criticisms, he said, were "examples of wishful thinking."[12]

Six months after the sharp criticism from the Chesapeake editors, Cooper presented the AP board with the new, anonymous criticisms shared by Ickes. Once again, the board sided with its correspondents in the field, concluding "the statements in the report were not substantiated by the facts and were in fact based on partial and misleading evidence."[13]

But even after the United States declared war on Germany, forcing Lochner's eventual return to the United States, the criticism didn't stop. In June 1942 Ickes received a letter from another Lochner critic, who objected to a Lochner story speculating about rumors that Hermann Göring might turn against Hitler.[14] Ickes replied that he had been suspicious of Lochner since World War I, when he had been an active pacifist and seemed (to Ickes) "to indicate distinctly pro-German sympathies." But when Ickes had written to AP about what he thought of Lochner, Ickes said, "I made no impression."[15]

Defending their Berlin bureau's journalism could be seen as blind trust or reflexive defensiveness on the part of AP leaders, but others who had warned the United States about Hitler's well-oiled war machine faced accusations similar to those targeting Lochner. When he visited Washington in the winter of 1939–40, Jacob Beam, third secretary at the U.S. Embassy in Berlin, sought to describe to American officials the verities of modern-day Nazi Germany. "They wanted to hear that there were severe food shortages, mass public dissatisfaction, shortage of essential war materiel," said Beam. "The last thing Washington upper circles wanted to be told was the truth, that Hitler controlled the world's most efficient war machine, made up of superbly trained and highly motivated soldiers."[16]

Beam said he was accused of being pro-Nazi for trying "to tell people in Washington that the German tanks were not immobilized from lack of oil and grease." When Beam returned to Berlin, he told American correspondents that they "had not done a good job of telling people at home how powerful Hitler's Germany had become."

If the men who worked with Lochner every day in the Berlin bureau were concerned about how he viewed the Nazis, they apparently kept such thoughts private. The only Berlin colleague known to have openly shared his views of Lochner was Lynn Heinzerling, who wrote years later for an AP book that was never published that the bureau chief had a "Germanic thoroughness" but "seemed to have considerable difficulty in getting his facts down on paper and he was not a good writer." Heinzerling's assessment noted that Lochner, who was hired abroad, was handicapped by not having passed through the domestic AP bureau system where journalists learned to report and write under fierce deadline pressure. Lochner, facing that kind of pressure most days after the war began, "occasionally at least, said things that reporters more versed in the AP Bible would have avoided," said Heinzerling.

For example, Lochner's "rather enthusiastic" account of German troops arriving at the English Channel in 1940, "champing to be sent on their errands of destruction," raised editorial eyebrows at home, though Heinzerling believed Lochner had simply "let the occasion overwhelm him and his better judgement." Then, noting Lochner's lifelong love of music (he performed a Beethoven piano concerto for his graduate examination at the Wisconsin Conservatory of Music), Heinzerling concluded: "He was a gracious, highly intelligent and kindly person who probably should have been a music critic."[17]

Outside the AP bureau, Lochner's competitors in Berlin generally avoided passing judgment on him, though they were not at all shy about rating and critiquing each other in books or private letters. Some of the more sharp-tongued descriptions appeared in *Berlin Diary*, the best seller published in 1941 by William Shirer of CBS. Shirer dismissed short, heavy-set Guido Enderis, bureau chief of the *New York Times*, as "aging in his sixties but sporting invariably a gaudy racetrack suit with a loud red necktie, minding the Nazis less than most."[18] International News Service bureau chief Pierre Huss, Shirer wrote, was "slick, debonair, ambitious, and on better terms with Nazi officials than almost any other." Lochner, Shirer noted, came "rarely if at all" to the Taverne, the Italian restaurant whose owner kept a corner table reserved for the American and British correspondents who showed up nightly to drink and talk shop. As a result, Lochner—who was far more likely to be found at the opera, a concert, or one of the numerous receptions and dinner parties on his packed social calendar—was spared one of Shirer's colorful critiques. But in other diary entries, Shirer made clear he had little time for correspondents like Lochner who accepted favors from the propaganda ministry.

In a far more detailed critique of the American press corps in Berlin, sent privately to his managing editor, *Christian Science Monitor* correspondent Joseph Harsch complained that the Germans used access to trips and interviews "as bait or reward," resulting "in a demoralization of the American press corps here." Lochner was among the main beneficiaries of this system, Harsch noted.[19] Harsch, who served two years in Berlin and filed for CBS when Shirer was away, said the American correspondents could be divided into "those who play the game and write as favorably as they can, and those who respect their integrity and write as honestly as they can." He placed Lochner, Huss, Enderis, and Max Jordan of NBC in the first group. On the other side, he said, were Shirer, Sigrid Schultze of the *Chicago Tribune*, and Ralph Barnes of the *Herald Tribune*, while Wallace Deuel of the *Chicago Daily News* "is the only one who manages somehow to retain his integrity while accepting some of the [Nazi] favors." "The most glaring single instance of how the system works," wrote Harsch, were the private briefings for a select few—Lochner and Huss among them—held an hour before each general press conference. "The entire staff of the Propaganda Ministry is under formal instructions to see to it that the AP and INS get all the news well in advance of the UP [United Press]."

That favoritism was also practiced on the road, where Karl Boehmer, a German Army officer, served as official minder on numerous trips to the western front with American correspondents.

There were always at least two cars to transport the Americans, according to Harsch, with Lochner, Huss, and Enderis riding with Boehmer. At the end of the day, when correspondents headed back to file their stories, Boehmer's car drove "at high speed, having ordered the follow-up car with UP, Herald Tribune, Chicago Daily News, CBS and other correspondents to follow at the official army speed limit, which was about 25 miles an hour."[20] This often gave Lochner and Boehmer's other "guests" a two- or three-hour beat over their competitors, an enormous advantage, Harsch said.[21]

Lochner's reputation also fared poorly in a history of United Press written years later, which praised UP bureau chief Frederick Oechsner for consistent skepticism of Hitler's public statements about peace. "The UP man was ostracized by the Nazi party, put at the tail end of motorcades, shunned and bullied," wrote the authors, while Lochner "was reporting the Fuhrer's pronouncements of non-aggression with the solemnity of a church warden reading from a bishop's manifesto."[22]

One example: Lochner's August 26, 1939, report that "a trustworthy and authoritative informant insisted Saturday that a compromise in the German-Polish crisis is underway and declared that the danger of a world war is definitely averted."[23] Lochner did not identify his informant, and though he hedged the claim a bit lower in the story, it's very possible he was passing on disinformation planted by the Nazis to conceal the timing of the planned German attack on Poland (which happened just days later). If so, it's hard to understand how Lochner fell for it. Not long before, he had written that the German-Polish conflict seemed set to explode, and just before his "war definitely averted" piece, he had received word from a high-ranking source in the anti-Nazi underground confirming that Hitler was about to invade Poland. But Lochner's voluminous files cast no light on his reporting of the August 26 story, and the hedging he put lower down in his text did little to alleviate the embarrassment for those who published it—such as the *Minneapolis Star*, which ran a front page, two-line banner headline:

BERLIN REPORTS "DANGER OF WORLD WAR HAS BEEN DEFINITELY AVERTED"

The *Star* provided its own hedge, though, with an introductory note beneath Lochner's byline. "Mr. Lochner is rated by newspaper men as one of the best-informed men in the world in German affairs," the *Star* noted. "In reading the following dispatch, it should be kept in mind, however, that he is presenting a view given by a German source he evidently trusts. It is definitely a German view, however."

In his memo about Berlin correspondents, Harsch, the *Christian Science Monitor* journalist, also criticized the "demoralizing effects" of Kent Cooper's management style on correspondents in AP bureaus in Europe. "They are hounded, bullied and badgered in a way which seems almost sadistic, sapping the morale of the organization and driving some of them to such devices as the pitiful plea here to the Propaganda Ministry for even more favors than the very substantial ones already arranged for them."[24]

Although Cooper was known to be an authoritarian figure, there is little evidence that he hounded Lochner, as Harsch frames it. In a sense, the two men needed each other. Lochner's German expertise—his encyclopedic knowledge of German affairs, near-native fluency in the language, and countless contacts high and low—made him all but irreplaceable. For his part, Cooper vigorously and repeatedly deflected Lochner's critics both inside and outside AP. But there is clearly a whiff of servility in Lochner's considerable correspondence with his boss, whom he addressed as "Dear chief." And in various writings during his time in Berlin and after, he portrayed his actions as responses to dictates from AP management: "Our orders from our bosses were to tell no untruth, but to report only as much of the truth without distorting the picture as would enable us to remain at our post," he wrote in a 1956 memoir.[25]

Despite the reference to "bosses," Cooper was clearly the boss Lochner sought most to please—and the one most determined to see the AP bureau remain in operation, despite Nazi pressures. Cooper could make the AP mission sound like a crusade for freedom. But he was also a businessman determined to expand his agency into a powerful global enterprise, even at the occasional expense of journalistic ethics. He considered foreign correspondents to be guests in the countries they covered and thus necessarily observant of local laws, even those aimed at repressing reporting. And he did not keep his early isolationist views on the war separated from news policy. At the September 1940 meeting, where the AP board unanimously supported Lochner, Cooper said AP's domestic staff had been instructed that reporting U.S. "government propaganda and material tending to lead public opinion to war should be excluded, except in the case of items of news value whose sources were clearly indicated."[26]

For his part, Lochner well understood that closure of the AP bureau in Germany would threaten Cooper's global ambitions and seriously disrupt German news coverage for its more than 1,200 American newspaper subscribers. When editors on the cable desk in New York challenged his copy or accused him of burying crucial news, he would trot out his standard justification: it needs to be written that way to avoid propaganda ministry repercussions, including possible closure of all AP operations in Germany. Though repercussions were a constant threat, Lochner probably was overstating how far the ministry might go. While the Nazis expelled or forced the departure of some individual foreign correspondents, their news organizations were allowed to send replacements. But Cooper did not question Lochner's warnings, and time after time, he backed his Berlin bureau chief in conflicts with AP editors.

So, did the AP Berlin bureau withhold important truths under Lochner's leadership? No rigorous academic study has assessed the AP coverage, which was voluminous throughout the 1930s as the bureau reported on all aspects of the growing Nazi menace. And any study of what was written and what newspaper readers actually saw would need to take into account the fact that AP itself was not a publisher. What its newspaper clients chose to print (or not print), how a story may have been rewritten or cut, and where each story was placed by AP's hundreds of newspaper subscribers were issues determined by editors at each paper.

Lochner readily acknowledged passing up some stories that he said could not be confirmed, or that he feared could trigger expulsion and closure of the bureau—like the photos of Nazi Brownshirts marching lawyer Michael Siegel through Munich in 1933. Even the reporting of Kristallnacht, he said, was understated by all U.S. correspondents, who omitted some stories they heard lest their sources be rounded up and tortured. And in writings after he left Germany, Lochner revealed that he let high-ranking officials review his stories, based on interviews with the officials, before they ran. While acknowledging that other journalists strongly disagreed with this practice, Lochner said "I feel that the approval of the interviewees is an insurance against later disavowal" of how he had quoted them. "Also," he wrote, "we foreign correspondents are, after all, guests in the country of our assignment. Why not be courteous and let our victims see what we intend to publish about them?"[27]

That view seemed torn from the Kent Cooper version of journalistic ethics, which argued that foreign correspondents, as "guests" of the countries where they worked, "should not abuse their hospitality." Lochner even gave Hitler editorial control when he interviewed him in 1932, the year before the Nazis took power. During the interview

Hitler said Jews must be eliminated from Germany because "we cannot as a people digest" them. Lochner apparently presented Hitler with a transcript of the interview and allowed him to edit his remarks. Hitler, he wrote in an article for the Wisconsin Historical Society in 1958, "must himself have noted what a fatal admission he had made, for with an angry gesture he crossed the whole passage out as he read my script. Incidentally, when I started him on the Jewish question, white saliva exuded from both sides of his mouth."[28]

In the postwar decades, books and conferences have critiqued, sometimes harshly, American media coverage of the Nazi policies that culminated in the Holocaust. During the Nazi era, though, what rankled Lochner's critics most was not how his bureau covered anti-Semitism's many forms. Rather, his exuberant descriptions of the German war effort fed the accusations that he was pro-Nazi. In his stories from the field, reported under German escort, he did include poignant portraits of refugees fleeing devastated landscapes. But his long-time pacifism and his war-is-evil views were expressed far more passionately in private letters home, and in public speeches Lochner made after leaving Germany in 1942.

In an address that year at the University of Virginia, Lochner painted devastating scenes he'd witnessed, describing the stench of the battlefields,

> where men and horse were rotting in the burning May and June sun; add the pitiful lowing of cows whose udders were bursting and paining them as they had not been milked for days, add the nerve-wracking roar of the planes above you, the swish of passing bullets, the holocausts of fire wherever shelling did its devastating work, the debris of once beautiful buildings that were brushed aside like card houses by the advancing, ruthless armored cars—add all this and you can understand, perhaps, why my last three years on the other side seem like a nightmare.[29]

Critics who saw Nazi leanings in Lochner's reporting likely would have been shocked to learn something Lochner's own employers probably didn't know: that the AP bureau chief in Berlin had long been in contact with members of the underground German resistance. In late August 1939 one of Lochner's connections passed him an explosive document: minutes from a secret meeting of Hitler and his top military commanders, just prior to the invasion of Poland. The document, taken from notes kept by an unnamed official at the meeting, not only revealed the planned timing of the Poland invasion but also quoted Hitler's determination "to send to death mercilessly and without compassion, men, women and children of Polish derivation and language. Only thus shall we gain the living space [Lebensraum] which we need."

According to the document, Hitler told the assembled commanders: "Our strength consists in our speed and in our brutality." Genghis Khan, he said, "led millions of women and children to slaughter—with premeditation and a happy heart. History sees in him solely the founder of a state. It is a matter of indifference to me what a weak western European civilization will say about me."[30] The version of the Hitler meeting given to Lochner also quoted Hitler as saying, "Who, after all, speaks today of the annihilation of the Armenians," a quote that did not appear in other accounts of the gathering. Scholarly research has generally argued that the quote is authentic, and it is included in an excerpt of the transcript given to Lochner that covers one wall in the United States Holocaust Memorial Museum in Washington, D.C.

The document came to Lochner from Ludwig Beck, who had resigned as German Army chief of staff in 1938 over differences with Hitler. Beck used a Social Democrat resistance figure well-known to Lochner to deliver it. Though the name of the actual minutes-taker was removed, some historians have concluded the source was

Admiral Wilhelm Canaris, chief of the Abwehr, the German military intelligence service, who had come to loathe Hitler and believed his plans should be exposed.

Lochner did not publish the document at the time, likely understanding that it would set off a firestorm, would be loudly denied and denounced by Nazi propagandists, and almost certainly would lead to executions of anti-Hitler underground figures. Instead, he took the text to the U.S. Embassy, where he met with Chargé d'Affaires Alexander Kirk. Kirk rejected the document outright, perhaps fearing it could somehow embroil the United States, still steadfastly neutral, in ongoing negotiations between Hitler and Britain.

Lochner described the meeting in testimony he gave to U.S. military war crimes investigators in July 1945:

> KIRK: Oh, take this out of here. That is dynamite.
> LOCHNER: Yes, but the American government ought to know about this whole thing.
> KIRK: Oh, we have so many troubles already, I don't want to get involved. I don't know whether our code isn't known, etc.[31]

Lochner subsequently gave the document to a British diplomat, who relayed it to London just days before September 1, 1939, when German troops began pouring over the border into Poland, as Lochner's source reported they would, triggering declarations of war from Britain and France. Three years later, in October 1942, AP finally published details of the document. By then Lochner was safely out of the country and about to publish his book, *What About Germany?*, which opens with the story of receiving the secret meeting minutes.

Ultimately the minutes were a footnote in the massive history of Nazi Germany, but the existence of the document did indicate—as noted by one historian—that before war broke out "there were highly placed Germans who were willing to go to the limit of treason to oppose the manifest danger emanating from their own country."[32]

In 1942, the same year the secret minutes were revealed, Lochner made a failed effort to set up radio contact between the U.S. government and other German resistance figures who advocated a military overthrow of Hitler and a return of the German monarchy. In Washington, he met with an agent of the Office of Strategic Services, the wartime intelligence agency, and with Allen Dulles, who later became the first civilian director of central intelligence. The agent, Emmy Rado, pushed for "higher-ups" to see Lochner, saying she was convinced he had more to say than he had revealed to her.

"He is very much on the defensive on account of being known as pro-German and is called pro-Nazi by many people," she wrote. "He might be very pleased if he were honored in some way."[33] Ultimately, though, Lochner's request for a personal meeting with President Roosevelt to outline the proposal for establishing contact with the resistance was rebuffed. The U.S. goal of Allied military victory and an unconditional German surrender did not call for working with resistance figures; the administration sent word to Lochner through AP's Washington bureau that he should drop the matter. Most of the resistance figures he had met with about the plan were later executed for complicity in a failed July 20, 1944, attempt to assassinate Hitler.[34]

9

PHOTO BLITZ

As the war in Europe exploded in the spring of 1940, AP's pictures of the first days of Nazi attacks on Germany's neighbors dominated the front pages of America's newspapers. They included photos of extensive bomb damage in Amsterdam; images of British "light dragon tractors" rumbling through Belgium to face the Germans; and a photo of a World War I–vintage artillery gun "effectively used by the French to slow down the smashing attacks of 80-ton German tanks," according to its caption.[1]

There was, too, on June 5, a dark, blurry glimpse of the last British troops passing burning debris as they lined up to board rescue ships on the French coast at Dunkirk.[2] A second photo captured the flight of the few remaining civilians at Dunkirk, while a third showed refugees in Paris, among the thousands "who have streamed into France from homes in Belgium, Luxembourg or France—homes which they may never see again," AP's caption said.[3] French censors approved the images of Dunkirk and the refugees in Paris, and the photos were quickly sent directly to New York from Paris.

At the outset of the blitzkrieg, AP boasted about its photo scoop on Amsterdam's devastation, "the first spot picture on yesterday's outbreak of war to reach America," and about another image showing an airport south of Rotterdam "converted into a series of craters" by Nazi bombers.⁴ "Associated Press photographs of the war in Holland scored a clean 'beat' in America today," an accompanying AP story ballyhooed.

The boastful prose about AP's speedy delivery of scenes of death and destruction expressed little sensitivity for those targeted, but it reflected the era's fierce competition among American photo agencies: being consistently first with exclusive photos could translate into more newspaper subscribers and greater revenues. In bragging about its exclusive images of the start of the blitzkrieg, the AP story added, rather breathlessly: "In thrilling sequence, the [AP] photographs from Amsterdam told the tale of destruction being wrought in Holland."⁵

AP's ability to score exclusives ceased, though, with Nazi occupation. A German censorship curtain fell across Holland and the other now-captive European countries during the spring and summer of 1940, cutting off access for non-German journalists but opening news columns in America and beyond for a flood of images produced under strict German military and propaganda auspices. Among them: a German U-Boat stationed in a French port just opposite the British Isles, and German soldiers on horseback riding past the iconic Arc de Triomphe in Paris.⁶

These were the work of German photographers who, starting in 1938, were drafted into military propaganda companies, known as Propagandakompanien, or simply PK. Recruited from German media outlets, they continued to receive salaries from their civilian employers, along with their military paychecks. But while media companies paid them, the photographers were now an integral part of the Nazi propaganda apparatus, their work controlled by the German military and the propaganda ministry. Employees of all German media were subject to PK recruitment. And so were those who worked for the last international photo agency still operating in Berlin: the AP GmbH, the photo subsidiary that had been incorporated as a German business in 1931.

By the time the PK units were formed, other international agencies had closed shop, most notably Keystone, a U.S. company with a German subsidiary, and the *New York Times*'s Wide World Photos, both of which departed in 1935 rather than face continued Nazi pressure. AP's decision to remain meant it had bowed to Nazi demands to dismiss its Jewish employees and to install a German owner-manager. And when the PK began drafting civilian photographers, AP bowed again. Its photographers went to work for the German military, as part of its propaganda effort, while remaining on AP's payroll.

PK warrior journalists "march with the infantry, go on scouting detail, stand watch, eat and sleep with other soldiers," AP reported in March 1940.[7] They were a vital part of the German war effort, wrote Phillip Knightley in *The First Casualty*, his history of war correspondence, "a combination of straight war correspondent, publicist, and master of what the British termed 'black propaganda.'"[8] The Wehrmacht's PK troops, first deployed in Czechoslovakia during the 1938 German annexation of the Sudetenland, may have helped inspire the Waffen-SS to establish its own SS-Kriegsberichter Kompanie, or SS-War Correspondent Company, in 1940.

Though the goal was propaganda, images taken by PK photographers could also have clear news value: the aftermath of battles, Hitler arriving in Nazi-occupied Poland, German soldiers parading through the streets of a vanquished Paris. The propaganda ministry distributed these photos to German media and to AP and its photo competitors outside Germany, who in turn sold them to newspapers in the United States and elsewhere. But while some of their work covered breaking news, PK photographers were clear about what was expected of them, and it was not objective journalism. Eric Borchert, one of the AP GmbH's photographers during Kristallnacht in 1938, a year later served in the PK covering the invasion of Poland. "We are no longer reporters or editors," he wrote in 1941. "We are soldiers of a new weapon of the Führer, the propaganda company."[9]

Two other photographers who were on the streets for AP the night of Kristallnacht, Gerhard Baatz and Franz Roth, also later served in the PK. Roth, a longtime ardent Nazi supporter, joined a notorious Waffen-SS fighting unit, the Leibstandarte SS Adolf Hitler, whose leader was later convicted of war crimes. Baatz volunteered at the outbreak of war as a PK photographer in Poland, where he worked the first month of the invasion. Even before Poland, at the same time that he worked for AP, Baatz said he covered political events for the propaganda ministry, including a trip Hitler made in 1938 to Italy, Austria, and Czechoslovakia. After the United States and Germany went to war against each other, he was hired to work for Büro Laux, the agency that would facilitate AP's wartime photo exchange with Nazi Germany. To hold the job, he also joined the Waffen-SS. But unlike warrior-photographer Roth, Baatz was based in Berlin and wore no uniform, though he apparently traveled extensively on photo assignments for Büro Laux, through "the entire German Reich and the adjacent countries of Hungary, what was formerly known as Yugoslavia, Poland, the protectorate of Silesia, Holland, Belgium, Denmark, Czechoslovakia and Greece."[10]

Wherever they traveled, the only PK photographer images that made it to public view were those that suited Nazi censors. And frontline access came at a personal price. PK photographers were expected to bear arms and take part in combat. Many were killed or wounded, including Borchert and Roth. Borchert was twenty-nine when he died on the German front lines at Tobruk, Libya, in 1941.[11] A Russian bullet hit Roth during a battle in Ukraine in 1943, and he died several days later. AP issued a brief obituary about Borchert, describing him as "one of Germany's outstanding feature photographers" who was working as a "German propaganda war cameraman" when he was killed. No mention was made of his dual employment with AP.[12] AP issued no obituary for Roth. Company records offer no explanation, but it's not hard to imagine some internal objections to publicly recognizing the Nazi photographer who also served AP.

Otto Dietrich, Hitler's personal press chief, claimed that in the first thirty months of the war, PK men wrote thirty-eight thousand war stories and made one million photographs.[13] PK text stories were seldom used in foreign newspapers, but the frontline images from PK photographers got wide distribution. Photos from war zones like Poland—the Führer walking along the Vistula River, joining troops at Kulm, arriving at an undisclosed Polish airfield—were shared by the propaganda ministry with the AP and its competitors.[14] But although it might be receiving the same images as rival agencies, the AP GmbH, with its substantial staff of editors and technicians, could outrace the competition to get the photos to New York (by radio or, for less urgent images, air shipment) and into the hands of U.S. newspaper editors.

AP was not shy about touting its speedy distribution system. "Even before complete word on the first day's developments had been received, Associated Press Wirephoto papers had the first action pictures from the front to reach America," an AP story boasted on the day after Germany's invasion of Poland in September 1939.[15] The photos showed German soldiers in action near Westerplatte at Danzig and the bombardment of the city's munitions depot.[16] Not included was a disclaimer the agency used, but not consistently, in the war years, stating that information provided with an image "was according to the Nazi caption accompanying this photo" or according to "the German caption accompanying this photo."[17] Some AP competitors were more explicit, at least some of the time, about images they distributed from Poland. International News, for example, revealed that a picture it shared of a Polish village in flames was "released by the German propaganda bureau," and a Central Press photo showing German troops herding Polish prisoners noted:

"This picture was passed by the Nazi censor and issued as propaganda for Germany."[18]

The lack of consistency on AP captions may be due in part to a view stated by Executive Photo Editor Al Resch in a December 12, 1940, memo to editors in New York: "The phrases 'According to British censor-approved caption,' or 'German sources say this picture shows,' have been vastly and needlessly overdone," Resch wrote. "Plain everyday judgment will dictate when reference properly should be made in a given caption to the source when occasion warrants, and it long since has ceased to be news that pictures from belligerent countries are passed by censor."[19]

Some analysts came to view Germany's takeovers in Europe as a brilliantly executed military strategy, supported by the most effective propaganda campaign of the twentieth century. In a 1941 study, "Photographs as News," Cyril Radcliffe, then director-general of Britain's Ministry of Information, examined why "our enemies' photographs," as he called them, appeared so frequently in American newspapers. One reason, he wrote, was that photos of German soldiers invading the Soviet Union were "immediate" and "alive"; they portrayed "exciting incidents."[20]

Another factor, cited by German historian Harriet Scharnberg, was the efficiency of press facilities the Germans provided their PK correspondents. While the military and the propaganda ministry moved material quickly, sluggish British censorship approved few countervailing photos from the Allied side, leaving the U.S. press inundated with images "from the immense flow of propagandistic, professionally produced and promptly distributed German photographs."[21]

Because all German war photos were released from the same source, the propaganda ministry, there were numerous occasions when two or more of the competing American agencies distributed the same images. There were also times when one agency distributed a photo that another held back. Even within AP, photo editors on different continents made different editorial decisions.

In early 1941, for example, the GmbH shipped a package of officially approved German photos to New York showing life in Nazi-created Jewish ghettos in Poland. The propaganda ministry–prescribed captions sent from Berlin gave racist descriptions of the content. The caption on an image of a "Jews only" trolley car said public transport was segregated "because most of the infectious diseases start in the thickly populated Jewish sections of the city, which are exceedingly dirty. The non-Jewish population is thus protected."[22] Another photo showed a water carrier in Lublin, a city with no running water, who, the caption alleged, had bought water from a public well and then resold it for twice what he'd paid.[23] In New York, the Jewish ghetto package was labeled "Nazi propaganda" and filed away in the photo library, its contents never distributed in the United States.

However, copies of the photos and captions were also relayed to AP photo editors in London, who decided to distribute them to British subscribers after a serious caption rewrite. The London editors, reflecting editorial practices of wartime Britain, described the Jewish ghettos as "containing all the worst features of those set up centuries ago," where "the helpless Polish Jews" experienced "indignities and sufferings of all kinds."[24]

Weeding out propaganda—from Nazi Germany as well as other war zones—was to become a major responsibility at AP's photo desk. Captions written by foreign bureaus were systematically rewritten in New York to conform to AP domestic standards overseen by Resch, the executive photo editor whose December 1940 memo had admonished colleagues not to overdo attributions such as "German sources say. . . ." In the same memo Resch urged AP editors to "SAY WHAT THE PICTURE SHOWS," citing a photo of an Italian bomber that crashed in England as an example of what not to do.

Though the photo showed a single plane, the caption stated an unverified claim made by British officials: "British Bag 13 Italian Planes in One Day." The caption, concluded Resch, "was rank propaganda."[25]

Though propaganda came from all sides during World War II, none matched the relentless Nazi disinformation efforts, particularly when it came to photos and photo captioning. An image of two women walking down a country path, dated August 27, 1939, offered a seemingly generic image from Poland days before Germany invaded—except for the caption, which alleged that the women were "running for their lives . . . seeking a hole in the barbed wire fence to cross the border" from Poland into Germany. The photo was made by Borchert, the AP photographer on assignment in Poland with the PK. The propaganda ministry released it, and an editor at the AP GmbH wrote the "running for their lives" caption, which identified it as an Associated Press photo from Berlin. Left unmentioned were the ministry's role and the fact that the cameraman was on assignment as a PK photographer.

The women Borchert photographed may or may not have been "running for their lives"; nothing in the image makes that clear. What was clear, though, was that the caption was designed to bolster Nazi claims of Polish persecution of Germans—the pretext for the invasion of Poland five days later, on September 1. This photo and another of men said to be Germans fleeing "from Polish terror" were blocked on arrival in New York, by editors who sent them to the AP photo library rather than distribute them. The photo of the men, still in library files today, bears an unknown editor's penciled notation: "Nazi propaganda." The image of the women is labeled "More Nazi propaganda."[26]

Willy Brandt, now officially owner of the GmbH, explained the new realities of the German photo operation to AP executives in

New York. While AP still paid Borchert and its other photographers, the GmbH had virtually no control over them or the images they produced once they joined PK units, he noted. It was a bizarre arrangement, one that made AP's photo operation at least a tacit part of the Nazi propaganda machine. But it also gave AP member newspapers continuing access to photos of events in Germany and beyond, keeping intact Kent Cooper's ambitious business dreams.

At the time, Assistant General Manager Lloyd Stratton seemed less concerned about moral compromise than about the loss of exclusive access to the work of AP photographers in Germany. "It does seem peculiar that you furnish the man, pay his salary and expenses and then have his production distributed to all" photo agencies by the propaganda ministry, he told Brandt.[27]

In October 1940 Brandt sought a partial solution to AP's demands for exclusive photos. The apparent result was an extraordinary contract, negotiated with the propaganda ministry, giving AP exclusive control of the work of Franz Roth. A copy of the contract, kept by Roth's family in Germany, is signed only by Roth and Brandt but contains considerable detail of an agreement that apparently had the blessing even of Heiner Kurzbein, the AP GmbH's longtime antagonist in the propaganda ministry's photo department. The contract terms said the ministry agreed that Roth's work while assigned to cover a Waffen-SS fighting unit "may exclusively be distributed by Associated Press GmbH, both nationally and abroad."[28] This gave the AP GmbH a significant advantage over its photo competitors in Germany while also providing AP in New York access to a selection of exclusive photos for distribution in the United States.

The contract also refers to a letter, written by Kurzbein, stating the agreement was made in appreciation "of the special status the Associated Press occupies in the United States picture press."[29] Kurzbein noted that the agreement made AP the sole picture news agency "to have its own Propaganda Company reporter," a privilege not even granted to the agency run by Hitler's personal photographer, Heinrich Hoffmann. Kurzbein's language suggests he saw AP as a vital conduit. Germany was anxious to keep the United States out of the war, and serving up Berlin's viewpoint to the American public and officials in Washington through the AP was a convenient channel for delivering the Nazi message.

Given his controlling management style, it is difficult to imagine that AP general manager Kent Cooper did not know that the agency had negotiated an agreement with the Nazi government. It also seems unlikely that Berlin bureau chief Louis Lochner would have failed to inform his boss of this breakthrough in AP's efforts to obtain exclusive photos from Germany. But Lochner makes no reference to the agreement in his voluminous papers, and no files have been found that would clarify Cooper's understanding of AP GmbH affairs.

Publicly, Cooper was pleased with the German subsidiary's photo operation. As 1940 came to a close, with the United States still not at war, he offered fulsome praise for photo coverage of the conflict produced by AP bureaus—London and Berlin—in countries at war with each other. Always with an eye on business, Cooper praised "the great record of pictorial performance abroad" but also the ability of both bureaus to maintain photo sales at a profitable level.

"These wholly owned subsidiaries not only demonstrated an inexhaustible initiative in producing news pictures under hitherto considered impossible conditions but managed as well to retain their markets of picture service on a self-sustaining cost basis," he told members of AP's board of directors in his end-of-year report. "To the staff members as well as the heads of these organizations who often risked life and danger in getting the pictures, we have frequently expressed admiration and high tribute for their devotion, loyalty and courage to the cause of news pictures."[30]

10

THE NAZI PHOTOGRAPHER

Franz Seraphicus Roth was an adventurous, larger-than-life Austrian photographer who worked off and on for the Associated Press GmbH from 1934 into the early war years. He was also a committed Nazi and later a soldier in a Waffen-SS unit, whose wartime actions he photographed while being paid by his government and—at least some of the time he was in military service—by AP. He was killed in battle on the Russian Front in 1943.

Roth was not the only German soldier-photographer who worked for AP while serving in the Nazi military.[1] But while others joined or were drafted into the armed forces after the war began, Roth's commitment to the Nazis dated back to 1933, when he signed up in Vienna with the Sturmabteilung (SA), the Nazi Party's paramilitary organization, the so-called Brownshirts. He was twenty-two.

Upon his death a decade later, when he held the rank of Untersturmführer (comparable to a U.S. military ranking of second lieutenant[2]) in the Waffen-SS, Propaganda Minister Joseph Goebbels sent a personal condolence letter to Roth's wife. The Nazi Party's weekly magazine *Illustrierter Beobachter* published a two-page tribute with several photos taken by "one of our most valued employees."

AP did not issue an obituary, nor has any personnel file for Roth been found in the agency's archives. Other company records, as well as sources from outside AP, contain sometimes contradictory information about the precise dates and status of his AP employment. But the records make clear that, while in the SA and later the Nazi Party, and during his years of service as a propaganda ministry and later Waffen-SS photographer, Roth was also at times employed by AP. It's also clear that his Nazi ties were known to AP managers who approved his hiring. At least two of the agency's managers raised objections to employing him, and others complained he was difficult to work with. Some of his most propagandistic photos were never distributed by AP.

But the relationship continued. Then, in the aftermath of war, Franz Roth's work with AP was lost to corporate memory—until historian Harriet Scharnberg's report in 2016 revealed that Roth was "receiving a good salary from AP in addition to his military pay" when he took pictures such as a series of portraits of Soviet prisoners of war that AP distributed in the United States.[3] After AP confirmed Scharnberg's findings about Roth and his Nazi connections, it identified some eighty digitized images credited to Roth that could be viewed on AP's online photo platform. Those photos are now blocked from view and purchase.

Roth's AP press passes and family photo albums reveal a tall, burly young man, neatly attired, with a broad smile and movie star good looks. At the time he joined the Brownshirts, he was struggling to establish himself in Vienna as a photographer. His break came in 1934, when the AP GmbH in Berlin hired him to work in Austria.[4]

Soon, growing tensions in East Africa leading up to Benito Mussolini's October 1935 invasion of Ethiopia offered more exciting photo opportunities. Or perhaps Roth was seizing the chance to get out of Austria, where he'd been arrested in 1934 for Nazi-related activities, according to a CV he wrote by hand in 1942.[5]

The arrest prompted Stanley Thompson, AP news photo editor for Central Europe, to wonder if "there is more to Roth's arrest than appears on the surface, and that he may have gotten us in bad." But the arrest did not stop AP from hiring Roth to go to Ethiopia when he asked for the assignment. When he left for Africa, Roth was armed with little more than his camera and an April 29, 1935, letter signed by Thompson stating that Roth was "authorized to take news and feature photographs for the Associated Press."[6]

Roth joined a swarm of foreign correspondents covering the gathering storm in Abyssinia. He photographed scenes of Emperor Haile Selassie's preparations for war, and on December 6, 1935, he captured on film the Italian bombing of Dessie (spelled Dessye at the time), a provincial capital that was home to Selassie's field headquarters. The air attack by nine Italian bombers unleashed one thousand bombs in seventeen minutes, according to AP's photo caption. The city was largely destroyed, and Roth's dramatic photos showed the smoking ruins as residents searched the wreckage for dead and wounded. Twenty-four days after the bombing, newspaper subscribers in Minneapolis saw his images atop the front page with a caption reflecting the communications challenges of the era: "These pictures were rushed by plane to Brindisi [Italy], carried by plane to Paris, by [ocean] liner to New York, and were flashed by Wirephoto to *The Minneapolis Tribune*."[7]

While in Dessie, Roth put down his camera at one point to assist Valentine Schuppler, a Viennese physician and superintendent of the Red Cross hospital there. The hospital itself was targeted by "a score" of Italian bombs, AP correspondent James Mills reported on December 7, but throughout the attack photographer Roth "anesthetized the patients while Dr. Schuppler performed operations."[8]

Volunteering for medical service in the midst of a bombing attack was very much in keeping with the daredevil image Roth painted of himself in a fourteen-thousand-word unpublished manuscript: fearless and ready to endure the most difficult conditions to get his pictures. The Roth portrayed in the memoir-manuscript, written around 1942, offers a stark contrast with his descriptions of the British and American correspondents covering the war, some of whom were the inspiration for *Scoop*, Evelyn Waugh's satirical novel in 1938 of foreign correspondents gone amok.

Roth's manuscript echoes Waugh's biting observations. Nearly all the foreign correspondents, Roth wrote, were not to be found in the trenches but instead gathered at the finer hotels, trading gossip and inventing stories while knocking back drinks at the bar. Of some 120 correspondents who had descended on Addis Ababa, only 5, including a German and a Dane, "thought at least a brief visit to the front was necessary."[9]

Roth even painted an unflattering portrait of his colleague Mills, a towering figure in AP journalism whose career included postings to Moscow, Vienna, Tokyo, and Bombay. When Mahatma Gandhi found Mills waiting for him as he was released from prison, he declared: "Why Mr. Mills, if I should die and start to enter Heaven, I should expect to see you waiting to interview me at the gates."[10] It was a line AP exploited for years in its promotional material.

In Roth's memoir, Mills comes off as a pampered spendthrift who, Roth alleged, made up some of the juicier details in his stories. According to Roth, Mills arrived in Dessie to cover war amply supplied with tins of lobster, "dozens of gin and whiskey bottles, Worcestershire and tomato sauce, two folding tables and four folding chairs, a live-in tent, a wash stand, a camp bed, mattress and pillows, a box of toilet paper and many other tidings of civilization in the wild." Roth said he set up "this private hotel" for Mills "and then rewarded myself with two tins of lobster."[11] Mills, in a personal diary about his time covering the war in Ethiopia, made no mention of tins of lobster but did agree with Roth on one point: only a handful of journalists did an honorable job of covering that story. Unlike Roth, though, Mills included himself in that elite group. The rest of the press corps, he wrote, were "incompetents, amateurs, adventurers, and fakers."[12]

When he returned to Europe from Ethiopia in early 1936, Roth transferred to the GmbH in Berlin, but his affiliation with the Nazi-supporting SA paramilitaries set off alarms at AP headquarters in New York. In a letter to Berlin bureau chief Louis Lochner, the head of the New York photo department, Wilson Hicks (who, in an earlier editorial position, had proposed asking Hitler to write columns for AP), noted "the file here contains adequate evidence of the inadvisability of permitting him to rejoin the staff."[13]

The Hicks note did not elaborate on the "adequate evidence," and the file it refers to—or any AP file devoted to documenting Roth's relationship with the agency—has not been found in company archives. Nor have any communications been uncovered to illuminate what happened next: Hicks's objection apparently was withdrawn, overruled, or simply ignored, because two months later the AP GmbH issued Roth an identification card dated July 9, 1936, and a press pass valid until December 31, 1936. The pass was then extended to the end of 1937. Roth was also in possession of a press pass valid until June 30, 1939, issued by the Associated Press of Great Britain. Another, undated, press pass identifies Roth as a staff photographer of the photo department of the Associated Press of Great Britain.[14]

The passes were likely issued to facilitate Roth's freelance coverage of the 1936–1939 Spanish Civil War, where he worked for both the AP GmbH and the Munich-based weekly Nazi Party magazine *Illustrierter Beobachter* (Illustrated Observer) covering the Nazi-backed forces of Francisco Franco. As he had in Ethiopia, Roth passed harsh judgment on the other journalists he encountered in Spain, including a Jewish photographer for the U.S.-based Keystone photo agency. Horace "Tubby" Abrahams "always emphasized that he was an Englishman," Roth noted in his memoir, then dismissed Abrahams as a "small, stocky, thoroughbred Jew with all the characteristics of that race," whose "pushiness and impudence" exceeded even that of the American reporters Roth so disdained.

Roth was freelancing for AP in Berlin in March 1938 when Nazi troops marched unopposed into his Austrian homeland. He went to Austria at the start of the Anschluss, though it's not clear in what circumstances. In a note dated March 14, 1938, the day after the Anschluss, W. F. Brooks—managing director of the Associated Press of Great Britain—told New York about the reassignment of Berlin-based photographers to cover "the Hitler Austrian coup story." Freelancer Roth was meant to be among them but "was jerked into the army and had to march into Austria," Brooks told management in New York.

In an update a week later, Brooks told New York that Roth "seems to have assumed a big position in Austria since the coup." According to Brooks, Roth was to be "the official party photographer in Austria," a position Brooks described as comparable to Heinrich Hoffmann, Hitler's personal photographer in Germany. "Roth said his position would not interfere with his accepting a full-time position with A.P.," Brooks wrote. According to Brooks, Berlin bureau chief Lochner, also nominally the manager of the photo operation, was ready to hire Roth full-time—until Brooks phoned him to say that having a Nazi photographer on staff "would not be good business for A.P."

"We can't get any coverage of anti-Nazi doings now to speak of, and you can imagine what it would be" with an official party photographer on the regular staff, Brooks wrote.[15]

Inexplicably, Brooks apparently didn't see the Nazi affiliation as an obstacle to having a less formal relationship with Roth. In his letter to Lloyd Stratton, AP deputy general manager in New York, Brooks recommended an arrangement in which the AP GmbH would have right of first refusal for Roth's photos—essentially, continuing to use him as a freelancer. Stratton signed off on the plan in May.[16]

Then within weeks, just as inexplicably, Brooks apparently backed down from his original objection, recommending that Roth be hired full-time. That decision almost certainly would have followed correspondence between Berlin, London, and New York, but the AP archives have yielded no documents explaining the reversal. It was up to Stratton again to give final approval, and in a July 21, 1938, letter to Brooks he did so, with some clear reluctance.

"Roth has been a difficult subject at times, not the least of which has been his aversion to discipline and any sense of discretion," Stratton wrote, without elaborating on specific Roth actions.[17] "It is also hard for us to recognize the desirability of employing a man so close politically to the government," he told Brooks, "but maybe our incomprehension is due to distance and lack of familiarity with new thought and conditions in Berlin." In the end, Stratton said, if Brooks had investigated the matter and still recommended hiring Roth, "of course we shall abide it." Roth was rehired by the AP GmbH on September 1, 1938.[18]

The few communications to be found in AP archives do not explain why some managers challenged, and then acquiesced to, rehiring Roth. Nor do they clearly identify who was pushing to bring him back to AP, beyond the Brooks note in which he reported telling Berlin bureau chief Lochner it "would not be good business for A.P." to have a Nazi photographer on the staff.

The men who decided on Roth's employment would have known of his Nazi connections, which he made no effort to hide. Shortly after the Anschluss, for example, Roth was photographed with other members of the Austrian Legion—a group of exiled Nazis he had joined in 1936—as they gathered in Vienna. An April 1, 1938, image, taken the day before the group paraded through the streets of the

Austrian capital to celebrate Hitler's annexation of their country, shows Roth with other legion members. He is sitting on the hood of a car, dressed in his Brownshirt uniform with a swastika armband and carrying a rifle.[19] One month later, Roth officially joined the Nazi Party.[20] And on October 2, just weeks after AP rehired him, he was issued a press pass by the Oberkommando der Wehrmacht, the High Command of the Armed Forces, which described Roth as a member of the pool of propaganda reporters and photographers certified by the propaganda ministry.[21]

It's not known what became of the "big position" as official party photographer that Brooks said Roth had been in line for in Austria. It may be that AP agreed to hire him only if he left Austria. Images credited to him in the AP photo library show that soon after his September hiring, he was in Czechoslovakia and Berlin. Later, he was one of the photographers out on the street in Berlin for AP during the November 1938 Kristallnacht pogrom.

Whatever the arrangement, Roth's photo work had now landed him a full-time job with America's largest news and photo agency at the same time that he received credentials as a propaganda photographer for the Nazi government. There is evidence that his two employers coordinated on some aspects of his assignments. A ministry memo from April 1940 informed Roth that a trip to southeastern Europe had been approved but noted: "Since a part of the costs will be borne by Associated Press, the financing must be structured accordingly."[22]

Such a relationship with the Nazis' chief purveyor of propaganda was, at the very least, ethically unacceptable by traditional journalistic standards, though it's not clear who within AP was aware of it. The ministry's letter about sharing costs with AP was addressed to Roth himself but the arrangment likely would have required approval from one or more of his superiors at the GmbH. Whether that information was shared with Lochner, who was nominally the chief of the GmbH, or with any AP executives in New York or London is unknown.

Photographer Roth clearly helped satisfy AP's desire for exclusive coverage of Nazi Germany and the war in Europe. Even before he joined a Waffen-SS unit, photographing its wartime battles, he had access to prewar military exercises that others likely were not given. In 1937, for example, AP distributed his photos of German warplanes pelting Berlin with smoke bombs "to show the effectiveness of their aim and to bring home to civilians what an actual air attack would mean."[23] The following year, two months after the Munich accords that dismembered Czechoslovakia, the agency distributed a trio of Roth photos showing tanks and soldiers participating in Nazi war games.[24] Exclusive photos like these would help fulfill the business imperative of General Manager Kent Cooper and his ambition to make AP "the world's greatest news and newsphoto agency."

The propaganda ministry may well have celebrated AP's decision to hire Roth, seeing it as a way to gain steady access to U.S. and British newspaper readers—though only to the extent that AP photo editors in New York and London considered his images worthy of further distribution. While Roth had a reputation for daring in Ethiopia and Spain, many of the photos he took as a Berlin-based photographer were simplistically propagandistic or of little interest to the American public. His output often reflected propaganda ministry priorities: Hitler's fiftieth birthday celebrations, preparations for war, and posed photos of Hitler Youth or the Nazi food rationing program. Many of his images still reside in AP's New York photo library, though most of the work Roth filed with the agency was never distributed.

Roth photos that did get distribution by AP, though, conveyed messaging clearly in line with propaganda ministry dictates. In 1940, when the ministry assigned him to cover the German occupation in France, AP sent out a series of four Roth photographs that portrayed a Paris returning to "business as usual." German soldiers were shown shopping and taking pictures while Parisians went about daily life "accepting the ways of its conqueror, so German sources say."[25] Ironically, Roth's propagandistic images were soundly contradicted a few months later by uncensored photos apparently smuggled from France and obtained by PIX, the photo agency founded in New York by Leon Daniel, AP's Jewish photo editor who fled Germany in 1935. Among the PIX images were a Paris restaurant window proclaiming "Jews Forbidden," a cinema open only to Germans, and a food line at Place de l'Opera captioned with a warning of famine to come. AP got rights to redistribute the PIX photos and made several available to subscribers.

In June 1940 Roth's career took another turn, when he became a propaganda company photographer in the Waffen-SS unit Leibstandarte Adolf Hitler, led by Kurt "Panzer" Meyer.[26] The Leibstandarte, originally Hitler's personal bodyguards, became the second-most decorated division of the Waffen-SS during World War II, with a dark reputation for murdering civilians and Allied prisoners. Some of the atrocities attributed to the Leibstandarte occurred when Roth would have been serving with the unit, though no evidence has surfaced that indicates his participation. After the war, Kurt Meyer was convicted in a war crimes trial for the killing of Canadian prisoners in 1944.

As a photographer in the SS unit, Roth photographed Meyer, his fellow soldiers, and scenes from battles and their aftermath. During the unit's action on the Eastern Front, Roth took a series of photographs of Soviet prisoners of war that became, according to historian Scharnberg, "perhaps the most frequently printed propaganda photos in National Socialist Germany." The faces of the exhausted, defeated prisoners were said by Nazi propaganda to show "the grotesque face of Bolshevism." The men are grim and hollow-eyed—or, shifty and conniving, as Nazi media presented them, under orders from Hitler that they run in every Nazi publication.

Copies of the photos in AP's London photo library are stamped on the back with a message in red from the propaganda ministry:

AUF WUNSCH DES FUEHRERS SIND UNSERE HEUTIGEN AUFNAHMEN, DIE WIR MIT ROTEN TEXTZETTELN VERSEHEN HABEN, UNBEDINGT ZU BRINGEN. 7.7.41[27]

The message instructs German media that "it is the wish of the Fuehrer that absolutely all of today's photos we have provided with red captions be used." AP would have been the financial beneficiary of that order, selling the photos to German media, noted Scharnberg. "Roth essentially produced German propaganda pictures bankrolled by the Americans and also for the American newspaper market, if the pictures found favor with AP and the editorial boards," she wrote.[28] AP did distribute the Soviet prisoner photos in the United States, with captions far different from those in the Nazi propaganda press. "Nazis say these are closeups of Russians captured in the battle of Lwow [today's Lviv]," read one.[29]

Roth's prisoner photos also appeared in a virulently propagandistic SS indoctrination handbook, *Der Untermensch* (The Subhuman), where they were used to illustrate "inferior people" of non-Aryan origin: Jews, Roma, and Slavs, including Russians.[30] "Second only to the Jews, Soviet prisoners of war were the largest group of victims of Nazi racial policy," according to the United States Holocaust Memorial Museum. Estimates put the number of Soviet POWs who died in Nazi captivity at more than three million: shot, burned alive, died of starvation or disease, or gassed in tests of techniques subsequently used in death camps for the wholesale slaughter of Jews.[31]

During the years he worked as a propaganda photographer and later as Waffen-SS soldier-photographer, Roth was also paid by AP, though precise dates for his several different periods of employment are not clear. An undated note from AP GmbH manager Willy

Brandt says Roth was employed full-time from September 1938 "until his conscription to the Waffen-SS at the end of 1941" and was paid a salary of 8,407 Reichsmarks in that final year.[32] Brandt's note appears to be correct about when Roth left AP employment, but it is not correct about his Waffen-SS conscription—which occurred July 25, 1940, nearly a year and a half before he left AP. Photos that AP distributed to U.S. newspaper clients did not identify Roth or the fact that the man behind the camera in these images was also working for the propaganda ministry and later the Waffen-SS. Brandt and at least some AP executives knew of his dual employment, but it's not clear whether editors writing photo captions in New York were aware of the relationship.

In his unpublished memoir, Roth writes about reporting to Leibstandarte's reconnaissance battalion in Metz, France, in July 1940. When he introduced himself to Kurt Meyer, Roth said, he told the commander he would "do my best, because our propaganda weapon must be better than that of the enemy!" Meyer's response: "Let's go! You'll see something here."

In April 1941 Roth accompanied Meyer's unit as it attempted to capture the well-fortified Klisura Pass in Greece. During the battle, a bullet grazed Roth's head. He ended up hospitalized but shipped rolls of his film to Berlin from his hospital bed, including a picture of himself, head bandaged, and a written account of the battle.

The AP Berlin bureau cabled the photos to New York, along with Roth's breathless text describing how he used his "camera with one hand and shot [a] pistol with [the] other" as German artillery fired on retreating Greeks. Then the bullet grazed him. "Thank God we had [a] doctor with our advance and he sewed up my head during [the] night," Roth wrote.[33]

The Berlin bureau's cable to New York identified Roth as a German soldier "but still active as cameraman" for AP's photo service. News editors in New York, perhaps dismayed by their daredevil photographer's description of active participation in battle, spiked both the story and the photos. But in Germany, Roth was awarded the Iron Cross second class medal for his wound, and Willy Brandt wrote to him: "Your willingness to sacrifice is indeed admirable considering that others with such an injury would have long since applied for home leave."[34]

During his first year with the Waffen-SS, AP had exclusive rights to distribute Roth's photos in Germany and the rest of the world. Those were the terms fixed in the deal Brandt had struck with the propaganda ministry in October 1940. But Roth's wartime photos were in great demand from the editors of German media, all under Nazi control. They complained bitterly about the U.S. company's monopoly over distribution of Roth photos inside Germany, and in September 1941 the government put an end to the monopoly.[35]

Under the new order, AP maintained its rights to distribute Roth's work abroad, but within Germany, his photos would go first to the Nazi weekly *Illustrierter Beobachter* and then to five Berlin photo news agencies.

"Our beautiful agreement that we reached with you and the Waffen-SS has once again been torpedoed and terminated without notice by our 'friends' at the Ministry of Propaganda," fumed Gerhard Meixner, chief editor at the AP GmbH.[36]

In February 1943 Franz Roth took a photo of a German tank destroyer and its crew in winter-camouflage overalls during the third Battle of Kharkov (now Kharkiv), a snowy scene of fellow members of the Leibstandarte Adolf Hitler.[37] It may have been his last. On February 21 a Russian bullet pierced both his lungs in fighting near Krasnograd, a day's journey from Kiev (today's Kyiv) in Ukraine.

"We pulled him to cover and then took him to a small house," where a doctor attended to him, Kurt Meyer said in a book published after the commander's war crimes conviction and imprisonment (Meyer was released in 1954).[38] Roth was rushed to the SS hospital in Kiev but then insisted on going to the airport in hopes of taking a plane to Berlin. After waiting in the cold for days, with no planes to accommodate him and no medical help, he was returned to the hospital, where he died March 17 of sepsis. "He had been one of our best photo correspondents," Meyer wrote. In his condolence note to Roth's widow, Propaganda Minister Goebbels said: "I will always appreciate the memory of your husband, whom I have come to know and appreciate as an outstanding photo journalist. Heil Hitler!"[39]

Roth was buried at Askold's Grave, a historic Kiev park on the right bank of the Dnieper River. In its two-page tribute, titled "SA.-Mann—Journalist—Soldat," (SA man—journalist—soldier), the *Illustrierter Beobachter* included what may be the final picture taken of Roth.[40] He is standing in snow and dressed in a fur hat and heavy, white sheepskin coat, an MP40 submachine gun in his right hand, a camera at the ready hanging from his neck.[41]

A collection of more than six hundred of Roth's wartime photos, recovered on contact sheets after the war, was published in 2008; the contact sheets are kept by the U.S. National Archives in College Park, Maryland. Some are versions of photos Roth provided AP, but others show the Waffen-SS and its officers at war, from Greece and the Soviet Union, including a startling series of eight photos depicting the execution of a Soviet political commissar.[42]

The collected images offer little insight into how AP's Nazi photographer thought about his work and whether he ever wrestled with the ethics and contradictions in serving his two bosses. That's typical, according to his granddaughter Tuya Roth. In wartime letters to his wife, Thea, "Everything is very unpolitical," said Tuya. "He never said, 'Today I have seen this and I think about it like this.'"

Tuya's father Hans was born in October 1942 to Franz Roth and his wife Thea Bohnsack, an actress who married the photographer in 1939. Hans never set eyes on the father who died in combat four months after he was born.

In 2018, at Hans's home in Bad Münstereifel, Germany, southwest of Bonn, Franz Roth's son and granddaughter offered insights from the carefully organized files and boxes they have maintained of the photographer's letters, unpublished manuscript, press passes, and personal photos. In one, Franz Roth is in an open-air jeep on a dirt road in Ethiopia, "The Associated Press" emblazoned on the door. Another shows him with a hundred or so propaganda company war photographers, attending a training session in Berlin in 1942. Roth is seated in the front, directly across from the lecturer, Propaganda Minister Goebbels.

The archives are sizable, but father and daughter did not agree on what they reveal. Hans Roth said that his father's family, once prosperous, faced near economic ruin in Austria after World War I. Coming of age in the turbulent postwar years, he said, made his father and others see Hitler and national socialism as the way out of their troubles. But Franz Roth was not a "typical Nazi," in his son's view. He dropped out of law school in Vienna to pursue photography and saw his AP assignment in Ethiopia as "a wonderful chance" for adventure. For Hans Roth, his father's letters home, devoid of anything political, are evidence that he was more of an adventurer than an avid Nazi.

"Shall I say," said granddaughter Tuya, "I have quite a different view on things." Her view: "He was an ardent Nazi," a fan of Hitler and especially Goebbels. There was anti-Semitism in the family, she added, and many Germans believed they had something to gain from Hitler: a better job, taking over the home or business of a Jewish neighbor, or, in Franz Roth's case, a successful career as a propaganda photographer.

The generational difference in this dialogue is one echoed in countless German homes since World War II, as families continue to grapple with the enormity of the crimes of the Nazi state and the role their parents or grandparents may have played. In the Roth family's dialogue, the back-and-forth was neither rancorous nor conclusive. Each descendant of Franz Roth pulled a document from a file, or showed a photo, or recalled a letter that shed light on some aspect of his character. Roth was not interested in doing something for the Nazi Party, his son argued; "his interest was to show that he was one of the best photographers."

"But he did this adventure for a dictatorship," Tuya Roth interjected. "And I think you can't excuse everything with this 'doing your own adventure' for a dictatorship." Tuya was troubled by suggestions in her grandfather's diary that there were combat situations at the Russian front when Roth shot not just photographs but also enemy soldiers. "I would not call him a murderer, but I think he murdered people as well to do his job," she said. "From my point of view there is a line, and he crossed the line."

On the other hand, her grandfather wrote caring letters from the front to his wife in Berlin. He would have been a great father, she said. But: "I'm very angry with my grandfather because he let himself shoot for Hitler."

Hans Roth, the son who never met his Nazi soldier-father, died in 2020.

11

OPERATION BARBAROSSA

For almost two years after Adolf Hitler and Joseph Stalin carved up Poland, German and Russian border sentries had faced each other at the international bridge in the Polish city of Brest-Litovsk.¹ On Sunday, June 22, 1941, instead of saluting one another at their usual 3 a.m. changing of the guard, the German border guards shot the Russian sentries dead.²

Two hours later, telephone calls from German officials rousted sleeping correspondents in Berlin to attend an early morning news conference at the Foreign Office. Seated at a long table, a row of uniformed but weary-looking Foreign Office and propaganda ministry officials faced a dense assembly of foreign correspondents.³ Even as Foreign Minister Joachim von Ribbentrop was confirming that the Nazi invasion of the Soviet Union was underway, German forces were smashing into Russian defenses at Brest-Litovsk using artificial fog, flame throwers, dive bombers, and a ferocious artillery attack. Ribbentrop told the reporters the assault eastward stretched along a 1,500-mile front, an arc reaching from Finland south to the Black Sea, the largest German military operation of World War II.

A year earlier, AP correspondents in Denmark and France had been able to cover the start of the German blitzkrieg as eyewitnesses. This time, only German reporters and photographers attached to Wehrmacht and Waffen-SS propaganda companies were on hand to witness the German onslaught on Joseph Stalin's Soviet Union. A series of entries in correspondent Lynn Heinzerling's diary describes how the lack of eyewitness access affected coverage by the AP bureau in Berlin. "We had word impending attack two weeks before, even to date, but of course unable to use.[4] Ribbentrop made usual announcement to press (summoned out of bed at 5 a.m.) and flock of documents to show Russian duplicity released. Then we left to learn what could about war from communiques, radio announcements. Sent first word to New York by telephone about 7.10 a.m."[5]

That first word appeared under banner headlines in the United States in a two-paragraph bulletin:

BY THE ASSOCIATED PRESS

Berlin (By Transatlantic Telephone to New York), Sunday, June 22— Adolf Hitler declared war at dawn today on Soviet Russia.

German troops massed in East Prussia already are on the march, along with soldiers from Finland and Norway in the north and Rumania to the south.[6]

Propaganda Minister Joseph Goebbels read Hitler's scorching denunciation of the Russians over the radio.[7] Ribbentrop then issued a formal declaration of war against the country with which he had signed a nonaggression pact just two years earlier. Hitler's speech conceded the Molotov-Ribbentrop Pact had been a strategic plan to prevent a war on two fronts, giving Germany peace with Russia while it conquered Poland, France, and (Germany had hoped) England. Once war was declared, the Soviet Embassy in Berlin was closed and fumigated, a propaganda stunt consonant with the Nazi view of Bolsheviks as subhuman.[8]

Reflecting on the difficulties in reporting on "Operation Barbarossa," the code name for the invasion, and his pending reassignment from Berlin to Spain and Portugal, Heinzerling wrote: "Attempting do own objective job reporting Berlin almost hopeless job. Stories held practically to official communiques and handouts at press conferences plus press editorials which dictated from above. Be glad to get out."[9]

For any on-the-scene reports, the Berlin foreign correspondents were reduced to relying on the accounts of PK reporters, who traveled and fought with German military units. The written accounts were considered little more than propaganda tracts and largely ignored, but AP and other American photo agencies snapped up the work of PK photographers in the German invasion.[10] Though Nazi censors also controlled the photo output, visual scenes from the front lines could convey news as well as propaganda. And many were full of the "exciting incidents" cited by Cyril Radcliffe, head of Britain's Ministry of Information, in his study in 1941 addressing why the German photos were so popular with American editors.[11] In one, a Russian is seen on his hands and knees surrendering to German infantry, while another shows a German soldier throwing a hand grenade at a Russian hideout.[12]

Most spectacular in those first days was an image of what was said to be German soldiers attacking a Russian machine gun nest, with village buildings aflame in the background.[13] The image was so popular that AP used it in another of its promotional ads, distributed to newspaper members so that they could share with their readers. "The Associated Press covers the war for you through (Name of your newspaper)," the ad declared, noting that an "impartial survey of hundreds of newspapers" showed AP's dispatches were "preferred over all others by a margin of 8 to 1." As for the highly competitive photo coverage, the AP ad said: "Starting with the first photographs of the press conference at which Germany announced the invasion, the AP Newsphoto Service has been consistently ahead with delivery of the best pictures of The Battle of Russia."[14]

What the AP ad and the original photo captions did not say was that the carefully crafted images of the Battle of Russia were made by unnamed German photographers, all of them attached to army or Waffen-SS units as part of the Nazi propaganda effort. But an editor at the *Daily News* in New York, an AP member, offered readers more transparency about the sourcing. A *Daily News* headline over two of the photos read: "Cameramen Illustrate Hitler's Oft-Told Tale: This Time the Fuehrer's Fotogs Send Berlin Scenes of Death, Violence and Destruction in Russia."[15]

After almost two weeks of producing stories based on little more than Nazi war claims in official communiques, foreign correspondents in Berlin were finally offered an escorted tour of the eastern front. It was a plum assignment, and Bureau Chief Louis Lochner sent Alvin Steinkopf, a seasoned correspondent whose text and photo coverage of Warsaw's Jewish ghetto the previous year was used widely in the American press—with disclaimers that the trip was made under Nazi escort.

Such trips were a tradeoff, as they always have been and still are today for journalists covering conflicts. Frontline access granted by one side or the other in the fighting comes with varying degrees of reporting restrictions. Even when the restrictions are relatively mild, they still aim to get journalists to report the escorting side in a positive light, while obscuring or covering up anything that might undercut that message. The German escorts to Nazi-held zones kept tight control of their correspondent "guests," limiting their ability to gather information beyond the official narrative. Even where access to civilians was possible, reporters said some were too frightened to speak openly—or to speak at all. Still, as Lochner had shown on his Nazi-escorted visit to Częstochowa in Poland two years earlier, even a limited eyewitness view could reveal far more than the propaganda-laden Nazi communiques churned out in Berlin.

Steinkopf was one of nine foreign correspondents who traveled as guests of the German High Command and the Ministry of Propaganda on a 660-mile tour of conquered Soviet territory. The group followed thousands of German tanks swarming the Soviet Union as Europe's two mightiest armies clashed. Speed in reporting was paramount, and Steinkopf dictated his stories over military phone lines to the bureau in Berlin, where Angus Thuermer, the junior member of the news staff, was often on duty when he called. Thuermer, impressed with how Steinkopf could create a compelling and coherent narrative on tight deadline, later described taking his dictation:

> Steinkopf was somewhere in Ukraine, tied to the Berlin bureau by a fading military communication wire, just back from being up where the armored troops were point-blanking it into Soviet defense positions. He didn't have a note. He didn't have a line on paper. The sound of battle was echoing down our wire—but he began dictating "Night Lead Russian Front—SOMEWHERE IN THE UKRAINE—" and as each graf came out of my typewriter, Herr Paul, the bureau's teletype man, began punching it through Bern, Switzerland to the AP's New York cable desk and out over the aa wire [the AP's primary newswire] to [newspaper] members.[16]

The opening paragraphs of Steinkopf's July 4 story were dictated to Thuermer by phone from Lwow, in what was then Soviet-occupied Poland.[17] To minimize transmission costs, he spoke in cablese, leaving out obvious words the cable desk editors in New York could later insert to the text as dictated to Thuermer:

> steinkopfs 10130 lwow direct uncounted hundreds Russian tanks smashed by German army lie disabled in southern Poland western Ukraine paragraph eye saw them on swift automobile tour of southern front as guest german high command paragraph thousands Russians

prisoners comma many barefooted comma are marching back along roads over which hang clouds of yellow dust.

steinkopfs 20130 eye saw four thousand Russian prisoners in one vast camp on conquered territory paragraph germans were putting them to work expanding camp paragraph preparations made this one place alone to accommodate fifty thousand Russians paragraph but many more than fifty thousand must cared for german officers said.[18]

Steinkopf said the many abandoned tanks and cannons spoke of a hasty Russian retreat, and the confused scene reminded him of the British flight from Dunkirk. Now, "all southern Poland and western Ukraine hums with sound of motors," he said—the motors of German columns moving endlessly eastward.

Steinkopf's on-the-ground account swept the front pages of many U.S. newspapers on Saturday, July 5, 1941.[19] A second Steinkopf story, released for afternoon papers, said several hundred civilians had been killed in Lwow, "and Germans said that in the last few days of Russian occupation hundreds of Ukrainians were bound up and shot. At the city prison I saw a basement in which there was an uncounted number of massed bodies."[20] Germans told Steinkopf the decomposing bodies would soon be sealed in with concrete, even though they remained unidentified.

Two days later, another dispatch described a somber parade of funerals held in Lwow on July 6, with civilians, many unidentified, buried in simple coffins side-by-side in long trenches. "The whole ghastly scene is a situation which any experienced correspondent would view with the greatest suspicion," wrote Steinkopf, whose story—like the reporting he had filed earlier—acknowledged he was under German escort. "It is a grisly episode which could be exploited by organized propaganda from one side or the other." His story went on to give what he said were "the cruel facts which are beyond dispute": that hundreds, possibly several thousand people were killed in Lwow and surrounding areas before the Germans arrived. "I saw scores of bodies," Steinkopf wrote. "Military pathologists turned them over and indicated the usual manner of execution—a shot in the back of the neck. In this city bodies were jammed for the most part into basements of three prisons."[21] Steinkopf said that when he asked who the dead were, "the usual answer is that they were Ukrainians who either were or were suspected of having been agents of the Ukrainian independence movement" suppressed by Lwow's Soviet occupiers.

Along with Steinkopf's stories, AP distributed striking photos of rows of corpses, as Lwow residents searched through them for missing loved ones. Newspapers labeled the images, taken by a PK photographer, with cautionary notes. "NAZIS ASCRIBE LWOW SLAYINGS TO RUSSIANS," a *Boston Globe* caption read, attributing the description to "German sources" while pointing out that "reports of mass executions have also come from Nazi-held Rumania and Yugoslavia."[22]

Steinkopf also made photos of the carnage in Lwow.[23] One showed foreign newsmen inspecting some of the bodies, another was of a mass grave being prepared to receive fifty of the victims, and a third showed family members mourning at a grave site in a cemetery dotted with newly erected wooden crosses. All three photos, with German language captions, were distributed July 9 by the AP GmbH in Germany but apparently were not circulated in the United States.[24]

Nazi propaganda mastermind Joseph Goebbels said he was pleased with "all the atrocity material from Lwow" filed by foreign correspondents and PK reporters and photographers. "Things there are totally horrific. Bolshevism is a scourge of humanity, a serious disease that must be eliminated," Goebbels wrote. Three days later he observed, "The great anti-Bolshevik campaign continues. The neutral press is cooperating. The Lwow case is our prime exhibit."[25]

When he dictated his first report from Lwow, Steinkopf noted that in the wake of the Nazi occupation an "especially terrified group [in the city] are numerous Jews who don't know what to expect" (though that phrase did not appear in his story as distributed by AP).[26] What Steinkopf and the other correspondents did not know was that anti-Jewish violence was already well underway in Lwow. The assaults and killings began before—and continued after—the brief, tightly controlled visit by the correspondents. Jews were beaten, humiliated before jeering crowds, and executed in the "frenzied atmosphere of the period," according to Adrian Gilbert's description in *Waffen SS: Hitler's Army at War.*

The killings, conducted by German forces and some roving Ukrainian mobs, marked "the first stage in a vicious and bloody pogrom against Jewish communities throughout the western Ukraine."[27] The U.S. Holocaust Memorial Museum estimates four thousand Jews were killed in Lwow in early July 1941.[28] More than two years later, AP carried a Polish Telegraphic Agency report that another thirty-five thousand Jews crowded into Lwow's ghetto at the beginning of 1943 had been annihilated—slain when the ghetto was destroyed or shipped to their deaths in concentration camps.[29]

Outside of Lwow, on the same German-escorted trip, Steinkopf reported seeing few refugees, compared with the masses he'd observed fleeing earlier fighting in Belgium and France. On the new eastern front, farmers stayed on their land and merchants remained in their shops. "For the civilian population the only escape was to Russia and very few chose to run in that direction," he wrote.[30] By July 10, less than a week after his first dispatch, Steinkopf's travels had ended. He was back in Berlin reporting the war based on communiques and looking for ways to convey his clear contempt for their propaganda content:

> Berlin, July 10 (AP)—The German High Command today continued its policy of "mystifying the enemy with silence" and for the third successive day described the great campaign on the Eastern Front with a one-line sentence.

Today it was "operations in the east are progressing relentlessly." Yesterday it was "the fights continue successful on the entire Eastern Front. Tuesday it was "operations on the Eastern Front are proceeding on schedule."[31]

When Steinkopf visited Lwow under German escort, photographer Franz Roth was already in the city, having accompanied the German invaders in late June as they thundered eastward capturing Lithuania, most of Latvia, Belarus, and part of western Ukraine. Though Roth traveled with the military, AP had exclusive rights to his photos under the agreement Willy Brandt had worked out with the propaganda ministry in late 1940. Among the Roth photos the agency distributed were a striking image of civilians huddled in a ravine to shelter from the fighting and another that captured German officers inspecting an abandoned Russian tank, its size dwarfing a farmer's passing horse-drawn wagon.[32]

On July 2 Roth sent photographs of Lwow residents throwing flowers as they cheered the arrival of the German occupation forces rumbling through the city in open-air trucks.[33] Later he made a very different image, showing corpses in a courtyard that were identified as prisoners who had been held by Russian secret police. That photo and a second one showing more corpses stacked in a prison cellar—apparently the same corpses Steinkopf saw—were distributed by the AP GmbH to German subscribers.[34] The prison cellar photo was published in the *Berliner Illustrierter Zeitung* credited to "SS-PK Roth—Associated Press."[35] There is no record of them being sent to AP subscribers in the United States.

Steinkopf, traveling with other foreign correspondents under Nazi escort, and Roth, accompanying Nazi troops, likely saw the corpses in the basement within a few days of each other. But there is no documentation that they encountered each other in Lwow, even though they were both AP employees and in the city at the same time. Steinkopf was a foreign correspondent, in Lwow under Nazi escort to report a first eyewitness account from the new battlefront for his American news agency. Roth was a propaganda photographer, on assignment from his other employer, Nazi Germany, to travel with the military and capture images that put the Nazis in a positive light. The two AP men were on very different missions.

In July, the same month Steinkopf and Roth were in Lwow, AP GmbH photographer Gerhard Baatz (now also a propaganda company photographer) was in Lithuania with German troops. AP distributed a photo Baatz made in Wilno, the Polish name for the Lithuanian capital of Vilnius, showing women wearing large letters "J" sewn on the back of their coats as Jews were rounded up into an urban ghetto.[36] It's not known to what extent, if any, Baatz was aware of the horrific events underway in the Lithuanian countryside, where local collaborators joined SS death squads known as Einsatzgruppen in the murder of Jews whose numbers had grown to some 250,000, swollen by refugees from Poland. "By the end of August 1941, most Jews in rural Lithuania had been shot," and by November the Germans had massacred most of the Jews in urban ghettos, in one of the war's worst Jewish slaughters.[37]

By mid-July the Nazi sweep into the Soviet Union had advanced almost three hundred miles, but the few remaining American correspondents in Germany were once more reduced to covering battlefield events based on official communiques. Then, in August, German military authorities offered another tour of Nazi-occupied territory, to Smolensk in western Russia. Once again, Steinkopf drew the assignment.

Looking down from the skies at the rolling steppe as he flew in with the German Army, Steinkopf was struck by the "hundreds of straw-thatched villages," the rye and wheat fields "gleaming golden in the sun," and the occasional sighting of a village left in blackened ruins.[38] "In this strange war, there was no sharply defined front. The foe was everywhere, behind and in front," he wrote. "In this headlong rush eastward the German army didn't pause to clean up every little pocket of resistance. When it could, it pushed forwards leaving a mop-up job that stretched backward a hundred miles." Steinkopf asked a German officer why they could not land at Minsk to get a closer look. "Because," he replied, "you are a guest of the German army, and the High Command would be irritated if I permitted you to be shot."[39]

On the ground in Smolensk, the correspondents walked through a city in ashes, "a wilderness of blackened chimneys standing like tree trunks after a forest fire."[40] German officers said most of the damage was "wrought by the Russians under orders of Premier Joseph Stalin for a 'scorched earth in the face of the enemy.'"[41] A photograph Steinkopf took of three women walking through the ruins ran on page one of the *Spokane Chronicle* in Washington state under the headline "Wirephoto from Smolensk After the Four Horsemen Rode Onward."[42]

While Steinkopf's Smolensk reports were widely used in the United States, some in the British press were skeptical of his account of the German victory there, according to CBS Berlin correspondent Howard K. Smith. Steinkopf was said to be "under the charm of the [Nazi] Propaganda Ministry," a common accusation against foreign correspondents who had not yet abandoned Berlin by 1941; any journalist still working there was suspected of having "sold out to Nazism," Smith wrote. Yet "Steinkopf was one of the most outspoken and adamant opponents of the Nazis in the American correspondents' corps," he wrote. "I once applauded Al as he poured fire on Goebbels' chargé for American affairs, Dr. [Hans] Froelich, whom he called a hypocrite and, using Bill Shirer's perfectly suited term, an oaf."[43]

In Berlin, correspondents took note of the public lack of enthusiasm for the new war front in Russia, though they wrote more candidly about it in private than in their news stories, for fear of violating the ill-defined rules of responsibility censorship. "No demonstrations whatever to indicate public interest or approval despite drummed up 'crusade' atmosphere in press," Heinzerling noted in his diary.[44] Thuermer wrote that "people just accepted it as something new, said nothing" as they moved quietly on the streets, "focused on just getting where they were going. There were no idle chit-chatters standing around." It was, said Thuermer, "the same sort of quiet" that descended on the stairwell of his apartment building the night the Gestapo arrested and hauled off a Jewish family that lived there.[45]

As Nazi troops battled their way eastward, they captured Kiev, laid siege to Leningrad, and unleashed special death squads to carry out mass executions of Jews. In Germany, Jews faced an increasingly dire existential threat. Residents of Berlin and other cities endured nighttime raids by British bombers. And nearly every German coped with shortages of nearly everything. But in the heavily censored German media, where "news" was dictated by propaganda ministry directives, little actual news was reported, beyond new military victories. In the accounts of German newspapers, all Germans die with a "joy in sacrifice," wrote one American reporter, which, he added, "the German front correspondents admit they find it impossible to describe."[46]

In August, *Time* magazine published a dubious account of a Radio Moscow report on Hitler visiting his troops along the eastern front. True or not, it quickly circulated among Berlin's malcontents. The Russians reported Hitler asked one of his soldiers what his last wish would be if a Russian shell landed near him. "I would wish," the soldier was said to have replied, "that my Führer stood beside me."[47]

12

BERLIN AT WAR

While Edward R. Murrow was delivering his dramatic "This is London" CBS radio broadcasts to U.S. audiences during the 1940–1941 Blitz, the war was also taking a toll on Berlin residents.

"I am still thinking of the girl in Berlin who wanted to see the fireworks and stood out in the open street, thrilled by the spectacular show of searchlights with myriads of bursting shells above," wrote Pierre Huss of International News Service, in an account of a nighttime raid by British bombers, whose arrival was greeted by German searchlights and anti-aircraft fire.

"The blackout hid her from the eyes of watchful police," Huss continued. "But not from that little nugget of anti-aircraft shell which fell, like a fiery pearl from the beautiful necklace floating around the British plane high in the heavens. It cut neatly through her from head to foot. She lay there as she had fallen, with a half-eaten apple in one hand."[1]

While Murrow's accounts from London had a you-are-there immediacy, Huss's story of the little girl was published some weeks after he departed Berlin in November 1941. It ran with a dateline from San Francisco, more than five thousand miles from Berlin. As war had escalated between Germany and Britain, so did Nazi media restrictions, ever more sharply curtailing what correspondents could write from Germany about nighttime bombings and the frightening air raid sirens when the Verdunklung (blackout) turned Berlin into a ghostly urban center.

Some of what correspondents described after leaving Berlin might have sounded familiar to those who endured London's Blitz. With streetlights switched off, cars crawled along, their headlights reduced to slits by heavy black paper pasted over them. Pedestrians wore luminous tokens on their coat lapels shaped as a dog or cat—or, in the case of some ardent Nazi Party members, a swastika—to avoid colliding with others on the sidewalks. Heavy drapes covered the entrances to restaurants, which closed ever earlier so patrons and staff could reach home before the mournful air raid sirens sounded.[2]

"It's like walking around in an ink pot," AP's Ed Shanke complained in a letter home. "People walk along the streets—the few that venture out—and hiss or whistle or scuffle their shoes to let you know someone is coming. To bump into a light pole or stumble over a curbing is nothing unusual."[3] At the U.S. Embassy in the refurbished Blücher Palace near Brandenburg Gate, blackout shades smothered the lamplight of late-night workers, and heavy sandbags protected the street level windows from bomb blasts. On the roof, the Americans had arranged large letters spelling out U-S-A, in hopes of directing Britain's bombers elsewhere during their raids.[4]

An early warning system detected British planes flying over the English Channel, and when a strike on Berlin was expected, key industrial plants, transportation hubs, and others got a warning an hour or so in advance. Journalists initially were included on the heads-up list until it was discovered that some of the Balkan correspondents—in exchange for free meals—were tipping off restaurants, giving them time to collect payment before their customers rushed for the bomb shelters.[5]

In addition to the bombing raids, basic living conditions in the Third Reich, even for the more privileged diplomats, were growing increasingly difficult. Hot water was scarce for most people—though it was steadily available at the Adlon and other elite hotels and at the U.S. Embassy, which installed tin bathtubs on an upper floor, one for men, one for women.[6] Cafés were still crowded along Kurfürstendamm, but only in the afternoons, before the blackout and early suspension of public transportation. And rationing was widespread. "If you can imagine Paris and Vienna without coffee, Danzig without whipped cream, Munich stores selling 'kuchen' on ration tickets, Berlin with weaker beer and the whole countryside waiting for more chickens to lay more eggs, you get a partial notion of the situation," AP correspondent Lynn Heinzerling reported in early 1941.[7]

Still, Heinzerling and the other foreign correspondents lived a privileged life compared to most Germans, who coped with shortages of nearly everything—soap, milk, bread, gasoline, frying pans, even shoelaces. The correspondents were given more generous ration cards, meant for those undertaking "heavy work," and they could eat at the restaurant of the Foreign Office's Auslands Presse Club, where rationing did not apply. In other restaurants, bread could only be sold after it was twenty-four hours old—to make it less appetizing and reduce demand. Even the amount of chocolate in Easter eggs was controlled.[8]

By May 1941 bars and restaurants began running short of beer, and signs appeared in shop windows declaring "Heute Tabakken Ausverkauft" (Tobacco sold out today).[9] At Easter the following year, shortages had become so dire that Propaganda Minister Joseph Goebbels told Germans the penalty for breaking the country's rationing laws was death. In what was seen as a political swipe at his rival and Hitler's designated successor, the decidedly overweight Hermann Göring, Goebbels warned that "hereafter it will not pay to risk one's head in order to take especially good care of one's belly."[10]

Nighttime entertainment was increasingly limited, though American diplomat Jacob Beam noted one strange diversion: the spectacle of the American-born William Joyce, who, as "Lord Haw

Haw," broadcast Nazi propaganda with "devastating" impersonations of a stereotypical British officer. "He performed occasionally in the Adlon bar in return for drinks," wrote Beam. "Viewing him from a discreet distance, I can fully appreciate British haste to get their hands on him and hang him as a traitor after the war."[11] That is, indeed, what the British did to Joyce.

At war's end, more than half a million Germans had died from Allied bombings, compared with fifty-eight thousand bombing deaths in Britain.[12] But in the early days, the British raids were pinpricks compared with the "Blitz" payloads Germany dropped on London, and the correspondents in Berlin understood the greater dangers faced by their colleagues working across the channel. In fact, while Hamburg and other major cities were targets in the initial rounds of British bombing, the Germans were cocksure that Berlin's defenses could not be breached. Göring was said to have boasted that if the Allies ever bombed Germany, "My name is Meyer," a common Jewish name.[13]

Nazi boasts and confidence collapsed on the night of August 25–26, 1940.

"On that night," wrote *Christian Science Monitor* correspondent Joseph C. Harsch, "Britain, driven from the continent of Europe with the ignominy of Norway and the agony of Dunkerque [*sic*] behind it, struck back at the very heart of the Nazi empire. It sent bombers over Berlin."[14] It was the first time the capital of Germany was directly attacked since the Napoleonic Wars at the start of the nineteenth century, and the Nazi press howled in anger with banner headlines condemning the "Banditen und Luftpiraten" (bandits and air pirates).[15] Foreign correspondents reported the raids based largely on official German statements, which downplayed damage and deaths (an early AP story noted censorship prohibited publishing casualty estimates). After a few days even the official reports began to give some German casualty figures. But, like Pierre Huss's account of the little girl hit by anti-aircraft shrapnel, foreign correspondents described the full import of that first raid only later, often in the books they published after departing Berlin and the heavy hand of Nazi censorship.

A year after the British raids began, and halfway through the overnight shift on September 2–3, 1941, an unhappy editor at the *New York Daily News* phoned the AP cable desk in New York.

"Aren't you going to have a stronger story on the Berlin raid than you have?" the irate editor demanded, referring to a piece filed by Berlin staffer Robert Schildbach that began: "British bombers attacked this capital Tuesday night with heavy explosives and incendiary bombs in one of the liveliest raids of the war. Three of the planes identified officially as British were reported shot down by anti-aircraft batteries." The article went on to cite an official Nazi communique that said that, while some apartment houses had suffered, the raid caused "insignificant damage."[16]

AP rival United Press, the editor said, perhaps sarcastically, "seemed to have a bit more detail."[17]

"Buildings shook and windows rattled during the night under the blasting of antiaircraft guns firing at British planes raiding the capital area," the UP story began. "Other British formations bombed areas in northern, central and southwest Germany," UP continued. "Motors of the big British craft could be heard over the city above the terrific din of the gunfire. Search lights flashed across the sky and at least one caught a British plane in its beams."[18] A few paragraphs later, the UP story noted that "correspondents in Germany are rigidly restricted to the sense of official statements and communiques." It went on to quote the language of the bland official communique, a jarring contrast with the story's vivid lead, but it also noted that the communique's use of the word "strongish" was an "indication of the force of the British attack."

When AP editors in New York requested more detail from Berlin to match UP's account, Bureau Chief Louis Lochner responded he was unable to "go beyond" Schildbach's story.[19]

His answer hit a frustrated nerve with an unidentified AP foreign desk editor, who forwarded the AP and UP stories to his superiors. The UP story "gives the impression that it is actually covering Berlin," the editor fumed, "whereas our coverage [is] confined almost entirely to relay of handouts." Then, acknowledging that the complaint was likely to get little traction with Lochner's chief defender, General Manager Kent Cooper, the editor noted that further pursuit of the issue would just result in yet another long Lochner memo to Cooper "about not sticking out necks and not appreciating the position of our men in Berlin." But the bottom line for AP, the editor warned, was that "both UP and INS are getting interesting copy from Berlin and AP is not."[20]

The editor's complaint did reach Cooper, and, as predicted, it led to a Cooper-Lochner exchange that featured a lengthy "not sticking our necks out" defense by the Berlin bureau chief. Lochner told his boss that UP's story had prompted a warning from the propaganda ministry for "flagrantly" violating rules that were then in place, requiring air raid reports to contain only information in official communiques. Continued violations, the ministry warned, could lead to a new regime, with Nazi bureaucrats demanding prior censorship of stories written by correspondents for UP, AP, and other foreign media.

Lochner closed with a somewhat petulant appeal:

IN VIEW THIS INCIDENT IF YOU STILL WANT US TAKE MORE DARING ATTITUDE OF COURSE WE CAN WRITE COPY AS COLORFUL AS UNIPRESS STOP ALL AIR RAIDS OVER BERLIN MAKE WINDOWS CLATTER STOP ALL PLANES ROAR STOP BUT WE'VE CONSISTENTLY TAKEN VIEW ITS WISER POLICY DASH ALSO REMEMBERING HARD STRUGGLE WHEREOF EYE

CAN ONLY TELL YOU PERSONALLY TO SAFEGUARD OUR FINANCIAL STAKES IN GMBH UNDASH TO OBEY SUCH DEFINITE RULES AS ARE IMPOSED AND TRUST TO OUR INGENUITY IN ALL OTHER RESPECTS TO PRESENT BALANCED PICTURE GERMAN SITUATION STOP[21]

This was typical Lochner. Faced with criticism that his bureau's coverage was soft-pedaling events, he returned to his standard argument: to go stronger risked offending Nazi authorities and could jeopardize the survival of both the news bureau and the "financial stakes" in Cooper's pet project, the AP GmbH.

Cooper's response to Lochner was also vintage Cooper: "LOCHNER CONTINUE PRESENT POLICY STOP IF UNIPRESS UNPAYS ATTENTION WARNING WILL ADVISE YOU."

The pressure to self-censor put a constant brake on reporting about the war's impact in Berlin. But the propaganda ministry didn't stop there. It staged guided propaganda tours of cleaned-up bomb sites, in an effort to convince correspondents that Britain's bombs really hadn't done much damage.

"There is an iron-clad rule in Germany that bombing repairs take precedence over all others," Lochner wrote, in a story published only in May 1942, after the United States and Germany declared war on each other and he was freed from German detention. On the morning after a bombing raid, Lochner said, workmen would arrive to replace broken windows "as the first step towards making a stricken area look normal again." Carpenters, masons, and plumbers quickly followed. While they worked, the area would be roped off so no one could see the extent of damage. By the second morning after a raid, a visitor "may be able to pass by without noticing much of anything untoward."[22]

The point of postraid tours, wrote UP's Fred Oechsner, "was, of course, to prove that the damage amounted to absolutely nothing at all."[23] William Shirer, the CBS correspondent, labeled the tours propaganda and declined to join them. His late 1940 diary entries bristled with complaints about the ever-tightening restrictions. "I think my usefulness here is about over," Shirer confided in his October 15, 1940, entry. "The new instructions of both the military and the political censors are that they cannot allow me to say anything which might create an unfavorable impression for Nazi Germany in the United States." Among the rules: "You cannot call the Nazis 'Nazis' or an invasion an 'invasion.' You are reduced to re-broadcasting the official communiques, which are lies, and which any automaton can do."[24] Despite the restrictions, Shirer's superiors urged him to stay. But by early December 1940 Shirer had smuggled his diary out of Berlin, buried in trunks under piles of his radio scripts that had the stamps of official censors. He headed to the United States, where his diary would become a best seller the next year.

Shirer and other radio journalists were forced to spar regularly with censors, who had to sign off on their scripts before they could be read on the air. Though print stories were not subject to the same prior censorship, the restrictions on how they could—and could not—be written were only slightly less onerous for those still reporting from Berlin into 1941.

"They became more and more repressive until finally a point was reached where we could send nothing that had not appeared in the High Command [of the Armed Forces] communiques, the DNB [Nazi press agency] reports or the German press," wrote Oechsner. "Anything else would be treated as 'military espionage.'"[25]

By late 1941 Oechsner, Lochner, and their UP and AP wire service staffs were almost the only Americans still filing stories from Berlin. Others had departed in frustration, several of them returning home where they could write, free of censorship, to warn America more clearly about the Nazi menace.

# 13

"WE LEAVE FOR THE JUG"

O n a cold, damp night in December 1941 with freezing rain in the forecast, Louis Lochner was guest of honor at a Sunday dinner party in Berlin with his wife, Hilde, his stepdaughter, Rosemarie, his parents-in-law, and Angus Thuermer, the junior member of the AP news staff (and Rosemarie's suitor until he enlisted in a U.S. Navy intelligence unit in 1942).

The war in Europe was now in its third year, and outside, the nightly blackout aimed at foiling British bombers had plunged the city into darkness. They were just starting dessert and coffee when the phone rang. On the line was Ed Shanke, working the night shift in AP's Berlin bureau.

Thuermer volunteered to take the call.

"Is the chief there?" Shanke asked. "We just got a cable from New York. The Japs have bombed Pearl Harbor . . ."

Known as a sometime prankster, Shanke made sure he was being taken seriously by reading the full message from New York: "JAPS BOMBED PEARL HARBOR NEED GERMAN FORN OFFICE REACTION SOONEST."[1]

Shanke remained in the office overnight, filing what official German reaction he could get, some of it provided by Lochner, who called his Foreign Office contacts at home. The next day there were the usual war communiques from the Oberkommando der Wehrmacht, the High Command of the Armed Forces. One of them, perhaps preparing the public for anticipated bad news to come, reported that frigid winter weather was slowing the progress of the Nazi onslaught on Moscow.

The official German commentary about the Pearl Harbor attack, from a Foreign Office spokesman, denounced the American president and declared: "Now Roosevelt has the war he wanted. Now American boys will be ploughed under."[2]

The outbreak of war with Japan left the small American colony of correspondents in Berlin to wonder what the December 7 Pearl Harbor attack—the "date which will live in infamy"—meant for them. Having stuck it out this long, they were not about to miss the finale, though their work must have often felt journalistically pointless. "Real news no longer flows out of Germany: it drips" was how *Time* magazine described the situation some months earlier. "Most correspondents have departed and those who remain are fettered by ever-tightening censorship."[3]

In the first five years of Nazi rule, a list Lochner kept of foreign journalists expelled or pressured to leave Berlin had grown to forty names.[4] By late 1940, as wartime censorship grew more heavy-handed, more were leaving—of their own volition, perhaps, but with deep frustration at the gap between what they knew and what they could actually report as long as they remained in the German capital.

Relations between the press and the Nazi government continued to spiral downward throughout 1941. American correspondents felt particular pressure, as the Nazis saw increasing signs that official U.S. neutrality was wavering. Congress passed the Lend-Lease Act in March, authorizing President Roosevelt to provide arms and other military aid to the British. And in August Roosevelt and Prime Minister Winston Churchill signed the Atlantic Charter, a statement of principles for a postwar, post-Hitler world. "Although the United

States was not about to declare war on Germany, as some in Britain had unrealistically hoped she might, the sixth article of the [Atlantic] Charter, which began, 'After the final destruction of the Nazi tyranny . . . ,' represented unequivocal language from a neutral party," noted British historian Andrew Roberts in his biography of Churchill.[5]

Roosevelt's reelection in November 1940 had been perhaps the most important signal that America's entry to the war on Britain's side was all but inevitable. No longer did German officials argue—as some had in the past—that having American correspondents reporting from Berlin could help keep the United States out of the war. "From that moment the German government treated us as future enemies," Joseph Harsch of the *Christian Science Monitor* wrote. "Freedom of movement was restricted. It became much harder to discover and report beyond the official German communiques."[6]

In the months after Roosevelt's reelection, several prominent U.S. correspondents left Berlin. Among the first to depart were William Shirer of CBS and Wallace Deuel of the *Chicago Daily News*, who returned home in December 1940 to write books with stories they could not tell from Berlin. Shirer had told CBS that year that he wouldn't continue if all he could report were German lies. His bosses responded that he should stay, "even if only reading official statements and newspaper texts," but he left anyway.[7] Edward R. Murrow, who had hired Shirer for the position, resented his decision and later criticized him for keeping the profits from a lecture tour and publication of his book, *Berlin Diary*. Shirer, said Murrow, was "making profits out of recounting the heroism of others, and then [putting] the money in the bank."[8] Shirer was replaced temporarily by Harry W. Flannery, who subsequently left Berlin in September 1941 to be replaced by Howard K. Smith—who then slipped out to Switzerland before the Pearl Harbor attack.[9]

Next to leave, in January 1941, were the *Christian Science Monitor*'s Harsch and Sigrid Schultz of the *Chicago Tribune*. Pierre Huss of the International News Service (INS) lingered long enough to report on Germany's sweeping attack on the Soviet Union in June 1941 but then departed that November. Reporter Hugo Speck replaced him.

These departures led to a small stream of books about the Nazis, some of them attempting to explain why the United States would, inevitably, be at war with Germany. Shirer's *Berlin Diary*, published June 20, 1941, was the first in the bookshops, while Harsch's *Patterns of Conquest* went on sale two days later, followed in 1942 by Huss's *The Foe We Face*. Deuel's *People Under Hitler* was published later that year. Despite his brief time there as Shirer's replacement, Flannery wrote an account of his Berlin days in *Assignment to Berlin*, published in 1943.

The exodus of seasoned, senior correspondents must have reinforced Lochner's sense that it was essential for AP to do what was necessary, including self-censorship, to "stay in the field." Other correspondents could depart, leaving their employers without dedicated coverage or with only newcomers covering the story. But their news organizations would still have AP's service to rely on, restricted though it might be by Nazi threats and edicts.

Lochner would have also had personal motivations for wanting to stay. He had a German wife and in-laws in Berlin, and he had cultivated a large network of sources for a story he knew better than probably any other Berlin-based correspondent. For years, his social calendar had overflowed with dinners and receptions hosted by diplomats, cultural figures, and even Nazi officials; he was a prominent member of the expat community, a status he likely wouldn't match if he moved to another AP bureau.

It's impossible to say how much those factors may have influenced his frequently made argument: that AP should remain in Berlin, even as the Nazi stranglehold on reporting grew tighter. Whatever the motives, Lochner's argument was always consistently accepted by the person he most relied on for support, AP general manager Kent Cooper.

The majority of the sixteen American journalists still in Berlin at the time of Pearl Harbor worked for news agencies, the so-called infantry of the press, usually the first in and the last out when it came to covering major world events. While the size of the AP bureau's news staff fluctuated over the years, on the day of Pearl Harbor four American reporters served under Lochner: Shanke, Thuermer, Alvin Steinkopf, and Ernest Fischer, along with the bureau's two longtime German reporters. Fred Oechsner of United Press (UP), the AP's chief rival, also had four Americans working for him, as well as an unknown number of German support staff. The other agency men were Hugo Speck of INS, owned by Hearst, and Jean A. Graffis of ACME News Service, a part of the E. W. Scripps Company.

By December 7, 1941, only four other Americans remained in the Berlin press corps: Alex Small, of the *Chicago Tribune*; Guido Enderis, of the *New York Times*; and two radio broadcasters, Paul Fisher, of the National Broadcasting Corp. (NBC), and John Paul Dickson, of the Mutual Broadcasting Co.

For the few who remained, Berlin now offered a rare story prospect: covering the outbreak of war against one's own country from inside the enemy's capital. That is, if they were allowed to stay.

On Tuesday, two days after Pearl Harbor, Shanke was working the late shift again when he called Lochner at home shortly before midnight with troubling news: the FBI had just arrested German reporters in America, part of a roundup of some four hundred German and Italian nationals.[10] Four of the five German reporters detained worked for the DNB, the Nazi national news agency.

Lochner spent the next morning consulting U.S. Embassy officials and the German Foreign Office on what was likely to happen next. "You may rest assured that whatever may become necessary in the way of reprisals will be done in the noblest manner," he was told by a Foreign Office official.[11] Meanwhile, in anticipation that Germany would declare war on the United States, American Embassy employees were burning so many documents in the furnace that the building superintendent came around and begged them to "take it easy—the chimney is glowing."[12]

When Lochner joined other reporters at the Foreign Ministry's daily press conference, "there was a tense atmosphere," he wrote later. "Little groups getting into huddles in various parts of the hall. Many a European correspondent with whom I had worked shoulder to shoulder for years came to say goodbye and to express the hope that America would bring freedom to a sorely tried European continent."[13]

There was a hush when Paul Schmidt, chief of the ministry's press department, entered the room. "One moment please!" Schmidt shouted. "The German correspondents in the United States have, contrary to custom and a gentleman's agreement, been arrested by the American authorities. I must, therefore, ask the American correspondents here present to leave the room and proceed forthwith to their homes." As the other reporters made way for the Americans to leave, shaking their hands as they trooped by, Schmidt also bid each farewell at the door, saying he regretted the step. Then he told the remaining correspondents, from countries either neutral or allied with Germany, that the American journalists "no longer exist for you and us."[14]

Ignoring the directive to go home, Lochner rushed from the ministry to the office, calling out "Get Berne!" as he peeled off his coat and headed to his typewriter. The AP bureau in the Swiss capital was the Berlin office's telex link to the outside world, since connections to New York via the Netherlands had been cut after the Nazi occupation of Holland in May 1940.[15]

The keys of the Berlin office's telex machine came alive, typing out "ASSOCIATED BERNE," the Swiss bureau's telex address, confirming it was ready to receive copy. Lochner hammered out his account of events at the Foreign Office, passing one take of the story after another to be punched up on telex tape for transmission to the Swiss bureau. He told his German staff that all American journalists were being placed under house arrest and that, in their absence, German reporter Rudi Josten and Willy Brandt, the managing director of the AP GmbH photo service, would carry on the bureau's business.[16]

The Swiss bureau transmitted Lochner's story to New York as the bureau chief contacted the rest of the American staff in Berlin, telling them they should consider themselves under house arrest. At 12:37 p.m., Thuermer, still lingering in the office, replied to a routine telex printer query from Switzerland. "Hurry Up. We leave for the jug," he typed. Asked who would take charge of the news bureau, Thuermer messaged back: "Rudy [Rudi Josten] will fill in. Lochner and I have to leave for home now." Asked if they would be interned, Thuermer answered: "We don't know. All American correspondents have been asked to leave for their homes in Berlin. Bye-bye, Old Man."[17]

Then, the line was cut.[18]

The Gestapo arrived at Lochner's home on December 11 at 12:50 a.m. Two men in plain clothes rang the doorbell. Lochner was expecting them and had packed a small overnight bag. He and his wife had spent the evening bidding sad farewells to her parents and to friends who called or visited them at the apartment.

"But how did you know we were coming?" one of the secret policemen asked Lochner as he grabbed his bag to leave.

"Why do you think I'm a newsman?" he retorted.[19]

Lochner was escorted to a waiting car after leaving a message in the bathroom for his wife to inform the embassy, the AP office, and the Foreign Press Association that he had been picked up. Minutes later, Thuermer, who lived nearby, was offering Chesterfield cigarettes and chatting up the same two early morning guests. "I guess we should move along," one of the Gestapo men finally suggested. "Your chief is in the car downstairs. We picked him up first."

An embarrassed Thuermer said he imagined his unhappy boss shivering in the cold car on the blacked-out street while waiting for him. But Lochner, he wrote later, "was too genteel to mention it more than once" as they headed slowly through the black night to Alexanderplatz in the heart of Berlin, to a Gestapo detention center.[20]

The two men were led to a large, third-floor room dominated by a grim photograph of Hitler and, on another wall, pictures of SS chief Heinrich Himmler and security chief Reinhard Heydrich.[21] Two other American reporters were already there: Alex Small, of the *Chicago Tribune*, and Mutual Broadcasting's Paul Dickson. More trickled in under escort, including AP reporters Shanke and Fischer. Fischer had been loaded into a tarpaulin-covered truck in front of his apartment just before 5 a.m., along with AP colleague Alvin Steinkopf, three UP reporters, and a highly intoxicated Hugo Speck of INS.[22]

The only American reporter not rounded up was Guido Enderis of the *New York Times*, who was allowed to remain in his hotel because of a bronchial infection, though he was not allowed to send stories. Later, he was permitted to move to Switzerland, where he resumed reporting. Enderis had been at AP in Germany when Lochner joined the bureau in 1924. When he moved to the *New York Times* four years later, Lochner replaced him as AP Berlin bureau chief. In 1940, when Lochner asked Kent Cooper what he and others in the AP bureau should do if the United States entered the war, Cooper dismissed the possibility of war as "remote." But if the

United States were to enter the conflict, he reminded Lochner that Enderis—then working for AP—had remained in Berlin throughout World War I. "Far from being molested, he lived comfortably at the Adlon Hotel," Cooper recalled.[23] While Enderis appeared to enjoy special status with Germany during both world wars, he got little respect from his fellow correspondents in Berlin—or from some of his *Times* colleagues, one of whom begged the paper to do something about "its Nazi correspondent."[24] In her book *Buried by the Times*, published several decades later, Laurel Leff described him as having "limited journalistic abilities and excessive German sympathies, as even his editors admitted."[25]

Howard K. Smith, the last CBS correspondent in Berlin before Pearl Harbor, was also not among the detainees, having left the country just before the attack. Back in the United States, he wrote the book *Last Train from Berlin*, a title that rankled some of his fellow correspondents, as did his preface's incorrect assertion, "I was the last American to get out of the country."[26]

On the afternoon of December 11, 1941, as the journalists sat under Gestapo guard, Hitler declared war on the United States and announced that Italy, Germany, and Japan were pledged in a new alliance to fight to the finish. His address to the Reichstag ran for ninety minutes and was delivered at the Kroll Opera House. Germany parked a sound truck in front of the American Embassy. The truck's loudspeaker broadcast Hitler's words to the diplomats inside at such high volume that it rattled the building's windows.[27]

With the American reporters detained, U.S. news agencies, newspapers, and broadcasters reported the outbreak of war either based on information provided by officials in Washington or by monitoring Berlin radio and Germany's Transocean news service from listening posts in London, New York, or Berne. AP's story, picked up from a German radio broadcast, began this way:

BERLIN, Dec. 11—(Official radio received by A.P.)—Adolf Hitler declared war against the United States today in a historic address before the Reichstag.

At the same time, he announced a new military alliance of Japan, Italy and Germany for a finish fight with the United States and Britain.[28]

Around the same time Hitler was speaking, the American reporters were being moved by truck to the Riviera Hotel in Grünau, about twelve miles away. During their Riviera stay, Josten and Robert Schildbach, the AP bureau's German reporters, arrived with canned goods and other food. A foreign office official who accompanied them said the State Department had agreed to treat German reporters detained in the United States as diplomats, and thus the Berlin-based American reporters would be treated similarly.[29] And Josten shared a telegram from Kent Cooper in New York, saying that detained American reporters and diplomats would ultimately be exchanged for those held in the United States, though no timetable was given.[30]

On the weekend, the journalists were told to return home, pack their belongings, and arrive at the U.S. Embassy at 9:00 the following morning. By the appointed hour, diplomats had already arrived, some with incongruous baggage: chests of drawers, china sets, bird cages, and lamps—all resembling a "disorganized flea market." Arthur Graubart, an American military officer, came with "three suitcases; one he filled with all the cigars he could find, one he filled with champagne, and one he used for clothes."[31]

In all, 114 people gathered in a light morning rain: diplomatic personnel (including Lochner's stepdaughter, who was a secretary at the consulate), journalists, and some spouses, Lochner's wife Hilde among them. They were taken under guard to a special train with two baggage cars to hold their more than one thousand pieces of luggage and transported to Bad Nauheim, a spa town about twenty-five miles north of Frankfurt.[32] In earlier years the families of both President Roosevelt and publisher William Randolph Hearst had visited the spa, known for its luxury hotels and mineral springs. Its six-story, four-hundred-room Jeschke's Grand Hotel, normally closed for the winter, was about to reopen as home for American diplomats and journalists rounded up from throughout Nazi-occupied Europe.

News of the internment of the Americans at Bad Nauheim prompted anxious queries about the conditions of their detention.

"We were treated with cold civility," Lochner wrote later, describing the five months the Americans spent at the resort as they waited to be exchanged for Axis detainees the United States was holding in White Sulphur Springs, West Virginia. But it would be "a mistake," Lochner said, to think of the Americans "as concentration camp inmates, as many inquiries to me have indicated."

"While constantly under surveillance, and while unable ever to stir from the hotel except under Gestapo guard, we were free as a little American community, to do pretty much as we pleased within the hotel itself," Lochner wrote. "This meant, in short, that we indulged in a most interesting experiment in self-government."[33]

Boredom, it turned out, was one of the worst aspects of the confinement, so the self-governors used their limited freedom to organize a full roster of diversions: evening lectures, Bingo, skits, and shipboard horse racing, a betting game.[34] On Saturdays there was a dance, and on Sundays Protestant church services were held in the hotel while Catholics were escorted to mass at a nearby church. Lochner reported that the journalists won, "hands down," a spelling bee against the diplomats. They were also victorious in a formal debate on the proposition: "Resolved, that the newspaper man is a greater menace to society than the diplomat." The "truth telling" journalists, Lochner noted, did not hesitate to expose their weaknesses, while the diplomats were trained for discretion.[35]

During the day, "Badheim University" offered classes in philosophy, history, religion, biology, and at least five languages.[36] Charlie Smith, a Sioux who had been serving as temporary embassy receptionist in Berlin, led classes on "Plains Indian Dancing." "His double-tailed eagle-feather war bonnet was sensational enough to be bright in my memory to this day," Thuermer wrote some years later.[37] Thuermer noted that as a detainee, he had maid and room service, including the option of tea and jam at 4 p.m. in his room.[38]

Personal animosities arose among the detainees, and there were extramarital flirtations and April Fools' Day pranks, but, despite the diversions, the war was never far away. The booms from bombing raids on nearby Frankfurt could be heard occasionally.

"Those were 'our' guys, out there, smashing a great German city to bits," Thuermer recalled later. "What went through our heads was: keep remembering Coventry [one of Britain's cities worst hit by German bombing raids] and who started it all. But that didn't mean we weren't aware" that the bombs were targeting "human beings who were being knocked to smithereens."[39]

The hotel, a spa resort built for summer accommodation, was hardly prepared for what was to be the coldest European winter of the twentieth century. The Americans appeared for dinner in overcoats on some nights, then rushed from the dining room to get under the bed covers. AP's Alvin Steinkopf noted in his diary that the temperature hit 24 degrees below zero on January 22, 1942.[40] Dining offerings were lean: fresh vegetables, eggs, and milk were rarities, and the often-served "Nauheim Pudding" was much reviled. Lochner described it as "screaming yellow" with "a faint odor of vanilla and ersatz eggs."[41] Thuermer claimed it was made of tires recycled by I. G. Farben, the German chemical company.[42] The dessert also inspired the name of the *Bad Nauheim Pudding*, an irregularly published, mimeographed newspaper produced by a few of the detained reporters. It offered a variety of news and gossip but always led with the latest word on repatriation possibilities, often provided by reports sent to Lochner from AP's German staff.

Most evenings a few of the journalists would attend "choir practice" in room 228, home for AP's Shanke, where they tuned in to the BBC's 9 p.m. news broadcast. The Germans had banned all radios, but Shanke had smuggled in a miniature, battery-operated model about the size of a cigar box, and the guards did not search the rooms.[43]

While detained, Lochner and his fellow journalists spent much of their time writing, preparing stories about Germany to be disseminated by their news organizations after their repatriation. Some worked on books they hoped to publish. The combined expertise of these correspondents in German affairs was seen as a rich resource for the Department of War in Washington, D.C., eager to develop an effective propaganda campaign aimed at the German public. The journalists agreed to complete a questionnaire on the subject, distributed by one of the embassy's military attachés. The report, based on their responses to seventeen questions, was marked "secret" and shared with the Military Intelligence Division of the War Department.

One of the report's main conclusions was that U.S. messaging targeted at Germans should avoid themes "pleading for consideration for Jews." "In the heat of the moment, anti-Semitism is not a subject which can be discussed," Steinkopf advised. "It's fixed German policy."[44] Others had similar advice. NBC's Paul Fisher suggested that Nazi atrocities and pogroms against Jews should not be a centerpiece of U.S. messaging. "I say this not in bigotry or any dislike for the race," the NBC correspondent wrote, "but merely because I know that anything which smacks of the Jewish angle or has a Jewish ring will be suspected and will not be well received in

Germany."[45] Lochner's questionnaire suggested targeting German soldiers with propaganda about the Nazi policy of euthanizing the disabled. His proposed message for them: "What guarantee has the maimed soldier that he won't be put out of the way once the war is over and he becomes a civilian like everybody else?"

In summarizing the journalists' responses, the report said the United States should develop a propaganda organization but be careful of how it was staffed. "Consequently, no Jew, however competent, should figure in any visible manner in the preparation of propaganda designed to reach the German people," the report said. "Nor should the threadbare stories of Jewish immigrants, who of course have their own adequate and personal reasons for hating and consequently misjudging Germans, have anything to do with this specialized department of propaganda."

On April 23, 1942, Leland Morris, the chargé d'affaires from the U.S. Embassy, posted a notice on the bulletin board reporting that the Swedish refugee ship *Drottningholm*, with 150 Americans on board, had sailed from Göteborg, Sweden, bound for New York. There, it would pick up Axis diplomats, deliver them to Lisbon May 14, and then stand ready to board the Bad Nauheim Americans. There was much celebration. "First thing I heard upon awakening at 6:30 a.m. was a bunch of drunks singing who had been celebrating since last night," wrote Ernest Fischer.[46]

On May 12, five months after their arrival in Bad Nauheim, the internees gathered in the hotel lobby and walked to the railway station, where they boarded third-class sleeping cars on a train sealed by the Gestapo and bound for Lisbon, via Frankfurt and occupied France. Two days later they arrived in Lisbon, where the journalists could finally send their first stories, without restrictions, describing conditions in Germany.

In his initial dispatch, Lochner wrote with an undercurrent of anger rarely found in the stories he had filed while in Berlin. "Hitler committed the greatest blunder of his career when he took upon himself the odium of declaring war upon the United States," Lochner wrote, adding that the Nazi leader "completely flabbergasted the German people" by doing so. "It was like an ice-cold shower to the German people," he wrote. "The rank and file of German people—even those millions who do not approve of his policies—thought Der Fuehrer too 'smart' ever to declare war."[47]

Lochner's story no doubt captured the mood among the many Berlin contacts who had called on him to bid farewell five months earlier. Left unsaid in the story was the fact that those contacts had little recourse for dissent in the brutal regime Hitler had built. Nor were there any foreigners from Allied countries left in Berlin to report on their current thoughts to the outside world.

In Lisbon the homeward-bound correspondents discovered a city awash in refugees who had fled Nazi takeovers of their homelands. There were Poles, Germans, Frenchmen, Englishmen, Italians, Romanians, Americans abandoning the Riviera, and Jews from everywhere crowding the streets, the bars, and the hotels. All were seeking an escape, and some would join the Americans when they boarded the *Drottningholm*.

The presence of the foreigners, particularly the European Jews who traveled with the Americans to the United States, triggered a series of shockingly racist and anti-Semitic entries in correspondent Ernest Fischer's private diary. In one, written in Portugal before boarding ship, Fischer noted he had turned down an invitation to appear on a BBC program in part because he was tired. Later, when he learned who had taken part, he wrote: "Glad now I did not appear on the program—with a Negro—twould have disgusted my southern 'public.'"[48]

Fischer was a Texas native, raised in a German-American community there, and attended German-English schools for several years. His remark about the "Negro" on the BBC program likely would have raised few eyebrows in what he called his "southern 'public.'" And the language in his several diary entries denigrating his Jewish shipmates reflected an all-too-common anti-Semitism of the era. At the time, depictions of Jews "as a universally unwanted burden struck a responsive chord in the American public," and opinion surveys in the early 1940s showed "that Jews were almost consistently seen as a greater menace to the welfare of the United States than were any other national, religious, or racial group," wrote historian Deborah Lipstadt in her book about American media coverage of Nazi anti-Semitism and the Holocaust.[49]

On board the *Drottningholm*, Fischer complained in his diary that the journalists were put in third-class quarters "along with a lot of dirty, flag-waving Jews. We have our 'diplomatic' friends to thank for that."[50] Upon learning that the ship would make more cross-Atlantic trips, bringing additional refugees to America, he railed against the diplomats and politicians who approved immigrant entry visas. They "should have to answer for the crimes against their own country," he wrote.

In another entry, Fischer said a fellow passenger, a former UP correspondent in Romania, suggested to him that "some such organization as the KKK would have to deal with America's Jew problem." Fischer wrote that he told the correspondent he was already "soliciting memberships" for a *Drottningholm* chapter of the KKK.

Whether and how Fischer's anti-Semitism affected his reporting for AP is not easily gauged. Company records of stories attributed to Fischer while he was a Berlin correspondent list just two with a focus on Jews. He may have avoided other assignments involving Jews, or he may have simply drawn assignments to cover the many other news stories handled by the Berlin bureau.

The two stories he wrote relating to Jews were both filed on an October 1941 reporting trip he made for AP, when official German escorts took more than two dozen correspondents on a tour of eastern European territories controlled by the Nazis. In Nazi-occupied Krakow, Poland, the reporters were shown (but apparently were not allowed to enter) the walled ghetto that their Nazi escorts said would be "living quarters" for the city's Jews. "German officials object to the term 'ghetto,'" Fischer wrote, in a story that described restrictions on ghetto residents and the ground rules for the reporting trip: no photos could be taken, and no questions could be asked without approval from the group's Nazi escorts.[51]

Another stop was the Ukrainian capital of Kiev, where the correspondents visited on October 10, less than two weeks after the first killings at Babi Yar, site of one of the most infamous Nazi massacres of Jews. But at that point it was not known to the outside world, and the German Army escorts were no doubt careful to keep the reporters far from any evidence of it. Thus Fischer and a small crowd of other foreign correspondents came and went from Kiev without learning of the Babi Yar atrocity—or of the suffering of Jews in Odessa, another German-occupied city on their itinerary. Instead, their stories focused on the aftermath of brutal combat that drove out the Soviet Army and brought the Ukrainian cities under Nazi control.

One reporter on the trip, UP's Fred Oechsner, did write that "it has not been possible to determine the fate of the Jews of Odessa." En route to the city, Oechsner said, "we heard frequently from German and Rumanian forces that there had been summary treatment of Jews in Kiev, Kherson and elsewhere. The Germans often remarked that the Ukrainians 'themselves took care of matters.'"[52] Fischer's stories did not include the "summary treatment" remarks, and a story he wrote from Kiev quoted an unnamed German officer as saying that 300,000 people had been evacuated from that city as the Germans closed in, but the story did not mention Jews.[53] A story by a reporter from Italy's *La Stampa*, who was also on the trip, said the group was told there had been 350,000 Jews in Kiev but none remained. "Where have the city's 350,000 Jews gone?" *La Stampa's* headline asked, but when a local official was asked that question, the answer, according to *La Stampa*, was simply: "They are no longer here."[54]

It's impossible to know why Fischer—and at least one other American reporter on the trip, Alex Small of the *Chicago Tribune*—did not speculate on the fate of the sizable Jewish populations in Odessa and Kiev. But it is chilling to read Fischer's diary entries and to know that he served in an AP bureau where the story of the plight of Jews was so central.

On May 22 most of the American reporters and diplomats left Portugal aboard the *Drottningholm* (Shanke, reassigned to London, was on the Lisbon dock to bid farewell to his AP colleagues). The ship's hull bore the word DIPLOMAT in huge letters, and, fully floodlit, it followed a course known to both sides so that both German U-Boats and Allied warships would allow it to cross the Atlantic unmolested.[55] It docked at Jersey City, New Jersey, June 1.[56]

Two days before the ship left Portugal, a U.S. State Department employee alerted the FBI that Lochner might be traveling home with a machine that automatically coded messages. "Lochner is reported to be pro-Nazi," warned the employee, who had been stationed in Berlin from 1938 to July 1941. While "pro-Nazi" suspicions were nothing new for the bureau chief, documents in his FBI file show the State Department employee's memo triggered an FBI investigation of him for possible espionage. When the *Drottningholm* docked in Jersey City, U.S. customs officials waiting at Pier F impounded the written material Lochner had brought with him.

But several days later, after a customs agent examined the impounded papers, "it was ascertained that the subject possessed no German propaganda or literature," according to a July 29, 1942, FBI report. That report gave details on Lochner's first two weeks in New York after his arrival, including the names of several people he spoke with by telephone; their names were searched through FBI records "with negative results." Since no coding machine was found and "a preliminary investigation has disclosed no espionage activities" by Lochner, "no further investigation is being conducted in this case," the report concluded.[57]

While the FBI case wrapped up quickly, another investigation would touch Lochner at war's end—this one involving his role in facilitating a wartime photo exchange with Germany that functioned through the AP bureau in Lisbon. At the dock when Lochner and the others left Lisbon in May 1942 was a key figure in that exchange: AP's Portuguese correspondent, Luiz Lupi, who had served both Reuters and AP after long experience as a reporter in South Africa and England.[58] With his somewhat pudgy figure, his suspenders, his goatee and mustache, the boutonniere he occasionally wore with his white suit, and the long pipe he gripped in his teeth, Lupi looked as if plucked from central casting for his new role as a behind-the-scenes facilitator. The war had just cast him as middleman in a stealthy photo exchange that endured throughout the remainder of World War II, between the German Foreign Office in Berlin and AP photo editors in New York and London.

A Berlin synagogue smolders during the November 1938 Kristallnacht pogrom. AP photographers took dozens of photos during the violence, but Nazi censors allowed only a few to be transmitted outside the country. This photo was widely published in the United States, in many cases on newspaper front pages.

Source: AP Images

Another AP Kristallnacht photo shows a man about to sweep up broken glass in front of a Jewish-owned Berlin store. The photo distributed by AP to member newspapers showed the storefront, the sweeper, and a few passersby, but not the three officials seen in the distance on the far right of this print. It's not known when or why the officials were cropped out of the version AP sent to its subscribers.

Source: AP Images

AP bureau chief Louis Lochner declined to buy this March 1933 photo of Jewish attorney Michael Siegel, paraded through Munich after an assault by Brownshirts. Had AP distributed it, Lochner told his superiors in New York, the Nazis would have expelled the agency from Berlin.

Source: Bundesarchiv, Bild 183-R99542/CC-BY-SA 3.0, CC BY-SA 3.0 DE, via Wikimedia Commons

An onslaught of anti-Semitic laws and actions targeted Germany's Jews as soon as the Nazis took power in 1933. On April 1 that year, Storm Troopers launched a nationwide boycott of Jewish businesses and professionals. AP described the Judenboykott as "the greatest organized antisemitic movement of modern times." These Nazis drove through Berlin in an open-air truck urging Germans to join the boycott.

Source: AP Images

The AP Berlin bureau in 1936. Bureau Chief Louis
Lochner is standing at far left.

Source: Wisconsin Historical Society, WHI-(157925)

AP Berlin bureau chief Louis Lochner at his desk in 1939.
Above the map of Germany hung photos from the receptions, cultural events,
and other social occasions that filled Lochner's calendar in the prewar years.

Source: Wisconsin Historical Society, WHI-(157924)

AP Berlin correspondent Lynn Heinzerling interviewing
General Omar Bradley in Berlin after World War II.

Source: Courtesy of the Heinzerling family

Correspondent Melvin Whiteleather in the
AP Berlin bureau, circa 1939.

Source: Courtesy of Jerry Whiteleather

AP correspondent Alvin Steinkopf in Berlin, 1940.
Source: Wisconsin Historical Society, WHI-(86818)

AP correspondent Edwin Shanke arrived in Berlin in 1937.
This photo was taken for his press pass there.

Source: Department of Special Collections and University Archives,
Raynor Memorial Libraries, Marquette University

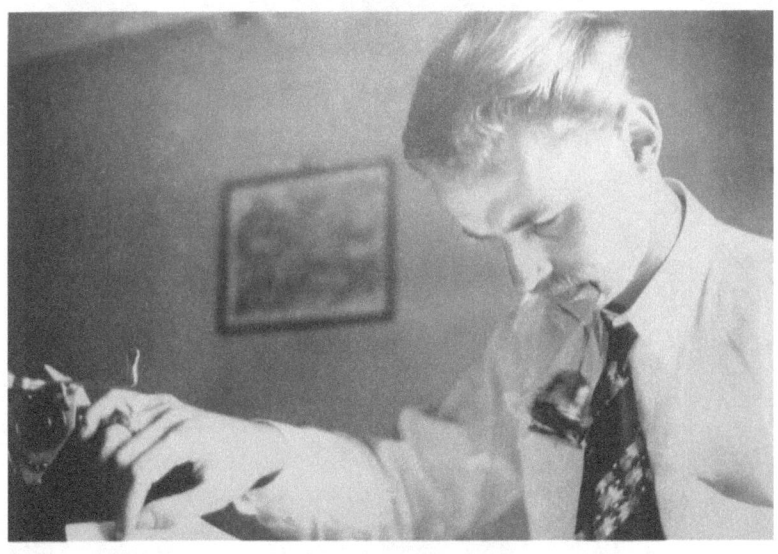

AP Berlin correspondent Angus Thuermer, in what his
family believes is a photo he took of himself while on assignment in
August 1939 to cover the anticipated Nazi invasion of Poland.

Source: Courtesy of the Thuermer family

Kent Cooper served as general manager of the Associated Press from 1925 to 1948. Shown here in 1936, he was a staunch defender of Lochner, the Berlin bureau chief, who came under fire from both AP editors in New York and editors at some of the agency's U.S. subscriber newspapers.

Source: AP Images

Joseph Goebbels, head of the Ministry of Public Enlightenment and Propaganda, in conversation with Lochner. The date and occasion are unidentified. As Berlin bureau chief, Lochner dealt frequently with Goebbels and after the war translated and edited some of the Nazi official's diaries. In a May 1942 entry, Goebbels—apparently offended by things Lochner reported after his expulsion from Germany—wrote that Lochner "is behaving in an especially contemptible way. His attacks are directed above all against German propaganda and he aims at me personally. I have never thought much of Lochner."

Source: Wisconsin Historical Society, WHI-(118602)

Over half the photos in the Nazi propaganda publication *Die Juden in USA* (The Jews in the USA) in 1939 came from the Associated Press. The images of prominent Americans had also been distributed as news and feature photos in the United States, but in *Die Juden*, the Nazis ran them with anti-Semitic captions. The unflattering cover photo shows New York Mayor Fiorello La Guardia, whose mother was Italian Jewish.

Source: Lebrecht Music & Arts/Alamy Stock Photo

Der Untermensch (The Subhuman) was a virulently propagandistic Nazi pamphlet that included several photos of Soviet prisoners of war taken by Franz Roth, who at times was employed simultaneously by AP and the Waffen-SS. German historian Harriet Scharnberg has written that the Roth prisoner of war images were "perhaps the most frequently printed propaganda photos in National Socialist Germany."

Source: SS Main Office, public domain, via Wikimedia Commons

The Nazis ordered all German media to publish Franz Roth's photos of Soviet prisoners of war. AP also distributed the photos to its U.S. subscribers. The *Los Angeles Times* ran four of them at the top right hand side of this picture page on July 25, 1941. The caption reads: RED FIGHTERS?— Nazi sources released and identified these close-up photographs as those of types of Russian soldiers taken prisoner by Germans in battle at Lwow.

Source: *Los Angeles Times*, Copyright © 1941

An undated AP press identification card for Franz Roth stating that he was a staff photographer of the photo department of the Associated Press of Great Britain, "an organization with international connections supplying photographs for Press purposes to practically every important newspaper in every corner of the world. Any courtesies extended to the bearer will be greatly appreciated."

Source: Courtesy of the Roth family

Franz Roth in uniform when he served as a war photographer with the Waffen-SS unit Leibstandarte Adolf Hitler. The photo is believed to have been taken in the summer of 1941 on the Eastern Front.

Source: Franz Roth/Privatarchiv Franz Roth, public domain, via Wikimedia Commons

As a soldier and photographer in the Waffen-SS unit Leibstandarte Adolf Hitler, Franz Roth carried both a camera and a gun. He was wounded during a battle on the Eastern Front in February 1943 and died the following month. Though Roth worked on and off for AP for nearly a decade, the agency issued no obituary for him, and no personnel file for him has been found in the company's archives.

Source: Archive Franz Roth, Bad Münstereifel / Germany, courtesy of the Roth family

Franz Roth traveled with his Waffen-SS unit as it fought in Soviet Ukraine. This photo attributed to him is described as showing horse-drawn German artillery and an armored car belonging to his Waffen-SS unit passing through a burning village on the Eastern Front. The photo credit is SS-PK-Roth-Scherl. 8/15/41.

Source: Bundesarchiv, Bild 183-L19830 / CC-BY-SA 3.0, CC BY-SA 3.0 DE. https://creativecommons.org/licenses/by-sa/3.0/de/deed.en, via Wikimedia Commons.

After Germany invaded Poland, Louis Lochner and other foreign correspondents could visit German-occupied territories only under Nazi escort, greatly limiting what they could observe. This undated photo is said to show Lochner "somewhere in Germany" with German soldiers and their artillery.

Source: Wisconsin Historical Society, WHI-(118609)

In June 1940 Louis Lochner and other foreign correspondents reached Paris ahead of the main German occupation force. A German photographer captured the journalists walking with their Nazi escorts down the Avenue des Champs-Élysées. Lochner, in suit and tie, is fifth from the left. Though he is not the only newsman in the photo, the image of him flanked by uniformed German press and propaganda officials may have added ammunition to the arsenal of those who already viewed Lochner as pro-Nazi.

Source: Bavarian State Library/Picture Archive

AP photographer Gerhard Baatz accompanied German troops invading Lithuania in July 1941. In the capital Vilnius, Baatz photographed Jews who had been ordered to sew the letter "J" on the back of their coats. As Jews in the capital were being forced into an urban ghetto, thousands were already being slaughtered in the Lithuanian countryside by SS death squads known as Einsatzgruppen and local collaborators. Estimates put the Jewish death toll in Lithuania at 250,000.

Source: AP Images

AP Berlin correspondent Alvin Steinkopf visited several Polish cities in October 1940, escorted by Nazi officials. After his trip, AP issued a series of photos showing a wall enclosing the Jewish ghetto in Warsaw and other street scenes of Jewish life in occupied Poland. The photographer, Steinkopf, was not identified. The *Minneapolis Star* ran six photos, showing the wall, a segregated street car, adults wearing white armbands mandated to show they were Jews, and a German officer lecturing children in the Lublin ghetto to wash their faces every day. Nazi occupation "has revived the Pale, if not the Pogrom," the paper wrote.

Source: Minneapolis Star Journal copyright © 1941

AP gave subscribers promotional ads to run in their newspapers, touting its news and photo coverage of World War II. This one boasts that the agency was "Ahead! with the story" that Germany was massing troops for a possible invasion of the Soviet Union in June 1941.

Source: AP Images

Another AP ad touted the credentials of bureau chief Louis Lochner, noting his 1939 Pulitzer Prize and his years of experience "as an observer of the German scene. He KNOWS Germany."

Source: Courtesy of the Oklahoma Historical Society

Luiz (or Luis, as his AP byline spelled it) Lupi in 1942, when, as AP's Lisbon bureau chief, he formed the crucial link in the wartime photo exchange between AP and Büro Laux, the German photo agency whose work was approved by the Nazi Foreign Ministry.

Source: United States Holocaust Memorial Museum, courtesy of National Archives & Records Administration

In November 1942 Helmut Laux (in uniform, far right) accompanied Foreign Minister Joachim von Ribbentrop to a meeting with Pierre Laval, then head of France's Vichy government. Laux, Ribbentrop's official photographer, used his connections with the Foreign Ministry to establish the Büro Laux agency, which exchanged photos with AP from 1942 to 1945, even though the United States and Germany were wartime enemies.

Source: Bavarian State Library/Picture Archive

Adolf Hitler greeted Italian dictator Benito Mussolini in April 1943. The photo was taken by Gerhard Baatz, who worked for AP before the war and was recruited by Helmut Laux after Germany and the United States went to war (Baatz worked for AP again after the war). Büro Laux sent the Baatz photo to AP, one of thousands it exchanged with the agency. AP distributed it to its U.S. newspaper subscribers, who published it with the explanation that it was "received from neutral Portugal."

Source: Bundesarchiv, Bild 183-B23938/Scherl Bilderdienst—Gerd Baatz (Laux)

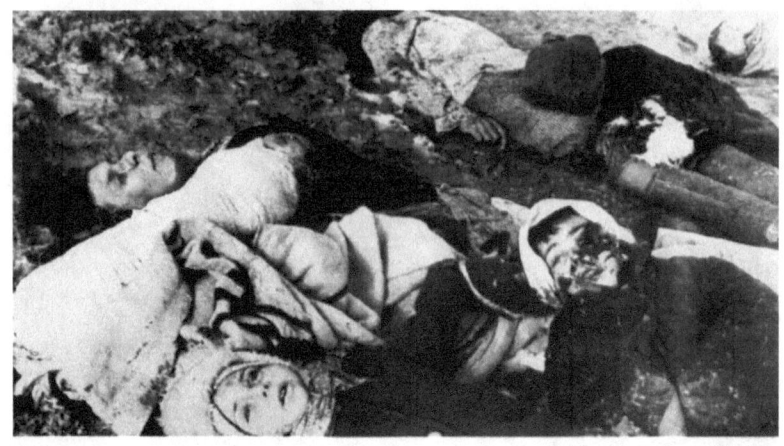

Mark Redkin, a Jewish Soviet photographer accompanying Soviet paratroopers as they recaptured territory from the Nazis, took this early 1942 photo of several victims of Nazi executions carried out in the Crimean city of Kerch. Published first in the Soviet Union, then sold to AP and other agencies for distribution to foreign media, the photo showed the world some of the first visual evidence confirming the atrocities of the Holocaust.

Source: AP Images

In the summer of 1944, Soviet forces were the first Allied troops to enter a Nazi death camp, at Majdanek in Poland. This photo of the ovens in Majdanek's crematorium and the skeletal remains of victims was distributed by the Soviet photo agency to AP and others. An estimated 80,000 to 110,000 victims died or were killed in the main Majdanek camp. The overwhelming majority were Jews.

Source: AP Images

As Western Allies liberated concentration camps in Germany in the spring of 1945, some military officials rounded up German civilians from nearby towns and forced them to witness the aftermath of Nazi atrocities. Lt. Col. Ed Seiller of the U.S. Army addressed some two hundred German civilians as he stood among the corpses of hundreds of Jewish prisoners at the Nazi concentration camp in Landsberg, Germany, a subcamp of Dachau. The photographer was AP's Jim Pringle.

Source: AP Images

Former Berlin bureau chief Louis Lochner was reunited with his former colleague, the AP GmbH's Willy Brandt, in the ruins of postwar Berlin. AP briefly rehired Brandt after the war but let him go after U.S. military officials in Germany said his wartime membership in the Waffen-SS made him unsuitable to serve as the top manager of the agency's reconstituted photo operation. In 1950 AP rehired Brandt as sales manager for its German news and photo service. He worked for AP until his retirement in 1978.

Source: AP Images

In October 1944 AP correspondent Joe Morton embedded with a secret Office of Strategic Services mission, landing behind enemy lines in Slovakia. Two months later the Nazis captured Morton and members of the OSS team. They were executed at the Mauthausen concentration camp in Austria. Morton is the only American journalist known to have been executed by Nazi Germany.

Source: AP Images

III

THE PHOTO DEAL

14

"CLOSE YOUR JUICE SHOP"

On the December 1941 morning when the American reporters in Berlin were placed under house arrest, Willy Brandt, the German left in charge of AP's photo operation there, was summoned to the office of Heiner Kurzbein, the hostile head of the propaganda ministry's photo section. "Machen Sie Ihren Saftladen zu" (literally, "Close your juice shop"), Kurzbein ordered, using a rude German insult to describe the AP GmbH as a business run by incompetents.[1]

Kurzbein's edict set off a fierce competition for control of the photo enterprise: its equipment, its staff of photographers and technicians, and its coveted photo archive. The archive, which AP likely inherited with its purchase of the Pacific & Atlantic photo agency in 1931, was estimated to contain one million or more images documenting German political and cultural life from World War 1 through Adolf Hitler's rise to power.[2] Almost immediately, predators began circling like vultures, ready to pounce on a profitable business whose earnings had helped AP finance its wartime reporting. The archive was particularly desired, since whoever controlled it would have a monopoly on early German pictorial history and could sell the contents in Europe's biggest newspaper market.

Soon after Brandt returned to the photo office from his encounter with Kurzbein, AP's German attorney visited, urging him to turn over the photo archive to Weltbild, the photo agency now owned by the Nazi news service DNB. Brandt rejected that proposal. But a bit later, just as Hitler was issuing his declaration of war on the United States, a more ominous demand arrived, this one from the Reich Association of the German Press, which was under the control of the propaganda ministry. A representative of the association announced that the group had expelled the AP GmbH, thus cutting off its access to cover news events. He demanded Brandt turn over the office keys. Brandt wrote later that when he refused, his visitor "looked at me astounded and quickly decided on retreat, no doubt not a little impressed" by the expression on Brandt's face.[3] It was a bluff on Brandt's part, since he had no means to stop a government takeover. "But I did not want to give up so easily," he said.

Next to arrive was Heinz Lorenz, head of the DNB's Weltbild photo service, who cited Kurzbein's authority in demanding that Brandt turn over the archive. This time Brandt offered a financial compromise: the archives would stay under his control, but Weltbild could sell clients use of archival photos, as long as it shared 50 percent of the proceeds with the AP GmbH.[4]

That did not end the war for control, though. The Foreign Office, eager to thwart the propaganda ministry's takeover efforts, installed a new manager of the GmbH. Karl von Lewinski, a former German consul general in New York and an authority on international law, was appointed trustee by a Berlin court on January 9, 1942.[5] He was tasked by the Foreign Office "to avoid an uncompensated move against American property despite the state of war with the USA."[6]

Lewinski's appointment offered protection from the covetous Weltbild and its supporters at the propaganda ministry, where Kurzbein, recognizing he had lost his bid for control, immediately retaliated. Brandt, who had held a deferment from military service, suddenly found himself drafted into the Luftwaffe on January 15.[7] He was ordered to begin training as a driver in an intelligence unit in Hannover ten days later.

Though Brandt was punished, the GmbH had escaped a propaganda ministry takeover thanks to the ministry's bitter rivalry with the vain, ambitious foreign minister Joachim von Ribbentrop. Before Hitler came to power in 1933, the Foreign Office and its press department had served as the official voice of the German government abroad. Joseph Goebbels, whose propaganda ministry took over as the megaphone of the Third Reich, swept that aside. By 1938, when Ribbentrop was appointed foreign minister, a small information office was all that was left inside his bureaucracy.

Desperate to increase his status by publicizing his activities at home and abroad, Ribbentrop in 1940 appointed his right-hand man, Paul Schmidt, as chief Foreign Office spokesman. Schmidt, a lieutenant colonel in the Allgemeine (General) SS, conducted the Tagesparole, the Foreign Office's daily 1 p.m. briefings for the international press corps, where he worked assiduously to promote his boss, Ribbentrop, while routinely referring to President Roosevelt as "the War Criminal," Winston Churchill as "Gravedigger of the Empire," and Joseph Stalin as "the mass-murderer."[8]

Schmidt was only slightly less derogatory about correspondents whose reporting angered him. At a news conference the day after AP's Ernest Fischer referred to him in a story as "the youthful spokesman" of the Foreign Office, Schmidt denounced Fischer's "poor, childish, asinine observations" that show "such a lack of grasp, such naivete as regards the political problems of our day that one can only stand here and cry silently. I want to say right here that such journalistic gangsterism has no place here."[9] United Press (and later CBS) correspondent Howard K. Smith described Schmidt as "vain as a peacock, and a guileless lover of personal publicity."[10] His press operation drew the ire of both Goebbels and Otto Dietrich, press chief of the Nazi Party. But he had impressed Hitler, who once described Schmidt as "the only political talent in the Foreign Office."[11]

Then, in 1942, Schmidt seized an opportunity to one-up Goebbels and the propaganda ministry and bring new prestige to his Foreign Office boss, using the remnants of the AP GmbH as a conduit for exchanging photos between two countries at war with each other.

In early May 1942, shortly before his release from internment at Bad Nauheim, Bureau Chief Louis Lochner wrote to Brandt wishing him well in "the hard days to come" and asking for news of the GmbH. "I want to express my deepest gratitude for the unfailing loyalty you have shown in these years to our company and to me personally," Lochner wrote.[12]

In a five-page response, Brandt recounted the recent history since Lochner's arrest: the jockeying for control of the GmbH archive, the Foreign Office appointment of trustee Lewinski, Brandt's conscription into the Luftwaffe, and—as the photo business remained in limbo—the departure of most GmbH employees. Then he described what had come next: an unexpected proposal from Ribbentrop's personal photographer at the Foreign Office, Helmut Laux. Though Germany was now at war with both Britain and the United States, Laux had a scheme to create a photo exchange, using neutral Portugal as a cordon sanitaire, that would help satisfy Ribbentrop's ambitions to increase his international profile while giving AP's New York and London offices a continuous flow of photos from Nazi-occupied Europe. Not coincidentally, the scheme was also designed to make money for Laux's own private business, a newly registered photo agency, Büro Laux.

Helmut Laux, the man at the heart of the scheme, had completed a Hitler Youth photography course just five years earlier. He began freelancing and quickly drew the attention of the Foreign Office with his many published photos of diplomatic functions. In 1939 he was assigned to cover the signing of the so-called Pact of Steel by Hitler and Italian leader Benito Mussolini, and soon he was accompanying Ribbentrop on all diplomatic trips. He was just twenty-six when he established Büro Laux, but he was already a prominent figure in the photographic world of Nazi Berlin. Mingling with high-ranking officials in his Hitler Youth uniform, however, was an embarrassment, Laux said after the war. The problem was resolved when an SS contact helped get him drafted into the Waffen-SS as a Sonderführer, a rank given to civilians with special skills (in this case, photography), where he served with a military deferment that allowed him to continue his work as a "war reporter," though far from the front lines of the actual war.

Laux was highly entrepreneurial and apparently not at all modest; he once described himself as the best photographer in Germany. Even before approaching Brandt with his Foreign Office–backed proposal, he had hired two of the AP GmbH employees, photographer Gerhard Baatz and darkroom technician Arthur von Brietzke, to work for Büro Laux. He hoped to take on other GmbH staff, along with the agency's photo equipment and its archive of images, but Laux knew that could happen only with the active support of Brandt, who enjoyed the trust of both GmbH staff and AP managers in London and New York. So he engineered a leave from the Luftwaffe for Brandt, allowing the AP manager to return to Berlin, where he could reunite with his wife and young son, and where he would hear the pitch for Büro Laux.[13]

Laux's connections with the Foreign Office meant his agency was in a position to supply AP with the "best possible pictures," from Japan as well as from Nazi-occupied Europe, Brandt wrote to Lochner. In exchange, Laux wanted AP's photo output from New York and London, which he would sell to German clients. After passing censorship in each country, photos would flow in both directions through the AP bureau in neutral Lisbon, as Laux had arranged with Luiz Lupi, AP's Portugal bureau chief. Between Lisbon and Berlin, the photo packages would travel in the German Embassy's diplomatic pouch.[14] Thus the flow of photos to and from AP would rely on the Foreign Office of a country that America was now at war with.

In his letter in 1942, Brandt told Lochner the exchange was already in operation, with photos flowing in both directions. "The only thing I would like to have for the whole scheme is your blessing and intercession," he wrote. Brandt reported that Laux had hired him and that, with Brandt's approval, Laux had already visited Lisbon to meet with Lupi, whose bureau was key to enabling the exchange.[15] "Lisbon is [the] relay station and supported by the German embassy there," Brandt told Lochner. "Lupi and Laux made an agreement which Lupi can show you when you see him." (Lochner and the others at Bad Nauheim were scheduled to stop in Lisbon on the first part of their exchange for Axis detainees.)

Ever the manager, Brandt included in the letter the GmbH's end-of-year financial statements for Lochner to take to New York. "Their main interest will, I suppose, be in receiving a further picture service from here, which they are receiving now through the arrangement with Laux. I dearly hope I did the right thing," Brandt wrote. And noting that this was likely the last letter exchange the two former colleagues could have until war's end, Brandt told Lochner: "I only want to say that I will never forget what you have done for me and that your name will be the first on my list of those to whom I am grateful for advice and support."

The next step in cementing the Büro Laux plan involved a face-to-face meeting between Laux and Lochner. The two had met briefly in 1940, during a Foreign Office trip for journalists from Germany to Finland. Now, Laux was set to join Lochner on his train ride from Bad Nauheim to Lisbon. Officially, Laux was there to photograph the detainee exchange for his new photo agency. Unofficially, he was there to get the former bureau chief to help persuade AP managers in New York to formalize his photo exchange scheme. No documentation of the Laux-Lochner train meeting has been found, but after the war, Laux told U.S. military interrogators that he and Lochner had reached a verbal understanding: that Laux would unite former members of the AP GmbH staff and "hold them together during the war" so the AP photo service could resume operations after the war with its former staff intact. To do that, the Büro Laux would establish a service providing photos to AP in New York and London, via Lisbon. In return, Büro Laux would receive the AP photo service, also via Lisbon. Neither side would pay for the photos it received.[16]

Lochner, according to Laux, "seemed very well pleased with such a plan." He told Laux to meet with Lupi and draft an agreement. Lochner also had a personal request: he asked that the agreement include a stipulation that he could use the photo exchange packages to send letters to his German mother-in-law, who remained in Berlin.[17]

"The details of this agreement with the A.P. were in both English and Portuguese, in triplicate and signed by Mr. Lupi and myself, as soon as the approval of the A.P. office in New York arrived, which took approximately three days," Laux said.[18] According to Laux, the agreement called for an exchange of photos between Berlin and Lisbon twice a week using a German Foreign Office diplomatic courier.[19] In later writings, Brandt confirmed that Laux and Lupi signed an agreement. But he said Laux had also asked AP managers in New York to sign a contract directly with him, and they declined. Laux kept that refusal secret, Brandt wrote, "and let the whole world believe that he was the only authorized representative of the AP in Germany."[20]

Other than Laux's postwar revelations under U.S. military interrogation, there is no known record of his meeting with Lochner. Details of the agreement he signed with Lupi are contained in a summary he wrote for interrogators, but the original agreement and any copies are not to be found in Lochner's extensive papers or in AP corporate archives. A sign-out sheet for a file labeled "Lisbon" in AP's archives, dated January 22, 1946, describes the content as "Arrangement whereby exchange of news pictures undertaken by AP + Berlin thru Lisbon (Marques Da Costa photo agent in Portugal)." According to the sheet, the contents were "delivered by hand by Mr. Kelly" to Lloyd Stratton, AP's corporate secretary at the time.[21] "Mr. Kelly" likely was Hugh V. Kelly, longtime executive clerk for AP. The file he delivered to Stratton remains missing.

In a lengthy document he wrote to Lochner after the war, Brandt said that Laux told him the Foreign Office supported his photo exchange scheme as a way of maintaining a connection with AP, despite the war. "You know that the way things are now, it is an accomplishment to get a picture of German origin into the neutral press or into the foreign press at all," Laux said, according to Brandt's account. The photo exchange through Lisbon would give Germany a conduit to "send out good German material through the channels of the AP."[22] Beyond the propaganda value, the Foreign Office would be the recipient of AP photos that it could share with high-ranking Nazis, perhaps enhancing Ribbentrop's prestige in the hierarchy, even though photos coming from AP had all been approved by Allied censors and often were already published in foreign media.

As for benefits to AP, Laux promised a constant, prioritized flow of photos from Germany. While other foreign agencies got some of the same pictures from the propaganda ministry, Laux vowed AP would get them first. AP also would have exclusive rights to photos taken by Laux and Baatz. In the highly competitive photo business, it was a huge advantage.[23]

Brandt wrote that his own goals in joining Büro Laux had been to protect AP's photo holdings in Berlin, so the company could resume business after the war, and to enable AP to get news images from

Nazi territories while the war continued. The propaganda ministry's residual anger with AP meant pictures with good news value were often withheld from the agency. The Laux deal would give AP "photo material that would be by far better and more varied than that which had been offered to us since the start of the war."[24] If Brandt saw legal or ethical issues in the Büro Laux arrangement, he did not express them in any writing that has survived.

Nor has any written record been found of AP managers in New York debating such issues. On April 29, 1942, even before Laux met Lochner and signed his agreement with Lupi, Executive Editor Alan Gould sent a memo to General Manager Kent Cooper announcing the resumption of photo traffic from Berlin, via Lisbon. Enclosed with Gould's note was a clipping from page 3 of that day's *New York Post* showing Hitler in the bomb-proof map room of his field headquarters. "This Hitler picture," Gould wrote, "was in the first batch we received via Lisbon, as a result of recent re-establishment of the relay arrangement there."[25] More followed quickly, including a series of Nazi-made photos recording the formal presentation of Germany's declaration of war to U.S. diplomat Leland B. Morris in Berlin on December 11, 1941. Though several months old when they arrived in New York, AP distributed the exclusive images of the historic moment. They were widely published in the United States, confirming the editorial hunger for photos from Germany that Cooper was eager to have AP satisfy.

U.S. and British censors would have been aware of the incoming photos, which passed from Berlin to Lisbon and then on to New York and London. From Lisbon to New York, for instance, photos were shipped on transatlantic flights that made a mandatory stop in Bermuda, where Britain had stationed about 1,500 agents at its Imperial Censorship station to check any material headed for the United States. But AP waited more than two months to inform the U.S. government about the photo exchange. No explanation for the delay has been found in AP communications.

And when AP did inform U.S. officials, its descriptions of the operation were far from transparent. In July Gould phoned N. R. Howard, head of the press division of the U.S. Office of Censorship (before the war, Howard was editor of the *Cleveland News* and president of the Associated Press Managing Editors association). In an internal July 13 memo about the call, Howard wrote that Gould had asked "if I could think of any reason why the AP should not make and/or renew loose photo exchange agreements with syndicates in Elizabeth [Lisbon], Portugal; Berne, Switzerland; and London, England,—none of them enemy countries." Howard said he saw no issue, as long as photos sent by AP passed through censorship first. "Mr. Gould said that was his expectation and he supposed the enemy countries would exercise censorship on what pictures they allowed to fall into the neutral syndicate hands."[26]

A day later, Gould followed up with a letter to Howard. He made no mention of Laux, Brandt, Lupi, the German diplomatic pouch, or other crucial details of what he termed "an experimental arrangement whereby an exchange of news pictures is being undertaken by the Associated Press with Marques Da Costa, a photographic agent in Portugal." Gould said that "from time to time" the photo agent supplied AP with news photos from Axis countries, and in exchange AP sent him images from the agency's news feed. He asked Howard for a note, for AP files, confirming the censor had no objection to the arrangement.[27] Howard obliged on July 18.[28]

Notes on Gould's letter to Howard indicate it was seen by Byron Price, the former AP executive editor, who was hired to head the new U.S. censorship office in December 1941.[29] Price took temporary leave from AP to accept the position, but he continued to draw an "allowance" from the agency that made up the difference between his government salary and what he had been making as a top AP executive. Others in the censorship office also received additional pay from their former media employers, Price pointed out, in a memo disclosing the arrangement to the federal government.[30]

The "Marques Da Costa" referred to in Gould's letter was Firmino Marques da Costa, a nationally known Portuguese photographer. His name was not mentioned in Brandt's postwar description of Büro Laux, nor did it appear in Laux's summary of the agreement he signed with Lupi, the AP Lisbon bureau chief. But da Costa became a key figure in the exchange, apparently recruited by Lupi.

Lupi was a wheeler-dealer, a gregarious charmer, and well plugged in to Portugal's political elite. He was also well regarded by AP management in New York. Gould judged him "extraordinarily competent," with easy access to all sources of news and rumor "in a capital which is a hotbed of gossip and intrigue."[31] Lupi may have asked da Costa to take on the mechanics of the photo exchange in order to protect AP's reputation—or his own—by putting a layer of distance between shipments from Büro Laux in Germany and AP.[32] Photos that came through the exchange to Lisbon, whether arriving from New York, London, or Berlin, bore a stamp on the back:

F. MARQUES DA COSTA—Fotografias—Reportagens
C/o Jornal "Comercio do Porto"
RUA DO ALECRIM, 81
TELEF. 27492—LISBOA

The workings of the Lisbon relay system can be seen in a photo from Berlin showing German troops amid the ruins of the railway station in the then-Soviet city of Sevastopol in Crimea, which surrendered to the Germans on July 4, 1942. The file in the AP New York photo library shows it was given the following caption in Lisbon:

For Associated Press only
German Troops in Sewastopol
Our picture shows the Sewastopol station where heavy fighting
   took place.
July 6, 1942.

Below the caption was the "F. MARQUES DA COSTA—Fotografias—Reportagens" stamp.[33] A penciled notation "Rcvd ap 8/1/42" indicated when it arrived in New York—twenty-six days after the caption was attached in Lisbon, an indication of how slow the Portuguese connection was, or possibly how bottlenecked the notoriously sluggish British censorship regime was in Bermuda. The day the Sevastopol photo was received, AP editors in New York distributed it in the United States with a new caption, used by the *Chillicothe (Ohio) Constitution-Tribune* and other papers:

AS NAZIS TOOK SEVASTOPOL GERMAN CAPTION SAYS THESE ARE NAZI TROOPS IN SEVASTOPOL, KEY CRIMEAN CITY WHICH THE RUSSIANS LOST AFTER MONTHS OF HEAVY FIGHTING. BUILDING IS DESCRIBED AS THE SEVASTOPOL RAILROAD STATION. PICTURE REACHED U.S. THROUGH NEUTRAL PORTUGAL.

Scores of German photos arrived in New York "via neutral Portugal" in the last half of 1942, offering a mostly exclusive glimpse of the world at war for American newspaper readers. Some newspapers ran captions clarifying the German origin of the photos. But details of how they were routed to AP, via Büro Laux, whose founder was a member of the Waffen-SS, were not disclosed. Nor did Kent Cooper describe the photo exchange system in his 1942 year-end report to the board of directors, where he boasted that AP's newsphoto service had been able to provide "exclusively for the most part—many pictures from Axis-occupied areas, obtained through neutral sources."[34]

15

BÜRO LAUX

After the war, Helmut Laux estimated that from 1942 to 1945, some ten thousand photos were exchanged between AP and Germany via Büro Laux. Of those, he said, some three thousand came from the United States. Among them were images of Winston Churchill and President Roosevelt meeting in Washington in June 1942; an American Flying Fortress bomber in Britain "preparing for action against the Nazis"; and official British photographs showing extensive damage to Germany's Krupps armament works in Essen, caused by a British bombing raid in 1943.[1] Copies of AP's incoming photos were routed to the very top of the Nazi political and military leadership, including the offices of Hitler, Heinrich Himmler, and Joachim von Ribbentrop, whose Foreign Office was chief sponsor of the Büro Laux photo exchange.[2]

One Foreign Office goal was to impress the other Nazi leaders that Ribbentrop was keeping them updated on Allied military activity, though it's not likely the Nazis gained critical insights from the AP photos, which had passed through U.S. or British censors and often were already published in those countries before they reached Berlin. But the exchange did supply the Nazis with photos from the U.S. side, which they could release to German media with captions rewritten to make their propaganda points.

Paul Schmidt, the patron of Büro Laux in the German Foreign Office, had secured financial backing for a special press unit through the SS-Führungshauptamt (SS-FHA), the operational and administrative headquarters of the Waffen-SS.[3] Laux persuaded two Büro Laux employees, Gerhard Baatz and Arthur von Brietzke, to join the Waffen-SS, which enabled their placement in the Foreign Office press unit. Though formally enlisted in a military body whose name became one of the most feared symbols of Nazi terror and brutality, they lived at home, dressed in civilian clothes, and did their wartime work within the Laux photo operation.[4]

Brandt resisted Laux's entreaties that he, too, join the Waffen-SS. But after several months, his Luftwaffe leave of absence was not renewed. Laux, fearful that Brandt would be called back to Luftwaffe service, which could jeopardize the Büro Laux connection with AP, arranged to have Brandt transferred to the Waffen-SS.

In his writings and interrogations after the war, Brandt repeatedly said Laux engineered the transfer without Brandt's knowledge. "You can imagine, Chief, what effect that had on me," Brandt wrote to Lochner after the war. "The idea of being taken over by the SS, which I detested, hated from the depth of my heart, was terrible."[5] But as with Baatz and Brietzke, Brandt stayed in Berlin, far from front lines, doing his service in the Waffen-SS by working in the office of the Büro Laux.

Laux himself had joined the Waffen-SS when he began photographing Foreign Office diplomats, but after the war he insisted to Allied military interrogators that it was a business decision and "not a voluntary action." As an officer, he had access to Waffen-SS funding and could arrange military deferments for Brandt and other AP GmbH employees, whom he needed to run the photo exchange and continue cooperation with AP. Laux told interrogators he was never assigned to a specific Waffen-SS unit "but carried on my function as a photographer on all diplomatic occasions."[6] He also said he entered the Waffen-SS "with the knowledge of the AP," including Louis Lochner.[7] "Of course, the name Waffen SS did not have in the days of 1942 that savor of war criminals that it got by the events of 1945 and especially by the discovery of the concentration camps," he told interrogators. His branch, the SS-FHA, was not connected to the camps or to Nazi political matters, he added, but was responsible for maintaining supplies of war materiel to other Waffen-SS divisions.[8]

Büro Laux initially operated out of its owner's seven-room apartment in Berlin's Schöneberg district.[9] After heavy air raids in November 1943, the office was moved to Laux's basement, but when bombing made work there difficult, it moved a final time, in February 1944, to a former bomb shelter for children in Berlin's Dahlem district.

The Foreign Office supplied the bureau daily with photos approved by the propaganda ministry and distributed by German photo companies, including frontline coverage by the military's PK photographers. Brietzke, the darkroom technician, made copies, Brandt wrote English captions, and the packages of German photos were sent via diplomatic pouch to the German Embassy in Lisbon.[10] In the afternoons, Brandt met with Schmidt at the Foreign Office to show him the latest batch of photos received from AP. "I always held myself back and watched my tongue because I felt Schmidt distrusted me," Brandt wrote.[11]

At one point Schmidt complained that the AP photos Brandt brought to him "hardly ever showed anything new" and took so long to arrive that they had already appeared in British magazines and newspapers, which the ministries in Berlin still received despite the war. AP also was unhappy with the sluggish relay of photos via Lisbon and had already begun supplementing the Büro Laux shipments with images purchased from Pressens Bild, a photo agency in Stockholm.

Sweden, like Portugal, was neutral, and beginning in 1942, Pressens Bild had become "an important relay station for German photos to AP and all the English and American correspondents in Stockholm during World War II days," according to a history of the agency.[12] Among the sources for Pressens Bild were Orbis, the photo arm of the German Transocean news service, and Heinrich Hoffmann, Hitler's personal photographer. These photos, like the ones that passed through Büro Laux, were taken by German propaganda photographers and censored by the propaganda ministry. Buyers from media in Allied countries would have known that, but the international demand for images from Germany and its occupied territories was so great that "as soon as a Hoffmann consignment arrived" in Stockholm, according to the Swedish agency's history, "we had to run to two dozen of the allied powers' journalists who lived at different hotels and addresses to show them the photos." In particular demand by foreign photo agencies, including AP, were Hoffmann photos taken in July 1944 of Hitler, just after an assassination attempt that failed to take the Nazi leader's life. The images showing Hitler alive "were of course a sensation," and within minutes the Pressens Bild office was "full of world press journalists" clamoring for copies.[13]

Unlike the Lisbon connection, which moved photos on flights from Berlin to Lisbon, then Lisbon to New York or London, Pressens Bild had the capability to transmit photos via radio technology from Stockholm to New York or London in a matter of minutes. The picture quality was not as good, but the speed with which the new radio technology could deliver photos was so impressive that in April 1944, Brandt went to Stockholm to negotiate a new, alternative relay station for the Büro Laux photo exchange, using Pressens Bild as a go-between, in addition to the AP Lisbon bureau.

From the start of Büro Laux in 1942 until 1945, the final year of war, AP received a constant flow of German photos—from Büro Laux itself, via Lisbon or Sweden, or from the photos Pressens Bild obtained from Hoffmann and other German photo services. Not all the photos AP received from Germany were distributed to subscribers, and some that AP did choose for news distribution were no doubt released by Nazi censors to convey propaganda messages: German troops with captured Allied parachutists in Holland;[14] Polish partisans who participated in the Warsaw Uprising, being marched to an internment camp in 1944;[15] Hitler shaking hands with Nazi officials and allies such as Italian leader Benito Mussolini and King Boris of Bulgaria. But the flow of photos also included images of clear news value and, as the war progressed, evidence of a faltering Nazi military effort. By early 1944 the photo exchange brought images to the United States of German soldiers crouching amid exploding Soviet shells and Nazi air raid police searching German bomb ruins for trapped victims.[16]

Captions on the photos AP sent to subscribers generally noted their German origins, with phrases such as "Nazi-produced photo" or "German photo." Sometimes newspaper editors added more context. On March 2, 1943, the *Minneapolis Star* ran three photos of German troops in Norway and the Soviet Union, noting that "since photos leaving belligerent countries are censored, naturally, they show only what the Germans care for the rest of the world to see."[17]

But the captions did not reveal how the photos got to AP from German hands. As with the Büro Laux photos coming through Lisbon ("via neutral Portugal"), those arriving from Sweden were identified as "received via Stockholm," or obtained by AP from "neutral Swedish photo agency Pressens Bild." Beginning with photos from around August 1944, a few dozen images found in the AP photo libraries in New York and London today have the words "Büro Laux" on the back, but there is no explanation of what that bureau was, where it was located, or who staffed it.

General Manager Kent Cooper used a similarly vague description of the photo operation in late 1943, when he reported to the AP board about "noteworthy firsts on distribution of pictures obtained from enemy territory via neutral capitals—including such copy as the first pictures of Berlin bomb damage." The board, made up of newspapermen driven by American journalism's imperative of getting the news before your competitors, does not appear to have questioned how photos from enemy territory in Germany ended up in the hands of AP.[18]

Laux's photo agency was a busy one but far from successful financially. Its list of German newspaper and magazine customers was significant but small, and Laux had ongoing conflicts with the Ministry of Propaganda over which AP photos he was allowed to sell to German media. The ministry's control was intense: Laux said AP's photo captions were altered as many as four times before the ministry allowed them to be released to German media.[19] Only a significant Foreign Office subsidy, funded by the Waffen-SS, kept the operation afloat, according to Brandt.[20]

Laux's efforts to sell AP images to Germany's Nazi-controlled media faced another big handicap. "By the time the Büro Laux began its work, the glory days of German success news was already over," Brandt wrote after the war. "As a result, the photo production was not usable for propaganda purposes anymore unless you resorted to faking the photos." Brandt said he was aware of just one such fake of an AP photo, published in a German magazine. The photo AP sent to Berlin showed three Allied flags—British, French, and American—raised after a victory in North Africa. Nazi retouchers took out the British and French flags, leaving only the American one, to send a Foreign Office-approved message: "that the intention of the Americans was not the liberation of Europe but the expansion of American 'imperialism.'"[21]

To boost his finances, Laux wanted more control over the AP GmbH and its assets. He pressured Brandt to give up the legal title of managing director of the suspended AP photo operation; if Laux had the title, he could exercise full control of the company's remnants. Brandt refused, writing later: "From this moment on, we were irreconcilable enemies. The only thing keeping us from a complete break was our joint interest in keeping the [Büro Laux] going."[22]

If Laux couldn't take over the managing director title, he still wanted control of the AP photo archive. Once the war was over, whether Germany won or not, he believed it would be a lucrative asset for the postwar photo agency he planned to operate. Brandt said that Laux also believed his work with AP, and keeping the former AP GmbH staff intact during the war, would help rehabilitate him in the eyes of Allied victors if things ended in defeat for the Nazis.[23]

The AP archive included thousands of photo prints and thousands more glass negatives, used in the early years of photography. In his first months working for Laux, Brandt had secretly stored the rare glass negatives and the contents of the news bureau in the basements of AP's Berlin office and another nearby building. Hiring help for the moves cost "thousands of cigarets [sic] obtained on the black market" at "substantially over going rates."[24]

With the negatives and news bureau equipment safely hidden away, Brandt agreed to let Laux "rent" the rest of the AP archives: photo prints of historic events and the life of Germany before Hitler came to power. Laux estimated the value of those prints at $500,000 (over $8.7 million in 2023 terms), and to protect this asset he persuaded Ribbentrop's ministry to designate them as official Foreign Office property. He then had the prints packed in boxes and labeled as "important army material."[25] In August 1943 he arranged their shipment by train and truck to a castle in western Poland owned by Nazi dramatist and author Hans Rehberg, where they remained until the closing months of the war.

That same year, in November, a phosphorous bomb dropped by the British bored through top floors of the AP's Berlin office building, destroying the AP newsroom and its GmbH office. Everything Brandt had put in basement storage, though—the glass negatives and the contents of the newsroom—survived unscathed. A month later, Brandt, his wife, and their son moved away from central Berlin to an apartment in Ziegenhals, about twenty miles southeast of the city. Brandt also moved the newsroom property and glass photo negatives, which he stored in a nearby hotel.[26] Months later, the two Berlin basements he had used for storage were destroyed in bombing raids.

 The war was coming closer, and despite German censorship, the photos exchanged from Büro Laux increasingly showed the Nazi military effort under siege. As the Soviet military marched from the east, reclaiming lands the Nazis had captured in earlier fighting, the German photo monopoly was collapsing. Soon, Soviet photographers, and later those from other Allied countries, would give the world visual proof of the horrific Nazi efforts to exterminate Europe's Jews.

IV

RECKONINGS

16

UNVEILING THE HOLOCAUST

Mark Redkin stood in an icy field, his camera lens taking in the corpses scattered across a bleak landscape outside the ancient Crimean city of Kerch. Redkin, a thirty-three-year-old Soviet Jew on assignment for TASS, the Soviet news agency, had joined paratroopers flown in on January 1, 1942, as they recaptured Kerch from Nazi invaders. Redkin pointed his camera down at several still figures by his feet. A woman and two children were lying face up, the eyes of the children still open, as if gazing lazily at clouds on a balmy summer's day. Another body, possibly the children's father, lay next to them.

Click.

Redkin had just made a so-called liberation photograph, which, when published a few weeks later, would give the world some of the first visual evidence of the atrocities of the Holocaust.

The site Redkin photographed that day was covered with corpses of some of the 7,500 Jews from Kerch, singled out by the Gestapo and shot to death at an antitank ditch after Germany occupied the city.[1] The "liberation" images were taken as the Soviet Army freed city after city from the Nazis, uncovering grim evidence of mass killings on an unimaginable scale. Redkin's photo from Kerch first appeared in the Soviet newspaper *Komsomolskaya Pravda* on January 20, 1942, and then in the Soviet weekly magazine *Ogonyok* in its issue of February 1, 1942. Though some Soviet photos and stories about Nazi atrocities identified victims as Jews, *Ogonyok*'s caption on Redkin's photo did not. "Hitler ordered his bandits to annihilate the peaceful Soviet population," it read. The "Hitlerite thugs," said *Ogonyok*, "showed no one any mercy."[2]

More than a month after Redkin took that image, the Soviet Information Bureau (Sovinformburo), a propaganda agency that supervised the work of Soviet war correspondents, approved it for release to foreign media, including AP and its rivals International News Photo and Central Press.[3] The agencies also received an image from Rostov-on-Don in southern Russia, where retreating Nazis had killed some one hundred Jews. The Rostov picture, taken by an unknown photographer, shows perhaps two dozen bodies scattered on the snow-covered ground, as if mowed down by machinegun fire. All three U.S. photo services distributed the images, and of the hundreds of U.S. newspapers that would have received them, at least several dozen published them beginning February 18, 1942. Captions used information provided by the Soviets that described the victims as "mothers and children" in Kerch and "people shot by Germans" in Rostov—not as Jews.[4]

The Kerch and Rostov photos from early 1942 were only the beginning of the Soviet uncovering of Nazi crimes as the Red Army pushed west to reclaim German-occupied parts of the Soviet Union. In July 1944 Soviet forces were the first to enter a Nazi death camp, at Majdanek in Poland. From there, Soviet journalists filed the first eyewitness reports and photographs of Nazi gas chambers and crematoriums used for mass murder of Jews. AP and other agencies, crediting Soviet media, wrote about the findings. A few weeks later an AP reporter produced a vivid firsthand account of Majdanek's horrors after the Soviets arranged a trip there for foreign correspondents.

The reporting on Majdanek was published in America nine months before the Allied liberations of the concentration camps at Buchenwald, Dachau, and Bergen-Belsen in 1945. (Teenage diarist Anne Frank had died of typhus at Bergen-Belsen just weeks before its liberation.) And yet for many Americans, the freeing of those camps is often remembered as the moment the world first viewed the full horror of the Holocaust.[5]

How did names such as Buchenwald and Dachau come to symbolize the unveiling of the Holocaust, and not Kerch, site of the first photo of a Nazi mass execution published in U.S. media in early 1942, or Majdanek, the first death camp to be liberated and described in media in 1944?

One explanation lies in the source of the Kerch and Majdanek revelations: the Soviet Union, whose communist system was widely detested and denounced in America. Though an ally in fighting Germany, the Soviet Union also was a notorious purveyor of propaganda and misinformation.[6] Soviet media were tightly controlled, and foreign correspondents based in Moscow faced severe restrictions, often reduced to little more than rewriting accounts that had appeared in the Soviet press. None of that built U.S. audience trust in information from Soviet sources, and it may have even created some doubt regarding the veracity of foreign correspondents whose reporting was based on visiting sites under Soviet escort.

In the cases of Nazi atrocities, the reporting was graphic, often presenting stories from firsthand accounts by the Soviet journalists who reported on the ground, perhaps foremost among them the Jewish writer Vasily Grossman, who covered the war for the Soviet Army newspaper *Krasnaya Zvezda* (Red Star). At war's end, the prosecutors at Nürnberg used Grossman's searing, deeply descriptive article, "The Hell of Treblinka," as evidence in making their case for Nazi war crimes.[7]

But while Grossman wrote about Treblinka as mainly "a slaughterhouse for Jews," Soviet media were inconsistent in identifying the Holocaust's victims. Some stories indicated the Nazis had targeted Jews for execution, but in other accounts Jews were listed as one of several categories of victims, all given more or less equal weight. And in some cases, likely reflecting both official anti-Semitism and official prioritizing of a unified "Soviet" identity, victims were described as "civilians," "Soviet citizens," or "the noncombatant population."

In its long, tortuous march to Berlin, the Soviet Union became the first of the wartime allies to expose the true savagery of Nazi occupation. And despite the limits on reporting from the Soviet side, correspondents in Moscow—including those from AP—filed some of the earliest accounts of Holocaust crimes for American newspaper readers. Along with photos the Soviets made available to AP and other agencies, these stories marked the beginning of the unveiling of the Holocaust, including revelations of mass executions by bullets and by gas.

Months later, when American and British soldiers liberated Buchenwald, Bergen-Belsen, and other camps in Germany, the corpses and living skeletons they found "seemed to convey the worst crimes of Hitler," wrote historian Timothy Snyder in *Bloodlands: Europe Between Hitler and Stalin*. But, wrote Snyder: "As the Jews and Poles of Warsaw knew, and as Vasily Grossman and the Red Army soldiers knew, this was far from the truth. The worst was in the ruins of Warsaw, or the fields of Treblinka, or the marshes of Belarus, or the pits of Babi Yar."[8]

Throughout the Nazi era, U.S. correspondents in Berlin, including the AP staff, had documented Germany's official anti-Semitism in their coverage of laws, violence, imprisonment, murder, and the banishing of vast Jewish populations to walled ghettos and concentration camps. Chilling threats about the elimination of Europe's Jews, made by Adolf Hitler and other Nazi officials, had been reported as breaking news as early as January 1939, when Hitler warned a new world war would lead to "the annihilation of the Jewish race in Europe."[9]

"Complete elimination of Jews from European life now appears to be fixed German policy," AP Berlin bureau chief Louis Lochner wrote in an October 1941 story that described mass deportations of Europe's Jews "eastward" to an unknown fate. "Many suicides are spoken of in Jewish circles," Lochner wrote.[10]

And yet, as accounts circulated in 1941 and 1942 describing a new level of Nazi brutality—mass murder by firing squad (the "Holocaust by bullets") and later by lethal gas—AP and other media struggled with how and what to report about things they could not see or independently verify. "Until the mass murder program began, relatively few attempts were made [by the Nazis] to hide what was being done to the Jews," wrote historian Deborah Lipstadt in *Beyond Belief,* her study of how the American press reported the Holocaust.[11] But the Final Solution was implemented well out of sight, and stories about the killing techniques were so barbarous that journalists often rejected them—as Lipstadt noted—as "beyond belief."

In November 1941 two small media outlets—the Overseas News Agency (ONA) and the Jewish Telegraphic Agency (JTA)—reported that in just two months after the Nazis took control of the Soviet city of Kiev, they had massacred fifty-two thousand Jews.[12] The statistic was astonishing, but the attribution was sketchy. The nearly identical agency stories each cited a single "unimpeachable," but unnamed, source, and ONA acknowledged that details were "scanty." Despite the thin sourcing, several ONA subscribers ran the story on page 1, including the *Boston Globe*.[13] AP could have distributed the story, attributing it to one or the other of the agencies, but it did not.

Two months later, though, on January 7, 1942, the Soviet news agency TASS released a far more detailed account, charging German troops had massacred more than ninety-five thousand people in thirteen Soviet cities and "countless hundreds elsewhere." The report, sourced to Foreign Minister Vyacheslav Molotov, said the largest toll was in Kiev—fifty-two thousand massacred, the same number used in the ONA and JTA stories. But while those earlier reports identified the Kiev victims as Jews, Molotov described them as "men, women, old folk and children," including "Ukrainians, Russians and Jews who in any way displayed their fidelity to the Soviet Government."[14] Molotov's report did include a description of one massacre of Kiev Jews, which AP cited in its story. According to "Soviet citizens who escaped from Kiev," Jews were rounded up in a Kiev cemetery, "stripped naked and beaten," then forced to lie face down in a ditch where they were shot with automatic rifles. After Germans covered the corpses with some dirt, "the next group of people awaiting execution was put on top of them in a second row and shot and so on."[15]

Later that year the Soviets released to AP and other outlets a gruesome picture, said to show a mass execution in progress. In the image, five people stand at the edge of a ditch, about to be shot. The ditch behind them is already packed with corpses.[16] The so-called trophy photo was taken, according to the Soviets, by a German soldier named Kurt Seidler who was killed on the front lines. The image was a seemingly compelling piece of evidence, showing a firing squad in action. But where the photo was made was unknown, and an AP caption writer injected a note of caution when the agency distributed it: "Russian sources claim that the five men standing on [the] embankment are Soviet citizens about to be executed by Nazis."

On June 25, 1942, a story in London's *Daily Telegraph* was among the first to report an alarming new murder weapon in use by the Nazis in Poland. "A special van fitted as a gas chamber was used into which were crowded 90 victims at a time," according to the report, which said about one thousand Jews a day were gassed and buried in a Polish forest during late 1941. The *Telegraph*'s story, headlined "Germans Murder 700,000 Jews in Poland," described other Nazi slaughters carried out by machine gun and hand grenade in an extermination frenzy.[17]

The information came from Szmul Zygielbojm, a Jewish member of the Polish National Council in London, who worked with a clandestine network of contacts in occupied Poland to gather eyewitness accounts. His report was chillingly detailed, and the *Telegraph*'s lengthy story called it evidence of "the greatest massacre in world history." But though the report broke news in revealing the Nazi use of gas, it gained little traction in U.S. media. United Press mentioned it in a single paragraph, tucked into the middle of a story focused on Italian dictator Benito Mussolini's foreign policy.[18] AP did not report the details at all when they first appeared, but four days later it distributed a two-paragraph story saying more than one million Jews had been killed or died of ill treatment in Poland, Lithuania, and the rest of Nazi-occupied Europe.

AP's brief account, which made no mention of gas chambers, came out of a World Jewish Congress press conference in London. UP, covering the same press conference, also did not mention gas but said the Nazis had established a "vast slaughterhouse for Jews," which had wiped out one-sixth of Europe's prewar Jewish population in less than three years. A number of papers, including the *New York Times*, published the UP story.[19] But far more newspapers favored AP's brief, 159-word account, among them the *Washington Post*, which published the story on page 2, while the *Chicago Tribune* ran it on page 6, and the *Los Angeles Times* on page 5.[20]

Why would the Associated Press put out a two-paragraph story about the slaughter of one million people—an extraordinary claim—without providing further available details, background, and context? One possible explanation is that the Holocaust atrocities were of such a scale as to be "beyond belief," despite numerous stories—some rumored, some published—that had circulated for months. Many in the press—including the editors at each paper, who ultimately decided which stories to run and where—simply refused to accept such barbarity could be true, especially since journalists could not see or verify stories by interviewing eyewitnesses. Whatever the reasoning, AP's abbreviated report may have suggested a lack of certainty, and that in turn may have influenced some local editors to downplay the story.[21]

American journalists covering the war were also made cautious by the plentiful German, British, Polish, and Soviet propaganda circulating as "information." Their skepticism was, in part, a hangover from World War I when the press gave credence to gory atrocity stories that were later exposed as fabrications or gross exaggerations. As a result, according to one study, many claims generated such great skepticism "that until proven true, atrocity reports were assumed false; they were regarded as narratives of exaggeration and propaganda and only later as potentially credible accountings of the ravages of war."[22]

There were also some editors and government officials who rejected Holocaust stories as special pleading, as a "Jewish story," reported by Jews, and therefore inherently untrustworthy because Jews were an "interested party." But it was also the sheer scale of the claims, regardless of who made them, that made some stories seem simply beyond comprehension. A British Foreign Office memorandum in 1943 reflected this view. "The Poles, and to a far greater extent the Jews, tend to exaggerate German atrocities in order to stoke us up," it said. "They seem to have succeeded."[23]

Historian Lipstadt offered another view: "One is loath to accept that as true, but it must be acknowledged that many government officials, members of the press, and leaders of other religions behaved as if Jewish lives were a cheap commodity."[24] The notion of Jews as "cheap commodity" may have been suggested when AP sent out just two paragraphs on the World Jewish Congress's claim that one million Jews had died in Nazi-occupied Europe. AP's story was likely brief because of the impossibility of independently verifying the information. But the brevity also may have left some readers thinking, "here's a story beyond belief." "The way in which the information was relayed enabled many people to categorize it as unverified rumors spread by unreliable sources," Lipstadt wrote, in describing American media coverage of the Nazi extermination program. "Ultimately the most formidable obstacle to the spreading and acceptance of news of the Final Solution was the nature of the information itself."[25]

Given Nazi anti-Semitism, isolated stories of murdered Jews were "fathomable," but "an actual extermination plan was not," noted Rebecca Erbelding, a historian at the U.S. Holocaust Memorial Museum. "It took time to realize that such stories were not only different—separate from wartime propaganda about the cruelty of the enemy—but also true."[26]

In November 1942, several months after AP ran the two-paragraph brief from the World Jewish Congress press conference, it distributed a far more detailed story attributed to the group's chairman, Rabbi Stephen Wise. Wise had gone to Washington, D.C., for a private meeting at the State Department with Undersecretary of State Sumner Welles, to discuss the latest disturbing stories his organization was hearing about the mass murder of Europe's Jews. From the State Department, Wise went to Washington's Union Station to board a train to New York. Waiting for him there was AP Washington correspondent Kenneth L. Dixon, to whom the rabbi gave an exclusive account of his meeting. Wise said the State Department had confirmed reports (which Wise also had received) that approximately two million of the estimated four million Jews living under Nazi control in Europe had been murdered in an "extermination campaign."[27] Warsaw's Jewish population, numbering more than 400,000 in the early part of 1942, had been reduced to 100,000, Wise said, and Hitler had ordered the elimination of all Jews in Nazi-held Europe by the end of 1942. (The estimated 300,000 Jews deported from the Warsaw ghetto between June and September 1942 were sent to the Treblinka death camp.)[28]

Dixon's story on Wise's revelations was published in hundreds of newspapers across the United States, displayed on page 1 in many, including the *Des Moines Register*, the *Arizona Republic*, the *Arkansas Gazette*, the *Hartford Courant*, and the *Miami Herald*.[29] Not every paper gave it such prominent treatment, though. The *New York Times* relegated the Wise story to page 10.[30] "The Atlanta Constitution put it on page 20 with the want ads and the train schedules, while the *Kansas City Star* and the *New Orleans Times Picayune* did not carry it at all," noted Lipstadt.[31]

The *Washington Post* carried the Wise story on page 6, running it with a separate AP story from London that cited the Polish government-in-exile as saying Jews were being sent to their deaths jammed into freight trains, 150 to a car. "The people are packed so tightly that those who die of suffocation remain in the crowd side by side with those still living," wrote AP. "Those surviving are sent to special camps at Treblinka, Belzec, and Sobibor [where] they are mass-murdered."[32] Four days later, AP reported from Washington that the United States and allied governments had condemned Germany's "bestial policy of cold-blooded extermination" of the Jews. Those responsible, it said, "shall not escape retribution."[33]

Nearly two years after the first reports of a massacre of fifty-two thousand people on the outskirts of Kiev, the Soviet Army forced the Germans to retreat from the shattered city. When the Soviets took control in the misty dawn of November 6, 1943, they soon discovered the ravine known as Babi Yar (Babyn Yar in Ukrainian), site of one of the largest mass killings carried out by Nazi firing squads. Three weeks after the discovery, Moscow organized a rare trip to Kiev for foreign correspondents, including AP's Eddy Gilmore. Gilmore reported that Babi Yar contained the remains of sixty thousand to eighty thousand Jews. The Soviet guide, an official in charge of Kiev's reconstruction, identified the dead as Jews, not the "Soviet citizens" terminology often used in Soviet accounts of Nazi atrocities.34 Researchers later documented that nearly thirty-four thousand Jews were killed at Babi Yar in two days in 1941, but the ravine continued to be an execution site for tens of thousands more Jews, Roma, Soviet war prisoners, and others.35

Gilmore, a balding, jovial, thirty-six-year-old native of Alabama best known for his southern drawl, good humor, and feature writing, might have seemed somewhat misplaced for such a dark assignment. He presented the scene in deceptively understated prose, announcing, "I'll let the story tell itself." His Soviet escort described how, in September 1941, Kiev's Jews were brought to the Babi Yar ravine, half a mile long and forty feet deep, and ordered to remove their clothes. Then, said the official escort, "in small groups they were mowed down by automatic gunners. Then they were buried. Recently they were dug up and burned by the Germans wanting to destroy all the evidence."

Gilmore wrote that as he walked in the ravine he found "fingers without hands," "a half-burned shoe with flesh inside," "several bones," "broken burned spectacles," and "several pairs of broken false teeth." He and the other correspondents were introduced to three Jewish men, Soviet Army soldiers who had been captured by the Nazis and brought to the ravine to help with the burning of the corpses. One of them told the journalists that he and other Soviet prisoners of war were given shovels and told to dig up the bodies.

"There were hundreds of them," the former prisoner said. "They made us take large tongs and drag these bodies up here. The Germans then made a layer of wood and then a layer of bodies and poured gasoline over them and set them on fire." Afterward, he said, the Germans used large instruments to crush the bones and destroy the evidence.

"That is the story as we heard it of Babii Yar," Gilmore concluded.[36]

A month later, in December 1943, Radio Moscow announced that more than fourteen thousand "absolutely innocent" inhabitants of the city of Kharkov (now Kharkiv) had been found slain, some shot, others executed in "death trap" trucks described as hermetically sealed with the exhausts connected inside.[37] Unlike Babi Yar, where the Germans sought to cremate the evidence, the Soviet military was able to disinter thousands of intact corpses in Kharkov. But although Gilmore and other reporters had visited Kharkov under Soviet escort earlier in 1943, they were not shown mass graves. Nor were foreign correspondents taken to Kharkov for the December 20, 1943, public hanging of three German soldiers and a Russian accomplice, convicted in the first Soviet war crimes trial.[38] AP, citing Moscow press accounts, reported that forty thousand Kharkov residents turned up to watch the executions.

Almost at the same time, the Soviets released a grisly picture of what was said to be the opened mass grave outside Kharkov—a long trench stuffed with hundreds of corpses, though the image is muddy and individual figures are difficult to make out. It appears to be the first Soviet photo depicting a mass grave, the skeletons identified in the photo caption as "persons asphyxiated in 'murder vans' or executed by firing squad." International News Photo and Central Press distributed it to their U.S. newspaper clients.[39] The *St. Louis Post-Dispatch* gave it front-page display, and other papers owned by the

Hearst newspaper chain (served by International News Photo) ran it on inside pages.[40]

It's not known why AP did not circulate the photo to its clients. Three months later AP did distribute a view of the Kharkov trench, taken from a Soviet propaganda film titled "Ukraine in Flames" (the Soviet photo caption, repeated by AP, erroneously described it as "Babi Yar ravine on the outskirts of Kharkov").[41] The agency may have considered the initial photo questionable propaganda or of such poor quality that it was not worth distribution. Or, in that period before widespread photo documentation of Holocaust crimes, editors may have deemed it too graphic for public consumption. In considering what to do with such a graphic image, it's likely photo editors would have discussed some or all of those issues, but corporate archives have not yielded documentation of such a conversation.

Eddy Gilmore's stark account of walking among the remains of corpses at Babi Yar offered shocking details, though some correspondents on the same trip found the evidence incredible and wrote more skeptical reports. Seven months later, in July 1944, the Soviets would liberate another site whose reality was perhaps even harder for some to grasp.

Since at least early 1943, rumors had persisted, unconfirmed, about atrocities at the Majdanek camp outside Lublin, Poland. That changed when the Soviet military arrived there during the night of July 22–23, 1944.

Word of what was revealed trickled out slowly through the Soviet press. In a first brief story, with few details, AP quoted Soviet media as describing a "medieval massacre" of "Ukrainians, Poles, and Jews" at Majdanek, though there were few details.[42] Then, on August 10, the Soviet army newspaper *Krasnaya Zvezda* reported that "hundreds of thousands of persons, principally Jews, were systematically and methodically killed there since the winter of 1941." By mid-August 1944 Sovfoto, the Soviet photo agency in New York, released a dozen or so images from Majdanek, at least three of which were distributed by AP to subscribers. In one, residents of Lublin gaze into a pit of bodies killed by Germans.[43] Another shows a row of cremation ovens with human skeletal remains in the foreground, and the third captures a mass funeral service held at a common grave beside medieval Lublin Castle—attended, Soviet media reported, by twenty-five thousand wailing mourners.[44] Hostile Poles screamed "murderers!" and "degenerates!" as German prisoners dug up many bodies of the victims, including a child, from an open ditch.

Eddy Gilmore in Moscow wrote AP's report, all of it attributed to Soviet press dispatches.[45] No trip to do firsthand reporting was on offer to foreign correspondents until a month later, August 27, when Soviet authorities opened the Majdanek camp to reporters from other Allied countries. AP correspondent Dan De Luce was among those who traveled with the Russian-Polish Atrocities Commission for a tour of what he called "perhaps the greatest horror in Nazi Europe."

De Luce, a tall, blond native of Yuma, Arizona, had been awarded the Pulitzer Prize for his coverage of Yugoslavia's partisan resistance in 1943. That night at Majdanek, "our clothes still reeking of the dead," De Luce wrote, the journalists gathered in a Lublin courtroom to hear four German prisoners tell their stories. The three SS officers and a German civilian, who spoke indifferently of Majdanek's scene of slaughter and blamed it on "orders from above," said men, women, and children from twenty-two countries had been gassed, hanged, shot, burned, drugged, or starved to death in the almost three years the camp was operational.[46]

Some of what De Luce described at Majdanek would become familiar some months later, when Americans read the accounts of journalists entering concentration camps with Western Allied military. But De Luce's story gave a first, vivid eyewitness account from the most horrific of Nazi creations: a death camp, one of six specially equipped for systematic murder. Majdanek had been the rail terminus for crowded cattle cars transporting Jews to their death from Vienna, Prague, Milan, Athens, Warsaw, and elsewhere. Russian and Polish officials estimated the camp "received more than half a million persons doomed to extermination," De Luce wrote.

"Majdanek is a ghastly fantasy," said De Luce. With its six concrete vaults used for execution by cyanide or carbon monoxide gas and its open-air crematorium, surrounded by skeletons, "it was established for murder on a vast but methodical scale." Mounds of human ashes mixed with manure were used to fertilize cabbage patches, and decaying bodies moldered in a burial ground in nearby woods. One survivor recalled a group of Polish women being marched up a hill to be shot. When they were ordered to disrobe, "one refused," the survivor said. "Two men tied [the prisoner's] hands and legs, put her on a steel stretcher and thrust her alive into the white-hot oven."

The Soviet Army overran three other extermination camps in the summer of 1944: Sobibor, Belzec, and Treblinka. Each had been shut down in 1943 by the Germans, who dismantled the camps, plowed the ground, and planted trees and crops to disguise their history. There were no foreign press visits to these areas as the Soviet Army continued its westward push toward Berlin, on a route that included the death camp at Auschwitz.

In January 1945, still months before the U.S. Army would reach Buchenwald, the Soviet army surrounded the Polish stronghold of Poznan and breached Nazi Germany's border just ninety-eight miles from Berlin. News of the Soviet advance flooded America's front pages the following day. Both AP and UP noted in a single paragraph, deep down in their accounts, that the Soviets had reached the

Nazi camps at Auschwitz (Oswiecim in Polish).[47] AP also distributed a brief separate story on Auschwitz's liberation, noting Polish underground reports that said 12,400 people, most of them women and children, were gassed to death there following the ill-fated Warsaw Uprising in the summer of 1944.[48]

Auschwitz was a complex of some forty camps, including some whose inmates were used for forced labor. Most of the killing took place in the gas chambers at the largest camp, Auschwitz II—Birkenau, the last major death camp liberated by the Soviets. An estimated 1.1 million people—nearly a million of them Jews—were gassed and cremated at Auschwitz, according to the U.S. Holocaust Memorial Museum. A first eyewitness report after its liberation ran in the Soviet daily *Pravda*. "Only now when Oswiecim has been liberated can one see with one's own eyes the whole of this terrible camp, its many dozens of square kilometers steeped in human blood and fertilized by human ashes," *Pravda* correspondent Boris Polevoy wrote. "I saw the thousands of tortured people whom the Red Army had saved—people so thin that they swayed like branches in the wind, people whose ages one could not possibly guess."[49]

AP picked up the story in London from Radio Moscow, which read the *Pravda* account over the air. But its version was no match for the more widely published UP story, which also was based on the *Pravda* report but included more chilling details. "During 1941, 1942 and early 1943, he [*Pravda*'s correspondent] said, five trains arrived daily at Oswiecim with Russians, Poles, Jews, Czechs, French and Yugoslavs jammed in sealed cars. The trains always left empty."[50]

Unlike Majdanek, which the Germans fled in haste, the Soviets did not take foreign correspondents to see the remains of the Auschwitz death camp, where the Germans had forced prisoners to destroy the death machinery before their retreat. Nor were Soviet journalists accompanying the Soviet Army when it liberated the camp, according to Yad Vashem, the World Holocaust Remembrance

Center in Jerusalem. A special photo exhibition that opened at Yad Vashem's museum in 2018 said that Soviet photographers were only brought to Auschwitz a week after its liberation. Yad Vashem has labeled their images of crowds of prisoners "staging of the liberation of the Auschwitz concentration camp."

Soviets made available at least one Auschwitz photo to foreign agencies, including AP. It shows emaciated men, including one in the foreground with stick-thin arms. The caption, used in a number of American newspapers that published the photo, described the men as "exhausted to an extent that it was impossible to determine their age," similar to the *Pravda* correspondent's observation that survivors were so thin their ages could not be guessed.[51]

AP's account of liberated Auschwitz was drawn entirely from Soviet media reports. But soon the agency's correspondents would file their own on-the-ground reports from other sites—concentration camps liberated by the Western Allies and opened to print reporters, photographers, and broadcasters. Earlier reporting had begun to unveil the horror of the Final Solution and the fate of Europe's Jews. But the scope of reporting now—the number of journalists traveling with Allied forces, the face-to-face access they had to camps and survivors, the newsreel cameras that provided a vivid new platform for journalism—was about to reveal the Holocaust horror in ever more detail.

AP correspondent Alvin Steinkopf witnessed his share of death in World War II—German butchery in Poland, a Soviet massacre in what is now Ukraine—but nothing prepared him for what he found when he arrived at Buchenwald in the spring of 1945. Steinkopf, one of many AP reporters and photographers sent to Europe to cover the final throes of the Nazi regime, was the first AP correspondent to reach the notorious camp and one of its satellites at Ohrdruf, forty miles from Buchenwald. (Ohrdruf, liberated on April 4, 1945, was one of the first of the Nazi camps in Germany reached by U.S. forces.)

A few days after the army's arrival, the officer in charge had rounded up forty of the town's leading citizens. They were ordered to accompany Steinkopf and other journalists on a tour of the carnage. "They saw bodies sprawling in the open space between the barracks, piled like timber in one building and heaped in a tangled mass in a wide pit in still another place where apparently some effort had been made to burn them," Steinkopf reported on April 11.[52] The appalling scenes were captured in a series of photos made by Byron H. Rollins, an AP photographer with the wartime still picture pool.[53]

"At first the Germans expressed disbelief, insisting, 'The SS isn't like that,'" wrote Steinkopf. "Later they voiced disgust, with one doctor saying 'It's the work of beasts.'" The next morning the Nazi mayor of Ohrdruf and his wife were found hanged in their home. The army said it was suicide.[54]

On April 16 Steinkopf reached the much larger main camp at Buchenwald, where he reported that twenty-one thousand "miserable, sick and ragged men" had still been alive when American troops arrived there four days earlier. "Tens of thousands of other prisoners had died before the Americans got there and many of the liberated were too far gone to be saved," Steinkopf wrote. "In the first 24 hours of American administration a few more than 150 succumbed to malnutrition and disease. In the next six hours, 39 more died."[55]

The first camps that Steinkopf and other correspondents entered with Allied liberators were not built for mass extermination by gassing, like Majdanek or Auschwitz-Birkenau. But Jews had died in them by the tens of thousands, of starvation, disease, beatings, and slave labor conditions. The liberators encountered piles of corpses and hundreds of prisoners who were little more than the walking dead. Their images were immortalized in both still photography and film.

American reporters, photographers, and broadcasters continued accompanying Allied troops as they moved eastward, liberating more camps as they progressed. AP's William Frye was with the British Second Army on April 20 when he arrived at Bergen-Belsen, with "its piles of dead and its aimless swarms of living dead." Frye said some of the estimated sixty thousand prisoners liberated by the British Second Army were dying of typhus, typhoid, or tuberculosis. But most were simply starving to death. An Irish major told Frye many were too far gone to be able to retain food. "[T]he flesh on their bodies had fed on itself until there was no flesh left, just skin covering bones and the end of all hope," Frye wrote. "Tragically, there is still hope inside these still breathing cadavers but no food, no care can save them. Ahead of them is nothing—nothing but that pit with the bulldozer waiting to cover them with earth."[56]

Frye was told of cannibalism, of beatings, of fingers being chopped off as punishment, and of SS women dancing around two prisoners, one dead, one alive, tied together on smoldering scraps of leather and worn-out shoes and boots. "I heard and saw more—but I cannot go on," he wrote.[57]

At Dachau, there were over sixty-five thousand registered prisoners, about a third of them Jews, when two columns of American infantry descended on the camp shortly after noon on April 30, 1945. AP's Howard Cowan, one of four American and British journalists riding just behind the troops, watched as a U.S. Army officer slipped the lock to the camp's main gate. At first there was no sign of life. "And then a tremendous human cry roared forth," Cowan wrote, as "a flood of humanity" poured across the yard and mobbed the American soldier. "He was hoisted to the shoulders of the seething, swaying crowd of Russians, Poles, French, Czechs and Austrians cheering the Americans in their native tongues." When two undetected SS guards fired into the mass from a tower, American infantrymen instantly riddled the Germans with bullets. Their bodies were hurled down into a moat "amid a roar unlike anything ever heard from human throats," Cowan reported.[58]

Official U.S. and British Army photographers arrived at the camps with the liberating troops, and most of the initial photos AP distributed were their work. Images of emaciated survivors, naked or in tattered prison uniforms, sent shock waves, as did photos of Germans forced to confront the gruesome camp scenes. In one, pairs of SS women at the Belsen concentration camp are seen being made to haul the lifeless remains of their former prisoners from a truck to a mass grave.[59] Another photo shows the camp commandant of Landsberg concentration camp No. 4, a subcamp at Dachau, forced to stand among the corpses of some of the four thousand Jews who perished there under his command.[60]

Weeks after Buchenwald's liberation, the camp had been converted from a death zone into a shelter for some twenty-one thousand war survivors. Some had survived Buchenwald itself. Others were displaced persons from many countries, awaiting decisions about their future. Louis Lochner, who had returned to Germany to help report the final days of the Third Reich, arrived at the main Buchenwald camp on May 31, where he met Romeo Boexelman. A young Jewish boy with sad eyes, dressed in an American uniform someone had shortened to fit his small frame, Boexelman told his story to Lochner:

> My mother was murdered by the Gestapo, and then burned. I was at the Auschwitz concentration camp for two years and then Buchenwald for one year. I worked in a quarry.
>
> My father was also at Buchenwald. He was removed with thousands of others just before the Nazis ran away. He's probably dead now. Maybe someday I can go to Palestine where I have an uncle.

Suddenly, noted Lochner, a satisfied smile crept over the boy's face. "Yesterday my comrade and I caught an SS man. He was dressed in civilian clothes and thought nobody would recognize him," Boexelman said. "But we reported him to the Americans—and now he is where he can do no harm. We'll get them all."[61]

The searing stories and graphic photos from AP and other American media offered irrefutable evidence of the Holocaust crimes. And yet many were met with the same initial skepticism as in years past, as stories simply too gruesome to be true. That is likely what inspired General Dwight D. Eisenhower, supreme commander of the Allied Expeditionary Forces in Europe, to summon seventeen U.S. newspaper publishers and editors, and a dozen congressional leaders, to come to Germany. Eisenhower wanted them to witness what he said was "almost impossible to describe in words."[62]

Among those who accepted the invitation and visited Buchenwald was Joseph Pulitzer, editor and publisher of the *St. Louis-Post Dispatch* and son of the legendary founder of the Pulitzer Prizes. "I came here in a suspicious frame of mind, feeling that I would find that many of the terrible reports that have been printed in the United States before I left were exaggerations, and largely propaganda, comparable to reports of crucifixions and amputations of hands which followed the last war, and which subsequently proved to be untrue," Pulitzer wrote in an April 28 story for his newspaper. "It is my grim duty to report that the descriptions of the horrors of this camp, one of many which have been and which will be uncovered by the Allied armies, have given less than the whole truth. They have been understatements," he added.[63]

AP distributed Pulitzer's article, as well as those by other editors, to the agency's newspaper members throughout the United States. Norman Chandler, publisher of the *Los Angeles Times*, wrote that he had seen the dying, the bodies, the gallows, the piles of dead stacked like cordwood. "There is no need of going into details," he wrote. "They have all been told. My purpose is merely to testify as to the accuracy of the American correspondents—they have told the truth. They have not exaggerated. Exaggeration, in fact, would be difficult."[64]

It was the photographs of this bestiality that had the greatest impact and told "the true story," Pulitzer wrote. "If the reader is still skeptical let him look at the photographs and when he does so let him remember that they picture only small parts of the mosaic of the Nazi policy of deliberate mass extermination."[65]

Pulitzer's doubts, finally erased by walking through Buchenwald, reflected the dilemma Western media had confronted throughout the war when faced with claims of mass murder—but with no means for independent confirmation. Despite the extraordinary reporting obstacles, however, "news of the mass destruction of the Jews came early, prominently and widely to America," wrote Ron Hollander, journalism professor and director of Jewish American Studies at Montclair State University, in "We Knew: America's Newspapers Report the Holocaust."[66]

In "We Knew," Hollander challenged a long-standing myth: that most Americans first learned about the Final Solution in April and May 1945 from media sources such as Fox-Movietone newsreels and CBS correspondent Edward R. Murrow's searing account of his visit to Buchenwald. In reality, wrote Hollander, "from 1942 on, we knew that the Germans were systematically exterminating specifically the Jews using gas chambers and crematoria. Nor was it just President Franklin Roosevelt and State Department officials with access to secret cables who knew. The American public itself read in its morning and evening newspapers that the Jews were being wiped out."

So if AP and other American media covered the story "early, prominently and widely," why didn't the public demand that the United States do more to try to save Europe's Jews? That is the central question in *Why Didn't the Press Shout*, the 2003 collection of academic studies and essays that includes Hollander's "We Knew" study.

Among the answers is this observation from journalist and professor Laurel Leff: "To know something requires more than the dissemination of information." Leff, whose study focused in-depth on the *New York Times*, argued that by seldom giving front-page play to stories of Nazi persecution of Jews, the *Times* minimized the story's importance; the information might be available, but its presentation cast doubts on its veracity.[67]

In other cities, stories of persecution, execution, and extermination of the Jews got prominent play in local newspapers—but readers may have found the Holocaust details too horrific to believe until the gruesome Movietone footage offered vivid confirmation.

Another reason cited by scholars: Allied war policy focused on winning Germany's unconditional surrender, rather than pursuing proposals such as bombing rail lines into Auschwitz to slow the slaughter. And public opinion polls at the time showed a significant minority of Americans held anti-Semitic views that left them unsympathetic to the plight of Europe's Jews. "Most journalists were like most other Americans—some anti-Semitic, some disbelieving, others indifferent," wrote journalist Marvin Kalb in his introduction to *Why Didn't the Press Shout?* "The Holocaust was not a burning story during the time of the Holocaust."

In the end, said Kalb, "the very nature of journalism itself" helped keep a veil on the Holocaust as it was unfolding. Trained to be skeptical and to verify every detail, American journalists struggled with how to write about atrocities they could not independently confirm. And once the United States went to war, their editors "wanted stories about the homefront and the war front," wrote Kalb. "They were not geared for stories—quite fantastic stories—about millions of Jews being gassed and burned to death as part of a systematic German campaign to exterminate a people. Now, with hindsight, we can second-guess the editorial limitations of the times—and say, tsk, tsk, you blew the story."[68]

17

THE COLLAPSE

In the final six months of the war, the photos flowing from Büro Laux in Berlin to AP in New York and London reflected ever grimmer scenes from inside the crumbling Third Reich. One showed children and middle-aged aged men and women digging long tank traps to blunt Allied advances from the west.[1] In another, civilian recruits reacted to Heinrich Himmler's announcement of the Volkssturm, a people's militia of armed men ages sixteen to sixty, who would erect street barricades and prepare for house-to-house, hand-to-hand combat.[2] Those refusing to join were hanged publicly.[3]

Though German-made and approved by German censors, these October 1944 images from Büro Laux made clear the tide of the war had turned decidedly against Germany. Now, the three men most responsible for AP's involvement in the Büro Laux arrangement would soon witness the war's climax from inside Germany. Afterward, an Allied military investigation would suggest the U.S. government consider legal action against AP for the Büro Laux operation. The same investigators even questioned Lochner's loyalty to America. The Allied victory and its aftermath would forever shape the postwar lives of Büro Laux founder Helmut Laux; of Willy Brandt, to whom AP had bequeathed the remnants of its Berlin photo agency (later absorbed into Büro Laux); and of Louis Lochner, the venerable bureau chief whose commitment to keeping AP operating in Germany had so often put him in the firing line of critics.

In the fall of 1944, with the Russians approaching from the east, Helmut Laux worried about the fate of the AP print photo archives that he had stored for safekeeping in a castle in western Poland. Laux understood his Waffen-SS affiliation would have serious personal consequences if Germany lost the war, but he somehow still imagined his small photo agency would not only survive but could expand and flourish in postwar Germany, no matter which side won. The print archives would be a significant boon for the future success of his business, Laux believed. So, claiming the archives were secret Foreign Office documents requiring safe haven, he used his authority as a military officer to requisition a railway car and four Waffen-SS guards. The soldiers moved the fifteen tons of crates and filing cabinets, crammed with print photos, from Poland to Treherz, a town in southern Germany.[4] Laux also tried to get the Foreign Ministry to transport the rest of his photo agency's property—the equipment in the Berlin bureau—to another safe haven outside the German capital. But as the Soviets closed in on Berlin, his telegrams to Paul Schmidt, the Foreign Office spokesman who had originally sanctioned the Büro Laux operation, were ignored or answered with "impossible."[5]

Meanwhile, Laux was sent to the Western front as a war correspondent in December 1944. There, he told American interrogators after the war, he became paralyzed with arthritis. Transferred from hospital to hospital, and later from town to town as the Allies closed in, he eventually reached Treherz, reuniting with the AP photo archive. In Treherz, he persuaded Wehrmacht soldiers to help him move the photo crates to a farm a few miles away, near the village of Steinental. On May 9 French troops occupied the village. Laux, shedding his Waffen-SS uniform for civilian clothes, "surrendered" to them. But in his typical wheeler-dealer style, he managed to convince the French not to confiscate the photo archives. Two weeks later the local French commandant gave Laux a pass allowing him to go search for U.S. military units that could take over protection of the AP photos—and, Laux hoped, help him connect with Lochner or others from AP who might vouch for him.[6]

As Laux obsessed over the fate of the print archives, Willy Brandt sought to protect AP's 70,000 glass negatives. In December 1943 Brandt and his family had fled Allied air raids on Berlin for the relative safety of Ziegenhals, southeast of Berlin. He also moved the glass negatives and other AP bureau contents to Haus Boehmer, a hotel outside Ziegenhals. But when the Soviet Army advanced into German territory, Ziegenhals was no longer safe. Brandt's wife burned his Waffen-SS *Soldbuch* or identity document, and the Brandts left to move further west, along with many others fleeing Berlin and its environs. "Refugees we met, whether they were military or civilians, German or foreigners such as Belgians, Dutch, Flemish, or French, all had just one question: Is the way to the West, to the Americans, still open?" Brandt wrote later. Brandt stayed safe, but the negatives he left behind were thoroughly plundered when Russian soldiers reached Haus Boehmer.[7]

When he arrived in the United States in 1942 after the five-month internment of Americans in Germany, Louis Lochner went on a lecture tour, did radio commentaries for the National Broadcasting Company, and wrote a book about covering the Nazis: *What About Germany?* By now "his lifelong commitment to pacifism, conciliation, arbitration and even 'appeasement' as preferable to war had crumbled in the face of totalitarianism and terror," according to Morrell Heald, who edited the letters Lochner wrote during his years in Germany.[8]

In the winter of 1944–45, AP assigned Lochner to return to Europe as a war correspondent. Like all journalists accredited to cover Allied forces as they moved east toward Berlin, he wore a U.S. Army uniform and traveled with the troops. To AP readers, Lochner was still the former Berlin bureau chief, a journalist with deep expertise after years of covering the Weimar Republic and the Nazi era before the United States and Germany declared war on each other. But now, as traveling war correspondent, his reporting again stirred the kind of controversy that dogged him through his years of covering the Nazis.

In February 1945 Lochner reported from the western German city of Aachen that field officers of the American Military Government overseeing the Allied occupation were questioning strict military orders that forbade them from any fraternizing with Germans. All invitations from Germans were to be declined, even if the invitation came from a local official "who, although thoroughly certified as non-Nazi, nevertheless is a German citizen and hence falls under the non-fraternization rule," Lochner wrote. Lochner said that when he spoke with American military officials in newly occupied zones, "almost the first question raised usually has been 'don't you think the non-fraternization order should be modified?'"[9]

The story's theme reflected Lochner's long-held view: Nazis should be held accountable for their crimes, but the Nazi debacle should not be blamed on all German society. It was a view that ran counter to Allied thinking as the war wound down, and in New York, his editors balked at putting out the story.[10] A rewrite was finally distributed with a paragraph added near the top to balance the complaints of officers with their higher ups' rationale for the nonfraternization order: "all Germans must share responsibility for Hitler; Naziism was overwhelmingly endorsed by the German people, its victories were generally acclaimed; there was no public protest against the inhumanity of the gestapo against the Jews and later the peoples of occupied countries."

Deeper in the story, Lochner's text pushed back on the notion of collective responsibility. Less than 10 percent of the American officers he spoke with felt that "all Germans are alike and must be barked at," he wrote. And, said Lochner, the no-fraternization policy made it "increasingly difficult to convince the bewildered Germans that the democratic way of life is better than what they have known."

The story immediately put Lochner in the crosshairs of William Shirer, the former Berlin correspondent for CBS, who rebuked "certain Americans" for trying to "draw a neat line between naziism and the German people."[11] In a clear assault on Lochner, Shirer wrote in his *New York Herald Tribune* syndicated column published on March 11: "I cannot help but think that he and a host of other American apologists for the 'German people'—for the people who almost won Hitler's war of bloody conquest for him—will cause a great deal of confusion in this country unless our memories are long."[12]

The no-fraternization story was only the first of a series of controversies stirred by Lochner's reporting during his travels with the military. As Allied forces moved further into Germany, Lochner renewed contacts with old sources from before the war—including, he said, one of the conspirators in the failed July 20, 1944, plot to kill Hitler. In March 1945, relying on the unnamed conspirator, whom he described as "a man I have known for years and in whose integrity and veracity I have a firm belief," Lochner produced three bombshell stories. One gave new details of the plot to kill Hitler in 1944.[13] Another recounted claims that Hitler was seriously ill and frequently couldn't speak.[14] The third said that Reichsmarschall Hermann Göring was regarded by his physician as physically and mentally finished, obsessed with holding on to jewels, precious stones, and priceless paintings he had "acquired" during the war.[15]

The Hitler plot story generated instant criticism after it appeared in newspapers across the United States. An editorial in the *Abilene Reporter-News* in Texas voiced the suspicion that stories about alleged resistance to Hitler were deliberately planted by Germany to convince the West that "the Nazis and the Nazis alone are responsible for Germany's conduct in this war, and that once we get rid of the Nazis we can deal safely and leniently with all other Germans. We fell for this line of bunk 25 years ago, and if we fall for it again—God have mercy on our souls."[16]

Time magazine, in its April 2, 1945, issue, mocked the breathless tone in some of Lochner's stories from Allied-occupied Germany.[17] It ridiculed his repeated used of the phrase: "I am able to reveal today" and chortled at the line: "As he [the late Baron von Bose] put it to me only a few hours before he was murdered by SS men."[18] *Time* compared Lochner's work to the often-dubious reports emanating during the war from neutral Stockholm, a "hotbed of unfounded rumors based on Swedish travelers in Germany."

Even more incendiary was the criticism from Geoffrey Parsons, Jr., editor of the Paris edition of the *New York Herald Tribune*, who refused to publish Lochner's story on the failed Hitler assassination. "It is a mistake for the Associated Press, no matter what experience and contacts Mr. Lochner has in Germany, to send back to Germany a man who was such a notorious apologist for the Nazis, even after the war began," he wrote in a letter shared with AP managers.[19]

Surveying the criticism, AP general manager Kent Cooper wrote a consoling but cautionary letter in late March 1945 to the beleaguered Lochner. "Your stories, particularly those on the Hitler plot, have been very widely published and accepted for what they are—the best accounts yet obtained by a correspondent especially qualified to obtain and write what has happened and is happening inside Germany," Cooper wrote. "By the same token, it is vital for you to make crystal clear that you are well aware what Germans who give information to Americans may be trying to accomplish, for personal reasons or bigger objectives."[20]

Lochner responded a few days later: "As to the charge that I make a distinction between Nazis and the German people, or certain sections of them, I plead guilty now as always." Then he offered his boss a potential way out of the controversy. "If you feel that I am in any way an embarrassment to AP, give me the signal and I'll return pronto; if desired retire on my pension; and lead the private life of one who has tried to do an honest job of reporting and can therefore grow old without regrets!"[21]

Cooper, ever loyal to his former Berlin bureau chief, made no move to recall Lochner, who continued his travels with Allied troops. Lochner reported on the vast destruction across Germany and, on July 3, 1945, was part of a multinational caravan of 140 correspondents riding into Berlin ahead of the Second Armored "Hell on Wheels" Division of the U.S. Army.

But Lochner's return to Germany also marked the beginning of his gradual exit from reporting. He found himself eclipsed by younger AP talent taking over the story he had reported for well over a decade. In Berlin, he was often relegated to covering features and "sidebar" stories, like exploring the much-visited remains of Hitler's bunker. Lead stories like the Big Three conference in Potsdam of Harry Truman, Winston Churchill, and Joseph Stalin, to map out Germany's future, were assigned to thirty-three-year-old rising star Daniel De Luce.

If Lochner had harbored hopes of returning to the helm in Germany, it was a bitter blow. A new generation would pick up the story of postwar Germany, led by Wes Gallagher, one of AP's top war correspondents. Gallagher had led the reporting team covering the U.S.-British invasion of North Africa and later oversaw AP's coverage of the Allied drive that began with D-Day in 1944. At war's end, Gallagher was acting Paris bureau chief; he was thirty-three when

Kent Cooper tapped him to lead AP's postwar Berlin bureau. Lochner recorded his reaction in a June 1945 diary entry: "Wes Gallagher is to be German chief—he doesn't know any German nor understand the people."²²

After receiving a travel pass from the French occupying forces in May 1945, Helmut Laux began a long and tangled odyssey through Germany as he pursued three goals. First and most immediate was to avoid almost-certain arrest if the Allies were to learn of his Waffen-SS affiliation. His second objective was to find Louis Lochner, now traveling with Allied military forces. Laux believed Lochner could vouchsafe his AP connection to American military authorities. He even trusted that Lochner would explain to the Americans that joining the Waffen-SS had been essential (in Laux's view) for AP and its photo exchange with Büro Laux. If Lochner could make a convincing argument, Laux believed, he could avoid arrest and get to work building his postwar photo business. Finally, Laux sought to retain control of the AP print photo archives that he saw as crucial to the success of that business.²³

When Laux told the French occupiers that he was safeguarding an extensive photo archive belonging to an American news agency, they agreed to put the archives under their protection and to allow Laux to contact military officials in a nearby American occupation zone.²⁴ On June 1, 1945, Laux met with U.S. Army Lieutenant Colonel Eugene P. Walters, commander of the American military government detachment at Memmingen, Bavaria. Walters arranged for the photo archives to be moved to U.S. protection at a monastery where art and other treasures looted by the Nazis were also under guard.²⁵

In a memorandum about his meeting with Laux, Walters made no mention of Laux's past as personal photographer for Foreign Minister Joachim von Ribbentrop, nor of his connection to both the Waffen-SS and the Foreign Office—connections that, if known by

Walters, almost certainly would have led to Laux's immediate arrest. Instead, Walters noted that he authorized Laux to travel further in occupied Germany. Walters also gave him a vehicle, seven cans of gasoline, and a letter indicating that Laux was an AP photographer, a mistake Laux did not correct.

Benefitting from Walters's assistance, Laux set off to find Louis Lochner. But as he searched, U.S. counterintelligence agents had begun an investigation that would lead them to the remnants of Büro Laux in Berlin and its creator. By September 1945, four months after his meeting with Walters and still unable to secure a meeting with Lochner, Laux was on a collision course that eventually led to the unraveling of the story of Büro Laux and its wartime photo exchange with AP.

A first arrest and detention in September ended with Laux being released by military authorities, who apparently again failed to discover his Waffen-SS affiliation. After spending Christmas with his mother and sister in Memmingen, he was summoned to report to the local U.S. Counter Intelligence Corps (CIC) office to check his identity papers. There, Laux denied having ever been in military custody and said "he was to be employed by AP and was to report to Louis Lochner" to take up his post.[26] It's unclear how Laux thought he could get away with lying about not having been in military custody, and there is no record that Lochner nor anyone else at AP ever intended to hire him after the war.[27]

"Subject was extremely uncooperative and insolent during the conversation," according to the CIC report, "and when informed he would have to go to jail pending verification of his story he flatly refused."[28] When Laux resisted arrest, military police escorted him to the local jail.

Laux's efforts to keep his Waffen-SS affiliation secret finally failed during his Memmingen interrogations. A CIC report on the questioning identified him by his SS rank and noted that Laux fell into the "automatic arrest" category for his work at the Foreign

Office, his SS membership, his service as Ribbentrop's photographer, and his status as "second to Hitler's photographer [Heinrich] Hoffmann for the Reich." The report said that Laux claimed AP had approved him to work for the company, but "it is the opinion of this agent that LAUX should never be associated with any U.S. business firm."[29] Further interrogation and a search of his home on January 5, 1946, confirmed that he had arranged for other Büro Laux staff to join the SS, that he had worked as a photographer at Hitler's headquarters and for Nazi publications, and that he had worked for Ribbentrop and Paul Schmidt at the Foreign Office.[30] The interrogation report noted that "Subject admitted membership in the Waffen-SS, claiming the SS Führungshauptamt was a 'fine' and 'innocent' organization until 'people began talking about concentration camps and that sort of thing.'"[31]

Laux told his interrogators that he failed to reveal his Waffen-SS membership when first interviewed by Colonel Walters "because it was impossible for him to believe my story" without Lochner there to verify it. "It was my plan from the very beginning to speak to Mr. Lochner and with him as a witness go to the next or highest CIC office and to clear my story there," Laux wrote.[32] But, he acknowledged, Lochner never agreed to meet with him, nor did AP ever respond to his efforts to contact executives in New York.

In fact, there is no evidence that Laux and Lochner had any contact after their 1942 encounter on the train to Lisbon. Lochner also turned down a request from Laux's mother, who wrote to him in November 1945 asking to meet to discuss her son's fate.[33] Lochner said that Laux's Waffen-SS membership, "regardless, how nominal this membership might have been," put him in a "categorial arrest" status that meant "I have to admit the impossibility of any help, now."[34]

A few days after Laux was interrogated in Memmingen, two of the investigating agents escorted him to the improvised, postwar bureau that Willy Brandt had set up for AP in Berlin. Laux had hopes that the Berlin trip would lead investigators to conclude his wartime operation was legitimate, including the SS connections, "for I am feeling responsible as the chief of the Bureau Laux in this respect towards all members of the bureau."[35]

Instead, the trip was a disaster for Laux. U.S. military officials had moved the photo archives he had spirited out of Berlin to the new bureau, removing them from Laux's control. And a CIC search of the Büro Laux office had turned up expense accounts, salary lists, financial records, and documentation of photo purchases by Nazi institutions.[36] But no copy was found of the document Laux had signed with AP's Luiz Lupi in Portugal in 1942, setting up the photo exchange with AP. Laux had believed that document would help exonerate him.

Paul J. Hoylen and Robert E. Gregg, the two CIC agents who escorted Laux to Berlin, used the subject line "Operation Pouch" for reports they wrote on Laux and his photo operation. The title referred to the Büro Laux use of German diplomatic pouches to relay photos to and from Berlin and Lisbon.[37] Their reporting included details of the visit they made to the Laux bureau in Berlin, where they found documentation that Laux had sold photos to, among others, the propaganda ministry, the Nazi Party, Foreign Minister Ribbentrop, and the German publisher Deutscher Verlag.[38] At the offices of Deutscher Verlag, the CIC agents found AP photos bearing the stamp of F. Marques da Costa, the Portuguese photographer who processed materials in the exchange. The English photo captions on most of the images had been rewritten in German to cast "an unfavorable light upon the United States or the Allies or was presented to the German public as a morale booster," their report stated.[39] One example: a German caption, approved by the propaganda ministry for an AP photo of a U.S. fighter plane, read in part: "The appearance of the plane was celebrated with typical American bluff. . . . Everywhere, where these giant planes appear over Europe, they become most welcome targets of our gunners."[40]

In a January 14, 1946, summary of their preliminary findings, Hoylen and Gregg said: "It is the opinion of these Agents that the definitive proof is likely to be found, upon which to substantiate a charge that the Associated Press, over a period ranging from 1942 to 1945, engaged in operations coming within the purview of the Trading With the Enemy Act." They described the use of German Foreign Office diplomatic pouches to transfer photos and said the AP photos reaching Germany via this route "were illegally placed at the disposal of the German authorities." As a result, "direct use of Associated Press news-photos as German propaganda possibly occurred during the war, through this highly questionable agreement."[41]

Besides their investigation of Laux, the two agents had probed Lochner's role in setting up the exchange, leading them to question his loyalty as an American.[42] Lochner, they wrote, was "apparently fully aware" of Laux's SS status and had sent personal mail to Germany via the diplomatic pouches that were key to the photo exchange.[43] Hoylen and Gregg also concluded that AP sought to cover up the existence of Büro Laux.[44]

A few weeks later, on February 23, the head of the Counter Intelligence Corps recommended that the U.S. War Department consult the Justice Department about possible "trading with the enemy" charges against AP.[45]

CIC's recommendation went to Brigadier General Edwin Sibert, head of the intelligence division of U.S. forces in Europe. In March Sibert forwarded the entire "File and Report on Helmut Laux" to the chief of the Military Intelligence Service in Washington for "any further action you may deem desirable." As for himself, Sibert wrote: "In view of the difficulties involved in pursuing this case further and negligible results to be anticipated, this office contemplates taking no further action."[46]

Sibert's note did not elaborate on the "difficulties" he saw in a potential legal case, and it is not known whether he or other military officials had contact with AP or the wartime censorship office before making his decision. Censorship officials had okayed the photo exchange during the war, though their approval appears to have been based on a vague description of the plan provided by AP, which did not mention Laux, his Waffen-SS membership, or the direct involvement of the Nazi government.

On March 15, a few days after Sibert forwarded the report to the Military Intelligence Service, a note was written on the investigative file stating: "Case is considered closed." The note, which is contained in the Operation Pouch files at the U.S. National Archives, gave no explanation for the closure.[47]

Louis Lochner continued to report in Germany as the war in Europe ended, and in July 1945 he was again the target of controversy. Rumors circulated in Britain that he was working directly for the American Military Government, helping it identify and capture leading Nazis in Germany. His claims to continued affiliation with AP were just a cover to hide his real mission, or so the story went. The rumors—ironically, the polar opposite of past charges that Lochner was pro-Nazi—reached Kent Cooper in New York, who quickly dismissed them as the work of other journalists jealous of Lochner's excellent military contacts. Lochner, Cooper wrote to a London colleague, is "an honest American citizen and if his own government asked him a question I assume and hope that he would answer it truthfully." But the notion that Lochner's real employer was now the U.S. government, and not AP, "is just simply a lie."[48]

When the International Military Tribunal hearings opened on November 20, 1945, at the Palace of Justice in Nürnberg, Lochner was one of some four hundred correspondents covering the prosecution of the surviving top Nazi leaders for crimes against humanity. But a few months later, in March 1946, Cooper wrote to tell him it was time to come home. Lochner took several weeks to respond, finally informing Cooper he would retire and making clear he felt AP had put him out to pasture. "If at my age of 59 and at this point in my AP work my contribution to our common effort was worth anything, it was naturally along the line of interpretive writing on Europe affairs. For that type of work, however, there is evidently no place for me within the AP."[49]

Lochner returned to the United States a bitter man, bristling for years at what he considered mistreatment by AP and variously referring to Cooper, his former boss and longtime protector, as the "Hitler of the AP" and "our Stalin," who "certainly played me dirt."[50] "The farther I can stay away from K.C. [Kent Cooper] the better I like it," he wrote to one former colleague.[51]

In the postwar years Lochner worked for a committee organizing relief supplies for the defeated Germans. He also edited and translated some of the diaries of Joseph Goebbels, whose propaganda ministry was the nemesis of both domestic media and foreign correspondents in the Nazi era. And he held jobs at the U.S. State Department and the United Nations, while continuing to write about Germany, including a memoir and various articles about his experiences covering Nazi Germany and the war.

Privately, Lochner criticized his former employer and the new tide of young journalists posted to AP bureaus abroad. In a letter to his long-time colleague Alvin Steinkopf in 1952, Lochner appeared to disparage the young "business men" newly assigned to AP's European bureaus, who were tasked with aggressively seeking subscribers to expand the company's rapidly growing international presence. In criticizing the idea of journalists taking on a role as salesmen, Lochner seemed to breezily distance himself from any responsibility for the activities of AP's German photo service in Nazi times.

"I recall that when KC offered to appoint me chief of Berlin, I made it a condition that I remain as the first correspondent on the staff, and not as the manager of the rest," he wrote. "And as I look back, I think we all tried in the Berlin bureau to be journalists and not businessmen. We left that to Willy Brandt."[52]

Lochner died in Wiesbaden, Germany, in 1975, a few years after he and his wife had returned to her homeland to live.

At war's end, Helmut Laux was sent to an internment camp that housed over eleven thousand other Germans, most of whom were arrested by Allied military authorities because of their affiliation with the Waffen-SS, the Gestapo, or other Nazi organizations. When he was released in 1947, he opened a photo agency in Frankfurt that eventually expanded into producing commercials for movies and television.[53]

Laux apparently managed to save at least some of his wartime photos, and in 1948 *Life* magazine published a dramatic three-page spread of images that he had carefully guarded for several years. The photos were taken in 1944 when Laux was on an assignment covering Hitler's meeting with the Hungarian prime minister in Salzburg. When the meeting was suddenly interrupted by word of the D-Day invasion in Normandy, Laux kept working his camera, capturing an iconic picture of Hitler intently examining a map of the coastline of France. "A remarkable record of the emotional impact of the invasion on the now-dead Nazi leaders," *Life* noted in its June 14, 1948, edition, "the pictures reveal the mixture of elation and concern with which Hitler and his aides greeted each battle report."

Laux died in 1987, according to his daughter Claudia. In an interview with AP in 2017, she said her father had never talked about his wartime activities. "During his whole life he was just interested in the future, not the past," she said.[54]

After Lochner reached Berlin with Allied forces, he reunited with Brandt, who showed his former boss the makeshift postwar office he had scrambled to put together for AP. At one point the two posed for a photo before the ruins of the Nazi Party headquarters.

In October 1945 Brandt was interviewed by the Army's Counter Intelligence Corps, the same body that had investigated Laux and his bureau and that had suggested the government consider charging AP with trading with the enemy. The CIC concluded that Brandt's claims were credible—that he was anti-Nazi and had joined the SS against his own free will. In November William F. Heimlich, the U.S. Army chief of intelligence in Berlin, issued a "To Whom It May Concern" letter, certifying that Brandt was "cleared for employment by agencies of the U.S. government and/or private firms of this or allied governments."[55] Brandt had already returned to the AP payroll, working with new bureau chief Wes Gallagher to revive the Berlin news and photo operations.

But soon, in March 1946, AP fired Brandt. Another military government office, the Information Control Division (ICD), had reviewed his affiliation with Laux and his membership in the Waffen-SS and deemed Brandt "unsuitable" to serve in the top position AP had rehired him for: as managing director of a reconstituted AP GmbH photo operation.

The ICD, charged with removing anyone with Nazi connections from German media, described Büro Laux as a "completely Nazified organization." It referred to Laux as a "violent Nazi" and noted that Brandt had failed to reveal his Waffen-SS affiliation at war's end.[56] "Even if Brandt was not a Nazi at heart, he certainly had chosen the worst place to wait for the liberation he claims to have been longing for," the agency concluded.[57]

Bureau Chief Gallagher and his predecessor Lochner, who was still reporting for AP in Berlin, objected to the report and sought a way to keep Brandt in charge of the photo agency. Gallagher wrote to Kent Cooper that the ICD investigation was "carried out in a witch hunt fashion" by investigators "who for the main part are former Jewish refugees who fled to America under Hitler and are not exactly impartial in their operations."[58] Brandt, wrote Gallagher, "is by far the most able German anyone of us has met thus far and his loss would be a severe blow to our photo and general operations."

"There is no lack of appreciation for that," Cooper responded, "but at this time we must act in accordance with realities" and dismiss Brandt.[59]

AP's decision to not appeal the military ban on Brandt likely was taken to avoid the possibility of being exposed for championing someone on the Waffen-SS payroll. In a February 26, 1946, letter to Gallagher, Lochner said the military had leaked its Brandt decision to a German-based reporter for *PM*, an afternoon tabloid newspaper in New York, "with the suggestion that he cut loose with a story on how AP maintains Nazis in its employ." Lochner said he had secured a promise from the reporter that he would not write a story for *PM* as long as AP removed Brandt from his managerial position.[60]

Two months after his firing, Brandt wrote Lochner that his hopes of returning to the AP had been destroyed "in a most cruel manner" and that the judgment against him had made it impossible to find work in Berlin.[61] He asked Lochner whether AP might consider turning over its German photo archives to him so he could exploit their commercial value to make a living. Lochner, who remained deeply loyal to Brandt and argued strenuously that he had always been anti-Nazi, passed on the proposal to Cooper's deputy, Lloyd Stratton.[62] No reply has been found.

For Brandt, who survived financially by working for his brother's medical supply business, there was the added bitterness that Helmut Laux was soon freed from the postwar internment camp and allowed to reestablish himself in business. And photographer Gerhard Baatz— who, like Brandt, had joined the Waffen-SS in order to work for Büro Laux—got a postwar clearance to work for the German news agency

Deutsche Allgemeine Nachrichten Agentur, which was supervised by the U.S. military. Later, after the U.S. Trading with the Enemy Act restrictions were eased in the summer of 1946, allowing AP to sell its news and photos to German media, Baatz returned to work for AP for several years. Gallagher, who went on to become one of Kent Cooper's successors as general manager in 1962, wrote to New York five years after Brandt's dismissal, in a new effort to bring him back to AP. "We need urgently a capable, aggressive man with a thorough knowledge of the newspaper and photo business, not only to sell photos but news as well," Gallagher wrote.[63] He proposed Brandt as the ideal candidate and repeated his view that Brandt "was the victim of an unfair persecution" by U.S. military authorities.

The passage of time apparently had lessened the sensitivity about Brandt's SS affiliation. With New York's approval, Brandt rejoined the reestablished AP GmbH as sales manager for its German-language news and photo service in October 1950. For the next quarter century, he spent much of his time on the road, selling AP's German-language news and photo services to publishers and editors throughout Germany and Switzerland. He built up a clientele second only to Germany's own national news agency, Deutsche Presse Agentur. By the time he retired in 1978, the postwar AP GmbH was the largest single AP news and photo operation outside the United States, serving more than two hundred subscribers.

The print photo archives, so valued and protected by both Brandt and Laux throughout the war, were largely destroyed afterward. Space was at a premium in AP's postwar offices, and Gallagher, the new bureau chief, was among those who considered "those thousands of pictures as merely cluttering up our new offices," Lochner wrote in 1946.[64] But many of the most significant photos had already been distributed to AP subscribers, and prints and negatives of those were stored in the New York and London photo libraries.

All the surviving photos in Germany were also sent to London when the AP GmbH was sold to the German agency DDP in 2009. Research for this book in the London photo library turned up numerous images with the AP GmbH stamp—some from Berlin, some from the postwar AP office in Frankfurt. Among them are the Franz Roth portraits of Soviet prisoners of war that were used extensively in German propaganda and distributed by AP in Germany and the United States. Some of the Roth portraits still bear a red strip with the Nazi propaganda ministry's order: that at the "request of the Fuehrer" all German papers publish the photos and identify "SS-PK Roth" as the photographer.

When Kent Cooper informed Lochner in September 1945 that he was putting Wes Gallagher in charge of the postwar AP Berlin bureau, he urged Lochner to "let the new corps of correspondents take over." That "new corps" would now help Cooper build toward a dream he had outlined to the AP board two years earlier: to bring true and unbiased news to every country in Europe, Africa, and Asia. Under the long-standing news cartel arrangement with Reuters and two other agencies, AP had been restricted to selling news only in the Americas until Cooper began his efforts to break up the cartel, including with creation of the AP photo agency in Berlin.

In 1944 the AP board authorized spending $1 million to establish the agency as a truly international news service. Before that, AP's news "wires" and photo circuitry reached a few dozen countries, but under Cooper's ambitious plans AP eventually would serve media in more than one hundred countries.

Postwar Germany was key to Cooper's expansion plans. He entrusted Gallagher not just to rebuild a Berlin bureau servicing mainly U.S. media but to create a new German operation that would be the leading source of news and photos for local media as well. Getting German newspapers to subscribe to AP in the postwar environment turned out to be a pretty easy sell. Godfrey Anderson, one of the AP journalists-turned-salesmen, reported the enthusiastic reception he got from a German editor. "Can you imagine what this means to us?" the editor said. "To be in contact with the world again, to have news from everywhere after years of Nazi propaganda?"[65]

Within AP, Cooper could be a tyrannical boss, running roughshod even over the company's highest-ranking executives. He often spoke of lofty news principles, then undercut his own message with dubious positions, for example, his insistence that foreign correspondents were guests of the countries where they worked and should obey all local rules, including censoring the news when demanded. His internal communications about the AP GmbH photo operation made clear that Cooper prioritized business over the moral and ethical issues that later led military investigators to suggest the photo exchange amounted to trading with the enemy.

Cooper stepped down as general manager in 1948. He wrote his memoir some years later and died in 1965, but assessments of his legacy did not mention AP's brush with accusations of "trading with the enemy." Kent Cooper was "a dominant figure in world journalism for a quarter-century," according to his lengthy AP-written obituary, which the *New York Times* published on page 1. Running AP "as a one-man show," the obituary said, Cooper changed almost everything about the agency, transforming it from a largely domestic news agency to one with international standing and a global audience. "He dreamed dreams," one of his competitors said. "Then he made them come true."[66]

EPILOGUE

The history of AP's entanglements with Nazi Germany includes one more important but long-forgotten story: the death of AP war correspondent Joseph Morton, the only American reporter known to have been executed by the Nazis. The details of Morton's death at the Mauthausen concentration camp in Austria were reported in July 1945 by Lynn Heinzerling, who was assigned to investigate after Morton disappeared while covering a secret OSS operation in Slovakia, a client state of Nazi Germany.

Like Heinzerling and other AP foreign correspondents in that era, Morton was a product of the Midwest. Born in St. Joseph, Missouri, he attended state universities in Nebraska and Iowa before launching his newspaper career at Midwestern newspapers. In 1937 he joined AP in Lincoln, Nebraska, and by 1940 he was promoted to work in New York as an editor in AP news features. When the first opportunity to go abroad came two years later, he seized it.

"Morton was fired with determination," AP wrote after his death, "to go where no other correspondent had gone, and get the story that no one else could get."[1]

A series of wartime assignments took him to West Africa, then flying with American bombers during a U.S. air assault on Rome, and on to Algiers to cover the war in North Africa.[2] From there, he wrote proudly to AP general manager Kent Cooper that he and his wife Letty would soon be parents. In his February 1944 response, Cooper urged the father-to-be to use more caution as a correspondent. "Don't risk your neck in stunts," he warned.

Morton continued his reporting, covering the war's impact across eastern Europe and often picking up scoops. In August 1944 he arrived in Bucharest, Romania, with a top official from the Office of Strategic Services (OSS), forerunner of the Central Intelligence Agency; he was the only Allied correspondent on hand to file the story of the Soviet liberation of Romania. The following month, Morton returned to Romania, catching a ride on a U.S. Air Force bomber. He raced off to the castle of Romanian King Michael, where he spent the day playing table tennis with the royal family and getting the young king's exclusive account of how he had engineered the arrest of Romania's pro-Nazi dictator, paving the way for surrender to the Allies.[3] Morton's story, the *New York Times* editorialized, had all the elements "of glamour, romance, comedy, dramatic suspense and rapid action." Added the *Times*: "Only the Balkans could produce it. The movies will not overlook it."[4]

Soon after, Morton filed exclusive stories on clandestine operations to rescue American pilots downed in Nazi territory. His reporting clearly came from OSS sources, and perhaps from accompanying secret missions that he may or may not have revealed to his superiors at AP.

In the last week of September 1944, Morton phoned his bureau chief in Rome, Noland "Boots" Norgaard, to request authorization to go on a mission. He couldn't give details, he told Norgaard, because of censorship and unsecured phone lines. But in a letter to his boss, written just before the mission departed, Morton told Norgaard it would be "the biggest story of my life." He would be flying with the OSS deep into the heart of Adolf Hitler's occupied Europe. Morton promised Norgaard he would go in with the undercover operatives and then return to Allied territory on the next available flight.[5]

The ostensible mission was an OSS rescue effort to pick up Allied pilots, downed behind enemy lines but protected by partisans in Slovakia. But the OSS was also delivering guns and ammunition to the partisans, who were using their precarious base in the Slovak city of Banska Bystrica to launch an uprising that they hoped would overthrow Nazi rule throughout their country. Each man on the mission was aware of Hitler's order to ignore the Geneva Convention on Prisoners of War and execute any Allied forces captured behind German lines.

Morton and the OSS unit flew into Banska Bystrica on October 7, 1944, in six Flying Fortress bombers loaded with machine guns, ammunition, medical supplies, and gasoline for the partisans. Morton brought his portable typewriter. Guided by smoke signals from bonfires, the planes landed at a makeshift airfield, greeted by scores of cheering Slovak partisans.

When the planes returned to Italy, the same day or shortly thereafter, Morton reneged on his promise to Norgaard. He gave a typewritten story to an OSS officer making the return flight but said he would stay on with the OSS men to cover the Slovak uprising. His last story apparently was never delivered to AP; military censors may have blocked it when the OSS officer returned to Italy.

Banska Bystrica was slowly being encircled by the German Army, seeking to snuff out the Slovakian rebellion, and on October 20 German Stukas heavily bombed it. A week later, with only hours to escape, Morton and the OSS men abandoned the town and joined long columns of soldiers, partisans, and civilians fleeing in panic into the Tatra Mountains. German planes strafed and bombed the roads, and German units with dogs followed in pursuit.

For the next six weeks, Morton, members of the OSS team, partisans, and British special operations agents fled through woods, dodging Nazis as they sought to reach the safety of the front lines of the advancing Soviet Army. Howling winds, a blizzard, crippling icy streams that froze boot leather to skin—all took their toll. Scores froze to death, including eighty-three of the partisans who led Morton and the OSS men through forests during the first two weeks of November.

As Christmas approached, Morton and some members of the OSS unit reached a hunter's lodge on a mountain above the Slovak village of Polomka. They stopped to rest, celebrating Christmas Day with carols. The day after Christmas, while several of the men and their partisan guide were away from the lodge hunting for food, a force of German soldiers, Ukrainian troops, and Slovakian Hlinka Guardists fired on the shelter from all sides. A local villager had betrayed Morton's group.

Four men who were not in the lodge at the time survived with partisan help and eventually were able to escape to Allied territory and tell the group's story. But Morton, nine OSS men, and four of the British special forces were captured and sent to the Nazi concentration camp at Mauthausen near Linz, Austria. They were put in the camp jail, whose basement housed execution rooms, including a gas chamber and a crematorium. Inmates at Mauthausen told investigators later that during the last three weeks of the war, more than five hundred bodies were burned daily.

Morton and the others were interrogated, and some were tortured. Throughout his questioning, Morton repeatedly identified himself as an AP reporter, according to the camp's German interpreter, who was later interrogated by Allied forces.[6]

On January 24, 1945, less than three weeks after their arrival, a telegram from Berlin, signed by Ernst Kaltenbrunner, chief of Reich police forces, ordered the execution of all members of the Slovak mission. That same day, the men were led to a room where a fake camera was set up. The prisoners, told they would be photographed, were taken in one at a time. After facing the camera, they were told to turn around. An SS guard then stepped up and shot each in the back of the neck.

Morton's colleagues in Europe, alarmed by his long absence and unaware of his fate, were prevented by transatlantic censorship from notifying AP in New York about the missing correspondent. That job fell to Heinzerling, who returned to the United States in December 1944 on home leave from covering the war in Europe. In New York, Heinzerling shared with editors what little was known about Morton and the OSS mission.

On January 24, 1945, the day the men were shot, the Germans announced on their Transocean propaganda channel that a group of Americans and British had been captured, sentenced to death for espionage, and executed. But there was no confirmation of their identities, and rumors continued to swirl—including one that reached Morton's wife, Letty, that Morton had been spotted, alive, in a prisoner of war camp in Bruck, Austria.

Then months of silence, until May 1945, when Allied investigators in Paris questioned a German prisoner who revealed he had served as interpreter at the interrogation of the captured men at Mauthausen. Heinzerling, who upon his return to Europe was assigned by AP to investigate Morton's fate, went to Paris to question the German prisoner. From there, he and a U.S. Army investigator went to Mauthausen, where they learned more from Wilhelm Ornstein, a Polish Jew and former camp prisoner who was assigned to work at the execution room. Ornstein said his job was to remove the bodies of Morton and the others after their executions. He presented a dog tag from one of the OSS men as proof of his account, telling Heinzerling that he watched each execution through a door peephole. After a prisoner was shot, he said, he hurried into the room, removed the body, and swabbed the floor.

Heinzerling's story for AP, delayed several days by U.S. censors, detailed the ill-fated mission and confirmed the death of Morton at age thirty-four. Later, Heinzerling said that, after his years of covering the Nazi terror and World War II battlefields, uncovering Morton's death at war's end was "the crowning sadness." The two had worked together in Cleveland years earlier and in Europe during the war.

In a condolence letter to Letty Morton, Kent Cooper wrote that her husband's three years of war correspondence "comprise one of the most brilliant chapters of the entire news coverage of the conflict.... Joe was absolutely fearless, and evidently nothing that I or anyone else could say would deter him on grounds of personal safety when he was on the trail of a great news story."[7]

At the Nürnberg trials, Kaltenbrunner, who had signed the execution order, was found guilty of war crimes and crimes against humanity. He was executed by hanging on October 16, 1946. Earlier, an American military court at Dachau had sentenced fifty-eight of the sixty-one operators of Mauthausen to die on the gallows.[8] Prosecutors told the court the defendants were responsible for seventy thousand deaths at Mauthausen and "the clock would be turned back 1000 years if the court condones these atrocities."[9]

In 1994, paralleling the fiftieth anniversary of the Slovak uprising, a plaque in Morton's honor was placed on a memorial replica of the hut in which he and the OSS men were captured. A small ceremony at the hut honoring the OSS men and Morton was attended by local Slovak officials; Steve Miller, then AP bureau chief in Germany; and U.S. secretary of state Madeleine Albright.

"Joe Morton came to this mountain in 1944 still trying to report a story no other correspondent could tell, and trying in his way . . . to bring freedom from oppression, light into darkness, and tell others of the brave deeds of courageous men and women," Miller told the gathering, which was covered on the front page of his hometown newspaper, Missouri's *St. Joseph News-Press*. Added Albright: Morton died "in pursuit of his calling and in quest for the truth."[10]

At the memorial ceremony in 1994, AP's Steve Miller said that, like the Slovak partisans and OSS operatives whose story he wanted to tell, Morton died "for a worthy cause." In the accolades, no one questioned his decision to stay in Slovakia.

But some undoubtedly will question AP's decision to keep its news bureau and its German photo agency operating in Nazi Germany as long as it did. It's a question worthy of debate today, as journalists around the world continue to confront authoritarian regimes that force them to decide whether it's better to leave—as William Shirer and other correspondents did—or to stay and try to work around repressive rules designed to block them from reporting the truth.

The fact that there is no consensus answer to the "stay or go" question continues to be evident in more contemporary situations. Some journalists in 2012, for example, sharply criticized AP for opening a bureau in North Korea; some authors have cited specific stories as evidence that AP has pulled its punches in reports from inside the world's most repressive state.[11] But four years later, with no letup in North Korea's repressive policies, the French wire service Agence France-Presse announced it would open a bureau there, too, because "AFP needs to be present all over the world to fulfill its mission of reporting news as fully as possible," the agency's CEO said.

More recently, when the notoriously censorious Iranian regime granted NPR correspondent Mary Louise Kelly a visa, enabling her to be the first Western reporter to visit after antigovernment protests began in September 2022, Twitter exploded with criticism. "Shame on you for partnering with the murderous government," wrote one. "How much did the mullahs pay you?" asked another, while as third wrote: "You have sold your soul."[12]

"I guess I always come down on the side of, well, what's the alternative? That we don't try? That we see nothing? That the only narrative we have is the one the government wants out there?" Kelly told an interviewer after her reporting trip. "There's no substitute in Iran now, or anywhere ever, for being on the ground, seeing what you can see, knowing at the same time that it's the narrowest slice, and that you're only seeing a tiny bit of a huge and vast and complex country."[13]

"There is nothing, nothing, that compares to being on the ground," the journalist Masha Gessen said in April 2023, lamenting the anti-press crackdown that sent domestic and foreign correspondents fleeing Russia in 2022 after it invaded Ukraine.[14]

Russia's war on Ukraine illustrated both the danger of staying and the importance of being on the ground. Some months after fleeing Russia, a few foreign correspondents decided to return—until authorities arrested *Wall Street Journal* reporter Evan Gershkovich and charged him with espionage. Meanwhile, in Ukraine, three AP journalists lived under constant threat for nearly three weeks, risking their lives to show the world the chaos and carnage as Russia laid siege to the eastern Ukrainian city of Mariupol. "You can't make the moment that captures the world if you're not there, and being there is often dirty and difficult and dangerous," said J. David Ake, AP's director of photography.

More than eighty years earlier, in a different place and a different context, Louis Lochner was making similar arguments for staying on the ground. AP's news bureau in particular needed to remain in Berlin, he often said, because of the unmatched number of U.S. newspapers that depended on the agency for international news. It doesn't take much more than a quick look at this book's endnotes to understand the breadth of AP's reach across America in the 1930s and 1940s. Using the online archive at newspapers.com to locate stories published by AP client newspapers, we were often directed to big-city dailies, such as those in Los Angeles, St. Louis, Atlanta, Chicago, New York, and Baltimore. But our searches also led to papers in off-the-beaten-track locales: Deadwood, South Dakota; Massillon, Ohio; Casper, Wyoming; Pottsville, Pennsylvania; Kokomo, Indiana; and Appleton, Wisconsin, among others. With more than 1,200 U.S. newspaper clients during most of the Nazi era, AP was the single most important news source for most Americans about the Nazi menace.

Despite that vast reach, AP's coverage has seldom been a primary focus for authors studying media coverage of the Nazi era. There are several likely explanations for this. Unlike newspapers, whose libraries often contain researchable issues going back decades, AP's news archive of original wire story content from the 1930s and 1940s was not readily available to the public until relatively recently. And while many AP stories from the Nazi era provided strong analysis and vivid detail, AP's output also reflected the agency's priorities of speedy and comprehensive coverage: report as much news as possible, as quickly (and accurately) as possible. In contrast, reporters for the "specials"—dailies like the *New York Times* or the *Chicago Tribune*, could usually devote their full time and attention to the top story of the day, polishing their work while leaving the rest of the news to "the wires," which their papers subscribed to.

Also, no matter how well reported or written AP stories were, there was no guarantee they would show up in client newspapers as AP sent them—or even show up at all; local editors could choose what to run and whether to alter AP stories and photo captions. Members could prominently feature AP stories on the front page or bury them deep inside the paper. "Altering" often meant cutting a story after just a few paragraphs, especially at smaller papers with less space for international news. The fabled inverted pyramid model, stacking all the "need to know" information at the very top of a story, was meant in part to ensure that readers would at least get the essence of the news, if not all the details or context that came in later paragraphs.

When AP's coverage of the Nazis did come under considerable scrutiny, in the wake of Harriet Scharnberg's report "The A and P of Propaganda" in 2016, the focus was on the wartime photo exchange with Germany, which was quickly denounced by some as collaboration with the enemy. AP, said one U.S. journalist, had made itself a "part of a pipeline for Nazi propaganda."[15] That was the same conclusion suggested decades earlier by the two postwar military investigators who recommended the United States consider whether AP should be charged with trading with the enemy. Their report disappeared into military files with no explanation: Did government officials reject it as a weak case, set it aside in favor of more pressing postwar issues, or simply bury what would have been explosive charges against a major American media institution? AP's own archives, and Lochner's voluminous papers at the Wisconsin Historical Society, shed no light on the military investigation or the shelving of the damning report. Indeed, the dearth of documentation by anyone at AP may suggest potentially controversial material was cleansed from files at some point.

Lost in the legitimate challenging of AP's role in the exchange is a complicated reality: with rare exceptions, the photos approved for release by German censors were the only images the world could see from German front lines and from inside Nazi-held Europe. (Photos AP sent to Germany during the war had also passed through U.S. censors for approval or rejection.) The Allies may not have liked what was revealed in late 1942 photos of devastation in Stalingrad, or the images from 1944 that showed Hitler had survived a failed assassination attempt. But these and other photos that AP distributed from the German exchange had legitimate news value.

The lack of study of AP's written coverage also has obscured the fact that it was remarkably comprehensive, despite concerted Nazi censorship, and particularly on the crucial story of the fate of Europe's Jews.

Louis Lochner's caution led him to err seriously in March 1933 when he chose not to purchase the explosive photos of beaten, humiliated Jewish lawyer Michael Siegel. But both before and after the Siegel beating, AP was reporting on the growing threat to Jews. Less than a month after the Siegel beating, Lochner's bureau reported that the Nazi boycott of Jewish businesses, the Judenboykott, was "the greatest organized antisemitic movement of modern times," and AP photos from the boycott showed the menacing Brownshirts enforcing it.

Throughout the period, AP offered comprehensive reporting on the major elements of the Nazi campaign to destroy European Jewry: from early Nazi violence against Jews; to the increasingly stringent Nazi laws and policies robbing Jews of property and rights; to the formation of early concentration camps where Jews and other Nazi targets were imprisoned; to the cordoning off of Jewish ghettos and the ever more menacing Nazi calls for eliminating Jews; to the deportation of Jews "eastward" to what turned out to be death camps and the implementation of the Final Solution. Not every newspaper client carried all of AP's reports or carried them in full. But America knew the scope of the Nazi menace, Montclair University professor Ron Hollander argued in 2003, because "the American public itself read in its morning and evening newspapers that the Jews were being wiped out." And depending on the city and the newspaper, much, probably most, of that coverage came from AP.

In hindsight, some of the decisions Lochner and his AP colleagues made decades ago—both in the field and back at New York headquarters—appear deeply flawed. The wartime photo exchange via Büro Laux clearly prioritized business over ethics. AP executives boasted to clients about the steady flow of photos out of Nazi-occupied Germany, without fully disclosing to those clients—and their audiences—how those photos were obtained.

But the day-to-day challenges for journalists in the news bureau were different and likely would seem sadly familiar to those working today under similar restrictions on their ability to do their jobs. How, and how much, should one joust with censorship? What restrictions on reporting are acceptable when traveling with one side or the other in a conflict? How can journalists assess the veracity of atrocity stories, and what sort of evidence is needed to support accusations of war crimes? Those who leave the scene may leave these questions behind. For those who stay, under difficult, dangerous, sometimes life-threatening circumstances, answering them will always be a challenge.

ACKNOWLEDGMENTS

Described here are some of the many people who helped Larry Heinzerling and Randy Herschaft with the original Covering Tyranny report and then later with their several years of continuing research on AP and Nazi Germany. Others helped after Larry's death in August 2021 as Randy and Ann Cooper worked to complete the book. But almost certainly some names are missing, in particular people who helped Larry along the way that we may not be aware of. We apologize for any omissions.

The main protagonists in this book are no longer alive, but several of their family members have generously shared their thoughts, documents, and photographs. We are grateful to Astrid Schulze, daughter of Willy Brandt; Hans Roth and Tuya Roth, son and granddaughter of Franz Roth; Angus, Tina, and Kitty, the children of Angus Thuermer; Jerry Whiteleather, son of Melvin Whiteleather; and Mimi Gosney, daughter of Joe Morton.

Many people at Associated Press gave generously of their expertise, time, and support of the original Covering Tyranny report and this book: John Daniszewski, vice president for standards and editor at large; Jessica Bruce, senior vice president for human resources and corporate communications; Valerie Komor, director of AP

Corporate Archives; Francesca Pitaro, AP archivist; Sarit Hand, digital archivist; Steve Ciaschi and Sean Thompson in AP's New York photo library; Katherine O'Mara and Kathryn Bubien in the AP London photo library; Aaron D. Jackson, photo editor manager; Charles Zoeller, former special projects manager; and AP Berlin correspondents David Rising, Ferdinand Ostrop, and David McHugh. Hal Buell, former head of AP photo services, now retired, shared thoughts. And a huge thank you to former AP German service staffer Frieder Reimold and to Gabriele Faeth-Reimold for invaluable help with translations and interpretations of the research from Germany.

From the academic world, Harriet Scharnberg shared advice, sources, and significant feedback throughout the process of reporting and writing. Joshua Zimmerman, the Eli and Diana Zborowski Professorial Chair in Holocaust Studies and East European Jewish History at Yeshiva University, gave insightful comments on key chapters, and Columbia Journalism School professor Ari Goldman and Columbia professor emeritus Robert Paxton offered helpful feedback on the Holocaust chapter. David Shneer, author of two books on Holocaust photos, gave crucial guidance to the authors. Historians Karel Berkoff and Martin Dean shared expertise on the Babi Yar massacre, and historian Richard Breitman was generous in answering questions and offering insights.

At the National Archives in College Park, Maryland, David Fort, deputy director of the Freedom of Information Act division, was helpful in efforts to declassify records. Greg Bradsher, William Cunliffe, Tab Lewis, Tom McAnear, Amy Reytar, Marqueta Troy, William Wade, and other National Archives staffers were also generous with their time and assistance.

Among those who gave generously of their assistance at other archives and libraries were Lee Grady and the staff at the Wisconsin Historical Society; William Fliss at Marquette University; Judith

Cohen, Raymond Florez, Andy Hollinger, Radu Ionaid, Megan Lewis, Paul Shapiro, Steven Vitto, and the staff at the United States Holocaust Memorial Museum; Emily McKibbon at the MacLaren Art Centre in Ontario, Canada, where part of the Sovfoto archive collection is housed; and Eleanor Yadin at the New York Public Library Dorot Jewish Division. Thanks also to the manuscript division staff at the Library of Congress; the staff of the Wiener Holocaust Library in London; the staff at the Leo Baeck Institute in Manhattan; the staff at the Fair Lawn Jewish Center Library in New Jersey; the staff at the Jewish Historical Institute in Warsaw; and the staff of the Yad Vashem Archives and Library in Jerusalem.

John Felton, Marty Gottron, and Carolyn Lee wielded their expert editors' pens over the entire manuscript. Carol Tannenhauser provided constant moral support and photo research, and Kaela Malig kept the photo files organized. Before she died in 2022, Anne Garrels offered a welcome writer's retreat and soul-boosting encouragement. Among the many others who gave advice and listened patiently to stories over the years were Deb Amos; Benton Arnovitz; Irwin Arieff and Debby Baldwin; Alex Beam; Elizabeth Becker; Allen Breed; Lisa Cohen; Eileen Cope; Susan Cornwell; Dorothea Degen; Francois Duckett; Nina Gafni, Arlene Getz; Ben, Gaby, and Kristen Heinzerling and Tom Minty; Aron Heller; Tami Herschaft; Henry Hemming; Logan Kleinwaks; Scott Kraft; Dru Menaker; Susan Osnos; Menachem Rosensaft; Robert Moses Shapiro; Joel Simon; Alison Smale; Judy Tellerman; and Abi Wright.

Columbia University Press editor Philip Leventhal provided early encouragement that helped push this project forward and then offered many thoughtful reviews as the manuscript progressed. Associate editor Monique Laban at Columbia University Press cheerfully and efficiently helped pull together all materials for the final draft. Susan Pensak and Anita O'Brien ably shepherded the manuscript into production.

Responsibility for any errors rests with the authors and not with the many who assisted in the reporting, writing, and production of the book.

From Ann: Without the encouragement, love, and spiritual support of Artyom and Maryam Keller, this book would never have been finished.

From Randy: I want to thank my wife, Tami, and ninety-nine-year-old dad, Jacques, for their endless love and support. And my mom, Jean, for being my lifelong inspiration, who is looking down from heaven and kvelling.

NOTES

INTRODUCTION

1. Report of the Executive Director, AP Annual Report, 1943, 55, Associated Press Corporate Archives, New York (hereafter APCA).
2. Richard Pyle, "Soldiers of the Press," in *Breaking News: How the Associated Press Has Covered War, Peace and Everything Else* (New York: Princeton Architectural Press, 2007), 219.
3. Lynn Heinzerling, "Hotel Windows Best Points for World-Shaking Events," *Rochester (N.Y.) Democrat and Chronicle*, March 2, 1941, 11.
4. Lynn Heinzerling, "Finns Cite Scandinavia's Lack of Aid," *Altoona (Pa.) Tribune*, March 14, 1940, 1.
5. Lynn Heinzerling, "Rotterdam a City of Ruins—Smoking Debris Forms Headstones for War Dead," *Philadelphia Inquirer*, May 23, 1940, 2.
6. Lynn Heinzerling, "The Heinzerlings: A Remembrance and a New Beginning," *AP World*, no. 1 (1972): 18, APCA.
7. AP Story, "War Writer Wounded," *Cincinnati Enquirer*, December 22, 1943, 3.
8. Lynn Heinzerling, "Allies Bomb Historic Abbey to Rout Nazis," *Huron (S.Dak.) Daily Plainsman*, February 15, 1944, 1.
9. Heinzerling, "The Heinzerlings," 20.
10. Lynn Heinzerling, "Inquiry Shows Nazis Executed A.P. Reporter," *St. Louis Post-Dispatch*, July 9, 1945, 1.
11. Lynn Heinzerling to Agnes Heinzerling, author's personal collection.

12. AP Story, "Gas Fumes Kill AP Writer's Son," *Arizona Republic* (Phoenix), June 21, 1947, 10.
13. Harriet Scharnberg, "The A and P of Propaganda, Associated Press and Nazi Photojournalism," in *Studies in Contemporary History* (Potsdam: Center for Contemporary History, 2016).
14. Larry Heinzerling, "Covering Tyranny: The AP and Nazi Germany: 1933–1945," 2017, AP28, Writings about the Associated Press, APCA, https://www.ap.org/about/history/ap-in-germany-1933-1945/.

1. KRISTALLNACHT

1. "Günter Beukert: Als Bildjournalist in der 'Reichskristallnacht,'" *Die Gleichschaltung der Bilder. Zur Geschichte der Pressefotografie 1930–1936* (Berlin: Frölich & Kaufmann, 1983), 191. In his detailed interview with Diethart Kerbs and Brigitte Walz-Richter, two of the editors of this book, Beukert says four photographers took pictures that night. None is identified on the images AP distributed, but in the AP London photo library the letter J is printed on the back of one photo—the letter AP used on other images to indicate they were taken by Jewish photographer Willy Jacobson. Jacobson is not one of the four photographers Beukert names, and no AP records exist that would show whether there was, in fact, a fifth photographer.
2. *Die Gleichschaltung der Bilder*, 148.
3. *Die Gleichschaltung der Bilder*, 191.
4. *Die Gleichschaltung der Bilder*, 191–93.
5. A sampling of the geographical spread of newspapers using the synagogue photo: "First Photos of Nazi Reign of Terror," *New York Daily Mirror*, November 11, 1938, 1; "Jewish Shop and Synagogue Wrecked by Nazis," *New York Times*, November 11, 1938, 3; "Nazis Loose Wrath on Jews," *Hattiesburg (Miss.) American*, November 12, 1938, 1; "Nazis Wreck Synagogues," *Freeport (Ill.) Journal-Standard*, November 12, 1938, 1; "Nazis Wreck Synagogues," *Bismarck (N.Dak.) Tribune*, November 12, 1938, 1; "Nazis Burn Jewish Synagogue in Reprisal," *New Orleans (La.) Times-Picayune*, November 12, 1938, 4; "Synagogue Fired by Nazis," *Newport News (Va.) Daily Press*, November 12, 1938, 8.
6. A sampling of the geographical spread of the newspapers using the storefront photo: "Wrecked by Nazi Violence," *Allentown (Pa.) Morning Call*, November 12, 1938, 1; "Wrecked by Nazi Violence," *Burlington (Vt.) Free Press*, November 12, 1938, 1; "Wrecked by Nazi Violence," *Newport News*

I. KRISTALLNACHT ⊗ 281

(Va.) Daily Press, November 12, 1938, 8; "Jewish Shop Windows in Berlin Smashed," *Rockford (Ill.) Morning Star*, November 12, 1938, 12.

7. "Brutal Nazi Wrecking Gangs Leave Path of Destruction," *Life*, November 28, 1938, 14–15.
8. AP story, "Nazis 'Justify' Looting, Arson," *Boston Daily Globe*, November 11, 1938, 1.
9. Louis P. Lochner, "Nazi Mobs Burn Synagogs [sic], Loot Stores of Jews," *Decatur (Ill.) Herald*, November 11, 1938, 1.
10. Alan E. Steinweis, *Kristallnacht 1938* (Cambridge, Mass.: Belknap Press of Harvard University Press, 2009), 60. Steinweis notes that many historians and others who write about Kristallnacht refer to it as the "November pogrom" or "Reich pogrom night," because the term *Kristallnacht* emphasizes the vandalism of Jewish property rather than the violence committed against Jewish people.
11. Morrell Heald, ed., *Journalist at the Brink: Louis P. Lochner in Berlin, 1922–1942* (N.p.: Xlibris, 2007), 328.
12. Deborah E. Lipstadt, *Beyond Belief: The American Press & the Coming of the Holocaust 1933–1945* (New York: Free Press, 1986), 99.
13. Daniel Greene and Frank Newport, "American Public Opinion and the Holocaust," *Polling Matters*, April 23, 2018.
14. Jacob Beam, "My Years in Berlin: 1935–1940," manuscript, 1992, 197–98, kindly made available by Alex Beam.
15. Louis Lochner to his children, November 28, 1938, Louis Paul Lochner Papers, Reel/Frame 15/616, Wisconsin Historical Society (hereafter WHS).
16. "What to Do If Your Moustache Falls Off: Fairly True Reports from a CIA Man," memoir, AP21.36, 399–400, Angus M. Thuermer Papers, Box 4, APCA.
17. Lochner to his children, Reel/Frame 15/616, WHS.
18. AP story, "Synagogues Destroyed in New Nazi Attack on Jews," *Massillon (Ohio) Evening Independent*, November 10, 1938, 1, 8.
19. Ernest G. Fischer, "Life Under the Nazis," 1943, chapter 10, 6, Ernest G. Fischer Papers, U.S. Mss 79AF, Box 1, Folder 4, WHS.
20. Time-Life Books, ed., *The Third Reich: The New Order* (Alexandria, Va.: Time-Life, 1989), 60.
21. "GERMANY: Ad Nauseam!," *Time*, December 5, 1938.
22. Wallace R. Deuel, *People Under Hitler* (New York: Harcourt, Brace, 1942), 119.

23. Louis Lochner, "Top for Sketch of Joseph Goebbels," Louis Paul Lochner papers, Reel/Frame 29/881, WHS.
24. Larry Heinzerling, "Covering Tyranny: The AP and Nazi Germany: 1933–1945," 2017, AP28, 63, Writings about the Associated Press, APCA, https://www.ap.org/about/history/ap-in-germany-1933-1945/.
25. Rudolf Herz, *Hoffmann & Hitler, Fotografie als Medium des Führer-Mythos* (Munich: Fotomuseum im Münchner Stadtmuseum, 1994), 54–56.
26. List of Nazi journalists, OSS Report, October 24, 1944, RG 319, Records of the Army Staff, Investigative Repository Records (hereafter IRR). National Archives and Records Administration, College Park, Md. (hereafter NARA). Beukert was included in a U.S. Army list of journalists who were "formerly democratically minded or have for some time expressed democratic ideals in private circles."
27. Heinzerling, "Covering Tyranny," 66.
28. Steinweis, *Kristallnacht 1938*, 3.
29. Figures are from the United States Holocaust Memorial Museum.

2. "IT IS MORE IMPORTANT FOR US TO REMAIN IN THE FIELD"

1. "The Story of Dr. Michael Siegel," *History Unfolded: US Newspapers and the Holocaust* (Washington, D.C.: United States Holocaust Memorial Museum).
2. *AP World* 9, no. 4 (Autumn 1954): 16, APCA. Siegel survived his ordeal and some years later moved to Peru, where he died in 1979.
3. "Heinrich Sanden: Das Foto ist von mir . . . ," in *Die Gleichschaltung der Bilder. Zur Geschichte der Pressefotografie 1930–1936* (Berlin: Frölich & Kaufmann, 1983), 126. Sanden was not identified as the photographer until after the war. According to U.S. Army Investigative Records Repository file 293217 from 1954, Sanden said that after he took the Siegel photos he worked for eight months at the Hoffmann press agency, owned by Hitler's official photographer, which required him to join the Nazi party. He was "denazified" in 1947, according to a personal history statement he made in 1951 when he applied for a German press card. After the war, Sanden worked for AP from at least 1948 to 1964. His son Heinrich Sanden Jr. also worked for AP, from 1954 to 1970.
4. "A Brand of Hitler 'Humane Justice,'" *Washington Times*, March 23, 1933, 1.

2. "IT IS MORE IMPORTANT FOR US TO REMAIN" 283

5. Louis Lochner to Kent Cooper, March 26, 1933, Louis Paul Lochner Papers, General Correspondence, Associated Press, Reel/Frame 1/863, WHS.
6. Joy Schaleben, "Louis P. Lochner: Getting the Story out of Nazi Germany, 1933-1941" (master's thesis, University of Wisconsin, 1967), 70.
7. Louis Lochner, *What About Germany?* (New York: Dodd, Mead, 1942), 238.
8. "Pen Pushing in War-Time," January 24, 1940, Louis Paul Lochner Papers, Reel/Frame 36/257, WHS.
9. Melvin K. Whiteleather, "The Foreign Press: Germany," *Journalism Quarterly* 16, no. 4 (December 1939): 395.
10. Ernest G. Fischer, "Life Under the Nazis," 1943, chapter 10, 43, Ernest G. Fischer Papers, U.S. Mss 79AF, Box 1, Folder 4, WHS.
11. Louis P. Lochner, "Adolf Hitler, Germany's Question Mark?," *Dothan (Ala.) Eagle*, July 28, 1932, 4.
12. AP story, "Paralyzed by Boycott in Germany," *Tacoma (Wash.) Daily Ledger*, April 2, 1933, 1; AP photos, "Eyewitness Describes Hitler's War on Jews," *Brooklyn Eagle*, April 14, 1933, 15.
13. Louis P. Lochner, "Jews Stripped of Citizenship," *Akron (Ohio) Beacon Journal*, September 16, 1935, 13.
14. AP story, "To Open Communist Camp," *Spokane (Wash.) Spokesman-Review*, March 21, 1933, 3; AP photo, "German Dachau Concentration Camp," March 23, 1933, AP Images.
15. Walter Brockman, "Nazi Imprisonment of 18,000 Dissenters Termed Training to Make 'Fit Citizens,'" *Frederick (Md.) Daily News*, May 20, 1933, 3.
16. AP story, "Nazi Vengeance on Jew," *Kansas City Star*, May 13, 1934, 5.
17. Frazier Hunt, "Inside a German Nazis Concentration Camp," *Belleville (Ill.) Daily Advocate*, December 19, 1935, 8.
18. AP story, "Jewish Terror Drive Spreads," *Los Angeles Times*, June 19, 1938, 1.
19. AP story, "Jews to Forfeit Fifth of Fortune to Pay Nazi Fine," *Bergen Evening Record* (Hackensack, N.J.), November 23, 1938, 1.
20. Louis P. Lochner, "Fuehrer Outlines Reich Objectives," *Akron (Ohio) Beacon Journal*, January 31, 1939, 1.
21. Lochner to Cooper, April 24, 1933, Reel/Frame 1/873, WHS. In this letter, which Lochner gave to someone leaving the country in order to avoid censorship, he told Cooper: "A Jewish attorney I know VERY WELL, and who would not lie to me, last night told me that the Jewish attorneys had considered in all seriousness what effect it might have on the German people and

the opinion of the world if SOME 500 UNMARRIED ATTORNEYS SCATTERED THROUGHOUT THE NATION WOULD ON THE SAME DAY COMMIT SUICIDE. A ghastly idea. They finally abandoned it because they felt that the government so absolutely controlled the channels of public opinion, especially radio and press, that the news in its full significance would never come out."

22. Lochner to Cooper, March 26, 1933, WHS.
23. Louis P. Lochner, "Shirt-Sleeve Ambassador," manuscript, 1945, Louis Paul Lochner Papers, Reel/Frame 40/141, WHS. Lochner was president of the Foreign Press Association for six years, from 1928 through 1930 and again from 1934 through 1936.
24. Fischer, "Life Under the Nazis," 42.
25. Dorothy Thompson, *I Saw Hitler!* (New York: Farrar and Rinehart, 1932), 13–14.
26. "Germany: Little Man," *Time*, September 3, 1934.
27. Jacob Beam, "My Years in Berlin: 1935–1940," manuscript, 1992, 347–48, kindly made available by Alex Beam.
28. AP story, "Correspondent and His Wife Leave Nazi Capital," *Appleton (Wis.) Post-Crescent*, November 20, 1939, 9; AP story, "Beach Conger Dies at 56; Reader's Digest Book Editor," *Central New Jersey Home News* (New Brunswick, N.J.), January 7, 1969, 25.
29. Larry Heinzerling, "Covering Tyranny: The AP and Nazi Germany: 1933–1945," 2017, AP28, 15, Writings about the Associated Press, APCA, https://www.ap.org/about/history/ap-in-germany-1933-1945/.
30. AP story, "Editor Describes Rioting in Berlin," *New York Times*, July 17, 1935, 4.
31. Burgomaster of Reinsdorf, "Reinsdorf Burgomaster Tells Story of Explosion," *St. Louis Post-Dispatch*, June 13, 1935, 1.
32. Heinzerling, "Covering Tyranny," 15.
33. The agency's main rivals in the United States were the for-profit United Press (UP), with just under 1,000 American newspaper subscribers, and the International News Service (INS), part of publisher William Randolph Hearst's media empire, which reached 388 U.S. subscribers (many newspapers subscribed to more than one wire service).
34. Jonathan Silberstein-Loeb, *The International Distribution of News: The Associated Press, Press Association, and Reuters, 1848–1947* (New York: Cambridge University Press, 2014), 67.

35. George A. Brandenburg, "E&P Circulation Survey Reveals All-Time High Reached in 1941," *Editor & Publisher*, December 27, 1941, 3.
36. AP promotional ad, "World Pictures with the Speed of Light," *Daily Oklahoman* (Oklahoma City), February 12, 1939, 64.
37. United States v. AP, 52 F. Supp. 362, 1943 U.S. Dist. LEXIS 2156 (D.N.Y. October 6, 1943).
38. AP story, "One-Half of Europe's Jews Slain: Dr. Wise," *Des Moines (Iowa) Register*, November 25, 1942, 1; AP story, "Plan to Kill All Jews Is Revealed," *Huntsville (Ala.) Times*, November 25, 1942, 1; AP story, "2,000,000 Jews Slain Wise Says," *Hartford Courant*, November 25, 1942, 1; AP story, "Wise Says Hitler Has Ordered 4,000,000 Jews Slain in 1942," *New York Herald Tribune*, November 25, 1942, 1; AP story, "2 Million Jews Slain, Rabbi Wise Asserts," *Washington Post*, November 25, 1942, 6; AP story, "Wise Gets Confirmations: Checks with State Department on Nazis' 'Extermination Campaign,'" *New York Times*, November 25, 1942, 10.
39. "Expanded Liberties: A Revived Identity Crisis," in *The League: The Story of the Associated Press and the Evolution of News*, AP28, 206, Writings about the Associated Press, APCA.
40. Kent Cooper to News Editors, Bureau Chiefs, and Correspondents, June 4, 1936, AP02A.03, Subject Files, Box 53, Folder: Circular Letters—General Manager, APCA.
41. Kent Cooper memo to news editors, June 3, 1940, AP01.04B, Records of Board President Robert McLean, Box 19, Folder 257, APCA.
42. Oral history interview with Alan J. Gould conducted by Rene Cappon, ca. 1985–1989, AP 20, Oral History Collection, APCA.
43. Kent Cooper to Robert S. Bates, September 20, 1939, AP01.04B, Records of Board President Robert McLean, Box 19, Folder 255, APCA.

3. THE NEWS BUREAU

1. Wilson Hicks to Louis Lochner, July 7, 1933, Louis Paul Lochner Papers, Reel/Frame 1/874, WHS.
2. Kathryn S. Olmsted, *The Newspaper Axis: Six Press Barons Who Enabled Hitler* (New Haven, Conn.: Yale University Press, 2022), 50–51.
3. Adolf Hitler, "Election Sign of New Peril, Says Hitler," *San Francisco Examiner*, September 28, 1930, K1.

4. Lochner to Hicks, August 5, 1933, Louis Paul Lochner Papers, Reel/Frame 1/875, WHS.
5. Louis Lochner, "Brushing Up Against a Dictator—My Encounters with Hitler," Louis Paul Lochner Papers, Reel/Frame 48/256, WHS.
6. Martha Dodd, *Through Embassy Eyes* (New York: Harcourt Brace, 1939), 112.
7. "Labor News Unit Ends Long Career," *New York Times*, December 11, 1956, 29.
8. Morrell Heald, ed., *Journalist at the Brink: Louis P. Lochner in Berlin, 1922–1942* (N.p.: Xlibris, 2007), 176–77.
9. Heald, 381, 344.
10. Heald, 369.
11. Melvin K Whiteleather, "On the Road from Damascus: A Journalist's Encounters with the Famous and Infamous," undated manuscript, 216, kindly made available by Jerry Whiteleather.
12. Melvin K. Whiteleather, "The Foreign Press: Germany," *Journalism Quarterly* 16, no. 2 (June 1939): 208.
13. Melvin K. Whiteleather, "Nazis Keep Tab on Every Voter," *Charlotte Observer*, March 12, 1939, sec. 3, 6.
14. Alvin J. Steinkopf, "Germans Eat Tho' Others May Starve," *Somerset (Pa.) Daily American*, October 5, 1942, 1.
15. AP story, "Britain Brutal in Ruling Colonies, Nazi Reply to Jew Violence Rap," *San Diego Evening Tribune*, November 15, 1938, 2A.
16. Lynn Heinzerling, "Nazis Propose Jewish Reservations in British Guiana or Madagascar," *La Crosse (Wis.) Tribune*, February 8, 1939, 2.
17. Edwin Shanke, "Another Hitler Sets Self Up," *Muncie (Ind.) Star Press*, March 25, 1938, 9.
18. Angus Thuermer to family, June 14, 1940, AP 21.36, Angus M. Thuermer Papers, Box 2, Folder 18, APCA. Julius Streicher, held accountable for inciting genocide, was convicted of crimes against humanity at Nürnberg and executed.
19. Rudolf Josten, "Bruno's Old Mother Asks F.D.R.'s Mercy," *New York Daily News*, February 15, 1935, 22.
20. AP story, "Nazis in 6 Years Kill Off Over 6,000 Publications," *Baltimore Evening Sun*, July 18, 1939, 2.
21. Robert F. Shildbach, "Berlin: Moribund Press," AP02.01, Records of General Manager Kent Cooper, Box 40, Folder 7B, APCA.

22. Deutsches Nachrichtenbüro Contract, August 31, 1934, AP03.04, Subsidiaries and Related Businesses, Box 3, Folder 45, APCA.
23. Thuermer to family, Box 2, Folder 17, APCA.
24. Lynn Heinzerling, "The Heinzerlings: A Remembrance and a New Beginning," *AP World*, no. 1 (1972): 20, APCA.
25. Edwin Shanke to parents, Edwin A. Shanke Correspondence, March 30, 1939, World War, 1939–1945, Box 1, Folder 1, Marquette University Libraries, Milwaukee, Wis..
26. Heald, *Journalist at the Brink*, 277.
27. Shanke, Correspondence, Box 1, Folder 1.
28. Heald, *Journalist at the Brink*, 14.
29. Heald, 373.

4. THE GMBH

1. Harriet Scharnberg, "The A and P of Propaganda, Associated Press and Nazi Photojournalism," in *Studies in Contemporary History* (Potsdam: Center for Contemporary History, 2016).
2. Kent Cooper, *Kent Cooper and the Associated Press* (New York: Random House, 1959), 8.
3. Reuters dominated the news agency cartel. Under the original nineteenth-century-agreement, it could sell its service in Great Britain, its colonies, and countries within its sphere of influence. Havas had France, Switzerland, Italy, Spain, Portugal, and Central and South America. Wolff had Germany, the Scandinavian countries, Holland, Russia, Austria, Hungary, and the Balkans, and Associated Press had North America.
4. Cooper, *Kent Cooper and the Associated Press*, 140.
5. Louis Lochner, "Berlin: Press Freedom I," December 14, 1937, AP02.01, Records of General Manager Kent Cooper, Box 40, Folder 7B, APCA.
6. Hans Ernst Albert Schmidt-Leonhardt/Peter Gast, *Das Schriftleitergesetz vom 4. Oktober 1933 nebst den einschlägigen Bestimmungen* (Berlin: Carl Heymanns Verlag, 1934), 53.
7. Lochner, "Berlin: Press Freedom I."
8. Louis P. Lochner, *Tycoons and Tyrant: German Industry from Hitler to Adenauer* (Chicago: Regnery, 1954), 215.
9. Lochner to Lloyd Stratton, September 18, 1934, AP03.04, Subsidiaries and Related Businesses, Box 1, Folder 19, APCA.

10. "Arthur von Brietzke: Vor die Linse mußten sie alle ... ," in *Die Gleichschaltung der Bilder. Zur Geschichte der Pressefotografie 1930–1936* (Berlin: Frölich & Kaufmann, 1983), 25.
11. Larry Heinzerling, "Covering Tyranny: The AP and Nazi Germany: 1933–1945," 2017, 54, AP28, Writings about the Associated Press, APCA. https://www.ap.org/about/history/ap-in-germany-1933-1945/.
12. Heinzerling, 55.
13. Sidney A. Freifeld, "Nazi Press Agentry and the American Press," *Public Opinion Quarterly* (Oxford University Press) 6, no. 2 (Summer 1942): 223.
14. Scharnberg, *The A and P of Propaganda*, 26.
15. Heinzerling, "Covering Tyranny," 56–58.
16. AP story, "La Guardia Stirs Hitler," *Los Angeles Times*, March 5, 1937, 3.
17. AP story, "Washington Apologizes: Regrets Sent Germany by State Department Over La Guardia Attack," *Los Angeles Times*, March 6, 1937, 1.
18. Heinzerling, "Covering Tyranny," 60–61.
19. "Covering World News," *Sioux Falls (S.Dak.) Daily Argus-Leader*, May 13, 1941, 6.

5. FIRST THEY CAME FOR THE JEWS

1. Hans Diebow, *Die Juden in USA* (Berlin: Zentralverlag der NSDAP, Franz Eher Nachf., 1939).
2. "The Jews Must Work," *Illustrierter Beobachter*, October 12, 1939, 1546.
3. Larry Heinzerling, "Covering Tyranny: The AP and Nazi Germany: 1933–1945," 2017, 4, AP28, Writings about the Associated Press, APCA. https://www.ap.org/about/history/ap-in-germany-1933-1945/.
4. Louis P. Lochner, *Tycoons and Tyrant: German Industry from Hitler to Adenauer*, (Chicago: Regnery, 1954), 215.
5. Lochner to daughter Betty, April 30, 1933, Louis Paul Lochner Papers, Reel/Frame 15/255, WHS.
6. Lochner to daughter Betty, September 21, 1933, WHS.
7. Raymond Geist to Cordell Hull, February 27, 1934, "Intervention of the Consulate General on behalf of the Associated Press G.m.b.H., Berlin," Record Group 59, Department of State, Central Decimal File: 362.1154/25, NARA.
8. "Wir zerschlagen eine Lüge" (We are smashing a lie), *Das Schwarze Korps*, August 24, 1935, 7.

9. Stanley Thompson to Lloyd Stratton, August 26, 1935, APo2A.o1, Bureau/Member Correspondence, Box 16, Folder: Berlin, APCA.
10. Heinzerling, "Covering Tyranny," 50.
11. "Wir Zerschlagen eine Lüge," *Das Schwarze Korps*, 10.
12. "German Father-Son Writing Team Sees Shore Friends on U.S. Tour," *Asbury Park (N.J.) Press*, August 22, 1955, 3.
13. Harriet Scharnberg, "The A and P of Propaganda, Associated Press and Nazi Photojournalism," in *Studies in Contemporary History* (Potsdam: Center for Contemporary History, 2016), 26.
14. Lochner, *Tycoons and Tyrant*, 91.
15. The PIX photo agency survived until 1969, when Daniel retired. Eisenstaedt won fame in the postwar years as a *Life* magazine photographer; his most iconic image captured an exuberant sailor kissing a nurse in Times Square, as they celebrated Victory over Japan Day in 1945. About two hundred of the photos he took for AP can be found on AP's online photo platform.
16. Lochner, *Tycoons and Tyrant*, 216.
17. Pacific & Atlantic Photos, the mother company owned by *New York Daily News* and *Chicago Tribune*, was sold the previous year to Scripps-Howard's Acme News Pictures.
18. Lochner to Kent Cooper, August 12, 1935, Louis Paul Lochner Papers, General Correspondence, Associated Press, Reel/Frame 1/915-917, WHS.
19. Willy Jacobson, "Als Bildreporter nur 'Nummern' waren," *Neue Deutsche Presse* 11, no. 13 (East) Berlin (1957): 37.
20. Alvin J. Steinkopf, "Million Thunder Welcome to Der Fuehrer at Vienna," *Atlanta Constitution*, March 15, 1938, 1.
21. Oliver Gramling, *AP—The Story of News* (New York: Farrar and Rinehart, 1940), 460.
22. Melvin K. Whiteleather, "Vienna Jews Flee from Nazi Terror," *Hackensack (N.J.) Record*, March 14, 1938, 1.
23. AP story, "Nazis in Vienna Hold 3 Newspaper Men," *New York Times*, March 17, 1938, 8.
24. Heinzerling, "Covering Tyranny," 51
25. Louis Paul Lochner Papers, Box-MCHC70-083, Folder-Lochner, circa 1945, WHS.
26. Bundesarchiv, Bild 183-2005-0721-521 - Allgemeiner Deutscher Nachrichtendienst (ADN), Berlin, 1945.

27. Louis Matzhold to Alvin Steinkopf, December 14, 1948, Alvin Steinkopf Papers, Box 1, Folder 52, WHS.
28. Matzhold to Steinkopf, March 23, 1950, WHS.
29. Email to AP Berlin bureau, August 2, 2016, from Britta Pawelke, Museologischer Dienst/Fotohek, Mahn-und Gedenkstätte Ravensbrück/Stiftung Brandenburgische Gedenkstätten, http://www.ravensbreuck.de; Willy Jacobson photos, German Historical Museum Foundation, Berlin.
30. Jacobson, "Als Bildreporter nur 'Nummern' waren," 34.
31. Scharnberg, "The A and P of Propaganda," 24–25.
32. Laurel Leff, *Buried by the Times: The Holocaust and America's Most Important Newspaper* (New York: Cambridge University Press, 2005), 54.
33. Bert Garai, *The Man from Keystone* (New York: Living Books, 1966), 177. In his book, Garai says the sale took place in 1937, but Scharnberg, "The A and P of Propaganda," n. 77, citing multiple German sources, puts the date as April 1935.
34. Willy Brandt, "Confession," 1945, manuscript written in German, trans. Steve Miller, March 10, 2001, 2, AP21.08, Willy Brandt Papers, APCA.
35. Vetting of Willy Erwin Hermann Brandt, Information Services Control Section, Office of Military Government (Berlin), January 18, 1946, AP21.08, Willy Brandt Papers, Box 1, Folder 2, APCA.
36. Astrid Schulze email to Larry Heinzerling, November 22, 2019, regarding her father's background.
37. Willy Brandt to Meyer, March 1946, Louis Paul Lochner Papers, Reel/Frame 3/913, WHS.
38. Vetting of Willy Erwin Hermann Brandt, January 18, 1946.
39. Gideon Seymour to Lloyd Stratton, March 1, 1937, AP21.08, Willy Brandt Papers, Box 1, Folder 2, APCA.
40. Memo to Lloyd Stratton from "sjm," October 17, 1950, AP21.08, Willy Brandt Papers, Box 1, Folder 2, APCA.
41. Cooper to Lochner, December 13, 1938, AP01.04B, Records of Board President Robert McLean, Box 34, Folder 654, APCA.
42. Heinzerling, "Covering Tyranny," 67.
43. Minutes of a Meeting of a Committee of Directors of the Associated Press of Great Britain on August 23, 1939, AP01.04B, Records of Board President Robert McLean, Box 34, Folder 655, APCA.
44. Lochner to Wes Gallagher, February 26, 1946, Louis Paul Lochner Papers, Box 1, Folder 23, WHS.

45. Memorandum of the AP GmbH's evolution from 1931 by Willy Brandt, February 18, 1946, kindly made available by Astrid Schulze.
46. Alien Personal History Statement, October 26, 1951; Waffen SS Personal History Statement, Life History (Lebenslauf), November 14, 1944, RG 319, IRR Baatz, Gerhard, XE 308711, NARA.

6. POLAND

1. Lynn Heinzerling, "Witness Tells How War Started in Danzig Before Hitler's 'Order,'" *Philadelphia Inquirer*, September 9, 1939, 2.
2. Lynn Heinzerling, "The World Goes to War at 4 a.m.," in *Reporting to Remember: Unforgettable Stories and Pictures of World War II by Correspondents of the Associated Press* (New York: Associated Press, 1945), 11.
3. "Fourth Estate: Censorship and Muddling Continue to Harry U.S. Press in Coverage of the War," *Newsweek*, September 18, 1939, 36.
4. Lynn Heinzerling, "Danzig Isolated by Nazi Forces," *Allentown (Pa.) Morning Call*, September 7, 1939, 1.
5. Louis P. Lochner, "Danzig Crisis Nearing Head," *Sioux City (Iowa) Journal*, August 19, 1939, 11.
6. Angus Thuermer to his parents, August 15, 1939, AP21.36, Angus M. Thuermer Papers, Box 2, Folder 17c, APCA.
7. "World Stumbles Toward War and AP Prepares," in *History of AP from World War II to Ronald Reagan*, 6, AP28, Writings about the Associated Press, Box 7, Folder 41, APCA.
8. Introduction of the Heilschreiber teleprinter in the bureau in 1937 marked a vast improvement over receiving carbon copies of DNB stories delivered hourly by messenger.
9. AP wire copy from Berlin bureau in September 1939 compiled by Edwin Shanke. Shanke, Edwin A. Correspondence, World War, Box 1, Folder 1, Department of Special Citations and University Archives, Marquette University Libraries, Milwaukee, Wis.
10. AP photo, "As Hitler Gave Fateful Word," *Chattanooga (Tenn.) Times*, September 2, 1939, 6.
11. AP story, "Hitler, Donning Uniform, Names Goering as His Heir," *Bergen Evening Record* (Hackensack, NJ), September 1, 1939, 1.
12. Lloyd Lehrbas, "Reporter Sees German Planes Bomb Capital," *Chippewa Falls (Wis.) Herald-Telegram*, September 1, 1939, 1.

13. Robert St. John, *Foreign Correspondent* (Garden City, N.Y.: Doubleday, 1957), 26.
14. Lehrbas later served as an aide to General Douglas MacArthur during World War II.
15. Alvin Steinkopf Papers, Box 2, Folder 12, Writings: Poland, 1940, WHS.
16. Max Hill, a chapter from the book *Writing Up the News* (New York: Dodd-Mead, 1939), as published in AP Circular no. 4, AP34.03, Box 1, Folder 1, APCA.
17. Elmer W. Peterson, "'Lightning War' Batters Poland," *Glenn Falls (N.Y) Post-Star*, September 14, 1939, 1.
18. The Black Madonna is a painting of the Blessed Virgin Mary and Child on wood adorned with precious jewels, housed in the Jasna Góra Monastery in Częstochowa since the 1380s.
19. UP story, "Shrine Bombs Draw Protest," *Rochester (N.Y.) Democrat and Chronicle*, September 5, 1939, 3.
20. Louis Lochner, "The First Big Lie of the Second World War," in *I Can Tell It Now* (New York: Dutton, 1964), 17.
21. Lochner, 18–19.
22. Louis P. Lochner, "Civilian Snipers Plague Nazis in Poland; American Reporter Describes Tour of German Front," *St. Louis Post-Dispatch*, September 6, 1939, 5.
23. AP photo, "Czestochowa, Poland," *Baltimore Sun*, September 6, 1939, 3.
24. Lochner, "The First Big Lie of the Second World War," 24.
25. Louis P. Lochner, *What About Germany?* (New York: Dodd, Mead, 1942), 123.
26. "Diverse Censorship," *Richmond (Va.) News-Leader*, September 13, 1939, 12.
27. Douglas Freeman to Frank Fuller, September 14, 1939, AP02A.03, Subject Files, Box 58, Folder: European War Coverage, APCA.
28. AP photo, "Smoke—After Smoke of Battle," *Boston Globe*, September 6, 1939, 14.
29. Nawench Morawski to Byron Price, September 6, 1939, AP02A.03, Subject Files, Box 58, Polish Agency Telegraphic, APCA.
30. Price to Morawski, September 8, 1939, AP02A.03, Subject Files, Box 58, Folder: Polish Agency Telegraphic, APCA.
31. Melvin K. Whiteleather, "Diary of a Berlin Correspondent: Intimate Glimpses Behind the Scenes While War Was Coming to Europe," *Scranton (Pa.) Times*, September 9, 1940. Whiteleather left Germany and AP in

1940. His diary from his last months in the country was distributed by the North American Newspaper Alliance.
32. "Calling All Chumps," *Miami Herald*, September 7, 1939, 4.
33. Cooper to News Editor Michelson (Kansas City), September 29, 1939, AP 02A.01, Bureau/Member Correspondence, Box 29, Folder: Foreign General, APCA.
34. AP story, "Today's Rumor Deflator," *Richmond (Va.) Times Dispatch*, August 7, 1941, 2.
35. Charles Honce to New York State Publishers Association, September 8, 1941, AP 28, Writings about the Associated Press, Box 19, APCA.
36. AP photos, "German Air Bombers Leave Warsaw Mass of Ruins," *Tampa (Fla.) Sunday Tribune*, September 17, 1939, 10.
37. AP story, "Tells Warsaw War Horrors," *Des Moines (Iowa) Register*, October 8, 1939, 23.
38. AP photo, "Bewildered Boy Returns to What Used to Be Home," *Wasau (Wis.) Daily Herald*, October 9, 1939, 5; AP photo, "War: Sister Mourns Sister," *Salem (Ore.) Capital Journal*, October 9, 1939, 8; "Tells Warsaw War Horrors," *Des Moines Register*, 23.
39. Daniel De Luce, "Lwow, Poland's 'Life Line' to Supplies, Is Fired by Nazi Bombs," *Madison (Wis.) Capital Times*, September 14, 1939, 1.
40. Louis P. Lochner, "2,000 Polish Troops Hold Out Near Gdynia 'Waiting for the British To Arrive,'" *St. Louis Post-Dispatch*, September 19, 1939, 4.
41. Melvin K. Whiteleather, "Newsman Sees Warsaw in Ruins as Bedraggled Poles March Out," *Atlanta Constitution*, October 1, 1939, 15.
42. Melvin K. Whiteleather, "Russians Follow Troops with Red Reading Matter," *Freeport (Ill.) Journal-Standard*, October 3, 1939, 12.
43. Melvin K. Whiteleather, "War Machinery Bogs Down in Red Invasion of Poland," *Atlanta Constitution*, October 2, 1939, 10.
44. "What to Do If Your Moustache Falls Off: Fairly True Reports from a CIA Man," memoir, AP21.36, 400, Angus M. Thuermer Papers, Box 4, APCA.
45. Louis P. Lochner, "Hitler Celebrates Warsaw Triumph," *Billings (Mont.) Gazette*, October 6, 1939, 1.
46. Louis P. Lochner, "Hitler States Peace Terms, London Cool, Paris Scornful," *Baltimore Evening Sun*, October 6, 1939, 1.
47. Louis P. Lochner, "Lochner Finds War Along Rhine Is Languid Affair," *Montgomery (Ala.) Advertiser*, September 29, 1939, 1.

48. Melvin K. Whiteleather, "The Foreign Press—Germany," *Journalism Quarterly* 16, no. 4 (December 1939): 397.
49. In addition, the Nazis maintained 30,000 slave labor camps, 1,000 prisoner of war camps, 980 concentration camps, 500 brothels filled with sex slaves, and thousands of other transit and other types of camps, according to the United States Holocaust Memorial Museum.
50. Lochner joined a short, escorted tour restricted to Krakow in April, concluding "that the Germans have come to stay—barring defeat," but he left the group early and returned to Berlin, he told his children, "because the chief of the government press office [Otto Dietrich, Hitler's personal press chief] . . . had arranged a sumptuous dinner for the American correspondents, members of the Embassy and Consulate staffs, and the secretary of the American Chamber of Commerce." See Morrell Heald, ed., *Journalist at the Brink: Louis P. Lochner in Berlin, 1922–1942* (N.p.: Xlibris, 2007), 424.
51. Alvin J. Steinkopf, "Warsaw—A Year Later," *Des Moines (Iowa) Register*, October 13, 1940, 1.
52. Alvin J. Steinkopf, "Writer Finds Warsaw Remains in Ruins Left by German Bombers," *Louisville (Ky.) Courier-Journal*, October 13, 1940, 4.
53. AP story, "Nazis Wall Off 500,000 Jews in Pole Capital," *Washington Post*, November 26, 1940, 7.
54. AP photos, "In Poland Under the Nazis," *St. Louis Post-Dispatch*, January 2, 1941, 23.
55. AP photo, "A Wall in Warsaw Built by Hitler," *New York Times*, January 3, 1941, 3.
56. AP photos, "The Clock Is Turned Back for the Jews of Poland," *Minneapolis Star*, January 2, 1941, 30.
57. Lloyd Stratton to Wilson Hicks, February 13, 1941, AP01.4B, Records of Board President Robert McLean, Box 32, Folder 332, APCA.

7. BLITZKRIEG

1. Louis P. Lochner, "Nazi Legions Thunder Forth to Decide Fate of Nation," *Boston Daily Globe*, May 11, 1940, 3.
2. Louis P. Lochner, "Lochner Reviews Dramatic Turns in European War," *Ironwood (Mich.) Daily Globe*, June 5, 1942, 1.
3. Andrew Roberts, *Churchill: Walking with Destiny* (New York: Viking, 2018), 486.

4. Louis P. Lochner, "Attack Blamed on Allies' Aims," *Bergen Evening Record* (Hackensack, N.J.), April 9, 1940, 1.
5. AP story, "Three AP Men Go to Europe," *Charlotte (N.C.) News*, March 2, 1940, 12.
6. Lynn Heinzerling, "War Swoops Down," *Baltimore Sun*, March 2, 1941, 11.
7. AP story, "Newsmen Describe German Occupation of Denmark by Hitler's Swift Moving Army," *Kokomo (Ind.) Tribune*, April 10, 1940, 1.
8. AP photo, "German Troops on Danish Soil," *Cincinnati Enquirer*, April 12, 1940, 2.
9. Louis P. Lochner, "Nazi General Tells How Denmark Fell," *Des Moines (Iowa) Register*, April 12, 1940, 4.
10. Pierre J. Huss, "Seizure of Danish Told by INS Man," *Santa Rosa (Calif.) Republican*, April 11, 1940, 1; Louis P. Lochner, "Nazi General Tells How Denmark Fell."
11. Frederick Oechsner, "Denmark Calm Under Nazi Rule," *Orlando (Fla.) Evening Star*, April 11, 1940, 15.
12. AP photo, "No More War for Them," *Hazleton (Pa.) Plain Speaker*, May 1, 1940, 1.
13. Wes Gallagher, "Organized Norwegian Resistance Collapses; Armistice Being Asked," *Sault Sainte Marie (Mich.) Evening News*, May 4, 1940, 1.
14. AP photo, "Writer Visits Front," *San Pedro (Calif.) News-Pilot*, June 8, 1940, 1.
15. Louis P. Lochner, "Lochner Describes Methods Used by German Air Force," *Casper (Wyo.) Star-Tribune*, May 20, 1940, 3.
16. Louis P. Lochner, "Speedy German Drive Leaves Path of Horror," *Los Angeles Times*, May 21, 1940, 1.
17. Louis P. Lochner, "German Forces' Main Objective Invasion of England," *Patterson (N.J.) News*, May 21, 1940, 12.
18. Louis P. Lochner, "Nazis Reach Channel," *Baltimore Sun*, May 23, 1940, 1.
19. Louis P. Lochner, "'Cocksure' Nazis Reveal Attack Plan," *Boston Globe*, May 27, 1940, 3.
20. Sidney A. Freifeld, "Nazi Press Agentry and the American Press," *Public Opinion Quarterly* (Oxford University Press) 6, no. 2 (Summer 1942): 223.
21. Louis P. Lochner, "Virtually No Opposition in Air Offered by Allies," *Huntsville (Ala.) Times*, May 26, 1940, 2.
22. Louis P. Lochner, "Nazi Attack Complete Surprise to the French," *Minneapolis Star*, May 31, 1940, 24.

23. AP story, "French Down 17 of Paris Raiders," *Cincinnati Enquirer*, June 4, 1940, 1.
24. Louis P. Lochner, "French Fight on as They Await 'Peace of Honor,'" *New York Daily News*, June 18, 1940, 55.
25. Louis P. Lochner, "Finds Paris 'Ghost City,'" *Des Moines (Iowa) Sunday Register*, June 16, 1940, 1.
26. Louis P. Lochner, "Lochner Finds Nazi-Held Paris Already Resuming Normal Life," *Minneapolis Morning Tribune*, June 18, 1940, 3.
27. AP photo, "Correspondents Walk in Conquered Paris," *Pottsville (Pa.) Republican*, July 3, 1940, 6.
28. William Shirer, *Berlin Diary* (New York: Popular Library, 1961), 310.
29. Taylor Henry, "Lack of Enthusiasm Aided French Defeat," *Boston Globe*, July 2, 1940, 3.
30. Henry C. Cassidy, "Nazi Troops Get Welcome of Conquerors," *Richmond Times-Dispatch*, July 24, 1940, 2.
31. Henry Cassidy, "France Set Back to 19th Century," *Minneapolis Star*, August 25, 1940, 4.
32. Louis P. Lochner, "Nazis Strew Flowers in Chief's Path," *Rochester (N.Y.) Democrat and Chronicle*, July 7, 1940, 1.
33. Louis P. Lochner, "Hitler's Drama Held Sway at Compiegne," *St. Louis Globe-Democrat*, July 14, 1940, 10.
34. Lynn Heinzerling, "Nazi Mosquito Fleet Floating Torpedo Tubes," *Port Huron (Mich.) Times Herald*, June 8, 1940, 2; Edwin Shanke, "German Parachute Troops Are Daring, Trained in Secret," *Oshkosh (Wis.) Daily Northwestern*, May 16, 1940, 5.
35. Lynn Heinzerling, "Rotterdam a City of Ruins—Smoking Debris Forms Headstones for War Dead," *Philadelphia Inquirer*, May 23, 1940, 2.
36. Louis P. Lochner, "War Drives Refugees on Never-Ending Trek," *Los Angeles Times*, June 6, 1940, 4.
37. Louis P. Lochner, "Nazi General Tells of 'Stern Battle' at Ghent; 'Enemies Resist Bravely, but Odds Are Greatly in Our Favor,'" *St. Louis Post-Dispatch*, May 24, 1940, 4.

8. LOCHNER UNDER FIRE

1. Minutes of fall meeting of the Chesapeake Association of the Associated Press, September 14, 1940, AP02A.01, Bureau/Member Correspondence, Box 33, Folder: Maryland Meeting, APCA.

2. Associated Press, Forty-First Annual Volume, Fiscal Year of 1940, 35–36, AP01.01, Records of the AP Board of Directors, APCA.
3. Larry Heinzerling, "Covering Tyranny: The AP and Nazi Germany: 1933–1945," 2017, 38, AP28, Writings about the Associated Press, APCA, https://www.ap.org/about/history/ap-in-germany-1933-1945/
4. "American News Sources in Nazi Germany," report of the Committee for National Morale, attachment to Arthur Upham Pope's March 12, 1941, letter to Harold Ickes, Harold Ickes Papers, Manuscript Division, Box 379, National Morale Committee 1940–1943, Library of Congress (hereafter LOC).
5. AP story, "Excerpts from the Official Translation of Hitler's Speech Before the Reichstag," *New York Times*, January 31, 1939, 6.
6. AP story, "Ickes Assails Ford, Lindy on Hitler Medals," *Wilmington (Del.) News Journal*, December 19, 1938, 13.
7. "American News Sources in Nazi Germany," LOC.
8. "American News Sources in Nazi Germany."
9. Heinzerling, "Covering Tyranny," 36.
10. "American News Sources in Nazi Germany."
11. "American News Sources in Nazi Germany."
12. Heinzerling, "Covering Tyranny," 37.
13. Associated Press, Forty-Second Annual Volume for the Fiscal Year of 1941, 17, AP01.01, Records of the AP Board of Directors, APCA.
14. Louis P. Lochner, "Lochner Discusses Loyalty of Goering to Hitler," *Salt Lake (Utah) Telegram*, June 6, 1942, 5.
15. Harold Ickes to Alfred Bergman, June 9, 1942, Harold Ickes Papers, Manuscript Division, Box 379, Folder 13, War-Bergman 1942–1943, LOC.
16. Joseph C. Harsch, *At the Hinge of History, a Reporter's Story* (Athens: University of Georgia Press, 2010), 47.
17. Lynn Heinzerling to John Hightower, October 23, 1973, AP21.54, Lynn Heinzerling Papers, Box 7, Folder: 1973, APCA.
18. William Shirer, *Berlin Diary* (New York: Popular Library, 1961), 35.
19. Note from Mrs. Roosevelt to President Roosevelt, June 11, 1940, accompanying *Christian Science Monitor* May 8 letter, FDR Presidential Library and Museum Digitized Collections.
20. Harsch, *At the Hinge of History*, 45.
21. Joseph C. Harsch, *Pattern of Conquest* (Garden City, N.Y.: Doubleday, Doran, 1941), 278.
22. Richard M. Harnett and Billy G. Ferguson, *UNIPRESS: United Press International- Covering the 20th Century* (Golden, Colo.: Fulcrum, 2003), xv.

23. Louis P. Lochner, "Berlin Reports 'Danger of World War Has Been Definitely Averted,'" *Minneapolis Star Tribune*, August 26, 1939, 1.
24. Mrs. Roosevelt to President Roosevelt, June 11, 1940, FDR library.
25. Louis Lochner, *Always the Unexpected* (New York: Macmillan, 1956), 252.
26. Minutes of fall meeting of the Chesapeake Association of the Associated Press, APCA.
27. Louis Lochner, "Shirtsleeve Ambassador," manuscript, circa 1945, Louis Paul Lochner Papers, Reel/Frame 40-214, WHS.
28. Louis P. Lochner, "Communications and the Mass-Produced Mind," *Wisconsin Magazine of History* 41, no. 4 (Summer 1958): 244–51.
29. Louis P. Lochner, "Inside Germany," in *Vital Speeches of the Day*, August 15, 1942, 652, Institute of Public Affairs, University of Virginia, Charlottesville.
30. Louis Lochner, *What About Germany?* (New York: Dodd, Mead, 1942), 2.
31. Testimony of Louis P. Lochner, taken by Colonel John H. Amen, IGD, July 25, 1945, RG238, Interrogation Records Prepared for War Crimes Proceedings at Nuremberg, NARA.
32. Klemens von Klemperer, *The German Resistance Against Hitler; The Search for Allies Abroad, 1938–1945* (Oxford: Clarendon Press, 1994), 133.
33. Emmy C. Rado to John P. O'Keeffe, Memorandum Re Mr. Louis P. Lochner, June 6, 1942, OSS IntraOffice Correspondence, 17, Central Intelligence Agency FOIA Electronic Reading Room.
34. Louis Lochner, "The Myth of the Prussian Generals' Revolt," manuscript, Louis Paul Lochner Papers, Reel/Frame 36/354. WHS.

9. PHOTO BLITZ

1. AP photo, "Smoke of Nazi War Sweeps Over Peaceful Holland, *Cincinnati Enquirer*, May 11, 1940, 8; AP photo, "British Ramble Into Belgium Again," *Tampa (Fla.) Tribune*, May 12, 1940, 11; AP photo, "Wirephoto: French Guns Slow Up German Drive," *Spokane (Wash.) Chronicle*, May 20, 1940, 2.
2. AP photo, "Wirephoto: Picture Sent from Paris Today Shows Last of Soldiers Ready to Leave Dunkerque," *Spokane Chronicle*, June 5, 1940, 1.
3. AP photo, "Evacuation," *Springfield (Mo.) Leader and Press*, June 5, 1940, 1; AP photo, "Misfortunes of War," *St. Johnsbury (Vt.) Caledonian Record*, June 5, 1940, 12.
4. AP photo, "Smoke of Nazi War Sweeps Over Peaceful Holland."

5. AP story, "A.P. Wirephotos Score Beat in Dutch Attack," *Spokane (Wash.) Spokesman-Review*, May 11, 1940, 12.
6. AP photo, "U-Boat Raids from French Port," *Louisville (Ky.) Courier-Journal*, August 13, 1940, 2; AP photo, "Hitler's Legions Before Arc de Triomphe," *Spokane Chronicle*, June 18, 1940, 1.
7. AP story, "Soldiers, Not Civilians, Report War Progress from U-Boats and Planes to German Papers," *Central New Jersey Home News* (New Brunswick, N.J.), March 23, 1940, 3.
8. Phillip Knightley, *The First Casualty* (Baltimore: Johns Hopkins University Press, 2004), 241.
9. Eric Borchert, *Entscheidende Stunden. Mit der Kamera am Feind* (Decisive hours: With the camera on the enemy) (Berlin: Wilhelm Limpert, 1941), 5.
10. Waffen SS Personal History Statement, Life History (Lebenslauf), November 14, 1944, RG 319, IRR Baatz, Gerald, XE 308711, NARA.
11. "Arthur von Brietzke: 'Vor die Linse Mußten sie alle . . . ,'" in *Die Gleichschaltung der Bilder. Zur Geschichte der Pressefotografie 1930–1936* (Berlin: Frölich & Kaufmann, 1983), 30.
12. AP story, "Borchert, German Photographer, Killed," *Des Moines Register*, October 19, 1941, 8.
13. Ernest G. Fischer, "Life Under the Nazis," 1943, chapter 10, 8, Ernest G. Fischer Papers, U.S. Mss 79AF, Box 1, Folder 4, WHS.
14. AP photo, "Hitler Walks Along the Vistula," *Miami News*, September 9, 1939, 12; AP photo, "Hitler Watches Troops on Polish Front," *Oakland Tribune*, September 6, 1939, 6; AP photo, "Latest Scene of War Caught by Cameras Across the World," *Oakland Tribune*, September 12, 1939, 10.
15. AP story, "Wirephoto First to Give Pictures from Warfront," *Chicago Tribune*, September 2, 1939, 2.
16. AP photo, "First Pictures of Fighting Brought by Radio and Wirephoto—Germans Claim Capture of Polish Stronghold," *Chicago Tribune*, September 2, 1939, 28; AP photo, "First War 'Action' Picture . . . Others Page 4," *Rochester (N.Y.) Democrat and Chronicle*, September 2, 1939, 1.
17. AP photo, "German Subs off American Coast," *Miami News*, June 29, 1942, 1; AP photo, "Nazis Say These Are Allied Prisoners," *Deadwood (S.Dak.) Pioneer-Times*, January 13, 1943, 1.
18. International News radiophoto, "Somewhere in Poland," *Dayton (Ohio) Herald*, September 5, 1939, 10; Central Press photo, "Poles Prepare for German Advance," *Richmond (Ind.) Palladium-Item*, September 4, 1939, 1.

19. Al Resch to New York Desk Editors, December 12, 1940, AP02A.03, Subject Files, Box 54, Folder: Newsphoto/Wirephoto, APCA.
20. Cyril Radcliffe, "Photographs as News," PRO INF/1/908/, July 1941, National Archives, UK.
21. Harriet Scharnberg, "The A and P of Propaganda, Associated Press and Nazi Photojournalism," in *Studies in Contemporary History* (Potsdam: Center for Contemporary History, 2016), 11.
22. WWII: EUROPE, Poland, People, Jewish Ghetto, E2297, AP New York Photo Library.
23. Poland, People, Jewish Ghetto, AP New York Photo Library.
24. AP photo (negative), "Nazis Recreated the Ghettos in Poland," negative envelope 234434, AP London Photo Library.
25. Resch memo to desk editors, APCA.
26. Poland, People, Jewish Ghetto.
27. Lloyd Stratton to Louis Lochner and Willy Brandt, September 9, 1940, AP02A.03, Subject Files, Box 48, Folder 402, APCA.
28. Copy of contract dated October 26, 1940, signed by Willy Brandt and Franz Roth, kindly provided by the Roth family.
29. Contract of October 26, 1940, Roth family.
30. Report of the General Manager to the Board of Directors, December 31, 1940, 58, Associated Press, Forty-First Annual Volume for the Fiscal Year 1940, AP01.01, Records of the AP Board of Directors, APCA.

10. THE NAZI PHOTOGRAPHER

1. From 1937 to 1939 the AP GmbH also employed as a photo salesman Rolf d'Alquen, a friend of Roth's (according to his granddaughter) and a Nazi Party member since 1931. D'Alquen later joined the Waffen-SS and led an SS war correspondent company headed by his brother, Guenther d'Alquen, editor of the SS publication *Das Schwarze Korps*. Paul Gandell, CIC Screening Staff to Assistant Chief of Staff, G-2 Headquarters, Subject: Internee D'Alquen, Rolf, September 19, 1946, RG 319, IRR, DW47022, D013541, XE013541, NARA.
2. Adrian Gilbert, *Waffen-SS: Hitler's Army at War* (New York: Da Capo Press, 2019), ix.
3. Harriet Scharnberg, "The A and P of Propaganda, Associated Press and Nazi Photojournalism," in *Studies in Contemporary History* (Potsdam: Center for Contemporary History, 2016), 20.

4. Letter from Harald Hall, former AP Vienna bureau news photo editor, March 28, 1936, kindly provided by the Roth family. Hall stated that Roth worked for AP News Photo Service from September 1934 to May 1935, when he left to go to Abyssinia.
5. Franz Roth, Lebenslauf [Anlage zum SS-Aufnahme- und Verpflichtungsschein], 25.9.1942, Bundesarchiv, SSO Franz Roth.
6. Stanley G. Thompson letter of April 29, 1935, kindly provided by the Roth family.
7. AP photo, "Ruins Left After Italian Planes Bombed Ethiopian City," *Minneapolis Tribune*, December 30, 1935, 1.
8. James A. Mills, "55 Slain, 300 Wounded by Italian Air Raiders," *North Adams (Mass.) Transcript*, December 7, 1935, 1.
9. Franz Roth, "Reporter," manuscript, circa 1942, kindly provided by Roth's granddaughter Tuya Roth.
10. AP story, "James A. Mills, A.P. Man, Dies," *Fort Worth Star-Telegram*, March 28, 1942, 13.
11. Roth, "Reporter."
12. James A. Mills, diary, Book No. 20, Abyssinia (1935), kindly provided by Jerry Whiteleather.
13. Larry Heinzerling, "Covering Tyranny: The AP and Nazi Germany: 1933–1945," 2017, 146, n. 155, AP28, Writings about the Associated Press, APCA, https://www.ap.org/about/history/ap-in-germany-1933-1945/.
14. Copies of press passes kindly provided by the Roth family.
15. Heinzerling, "Covering Tyranny," 73.
16. Lloyd Stratton to W. F. Brooks, May 17, 1938, AP01.04B, Records of Board President Robert McLean, Box 34 Folder 655, APCA.
17. Stratton to Brooks, July 21, 1938, APCA.
18. Copy of affidavit by Wilhelm Brandt, believed written on behalf of Roth's widow for tax purposes, kindly provided by the Roth family.
19. "SA–Mann—Journalist—Soldat!" *Illustrierter Beobachter*, May 6, 1943, 4.
20. SS Officer Personnel Files, Microfilm Publication A3343, Series SSO, Franz, Roth, D.O.B. 5.4.11, roll # 049B frames 126-149, NARA. Roth's party number was 6123241.
21. Oberkommando der Wehrmacht Press Pass no. 242, dated October 2, 1938, kindly provided by the Roth family.
22. Letter from the Reich Ministry for Public Enlightenment and Propaganda, April 10, 1940, kindly provided by the Roth family.
23. AP photo, "German Bombers Show Berlin What War Would Mean," *Baltimore Evening Sun*, September 29, 1937, 22.

24. AP photo, "Germany Continues War Games," *Tampa (Fla.) Tribune*, December 13, 1938, 6.
25. AP photos, "While Bombs Rain on England," *Indianapolis Star*, August 20, 1940, 15.
26. Franz Roth biographical sketch kindly provided by Roth's granddaughter Tuya Roth.
27. AP photos, Box: WWII POW, Envelope: russische Kriegsgefangene [Russian prisoners of war], AP London Photo Library.
28. Scharnberg, "The A and P of Propaganda," 27.
29. AP Photo, *Louisville (Ky.) Courier-Journal*, July 24, 1941, 26.
30. "Der Untermensch," translation of the German document by the Holocaust Education & Archive Research Team, http://www.holocaustresearchproject.org/holoprelude/deruntermensch.html.
31. "The Treatment of Soviet POWs: Starvation, Disease, and Shootings, June 1941–January 1942," *Holocaust Encyclopedia* online, United States Holocaust Memorial Museum.
32. Copy of affidavit by Wilhelm Brandt, kindly provided by the Roth family.
33. Cable from Ernest Fischer to New York, April 23, 1941, Louis Paul Lochner Papers, Reel/Frame 32/200, WHS.
34. Willy Brandt to Franz Roth, May 2, 1941, kindly provided by the Roth family.
35. Memorandum to SS-War Correspondents Company, September 5, 1941, kindly provided by the Roth family.
36. Gerhard Meixner to Roth, September 11, 1941, kindly provided by the Roth family.
37. Battle for Kharkov: Men of Panzer Regiment 1 of the Waffen SS Division "LSSAH" (Leibstandarte SS Adolf Hitler) attacking Kharkov, tank destroyers "Marder III" and infantry in winter camouflage suits in snowy terrain, Franz Roth, SS PK, File: Bundesarchiv, Bild 101III-Roth-173-01/ Roth/ Franz/CC-BY-SA 3.0, Wikimedia Commons.
38. Kurt Meyer, *Grenadiers: The Story of Waffen SS General Kurt 'Panzer' Meyer* (Mechanicsburg, Pa.: Stackpole Books, 2005), 177
39. Joseph Goebbels to Thea Roth, April 15, 1943, kindly provided by the Roth family.
40. The photo fills the cover of Charles Trang's *Kriegsberichter Franz Roth* [War correspondent Franz Roth] (Bayeux, Fr.: Editions Heimdal, 2008).

41. "Dem Journalisten und Kriegberichter Franz Roth zum Gedenken," *Illustrierter Beobachter*, May 6, 1943.
42. Trang, *Kriegsberichter Franz Roth*, 49.

11. OPERATION BARBAROSSA

1. The Brest-Litovsk border marked the new German-Soviet border after the dismemberment of Poland in 1939. Brest is located in modern day Belarus, formerly a republic in the Soviet Union.
2. Frederick Cable Oechsner, *This Is the Enemy* (Boston: Little, Brown, 1942), 177–78.
3. "What to Do If Your Moustache Falls Off: Fairly True Reports from a CIA Man," memoir, AP21.36, 456, Angus M. Thuermer Papers, Box 4, APCA.
4. A likely reference to the Propaganda Ministry's Karl Boehmer leaking the invasion plans while inebriated at a diplomatic reception.
5. Lynn Heinzerling Diaries, June 22, 1941, AP 21.54, Lynn Heinzerling Papers, Box 4, Folder: 1941, APCA.
6. AP Story, "Germans Invade Russia," *Baltimore Sun*, June 22, 1941, 1.
7. Joseph Goebbels, *The Goebbels Diaries 1939–1941*, trans. and ed. Fred Taylor (London: Sphere Books, 1983), 425.
8. Harry W. Flannery, *Assignment to Berlin* (London: Right Book Club, 1943), 256, 260.
9. Heinzerling Diaries, June 23, 1941.
10. While annual, year-to-year figures have not been found, a memo dated October 8, 1941, from photo editor Al Resch to assistant general manager Lloyd Stratton, shows there were just 64 photo transmissions from abroad by radio and cable in the first three months of 1941, before the invasion: 25 from London and 39 from Berlin. From July 8, when radio transmission from Moscow became available and the invasion of Russia was well underway, a similar three-month period saw a total of 320 photo transmissions, most from Berlin and Moscow—a 500 percent increase. These numbers did not include less urgent photos sent by mail.
11. Cyril Radcliffe, "Photographs as News," PRO INF/1/908/, July 1941, National Archives, UK.
12. AP photo, "Nazis Take a Prisoner on Eastern Front," *Orangeburg (S.C.) Times and Democrat*, June 28, 1941, 1; AP photo, "Berlin Radios Views of

German Invasion of Russia Along 2,000-mile Front," *Hackensack (N.J.) Record*, June 27, 1941, 4.

13. AP photo, "German Soldiers Attacking Russian Machine Gun Nest," *Saint Joseph (Mich.) Herald-Press*, June 27, 1941.
14. "AHEAD! with the Story—and the Pictures," *Arizona Republic* (Phoenix), July 23, 1941, 4.
15. AP photo, "Cameramen Illustrate Hitler's Oft-told Tale," *New York Daily News*, June 27, 1941, 30.
16. Angus Thuermer to Dean, University of Illinois School of Journalism, October 17, 1994, Alvin Steinkopf Papers, Box 1, Folder 1A, WHS.
17. The city was part of Poland before World War II and became part of Ukraine when Stalin shifted postwar borders westward. Its name is Lviv in today's Ukraine and was Lwow when it was part of Poland, Lvov during the Soviet era, and Lemberg when under German control.
18. Louis Paul Lochner Papers, Bureau Journal, 1940–1941, Reel/Frame 32/709. WHS.
19. Alvin J. Steinkopf, "An Eyewitness Story of Fury in Red-Nazi War," *Chicago Daily Tribune*, July 5, 1941, 1.
20. Alvin J. Steinkopf, "Reds Rushed Off Feet by Speed of Hitler's Opening Attack," *Muncie (Ind.) Evening Press*, July 5, 1941, 11.
21. Alvin J. Steinkopf, "Lwow City of Funerals After Mass Executions," *Boston Globe*, July 7, 1941, 1.
22. AP photo, "Nazis Ascribe Lwow Slayings to Russians," *Boston Globe*, July 7, 1941, 3.
23. A Steinkopf scrapbook among his papers at the University of Wisconsin Historical Society contains numerous such photos.
24. "Auslandsjournalisten an der Statte der G.P.U. Morde in Lemberg, BER/STEIN," photo #59597, 59598, July 9, 1941, AP London Photo Library, WWII, Folder Lemberg.
25. Goebbels, *The Goebbels Diaries*, 450, 454.
26. Lochner Papers, Bureau Journal, WHS.
27. Adrian Gilbert, *Waffen-SS Hitler's Army at War* (New York: Da Capo Press, 2019), 134.
28. "Lvov," *Holocaust Encyclopedia* online, United States Holocaust Memorial Museum.
29. AP story, "Lwow Jews Reported Wiped Out by Nazis," *Baltimore Sun*, October 29, 1943, 3.

30. Alvin J. Steinkopf, "Poles Simply Watch," *Baltimore Evening Sun*, July 7, 1941, 2.
31. Alvin J. Steinkopf, "Nazis Continue Silent; Drive 'Progressing,'" *New York Daily News*, July 11, 1941, 3.
32. AP photo, "Ukrainian Refugees Seek Shelter in Ravine," *Indianapolis Star*, June 29, 1941, 3; AP photo, "Nazis Inspect Big Russian Tank," *Boston Globe*, July 3, 1941, 1.
33. AP photo, "Berlin Pictures Nazis Being Welcomed at Lwow," *Rochester (N.Y.) Democrat and Chronicle*, July 3, 1941, 2.
34. On the back was a propaganda ministry order, instructing all German media to run the image of the corpses.
35. *Berliner Illustrierter Zeitung*, July 17, 1941, 765.
36. AP photo, "Lithuania's Jewish Girls Wear Racial Brand," *Miami Herald*, August 18, 1941, 3.
37. "Lithuania," *Holocaust Encyclopedia* online, United States Holocaust Memorial Museum.
38. Alvin J. Steinkopf, "Smolensk Ruins Held by Nazis, Reporter Finds," *St. Louis Post-Dispatch*, August 11, 1941, 1.
39. Alvin J. Steinkopf, "The Surge Upon Smolensk," *Miami Herald*, July 5, 1942, 36.
40. Alvin J. Steinkopf, "Nothing Left of Smolensk but Blackened Chimneys; Germans Claim to Have Duplicated Napoleon's Feat," *Sioux City (Iowa) Journal*, August 14, 1941, 1.
41. Alvin J. Steinkopf, "U.S. Reporter Tours City, Still in Battle Zone—Finds That Russians Obeyed Stalin Scorched-Earth Order," *New York Times*, August 12, 1941, 3.
42. AP photo, "Wirephoto from Smolensk After the Four Horsemen Rode Onward," *Spokane (Wash.) Chronicle*, August 14, 1941, 1.
43. Howard K. Smith, *Last Train from Berlin* (London: Phoenix Press, 2000), 172.
44. Heinzerling Diaries, June 22, 1941, APCA.
45. Thuermer, "What to Do If Your Moustache Falls Off," 474.
46. Edward W. Beattie, Jr., *Diary of a Kriegie* (New York: Crowell, 1946), 132.
47. "World War: Last Wish," *Time Magazine*, August 25, 1941.

12. BERLIN AT WAR

1. Pierre J. Huss, "Back from Berlin, Finds Frisco Is Too Casual About Grim Business; Warns That Perils of Anti-Aircraft Shells Are Ever Present," *Wilmington (Del.) News Journal*, December 10, 1941, 6.
2. William Russell, *Berlin Embassy* (New York: Carroll & Graf, 2005), 61.
3. Edwin Shanke to parents, September 13, 1939, Shanke, Edwin A. Correspondence, World War, Box 1, Folder 1, Department of Special Citations and University Archives, Marquette University Libraries, Milwaukee, Wisconsin.
4. See photo by Hanns Hubmann/ullstein bild via Getty Images.
5. Ernest G. Fischer, "Life Under the Nazis," 1943, chapter 10, 40, Ernest G. Fischer Papers, U.S. Mss 79AF, Box 1, Folder 4, WHS.
6. Harry W. Flannery, *Assignment to Berlin* (London: The Right Book Club, 1943), 169.
7. Lynn Heinzerling, "No Place for Gourmets, but There Is Food," *Minneapolis Star Tribune*, February 26, 1941, 2.
8. Wallace R. Deuel, *People Under Hitler* (New York: Harcourt, Brace, 1942), 151.
9. Flannery, *Assignment to Berlin*, 186.
10. Fischer, "Life Under the Nazis," chapter 5, 50, M92-026, Box 1, Folder 3.
11. Jacob Beam, "My Years in Berlin: 1935–1940," manuscript, 1992, 285, kindly made available by Alex Beam.
12. Andrew Roberts, *Churchill: Walking with Destiny* (New York: Viking, 2018), 598.
13. "What to Do If Your Moustache Falls Off: Fairly True Reports from a CIA Man," memoir, AP21.36, 433, Angus M. Thuermer Papers, Box 4, APCA.
14. Joseph C. Harsch, *Pattern of Conquest* (Garden City, N.Y.: Doubleday, Doran, 1941), 27.
15. Frederick Cable Oechsner, *This Is the Enemy* (Boston: Little, Brown, 1942), 207.
16. AP story, "'Liveliest' British Air Raid on Berlin," *Des Moines Register*, September 3, 1941, 1.
17. Cable desk memo, September 3, 1941, AP02A.01, Bureau/Member Correspondence, Box 36, Folder: Berlin, APCA.
18. UP story, "Berlin Hints Raid by R.A.F. Heavy," *Boston Globe*, September 3, 1941, 7.

19. Louis Lochner cable to New York, September 3, 1941, AP02A.01, Bureau/Member Correspondence, 1938–1941, Box 25, Folder: Berlin, APCA.
20. Cable desk memo, September 3, 1941, AP02A.01, Bureau/Member Correspondence, 1938–1941, Box 36, Folder: Berlin, APCA.
21. Lochner to Kent Cooper, September 5, 1941, AP02A.01, Bureau/Member Correspondence, 1938–1941, Box 36, Folder: Berlin, APCA.
22. Louis P. Lochner, "British Raids Lower Morale, Cut War Production in Reich," *New Brunswick (NJ) Daily Home News*, May 22, 1942, 2.
23. Oechsner, *This Is the Enemy*, 207.
24. William L. Shirer, *Berlin Diary* (New York: Popular Library, 1961), 35.
25. Oechsner, *This Is the Enemy*, 209.

13. "WE LEAVE FOR THE JUG"

1. "What to Do If Your Moustache Falls Off: Fairly True Reports from a CIA Man," memoir, AP21.36, 430, Angus M. Thuermer Papers, Box 4, APCA.
2. AP story, "Roosevelt Blamed by Nazis for War," *Roseburg (Ore.) News-Review*, December 8, 1941, 1.
3. "Foreign News: Germany, News from Inside," *Time*, August 11, 1941, 19.
4. Joy Schaleben, "Louis P. Lochner: Getting the Story out of Nazi Germany, 1933–41" (master's thesis, University of Wisconsin, 1967), 74–76.
5. Andrew Roberts, *Churchill: Walking with Destiny* (New York: Viking, 2018), 640, 676.
6. Joseph C. Harsch, *At the Hinge of History* (Athens: University of Georgia Press, 2010), 56.
7. Steve Wick, *The Long Night: William L. Shirer and the Rise and Fall of the Third Reich* (New York: Palgrave Macmillan, 2011), 198.
8. Stanley Cloud and Lynne Olson, *The Murrow Boys* (Boston: Houghton Mifflin, 1966), 143.
9. Smith remained in neutral Switzerland until the liberation of France in 1945, unable to move because it was surrounded by Germany, Austria, Italy, and German-occupied France.
10. Louis P. Lochner, *What About Germany?* (New York: Dodd, Mead, 1942), 360.
11. Lochner, 360.
12. Ernest Fischer, "An Internment Diary," Ernest G. Fischer Papers, U.S. Mss 79AF, Box 1A, Folder 1, (1941–1942), WHS, 224.

13. Lochner, *What About Germany?*, 360.
14. AP story, "U.S. Correspondents in Berlin Forced by Nazis to Go Home," *East Liverpool (Ohio) Evening Review*, December 11, 1941, 6.
15. Thuermer, "What to Do If Your Moustache Falls Off," 431.
16. Thuermer, 433.
17. "U.S. Correspondents in Berlin Forced by Nazis to Go Home."
18. Reflecting the closure of not only the AP's Berlin bureau but others in the Axis and occupied countries, a January 27, 1942, memo to Cooper reports a sharp drop in foreign news collection costs for December 1941, including a decrease of $13,000 in cable tolls. Financial statements from the Kent Cooper collection, APCA.
19. Lochner, *What About Germany?*, 365.
20. Thuermer, "What to Do If Your Moustache Falls Off," 436.
21. Lochner, *What About Germany?*, 363–64.
22. Fischer, "An Internment Diary," WHS, 1.
23. Kent Cooper to Lochner, October 28, 1940, AP01.4B. Records of Board President Robert McLean, Box 20, Folder 275, Administrative & Bureau Correspondence—Foreign News Service 1938–1940, APCA.
24. Laurel Leff, "The New York Times' Nazi Correspondent," *Tablet*, June 3, 2021.
25. Laurel Leff, *Buried by the Times* (New York: Cambridge University Press, 2005), 55.
26. Thuermer, "What to Do If Your Moustache Falls Off," 457; Howard K. Smith, *Last Train from Berlin* (London: Phoenix Press, 2000), preface.
27. Charles B. Burdick, *An American Island in Hitler's Reich: The Bad Nauheim Internment* (Menlo Park, Calif.: Markgraf Publications Group, 1987), 9.
28. AP story, "Germany and Italy Declare War Today on United States," *Sedalia (Mo.) Democrat*, December 11, 1941, 1. Another historic report by Transocean would come on June 6, 1944, when it reported that Allied parachute troops were landing on the French coast, a story picked up by AP. It was the first news that Operation Overlord, the Allied invasion of Nazi-occupied Europe, was underway.
29. Lochner, *What About Germany?*, 367.
30. Larry Heinzerling, "Covering Tyranny: The AP and Nazi Germany: 1933–1945," 2017, 92, AP28, Writings about the Associated Press, APCA, https://www.ap.org/about/history/ap-in-germany-1933-1945/.
31. Burdick, *An American Island in Hitler's Reich*, 13.

32. Burdick, 33.
33. Louis P. Lochner papers, Reel/Frame 36/383-385, WHS.
34. Thuermer to family, December 19, 1942, Angus M. Thuermer Papers, 1938–1947, AP21:36, Box 2, Folder 20. APCA.
35. Lochner papers, Reel/Frame 36/383–385, WHS.
36. Lochner papers, Reel/Frame 36/384.
37. Thuermer, "What to Do If Your Moustache Falls Off," 446, 440.
38. Thuermer to family, December 19, 1942.
39. Thuermer, "What to Do If Your Moustache Falls off," 439.
40. Alvin Steinkopf, "The Last Chapter—Play by Play," manuscript, Alvin Steinkopf Papers, Box 5, Folder 2, 6, WHS.
41. Lochner, *What About Germany?*, 371.
42. Thuermer, "What to Do If Your Moustache Falls Off," 445.
43. Burdick, *An American Island in Hitler's Reich*, 47.
44. Study of War Propaganda, March 6, 1942. RG165, Records of the War Department General and Special Staffs, Military Intelligence Division, Regional File, 1922–1944, Germany 2910–2950, Entry 77, Box 1074, NARA.
45. Richard Breitman, *Official Secrets: What the Nazis Planned, What the British and Americans Knew* (New York: Hill and Wang, 1998), 125.
46. Fischer, "An Internment Diary," 214.
47. Louis P. Lochner, "Fuehrer's Act Biggest Error of His Career, Lochner Says," *St. Louis Post-Dispatch*, May 17, 1942, 1.
48. Fischer, "An Internment Diary," 245.
49. Deborah E. Lipstadt, *Beyond Belief: The American Press & the Coming of the Holocaust 1933–1945* (New York: Free Press, 1986), 127.
50. Fischer, "An Internment Diary," 248.
51. Fischer, "Writers See Walled City Built By Nazis; 600,000 Segregated in Polish Ghettos; Foreign Newsmen Shown Quarters at Krakow," *San Francisco Examiner*, October 15, 1941, 3.
52. Frederick Oechsner, "Graves Line Ukraine Roads, Soldiers Grim and Dazed," *Pittsburgh Press*, November 2, 1941, 35.
53. Ernest G. Fischer, "Blitz Backfires: Kiev Burns—Nazis 'Burn'—Reds Skipped with Fire Trucks," *Minneapolis Star Tribune*, October 23, 1941, 1.
54. Felice Bellotti, "Where Are the 350,000 Jews of the City?" *La Stampa (Turin)*, October 31, 1941, 3.
55. Thuermer, "What to Do If Your Moustache Falls Off," 254.

56. AP photo, "Correspondents Arriving on Drottningholm," *Fort Worth (Tex.) Star-Telegram*, June 2, 1942, 2.
57. Report by J. R. Ylitalo, July 29, 1942, Louis P. Lochner FBI file, Federal Bureau of Investigation, U.S. Department of Justice.
58. "AP's Frontline Press," 1943, 19, AP34.06, Box 2, Folder 23, APCA.

14. "CLOSE YOUR JUICE SHOP"

1. Willy Brandt, "Confession," 1945, manuscript written in German, trans. Steve Miller, March 10, 2001, 3, AP21.08, Willy Brandt Papers, APCA. Brandt wrote his "Confession," or "Geständnis," in German in 1945 to Louis Lochner, explaining what he had done during the war after Lochner's expulsion. A Lochner translation is in his papers at the Wisconsin Historical Society, and another, translated by former AP Frankfurt bureau chief Steve Miller in 2001, is in AP Corporate Archives. Quotes here are from the Miller translation.
2. Wes Gallagher, "Two Views of Berlin," *AP World*, Summer 1990, 12, APCA.
3. Brandt, "Confession," 4.
4. Brandt to Louis Lochner, May 8, 1942, letter kindly provided by Astrid Schulze.
5. Copy of a January 9, 1942, entry in the German Trade Register, AP 18.23, Berlin Bureau Records, Box 4, folder 3, APCA. Karl von Lewinski, who withdrew from public service when Hitler came to power and returned to Germany to practice general law, was appointed administrator of many American properties in Germany during the war. After the war he eventually returned to the United States and worked for the Department of Justice as an expert on German law.
6. Brandt, "Confession," 4.
7. Memorandum for Officer in Charge, October 17, 1945, Subject: Brandt, Willy Hermann Erwin, Holtzendorffstr. 6, Berlin, Charlottenburg, RG319, IRR LAUX, Helmut, X 8502334, Box 456, NARA.
8. Notes on German Propaganda, the Press and the Foreign Office, File#D-152515, RG 319, Records of the Army Staff, IRR, NARA.
9. Ernest G. Fischer, "Life Under the Nazis," circa 1942, Ernest G. Fischer Papers, Box 1A, Folder 1, WHS.
10. Howard K. Smith, *Last Train from Berlin* (London: Phoenix Press, 2000), 156.

14. "CLOSE YOUR JUICE SHOP" ⚭ 311

11. Notes on German Propaganda, the Press and the Foreign Office, NARA.
12. Lochner to Brandt, May 4, 1942, letter kindly provided by Astrid Schulze.
13. Brandt to Lochner, May 8, 1942.
14. Brandt to Lochner, May 8, 1942.
15. Lupi spelled his first name as Luiz on business cards and for other uses, but his byline on AP stories usually was rendered Luis Lupi.
16. Memorandum Report, January 14, 1946, Subject: Operation POUCH, "Agreement Between the Associated Press and Bureau Laux," RG319, IRR LAUX, Helmut, X 8502334, Box 456, NARA.
17. Laux told his U.S. military interrogators that Brandt maintained all contact between Lochner in New York and his mother-in-law in Berlin (Emma Buechner Steinberger) between 1942 and 1945. Several letters were sent to and from Berlin via German diplomatic pouch, and Brandt sent several personal photographs of Lochner's mother-in-law to Lochner. See Memorandum for the Officer in Charge, February 5, 1946, Subject: Operation POUCH, RG319, IRR LAUX, Helmut, X 8502334, Box 456, NARA.
18. Agreement Between the Associated Press and the Bureau Laux, Memorandum Report, January 14, 1946, Subject: Operation POUCH, NARA.
19. Memorandum for the Officer in Charge, February 5, 1946, Subject: Operation POUCH, NARA.
20. Brandt, "Confession," 13.
21. Out Sheet: January 22, 1946, AP02A.2, Foreign Bureau Correspondence, Box 4, Folder: Portugal-Lisbon, APCA.
22. Brandt, "Confession," 12.
23. Brandt, 12.
24. Brandt, 13.
25. Alan Gould to Kent Cooper, typescript note enclosing clipping, April 29, 1942, AP02A.03, Subject Files, Box 56, Folder: Newsphoto/Wirephoto, APCA.
26. N. R. Howard office memorandum, July 13, 1942, RG 216, Office of Censorship, Index to Administrative Subject File "Howard, N. R.," Box 1140, NARA.
27. Gould to Howard, July 14, 1942, AP02A.02, Foreign Bureau Correspondence, Box 2, Folder: Lisbon, APCA
28. Howard to Gould, July 18, 1942, RG 216, Office of Censorship, Administrative Subject File, Portugal, Box 113, NARA.
29. AP story, "Wartime Censorship Announced; Byron Price Will Be in Charge," *St. Louis Post-Dispatch*, December 16, 1941, 1. The Pulitzer Prizes

in 1944 included a special citation for Price honoring his work in the censorship office. "A censor who gets a Pulitzer citation should be very proud," a colleague wrote to Price.

30. Byron Price Memorandum for Mr. Stephen Early, January 20, 1942, Byron Price Papers, Box 1, Folder 2, WHS.
31. Gould Memorandum on Luiz Lupi, March 17, 1944, AP02A.2, Foreign Bureau Correspondence, Box 2, Folder: Lisbon, APCA.
32. Wilton Fonseca and Mario Carvalho, Conferência Internacional "República e Estado Novo," in Revista Portuguesa de História da Comunicação, no. 1, July 2017, Oporto, Portugal, 69–79.
33. WWII: RUSSIA German Army Occupies Cities & Towns, S-T Sectors, R75, AP New York Photo Library.
34. Report of the General Manager, December 31, 1942, Forty-Third Annual Volume for the fiscal year 1942, 80, AP01.01, Records of the AP Board of Directors, APCA.

15. BÜRO LAUX

1. AP photo, "Churchill and Roosevelt Meet with War Council," *Tampa (Fla.) Tribune*, June 26, 1942, 1; AP photo, "Wirephoto: An American Contribution for a Second Front—a Flying Fortress Over Britain," *Spokane (Wash.) Daily Chronicle*, July 25, 1942, 2; British Official Photographs nos. C3438 and C3440, "Damage to Krupps Works, Essen," March 5–6, 1943, Box: WWII Destroyed German Cities, AP Photo Library, London.
2. Willy Brandt, "Confession," 1945, manuscript written in German, trans. Steve Miller, March 10, 2001, 16, AP21.08, Willy Brandt Papers, APCA.
3. Brandt, 7.
4. Brandt, 10.
5. Brandt, 15.
6. Helmut Laux, Memorandum Report, Subject: Operation POUCH, January 14, 1946, Exhibit H, RG 319, Operation Pouch, vol. 1, IRR, XE-10063, NARA.
7. Helmut Laux, "Story of Life," December 27, 1945, Exhibit A, RG 319, IRR, X8502334, Box 456, NARA.
8. Memorandum for the Officer in Charge, Subject: Helmut Laux, SS Sonderführer, Legationssekretär and personal photographer for Ribbentrop,

January 6, 1946, Attachment: Activity of BÜRO LAUX during the war, RG 319, IRR, LAUX, Helmut, X8502334, Box 456, NARA.

9. Brandt, "Confession," 8, 24. Brandt said that Laux used prisoners from the Sachsenhausen concentration camp to build a villa for himself near the bureau's offices.
10. Brandt, 13.
11. Brandt, 17.
12. Jörgen Carlsson, "Pressens Bild 50 Years Old," kindly made available by Tobias Röstlund, photo manager of Sweden's TT news agency.
13. AP photo, "Hitler and Mussolini Look at Bomb Damage," *Allentown (Pa.) Morning Call*, July 25, 1944, 1; AP photo, "Hitler Confers with Goebbels," *Rocky Mount (N.C.) Evening Telegram*, July 28, 1944, 1.
14. AP photo, "Germans Say These Are Captured Allied Paratroopers," *Albuquerque Journal*, October 1, 1944, 1.
15. "Polish Patriots Marching Into German Internment," October 7, 1944, AP Photo Library, E2311, WWII: Europe, Poland, Print Folder.
16. AP photo, "German Infantrymen Amid Exploding Soviet Shells During an Attack on Soviet Positions Somewhere at the East Front," *Vancouver (B.C.) Sun*, February 3, 1944, 1; AP photo, "Members of a Nazi Air Raid Police Patrol Searching the Ruins of Bombed Buildings in Germany for Trapped Victims," *New York Daily News*, April 25, 1944, 3.
17. AP photos, "Behind the German Lines," *Minneapolis Star Tribune*, March 2, 1943, 24.
18. Report of the General Manager, December 31, 1943, Associated Press Annual Report for fiscal year 1943, 80, AP01.01, Records of the AP Board of Directors, APCA.
19. Memorandum for the Officer in Charge, Subject: Operation POUCH, January 14, 1946, RG 319, IRR, LAUX, Helmut, X8502334, Box 456, NARA.
20. Brandt, "Confession," 18.
21. Brandt, 18.
22. Brandt, 16.
23. Brandt, 9.
24. Brandt, 26.
25. Helmut Laux, Memorandum Report, Subject: Operation POUCH, January 14, 1946, NARA.
26. Brandt, 26, 27.

16. UNVEILING THE HOLOCAUST

1. David Shneer, *Through Soviet Jewish Eyes: Photography, War, and the Holocaust*, (New Brunswick, N.J.: Rutgers University Press, 2012), 100.
2. David Shneer, *Grief: The Biography of a Holocaust Photograph* (Oxford: Oxford University Press, 2020), 40.
3. A number of earlier Nazi atrocity photos from Poland of uncertain provenance surfaced in several U.S. newspapers in June 1941. The most widely published showed German soldiers leading women into a forest supposedly to be executed. Others show a firing squad, a pit of bodies, a man hanged, and more. Some appeared in the *Lancaster (Pa.) New Era*, which cited the source as the British Press Service in New York. Some of the same photos were distributed by the Wide World Photos service of the *New York Times* and by the United Features Syndicate (UFS), part of the E. W. Scripps Co. Both said the images had been smuggled out of Nazi-occupied Poland and obtained from a Gestapo agent or agents. It seems likely AP would have had access to the photos, but it does not appear to have distributed any of them.
4. AP photo, "The Nazi Way—Young and Old Shot Down," *Des Moines (Iowa) Register*, February 19, 1942, 3.
5. Of the 6 million Jews estimated to have died in the Holocaust, as many as 1.5–2 million are believed to have been murdered by firing squads called Einsatzgruppen ("mobile killing units") and local collaborators in Nazi-occupied areas. When the Nazis deemed the firing squad executions too inefficient to achieve Adolf Hitler's avowed goal of annihilating all of Europe's Jews, the Nazi Final Solution turned to gas, used to kill another three million, most of those at the Soviet-liberated death camps of Auschwitz and Treblinka. Other Jews died in concentration camps from starvation, disease, or other causes.
6. Perhaps the boldest lie told by the Soviet Union during the war involved the Katyn massacre, in which some twenty-two thousand Polish military officers, police, lawyers and other members of the country's intelligentsia were killed and buried in mass graves, including in the Katyn Forest outside the Russian city of Smolensk. Germany announced the discovery of the graves in April 1943 and charged that the Red Army had killed the victims after it marched into eastern Poland in 1939. For decades the Soviet Union denied the charge, blaming the Nazis instead. Nearly half a century later, in 1990,

Mikhail Gorbachev, the last leader of the Soviet Union, acknowledged Soviet forces had carried out the killings.
7. Vasilii Grossman," profile at website of Yad Vashem, The World Holocaust Remembrance Center.
8. Timothy Snyder, *Bloodlands: Europe Between Hitler and Stalin* (New York: Basic Books, 2010), 312.
9. Louis P. Lochner, "Fuehrer Outlines Reich Objectives," *Akron (Ohio) Beacon Journal*, January 31, 1939, 1.
10. Louis P. Lochner, "Total Elimination of Jews in Europe Pressed by Hitler," *Baltimore Sun*, October 28, 1941, 2.
11. Deborah E. Lipstadt, *Beyond Belief: The American Press & the Coming of the Holocaust 1933–1945* (New York: Free Press, 1986), 136.
12. JTA story, "Nazis Execute 52,000 Jews in Kiev; Smaller Pogroms in Other Cities," *JTA Daily Bulletin*, November 16, 1941.
13. ONA story, "52,000 Jews Reported Slain in Kiev," *Boston Globe*, November 15, 1941, 1.
14. "The Molotov Paper on Nazi Atrocities," American Council on Soviet Relations, New York, 1942.
15. AP story, "Savage Cruelties Laid to Nazis by Molotoff," *Boston Globe*, January 7, 1942, 1.
16. Among many examples, see AP Photo, "Mass Execution by Nazis," *Minneapolis Star*, September 7, 1942, 28; and "Mass Execution," *Philadelphia Inquirer*, September 7, 1942, 14.
17. "Germans Murder 700,000 Jews in Poland," *Daily Telegraph*, London, June 25, 1942, 5. Szmul Zygielbojm, the source for the story, killed himself in London in May 1943. He left a note saying he intended his suicide as the "most profound protest against the inaction in which the world watches and permits the destruction of the Jewish people."
18. UP story, "Mussolini Seeks Latin Alliance," *Wisconsin State Journal* (Madison), June 25, 1942, 28.
19. UP story, "1,125,000 Jews Slain by Nazis During War, Spokesman Says," *Philadelphia Inquirer*, June 30, 1942, 3.
20. AP story, "Nazi Toll of Jews Put at Million," *Washington Post*, June 30, 1942, 2; AP story, "Estimate 1,000,000 Jews Died Victims of Nazis," *Chicago Tribune*, June 30, 1942, 6; AP story, "Nazis Kill Million Jews, Says Survey," *Los Angeles Times*, June 30, 1942, 5.
21. Lipstadt, *Beyond Belief*, 139.

22. Barbie Zelizer, *Remembering to Forget: Holocaust Memory Through the Camera's Eye* (Chicago: University of Chicago Press, 1998), 31.
23. Janina Struk, *Photographing the Holocaust: Interpretations of the Evidence* (London: Routledge, 2004), 46.
24. Lipstadt, *Beyond Belief,* 276.
25. Lipstadt, 141–42.
26. Rebecca Erbelding, *Rescue Board: The Untold Story of America's Efforts to Save the Jews of Europe* (New York: Doubleday, 2018), 19.
27. AP story, "One-Half of Europe's Jews Slain: Dr. Wise," *Des Moines Register*, November 25, 1942, 1.
28. "Deportations to and from the Warsaw Ghetto," *Holocaust Encyclopedia* online, United States Holocaust Memorial Museum.
29. AP story, "Fiendish Hitler Plot to Slay All Jews Told," *Arizona Republic* (Phoenix), November 25, 1942, 1; AP story, "Declares Half of Jews in Europe Slain," *Arkansas Gazette* (Little Rock), November 25, 1942, 1; AP story, "2,000,000 Jews Slain Wise Says," *Hartford (Conn.) Courant*, November 25, 1942, 1; AP story, "2,000,000 Jews 'Exterminated' by Nazis, Dr. Wise Reports," *Miami Herald*, November 25, 1942, 1; Kenneth L. Dixon, "Committee Gets Details of Nazi Campaign to Kill All Jews in German Grip," *Albuquerque (N.Mex.) Tribune*, November 25, 1942, 1.
30. AP story, "WISE GETS CONFIRMATIONS, Checks with State Department on Nazis' 'Extermination Campaign,'" *New York Times*, November 25, 1942, 10.
31. Lipstadt, *Beyond Belief,* 181.
32. AP story, "Half of Jews Ordered Slain, Poles Report," *Washington Post*, November 25, 1942, 6.
33. AP story, "Warns Nazis They Will Pay for Slaughter," *Des Moines (Iowa) Tribune*, December 17, 1942, 3.
34. Eddy Gilmore, "Nazi-Styled Horror at Kiev Related," *Birmingham (Ala.) News*, November 29, 1943, 18.
35. According to the United States Holocaust Memorial Museum, executions at Babi Yar were led by a unit of the Einsatzgruppen, whose headquarters in Berlin recorded that SS, German police units, and their auxiliaries executed 33,771 Jews there on September 29–30, 1941.
36. Gilmore, "Nazi-Styled Horror at Kiev Related."
37. AP story, "Russians Try Nazis for Many Atrocities," *Wisconsin Rapids Daily Tribune*, December 16, 1943, 9.

16. UNVEILING THE HOLOCAUST ⬥ 317

38. AP story, "Four War Criminals Hanged," *Casper (Wyo.) Star-Tribune*, December 20, 1943, 1.
39. INP photo, "Victims of Nazi Barbarism," *Binghamton (N.Y.) Press and Sun-Bulletin*, December 23, 1943, 10.
40. INP photo, "Russian Radio Photo of Nazi Murder Pit at Kharkov," *St. Louis Post-Dispatch*, December 23, 1943, 1.
41. AP photo, "The News in Pictures," *Fort Worth (Tex.) Star-Telegram*, March 31, 144, 10.
42. AP story, "Russians Reveal Nazis Massacred Jews in Lublin," *Newark (Ohio) Advocate*, July 28, 1944, 14.
43. AP photo, "Bereaved Families Mourn Lublin Dead," *Vineland (N.J.) Daily Journal*, August 15, 1944, 3.
44. AP photo, "Nazi Crematory, Reds Say," *St. Louis Post-Dispatch*, August 14, 1944, 19; AP photo, "Funeral Service for Victims of German Terror," *Cedar Rapids (Iowa) Gazette*, August 15, 1944, 16.
45. Eddy Gilmore, "Captured Nazis Dig Up Bodies of Victims as Lublin Poles Mourn," *St. Louis Post-Dispatch*, August 12, 1944, 8.
46. Daniel De Luce, "Bored Germans Tell Story of Unimaginable Atrocities," *Atlanta Constitution*, August 30, 1944, 1.
47. AP story, "REDS SWEEP ON 43 MILES!" *Chicago Tribune*, January 28, 1945, 1–2; UP story, "Red Army Overruns Silesian War Arsenal Surrounds Posen and Closes on Brandenburg; 3rd Army Drives 4 Miles to German Border," *New York Times*, January 28, 1945, 1–3.
48. AP story, "Reds Capture Nazis' Gas Death Camp," *Los Angeles Times*, January 29, 1945, 2.
49. AP story, "Red Army Troops Free Thousands Nazis Tortured," *St. Louis Post-Dispatch*, February 2, 1945, 2.
50. Henry Shapiro, "Details Are Revealed of Nazi 'Murder Plant,'" *Knoxville (Tenn.) News-Sentinel*, February 2, 1945, 9.
51. AP photo, "Wirephoto: Red Army Doctors Examine Freed Prisoners," *Spokane (Wash.) Spokesman-Review*, February 22, 1945, 1
52. Alvin Steinkopf, "Nazi Civilians Taken on Tour of Death Camp," *Decatur (Ill.) Daily Review*, April 11, 1945, 9.
53. AP photo, "Slain Internees in German Camp," *Vineland (N.J.) Daily Journal*, April 10, 1945, 1.
54. Steinkopf, "Nazi Civilians Taken on Tour of Death Camp."
55. Alvin J. Steinkopf, "21,000 Freed!" *Cincinnati Enquirer*, April 17, 1945, 1.

56. William Frye, "Piles of Naked Corpses Are Found When British Take Nazi Hell Camp," *Louisville (Ky.) Courier-Journal*, April 21, 1945, 1.
57. Descriptions of the camp by Richard Dimbleby, war correspondent for the BBC, were so graphic that the BBC refused to broadcast his report for four days until he threatened to resign.
58. Howard Cohen, "Dachau Prison Camp Taken, 32,000 Set Free by Yanks," *Baltimore Evening Sun*, April 30, 1945, 2.
59. AP photo, "German SS Women Forced to Bury Their Victims," *Davenport (Iowa) Daily Times*, April 28, 1945, 2.
60. AP photo, "A Nazi and His Handiwork," *St. Louis Post-Dispatch*, May 11, 1945, C1.
61. Louis P. Lochner, "Buchenwald Transformed Into a Refugee Center," *Des Moines (Iowa) Register*, June 1, 1945, 2.
62. AP story, "To View Horror," *Kansas City Star*, April 22, 1945, 14. Among the other media executives were publishers or editors from the *New York Times, Washington Star, Detroit Free Press, New Orleans Times Picayune, Kansas City Star, Minneapolis Star-Journal, Chicago Sun, Saturday Evening Post*, and *Reader's Digest*.
63. Joseph Pulitzer, "Nazi Horror Camps Even Worse than Reported, Pulitzer Says," *Pittsburgh-Post Gazette*, April 30, 1945, 2.
64. Normal Chandler, "That America May Know the Truth," *Dayton (Ohio) Journal Herald*, April 28, 1945, 1.
65. AP story, "Nazi Horror Camps Even Worse than Reported, Pulitzer Says," *Pittsburgh Post-Gazette*, 2.
66. Ron Hollander, "We Knew: America's Newspapers Report the Holocaust," in *Why Didn't the Press Shout? American & International Journalism During the Holocaust* (Newark: Yeshiva University Press in association with KTAV Publishing House, 2003), 41.
67. Laurel Leff, "When the Facts Didn't Speak for Themselves: The Holocaust in the *New York Times*, 1939–1945," in *Why Didn't the Press Shout?*, 53.
68. Marvin Kalb, "Introduction," in *Why Didn't the Press Shout?*, 8.

17. THE COLLAPSE

1. AP photo, "Germany Digs In," *Richmond (Va.) Times-Dispatch*, October 18, 1944, 4.
2. AP photo, "Germany's New Folk Army," *Casper (Wyo.) Star-Tribune*, October 25, 1944, 2.

3. Erich Schneyder, "The Fall of Berlin," trans. Louis P. Lochner, *Wisconsin Magazine of History* 50, no. 4 (Summer 1967), WHS.
4. Activity of Büro Laux during the war, attachment to Memorandum for the Officer in Charge, Subject: Helmut Laux, January 6, 1946, Operation POUCH, RG 319, IRR, Laux, Helmut, X8502334, NARA.
5. Willy Brandt, "Confession," 1945, manuscript written in German, trans. Steve Miller, March 10, 2001, 29, AP21.08, Willy Brandt Papers, APCA.
6. Helmut Laux life summary, Memorandum Report, Subject: Operation POUCH, January 14, 1946, Operation POUCH, RG 319, IRR, XE10063, NARA.
7. Brandt, "Confession," 30.
8. Morrell Heald, ed., *Journalist at the Brink: Louis P. Lochner in Berlin, 1922–1942* (N.p.: Xlibris, 2007), 508.
9. Louis P. Lochner, "A.M.G. Aides Find It Hard to Shun Friendly Germans," *Des Moines (Iowa) Register*, February 11, 1945, 4.
10. Kent Cooper to Louis Lochner, March 27, 1945, Louis Paul Lochner Papers, AP Correspondence, Reel/Frame 2/43, WHS.
11. William Shirer, "Americans Need Beware Nazi Civilian Whinings," *Birmingham (Ala.) News*, March 11, 1945, 45.
12. William Shirer, "Propaganda Front," *New York Herald Tribune*, March 11, 1945, A1.
13. Louis P. Lochner, "Conspirator Reveals Details of Plot to Kill Adolf Hitler," *Richmond (Va.) Times-Dispatch*, March 20, 1945, 1.
14. Louis P. Lochner, "Hitler, Ill Since Attempt on His Life, Knows He's Lost War," *Honolulu Star-Bulletin*, March 19, 1945, 5.
15. Louis P. Lochner, "Goering's Mind Is Slipping," *Des Moines (Iowa) Tribune*, March 20, 1945, 1.
16. "Beware This Propaganda Line," *Abilene (Tex.) Reporter-News*, March 21, 1945, 9.
17. "I Am Able to Reveal," *Time*, April 2, 1945, 68.
18. Louis P. Lochner, "Hindenburg Didn't Want Hitler as Successor, Portion of Statesman's Will Withheld—Lochner," *Poughkeepsie (N.Y.) Journal*, February 11, 1945, 8.
19. Geoffrey Parsons to Edward Kennedy, March 20, 1945, Louis Paul Lochner Papers, General Correspondence, Associated Press, Reel/Frame 2/40, WHS.
20. Cooper to Lochner, March 27, 1945, Louis Paul Lochner Papers, AP Correspondence, Reel/Frame 2/43, WHS.

21. Lochner to Cooper, April 6, 1945, Louis Paul Lochner Papers, AP Correspondence, Reel/Frame 2/50, WHS.
22. Lochner, entry dated June 11, 1945, Louis Paul Lochner Papers, Diaries 1940–1948, Reel/Frame 47/1, WHS.
23. Memorandum for the Officer in Charge, Subject: Interview with Helmut Laux, September 19, 1945, Operation POUCH, RG 319, Records of the Army Staff, NARA.
24. Note du Government Militaire, Armée Français, June 1, 1945, Operation POUCH, XE10063, NARA.
25. Helmut Laux life summary, in Memorandum Report: Subject: Operation Pouch, January 14, 1946, Operation POUCH, RG319, IRR, XE10063, NARA.
26. Memorandum for the Officer in Charge, Subject: Helmut Laux, Re: Return of subject to Memmingen on 24 December 1945 and apprehension by this office 26 December 1945, December 27, 1945, RG 319, IRR, Laux, Helmut, X8502334, NARA.
27. Laux to Lochner, January 4, 1946, in Memorandum Report, Subject: Operation Pouch, File XE10063, NARA.
28. Memorandum for the Officer in Charge, Return of subject to Memmingen, NARA.
29. Memorandum for the Officer in Charge, Return of subject to Memmingen.
30. Memorandum for the Officer in Charge, Subject: Helmut Laux, Re: Arrest and Additional Information, January 6, 1946, Operation POUCH, RG 319, IRR, XE10063, NARA.
31. Memorandum for the Officer in Charge, Arrest and Additional Information.
32. Helmut Laux life summary, January 14, 1946, NARA.
33. Lene Laux to Lochner, November 29, 1945, Memorandum Report, Subject: Operation POUCH, January 14, 1946, IRR, XE10063, NARA.
34. Lochner to Mrs. Lene Laux, December 8, 1945, Memorandum Report, Subject: Operation POUCH, January 14, 1946, IRR, XE10063, NARA.
35. Helmut Laux, Report of the Berlin trip, 13–18 January, 1946, in Memorandum to the Officer in Charge, Subject: Operation POUCH, Re: Investigation in Berlin, February 1, 1946, NARA.
36. Memorandum for the Officer in Charge: Subject: Operation Pouch, Re: Investigation in Berlin, February 1, 1946, RG 319, IRR, XE10063, NARA.

37. Authorization to Travel out of Germany, January 16, 1946, Operation POUCH, RG 319, NARA.
38. Memorandum for the Officer in Charge, Subject: Operation POUCH, Re: Investigation in Berlin, February 1, 1946, RG 319, IRR, XE10063, NARA.
39. Memorandum for the Officer in Charge, Subject: Operation POUCH, February 1, 1946.
40. Operation POUCH RG 319, IRR, D10063, NARA.
41. Memorandum for the Officer in Charge, Subject: Operation POUCH, Re: Supplemental Investigation, January 14, 1946, RG 319, IRR, XE10063, NARA.
42. Memorandum for the Officer in Charge, Supplemental Investigation.
43. Memorandum for the Officer in Charge, Subject: Operation POUCH, January 14, 1946, NARA.
44. Memorandum for the Officer in Charge, Subject: Operation POUCH, February 1, 1946, NARA. 45. Among the main evidence they cited for the alleged cover-up: recovery of AP photos in Büro Laux that were dated after the United States and Germany went to war against each other; Willy Brandt's failure to divulge the existence of the photo exchange when seeking clearance for his employment at AP; and Brandt's transport "under questionable circumstances" of documents and AP photos received from Lisbon, "all of which constituted Bureau Laux property," to the AP address in Berlin.
45. CIC, February 23, 1946, Operation POUCH, RG319, IRR, XE10063, NARA.
46. Edwin L. Sibert to Assistant Chief of Staff, G-2, War Department, Washington, D.C., Subject: File and Report on Helmut Laux, March 8, 1946. RG 319, IRR, Laux, Helmut, X8502334, NARA.
47. CIC Weekly Report, March 15, 1946, Operation POUCH, RG 319, IRR, XE10063, NARA.
48. Cooper to Robert Bunnelle, July 11, 1945, AP01.4B, Papers of Board President Robert McLean, Box 23, Folder 27, APCA.
49. Larry Heinzerling, "Covering Tyranny: The AP and Nazi Germany: 1933–1945," 2017, AP28, 132, Writings about the Associated Press, APCA, https://www.ap.org/about/history/ap-in-germany-1933-1945/.
50. Lochner to Eddie Shanke, August 2, 1947, Louis Paul Lochner Papers, Reel/Frame 2/141, WHS; Lochner to Ernest Fischer, December 11, 1953, Louis Paul Lochner Papers, AP and former AP staffer correspondence 1948–1956, Reel/Frame 2/270-271, WHS.

51. Lochner to John Evans, November 21, 1949, Louis Paul Lochner Papers, AP and former AP staffer correspondence 1948–1956, Reel /Frame 2/224-225, WHS.
52. Lochner to Steinkopf, January 16, 1952, Alvin Steinkopf Papers, Box 1, Folder 49, WHS.
53. Heinzerling, "Covering Tyranny," 134.
54. Heinzerling, 134.
55. Heimlich, W. F. (U.S. Army Headquarters, Berlin District) to Whom It May Concern, November 2, 1945, AP21.08, Willy Brandt Papers, Box 1, Folder 2, APCA.
56. Office of Military Government, Subject: Circumstances surrounding the investigation of Willy Brandt, January 24, 1946, Louis Paul Lochner Papers, Reel/Frame 3/912. WHS.
57. Office of Military Government, Subject: Vetting of Willy Erwin Herrmann Brandt, January 18, 1946, Louis Paul Lochner Papers, Reel/Frame 3/910. WHS.
58. Wes Gallagher to Kent Cooper, March 2, 1946, AP21.08, Willy Brandt Papers, Box 1, Folder 2, APCA.
59. Cooper to Gallagher, March 25, 1946, AP21.08, Willy Brandt Papers, Box 1, Folder 2, APCA.
60. Lochner to Gallagher, February 26, 1946, Louis Paul Lochner Papers, Reel/Frame 2/117, Gallagher Correspondence, WHS.
61. Brandt to Lochner, May 19, 1946, Louis Paul Lochner Papers, Reel/Frame 3/927, WHS.
62. Lochner to Stratton, July 4, 1946, Louis Paul Lochner Papers, Reel/Frame 2/119, WHS.
63. Heinzerling, "Covering Tyranny," 129.
64. Lochner to Stratton, July 4, 1946, WHS.
65. "British AP Man Moves to Texas," *AP World*, 27, no. 2 (Summer 1970): 6, APCA.
66. AP story, "Former A.P. Chief Kent Cooper Is Dead at 84," *New York Times*, January 31, 1965, 1.

EPILOGUE

1. AP story, "AP's Joseph Morton Executed by Germans," *Atlanta Constitution*, July 9, 1945, 3.

2. Joseph Morton, "Tokyo Veterans on Raid; Bombs Are Well Placed," *Dayton (Ohio) Journal Herald*, July 20, 1943, 1.
3. Joseph Morton, "Romania's King Stars in Courageous Coup d'Etat," *Richmond (Va.) Times Dispatch*, September 10, 1944, 1.
4. "King Michael's Story," *New York Times*, September 11, 1944, 16.
5. Much of this account of the Morton tragedy is taken from Larry Heinzerling's "The Execution of Joe Morton," manuscript, 1996, Larry Heinzerling Papers, APCA.
6. AP story, "Nazis Executed A.P. Man and 13 More in Party," *Spokane (Wash.) Daily Chronicle*, July 10, 1945, 10.
7. Cooper to Letty Morton, July 9, 1945, kindly made available by Morton's daughter, Mimi Gosney.
8. AP story, "58 Nazi Killers Sent to Gallows," *Spokane (Wash.) Spokesman-Review*, May 14, 1946, 9.
9. AP story, "61 SS Men Guilty of Camp Atrocities," *Knoxville (Tenn.) News-Sentinel*, May 12, 1946, 11.
10. AP story, "Americans Slain by Nazis Honored for Efforts," *St. Joseph (Mo.) News-Press*, August 29, 1994, 1.
11. Isaac Stone Fish, "The Controversy Over Pyongyang's Associated Press Bureau," *Foreign Policy*, December 24, 2014.
12. Mary Louise Kelly, "Why I Went to Iran," *Atlantic*, February 17, 2023.
13. Jason Rezaian, "NPR's Mary Louise Kelly on the Challenges of Reporting from Iran," *Washington Post*, March 8, 2023.
14. "I Wish We'd Known That: Leading Journalists Look Back at the Russian Story," April 11, 2023 panel, Craig Newmark Graduate School of Journalism, City University of New York.
15. "Axis Journalism," *On the Media*, WNYC Studios, June 9, 2017.

BIBLIOGRAPHY

ARCHIVAL SOURCES

Associated Press Collections
Associated Press Collections Online
Associated Press Corporate Archives (APCA), New York
Associated Press London Photo Library
Associated Press New York Photo Library
British Newspaper Archive (online)
Franklin D. Roosevelt Presidential Library and Museum digitized collections
Herbert Hoover Presidential Library, West Branch, Iowa
History Unfolded: US Newspapers and the Holocaust (online)
Hoover Institution Library and Archives, Stanford, Calif.
Jewish Historical Institute, Warsaw, Poland
Jewish Telegraphic Agency digital archive
Library of Congress (LOC), Washington, D.C.
National Archives (NARA), College Park, Md.
National Archives (United Kingdom)
Newspapers.com (United States)
New York Public Library
United States Holocaust Memorial Museum, Washington, D.C.
Wiener Holocaust Library, London
Wisconsin Historical Society (WHS), Madison, Wis.
Yad Vashem, Jerusalem, Israel

OTHER SOURCES

Associated Press, ed. *Breaking News, How the Associated Press Has Covered War, Peace and Everything* Else. New York: Princeton Architectural Press, 2007.

Beam, Jacob. "My Years in Berlin: 1935–1940." Manuscript. 1992. Courtesy of Alex Beam.

Beattie, Edward W., Jr. *Diary of a Kriegie*. New York: Crowell, 1946.

Borchert, Eric. *Entscheidende Stunden: Mit der Kamera am Feind*. Berlin: Wilhelm Limpert, 1941.

Breitman, Richard. *Official Secrets: What the Nazis Planned, What the British and Americans Knew*. New York: Hill and Wang, 1998.

Brown, David, and W. Richard Bruner, eds. *I Can Tell It Now*. New York: Dutton, 1964.

Burdick, Charles B. *An American Island in Hitler's Reich: The Bad Nauheim Internment*. Menlo Park, Calif.: Markgraf Publications Group, 1987.

Byers, Catherine P. "Reporting Wartime Germany: Perceptions of American Journalists in Berlin, 1939–1945." Ph.D. dissertation, Ball State University, 1986.

Cloud, Stanley, and Lynne Olson. *The Murrow Boys: Pioneers on the Front Lines of Broadcast Journalism*. Boston: Houghton Mifflin, 1996.

Cooper, Kent. *Barriers Down: The Story of the News Agency Epoch*. New York: Farrar & Rinehart, 1942.

———. *Kent Cooper and the Associated Press: An Autobiography*. New York: Random House, 1959.

Deuel, Wallace R. *People Under Hitler*. New York: Harcourt, Brace, 1942.

Diebow, Hans. *Die Juden in USA*. Berlin: Zentralverlag Der NSDAP, Franz Eher Nachf., 1939.

Dodd, Martha. *Through Embassy Eyes*. New York: Harcourt Brace, 1939.

Domeier, Norman. "Secret Photos: The Cooperation Between Associated Press and the National Socialist Regime, 1942–1945." *Zeithistorische Forschungen/Studies in Contemporary History* 14 (2017).

Dussel, Konrad. *Bilder als Botschaft: Bildstrukturen deutscher Illustrierter 1905–1945 im Spannungsfeld von Politik, Wirtschaft und Publikum*. Cologne: Herbert von Halem Verlag, 2019.

Erbelding, Rebecca. *Rescue Board: The Untold Story of America's Efforts to Save the Jews of Europe*. New York: Doubleday, 2018.

Flannery, Harry W. *Assignment to Berlin*. London: Right Book Club, 1943.

Foster, Kevin. "Deploying the Dead: Combat Photography, Death and the Second World War in the USA and the Soviet Union." *War, Literature & the Arts* 26 (2014).

Garai, Bert. *The Man from Keystone*. New York: Living Books, 1966.

Gilbert, Adrian. *WAFFEN-SS: Hitler's Army at War*. New York: Da Capo Press, 2019.

Goebbels, Joseph. *The Goebbels Diaries 1939–1941*, ed. and trans. Fred Taylor. London: Sphere Books, 1983.

Gramling, Oliver. *AP: The Story of News*. Ann Arbor, Mich.: University Microfilms, 1968.

Harsch, Joseph C. *At the Hinge of History, a Reporter's Story*. Athens: University of Georgia Press, 1993.

——. *Pattern of Conquest*. Garden City, N.Y.: Doubleday, Doran, 1941.

Harnett, Richard M., and Billy G. Ferguson. *UNIPRESS: United Press International Covering the 20th Century*. Golden, Colo.: Fulcrum, 2003.

Heald, Morrell, Ed. *Journalist at the Brink: Louis P. Lochner in Berlin, 1922–1942*. N.p.: Xlibris, 2007.

Heinzerling, Larry. "Covering Tyranny: The AP and Nazi Germany 1933–1945." 2017. https://www.ap.org/about/history/ap-in-germany-1933-1945/ap-in-germany-report.pdf.

Herz, Rudolf. *Hoffmann & Hitler: Fotografie als Medium des Führer-Mythos*. Munich: Fotomuseum in Münchner Stadtmuseum, 1994.

Hoffmann, Peter. *The History of the German Resistance 1933–1945*. Montreal: McGill-Queen's University Press, 1996.

Huss, Pierre J. *The Foe We Face*. Garden City, N.Y.: Doubleday, Doran, 1942.

Jacobson, Willy. "Als Bildreporter nur 'Nummern' waren." *Neue Deutsche Presse* 11, no. 13 (1957).

Kerbs, Dieter, Walter Uka, and Brigitte Walz-Richter, eds. *Die Gleichschaltung der Bilder. Zur Geschichte der Pressefotografie 1930–1936*. Berlin: Frölich & Kaufmann, 1983.

Knightley, Phillip. *The First Casualty*. Baltimore: Johns Hopkins University Press, 2004.

Leff, Laurel. *Buried by the Times: The Holocaust and America's Most Important Newspaper*. New York: Cambridge University Press, 2013.

Lipstadt, Deborah E. *Beyond Belief: The American Press & the Coming of the Holocaust 1933–1945*. New York: Free Press, 1986.

Lochner, Louis P. *Always the Unexpected: A Book of Reminiscences*. New York: Macmillan, 1956

———. "News Gathering in Nazi Germany." *Quill* (August 1939).

———. "Round Robins from Berlin: Louis P. Lochner's Letters to His Children, 1932–1941." *Wisconsin Magazine of History* 50 no. 4 (Summer 1967).

———. *Stets das Unerwartete: Erinnerungen aus Deutschland 1921–1952*. Darmstadt, Ger.: Franz Schneekluth Verlag, 1955.

———. *Tycoons and Tyrant: German Industry from Hitler to Adenauer*. Chicago: Regnery, 1954.

———. *What About Germany?* New York: Dodd, Mead, 1942.

Lower, Wendy Morgan. "From Berlin to Babi Yar." *Journal of Religion & Society* 9 (2007).

Meyer, Kurt. *Grenadiers: The Story of Waffen SS General Kurt "Panzer" Meyer*. Mechanicsburg, Penn.: Stackpole Books, 2005.

Mills, James A. Diary, courtesy of Jerry Whiteleather.

Morris, Joe Alex. *Deadline Every Minute: The Story of the United Press*. Garden City, N.Y.: Doubleday, 1957.

Moseley, Ray. *Reporting War: How Foreign Correspondents Risked Capture, Torture and Death to Cover World War II*. New Haven, Conn.: Yale University Press, 2017.

Nafziger, Ralph O. *International News and the Press; an Annotated Bibliography*. New York: Wilson, 1940.

Nagorski, Andrew. *1941: The Year Germany Lost the War*. New York: Simon & Schuster, 2019.

———. *Hitlerland: American Eyewitnesses to the Nazi Rise to Power*. New York: Simon & Schuster, 2012.

Novick, Peter. *The Holocaust and Collective Memory: The American Experience*. New York: Bloomsbury, 2001.

Oechsner, Frederick. *This Is the Enemy*. Boston: Little, Brown, 1942.

Olmsted, Kathryn S. *The Newspaper Axis: Six Press Barons Who Enabled Hitler*. New Haven, Conn.: Yale University Press, 2022.

Reporting World War II: American Journalism, 1938–1944. N.p.: Library of America, 1995.

Roberts, Andrew. *Churchill: Walking with Destiny*. New York: Viking, 2018.

Roth, Franz. "Reporter." Manuscript. Circa 1942. Courtesy of Tuya Roth.

Russell, William. *Berlin Embassy*. New York: Carroll & Graf, 2005.

Sachsse, Rolf. *Die Erziehung zum Wegsehen: Fotografie im NS-Staat*. Dresden: Philo Fine Arts, 2003.

Schaleben, Joy. "Louis P. Lochner: Getting the Story Out of Nazi Germany, 1933–1941." Master's thesis, University of Wisconsin, 1967.

Scharnberg, Harriet. "The A and P of Propaganda, Associated Press and Nazi Photojournalism." *Zeithistortische Forshungen/Studies in Contemporary History* 13 (2016).

———. *Die "Judenfrage" im Bild: Der Antisemitismus in nationalsozialistischen Fotoreportagen*. Hamburg: Verlag des Hamburger Instituts für Sozialforschung, 2018.

Schneyder, Erich. "The Fall of Berlln." *Wisconsin Magazine of History* 5, no. 4 (1967).

Shapiro, Robert Moses, ed. *Why Didn't the Press Shout? American and International Journalism During the Holocaust*. Newark, N.J.: Yeshiva University Press in association with KTAV, 2003.

Shirer, William L. *Berlin Diary. 1941*. New York: Popular Library, 1961.

———. *The Nightmare Years: 1930–1940*. Boston: Little Brown, 1985.

———. *The Rise and Fall of the Third Reich*. New York: Simon & Schuster, 1959.

Shneer, David. *Grief: The Biography of a Holocaust Photograph*. New York: Oxford University Press, 2020.

———. *Through Soviet Jewish Eyes: Photography, War, and the Holocaust*. New Brunswick, N.J.: Rutgers University Press, 2011.

Smith, Howard K. *Last Train from Berlin: An Eye-Witness Account of Germany at War. 1943*. London: Phoenix Press, 2000.

Snyder, Timothy. *Bloodlands: Europe Between Hitler and Stalin*. New York: Basic Books, 2010.

St. John, Robert. *Foreign Correspondent*. Garden City, N.Y.: Doubleday, 1957.

Steinweis, Alan E. *Kristallnacht 1938*. Cambridge, Mass.: Belknap Press of Harvard University Press, 2009.

Struk, Janina. *Photographing the Holocaust: Interpretations of the Evidence*. London: Tauris, 2004.

Thompson, Dorothy. *I Saw Hitler!* New York: Farrar and Rinehart, 1932.

Trang, Charles. *Kriegsberichter Franz Roth*. Bayeux, Fr.: Editions Heimdal, 2008.

Von Klemperer, Klemens. *German Resistance Against Hitler: The Search for Allies Abroad, 1938–1945*. Oxford: Clarendon Press, 1992.

Von Wedel, Hasso. *Die Propagandatruppen der Deutschen Wehrmacht*. Neckargemünd, Ger.: Scharnhorst Buchkameradschaft, 1962.

Whiteleather, Melvin K. "The Foreign Press: Germany." *Journalism Quarterly* 16, no. 2 (1939).

———. "The Foreign Press—Germany." *Journalism Quarterly* 16, no. 4 (1939).
———. "The Foreign Press—Germany." *Journalism Quarterly* 17, no. 1 (1940).
———. "On the Road from Damascus: A Journalist's Encounters with the Famous and Infamous." Manuscript. Courtesy of Jerry Whiteleather.
Wick, Steve. *The Long Night: William L. Shirer and the Rise and Fall of the Third Reich*. New York: Palgrave Macmillan, 2012.
Zelizer, Barbie. *Remembering to Forget: Holocaust Memory Through the Camera's Eye*. Chicago: University of Chicago Press, 1998.
Zeltser, Arkadi, "The Subject of 'Jews in Babi Yar' in the Soviet Union in the Years 1941–1945." International Institute for Holocaust Research, Yad Vashem.

INDEX

Abilene Reporter-News, 248
Abrahams, Horace, 143–44
ACME News Service, 179
Albright, Madeleine, 268
Allen, Jay, 33
"American News Sources in Nazi Germany" (anonymous report), 114–16
Amsterdam, 129–30
Anderson, Godfrey, 262
Anderson, Terry, 5
anti-Semitism: American anti-Semitism, 189–192, 241; AP reporting on anti-Semitism and Hitler's plans to eliminate the Jews of Europe, 29–31, 222–23; AP's prewar reporting on Nazi anti-Semitic actions, 29, 47, 222–23; Fischer's anti-Semitism, 189–192; and Holocaust victims not identified as Jews in Soviet press, 220, 222, 224; Nazi lack of concern over stories revealing anti-Semitism, 28; and U.S. propaganda aimed at German population, 187–88. *See also* Kristallnacht
AP. *See* Associated Press and specific bureaus
AP Berlin news bureau, 41–52; American leaders and staff, 42, 46–49, 179; arrest and detention of American staff, 181–87; and beginning of WWII, 83, 87–88; and British bombing raids, 170, 215–16; and decision to maintain a presence in Nazi Germany, xii, xiii, 25–40, 178–79, 269; German staff, 42, 49, 184; and Hitler's declaration of war on U.S., 183–84; lack of eyewitnesses to German invasion of Soviet Union, 156; location and physical layout, 50; Lochner as head of, 42–46; Lochner replaced by Gallagher as bureau chief, 249–50, 261; and Lochner's handling of wartime stories, 121–24; and Operation Barbarossa, 157–166; and

AP Berlin news bureau (*continued*) photographs; prewar news exchange agreement with DNB, 49–50; and prewar reporting, 12–13, 29; reporting limited to official statements and censored photos and reports, 87–88, 111, 157–58, 170, 172, 174; reporting on anti-Semitism and Hitler's plans to eliminate the Jews of Europe, 29–31, 222–23; and responsibility censorship, 27, 54, 81, 166; routes for sending German news and photos out of the country in wartime, 95; Rust's order to boycott AP (1935), 34–35; speedy coverage, 159; understaffing problems, 50–51. *See also* AP GmbH; Fischer, Ernest; Gallagher, Wes; Heinzerling, Lynn; Josten, Rudolf; Kristallnacht; Lochner, Louis; photo exchange between AP and Nazi Germany; Schildbach, Robert; Shanke, Edwin; Steinkopf, Alvin; Thuermer, Angus; Whiteleather, Melvin

AP Budapest bureau, 86

AP GmbH (photo agency), xii, 53–61; agreement about first refusal of Roth's photographs, 144–45, 151, 163; Beukert as chief editor, 22; and Blitzkrieg photographs, 103; Brandt placed in charge of, 1, 73–77; and Brandt's postwar career, 260; caption issues, 57–60, 64–65, 133–36; charges of cooperation in Nazi vilification of Jews, 63; charges of disseminating Nazi propaganda, 114–16; charges of unethical compliance with Nazi anti-Semitic laws, 65; closure considered, 59, 61; compliance with Nazi edicts, 72–76; and Cooper's business ambitions, 39, 54–55, 61, 75, 137, 138, 147, 173; and "Covering Tyranny" account, 8; creation of, 54–55; dual employment of photographers with PK companies and AP GmbH, 130–31, 137, 139–40, 143, 149–50; and Editor's Law, 55–56, 59; end of AP monopoly on distribution of Roth's photos within Germany, 151; exclusive photographs, 129–30, 137–38, 147, 151, 204; fate of Jewish employees, xiii, 8, 54, 65–66, 69, 131; as German company subject to racist rules, 54, 55; Jewish employees, 65–71; and Kristallnacht, 11–12, 13–18, 21–23; Lochner as nominal head of, 42, 56–57, 65; and Lochner's battles with propaganda ministry, 57–60; and maintaining a presence in Nazi Germany, 26–27, 31; Nazi control over photographs and photographers, 137; and Nazi propaganda, xii–xiii, 5, 53, 60, 63–64, 114–16, 134–38; Nazi raid on offices, 26; and Nazi war photographer Franz Roth; office destroyed in bombing raid, 215–16; and Operation Barbarossa, 161; photo archive, 197–98, 204–5, 215–16, 250, 253, 260–61; photographers and staff, xii, 13, 23, 60–61, 65–67, 116, 300n1; photos passed up by, 26; postwar investigation of, xiii, 76, 251–55, 272; relations with Nazi government, xiii, 21–23, 53, 61, 63, 68, 76–77, 116, 137–38; Roth's dual employment with, 139–40, 145–46; sold to German agency DDP, 261; as sole foreign photo service following closure or absorption of other photo services, 72–73, 131; speedy distribution of photos, 36, 133; staff employed at Büro Laux, 201–5; struggle for control over, 197–99, 214–15; von Lewinski installed as new manager, 198–99; and wartime photo exchange with Nazi Germany, xiii, 5, 6, 77, 132, 200–8; and Wide World Photos, 72. *See also* Baatz, Gerhard; Beukert, Guenther; Boecker, Kurt; Borchert, Eric; Brandt, Wilhelm "Willy"; Brietzke, Arthur von; d'Alquen, Rolf; Daniel, Leon; Eisenstaedt, Alfred; Jacobson, Willy; Jordan, Lisa; Josten, Rudolf; Kuchuk/Kutschuk, Cecile; Lange, Eitel; Meixner, Gerhard; photo exchange between AP and Nazi Germany; Roth, Franz; Seidenstein, Berthold Leopold

AP Lisbon bureau, 193, 200, 202, 203, 205. *See also* Lupi, Luiz
AP London bureau, 86, 200; photo library, 17–18, 149, 261
AP Moscow bureau, xi, 45, 95, 221, 222, 230, 232
AP New York bureau, 36–37; photo library, 147; and wartime photo exchange, 200, 203
AP Swiss bureau, 181
AP Warsaw bureau, 85, 87
Arizona Republic, 228
Arkansas Gazette, 228
arrest and detention of journalists: arrest and detention of Evan Gershkovich in Russia, 270; arrest and detention of journalists in Germany and occupied territory, 4, 33, 70–71, 181–87; arrest of German reporters in America, 179–80; capture of Joe Morton during OSS mission, 266; and Kristallnacht, 13
Assignment in Berlin (Flannery), 178
Associated Press (AP): anti-trust case, 36; and avoiding misinformation, 64–65, 92, 135–36; circulation in 1941, 35; Cooper as general manager, 38–39; daily operations described, 37; influence in the Nazi era, xiv, 270; lack of study of AP's written coverage, 272–73; and local gatekeeping by editors at subscriber newspapers, xv, 37, 271; and maintaining a presence in Nazi Germany in spite of ethical issues, 25–40, 122, 269–71;

Associated Press (*continued*)
need for speedy coverage, xv, 36, 271; news archive from the 1930s and 1940s, 271; origins of, xiv; postwar expansion of, 261–62; and postwar military investigation, 243, 251–55, 272; recommended charges against not pursued, 254–55; reporting on the Holocaust, 225–27, 231, 234–40; reporting on threat to Jews, 29–31, 222–23, 272–73; reporting standards and ethics, xv, 39, 123; reports playing differently in different newspapers across the country, 37–38, 271; rivalry with other agencies, 38, 54, 119, 172, 284n33; unique position in American journalism, 31–32; and wartime news downplayed during World Series, 95–96. *See also* Cooper, Kent; exchange between AP and Nazi Germany
Associated Press Gesellschaft mit beschränkter Haftung. See AP GmbH
Atlantic Charter, 176–77
atrocities: criticisms of journalists as ignoring atrocities, 91; difficulties of verifying and reporting on atrocities, xv–xvi, 91–92, 223, 224, 226–27, 240, 241; Holocaust, 219–41; initial Holocaust atrocity photos not identified as being of Jews, 220, 222, 224; journalists and congressional leaders summoned to witness Holocaust evidence, 239–40; skepticism about Holocaust reports and photos, 221, 223, 226–27, 231, 239, 241; and U.S. propaganda aimed at German population, 187; and World War I propaganda, 226; *See also* concentration camps, death camps, and execution sites; Holocaust

Auschwitz concentration camp, 6, 233–36, 238, 241

Austria: Hitler's takeover of, 12–13, 69–70, 144; Roth in, at the start of the Anschluss, 144–46; Roth's arrest in, 140–41

Baatz, Gerhard: at AP GmbH, 23, 76–77; at Büro Laux, 201; and invasion of Poland, 84; and invasion of Soviet Union, 164; and Kristallnacht, 13; as PK photographer, 132; postwar career, 259–60

Babi Yar execution site, 191, 222, 229–31, 316n35

Bad Nauheim, journalists detained at, 185–88

Banska Bystrica, 265

Barnes, Ralph, 119

Beam, Jacob D., 19–20, 117, 169–70

Beck, Ludwig, 125–26

Belarus, 163

Belgium, 102–5

Belsen. *See* Bergen-Belsen concentration camp

Belzec death camp, 228, 233

Bergen-Belsen concentration camp, 221, 222, 237–38, 318n57
Berlin: bomb sites promptly cleaned up, 173–74; British bombing raids, 166–68, 170–73; and Kristallnacht, 11–23; lack of public enthusiasm for war on eastern front, 165–66; life in wartime Berlin, 167–74; U.S. embassy, 168–69, 179–80. *See also* AP Berlin news bureau; AP GmbH
Berlin Diary (Shirer), 118, 177, 178
Berliner Illustrierter Zeitung, 163
Beukert, Guenther, 60–61, 280n1, 282n36; as chief photo editor of AP GmbH, 22; dismissed from AP, 22–23; and Kristallnacht, 11–15, 17–18
Beyond Belief: The American Press & the Coming of the Holocaust 1933–1945 (Lipstadt), 19, 223
Birchall, Frederick, 72
Black Madonna of Częstochowa, 88–90
Blitzkrieg, 101–12, 114, 129
Bloodlands: Europe Between Hitler and Stalin (Snyder), 222
Boecker, Kurt, 11, 13
Boehmer, Karl, 110, 111, 119–20, 303n4
Boexelman, Romeo, 238–39
Bohnsack, Thea, 152
Bolgar, Julius, 71–72
Borchert, Eric, 76–77; and anonymous critique of AP GmbH, 116; death in combat, 132; and Kristallnacht, 13; as PK photographer, 23, 131, 136

Boston Globe, 223
Brandeis, Louis, 63
Brandt, Wilhelm "Willy," 1–2, 8, 310n1; and agreement on AP GmbH's exclusive control of Roth's photographs, 137, 163; and AP Berlin bureau following arrest of American journalists, 181; background and career summary, 73–74; conflicts with Nazi officials, 77; dismissed from AP following ICD investigation, 258–59; drafted into the Luftwaffe, 199; and end of the war, 243, 245; Gallagher's defense of, 258–59; and German propaganda photo operation, 136–37; Laux and, 200–202, 204–5, 214–15, 311n17, 313n9; military deferment, 198–99, 201, 210–11; move from Berlin to Ziegenhals, 216, 245; placed in charge of AP GmbH, 1, 73–77; postwar career, 258–60; postwar letter to Lochner, 204–5; and postwar military investigation, 258, 321n44; and protecting AP photo archive, 204–5, 215–16, 245; reunited with Lochner, 257–58; Roth and, 149–50, 151, and struggle for control over AP GmbH, 197–98, 214–15; and Waffen-SS affiliation, 210, 258; and wartime photo exchange, 77, 200–5, 211, 212, 321n44
Brest-Litovsk, 94–95, 155, 303n1
Brietzke, Arthur von, 201, 210, 211

Brooks, W. F., 144–45
Brownshirts, 11, 17, 25, 29, 123
Bryan, Julien, 93
Buchenwald concentration camp, 23, 30, 221, 222, 235–36, 238–39
Bullitt, William C., Jr., 108
Buried by the Times (Leff), 183
Büro Laux (photo agency), 132, 209–16; business prioritized over ethics, 273; daily operations described, 211; difficulties of selling images to German media, 214; establishment of, 201; and final months of WWII, 243; finances of, 214–15; ICD assessment of, 258; and Laux's Waffen-SS affiliation, 210–11, 250; and postwar military investigation, 251–55; and Pressens Bild as go-between, 211–12; Schmidt and, 210; and wartime photo exchange, 200–5, 209–16

Canaris, Wilhelm, 126
Cassidy, Henry C., 109
CBS, 35, 119, 120, 167, 177, 183. *See also* Flannery, Harry W.; Murrow, Edward R.; Shirer, William; Smith, Howard K.
censorship: and AP Berlin bureau, 170; and AP GmbH, 54, 59; and British bombing raids, 173; censorship of casualty estimates, 170; consequences of transgressions, 28–29, 31–34, 59; Cooper's views on, 262; and DNB (official German news agency), 50; and Lochner's determination to avoid expulsion, 26–28, 178; Nazi lack of concern over stories revealing anti-Semitism, 28; and Nazi takeover of Austria, 13; and Operation Barbarossa, 166; and photographs, 130, 134, 205–6, 209; and print stories, 174; and professional frustrations of wartime reporting, 176–77; and radio broadcasts, 32, 174; "responsibility censorship," 27, 54, 81, 166; self-censorship, xi, 27–28, 173, 178; and sensitivity of military information, 28; Seymour's anticensorship position, 59; Shirer on Nazi rules about, 174; U.S. and British censorship, 205–6, 209
Central Press, 230
Chesapeake Association of the Associated Press, 113–14
Chicago Daily News, 32–33, 120. *See also* Deuel, Wallace R.
Chicago Tribune, 35, 179, 225. *See also* Schultze, Sigrid; Small, Alex
Christian Science Monitor. *See* Harsch, Joseph
Churchill, Winston, 50, 102, 176–77, 199, 209
CIC. *See* Counter Intelligence Corps, U.S.
Colbert, Claudette, 64
concentration camps, death camps, and execution sites, 294n49; AP's prewar reporting on, 29–30;

Auschwitz concentration camp, 6, 233–36, 238, 241; Babi Yar execution site, 191, 222, 229–31, 316n35; Belzec death camp, 228, 233; Bergen-Belsen concentration camp, 221, 222, 237–38, 318n57; Buchenwald concentration camp, 23, 30, 221, 222, 235–36, 238–39; Dachau concentration camp, 23, 29–30, 221, 237–38; and execution of journalist Morton, 4, 266–68; Kerch execution site, 219–220; Kharkov execution site, 230; and Kristallnacht, 23; Majdanek death camp, 220–21, 231–33; massacre of Jews of Kiev, 223–24; Mauthausen concentration camp, 4, 263, 266, 268; Oranienburg concentration camp, 30; photographs, 219–21, 224, 230–32, 235–36, 238, 240, 314n3; press tours to concentration camps, death camps, and execution sites, 229–30, 232–33, 235–36, 239; prewar arrest campaigns, 30; Rostov-on-Don execution site, 220; Sachsenhausen concentration camp, 23; Sobibor death camp, 228, 233; Treblinka death camp, 99, 221–22, 228, 233

Conger, Beach, 33–34, 114

Cooper, Kent, xii; and anticipating consequences of U.S. entry into war, 182–83; as AP general manager, 38–39, 54, 138, 147, 213, 262; and AP GmbH's agreement with Nazi government on exclusive photographs, 138; and AP's reporting standards, 39; business ambitions, xiii, 54–55, 61, 75, 122, 137, 138, 147, 173, 261, 262; and complaints about reporting on bombing raids, 172; and creation of AP GmbH, 39, 54–55; death of, 262; and decision to maintain a presence in Nazi Germany, xiii, 31, 38, 179; defense of AP Berlin bureau, 116–17; defenses of Lochner, xii, 38, 113–14, 121–23; embrace of technological advances, 36; falling out with Lochner, 256; and gatekeeping, 38, 40; and ICD investigation of Brandt, 258–59; and journalistic ethics, 39, 122, 123, 262; and Lochner's decision to reject Sanden's photos, 26; management style, 121–22, 262; and misinformation, 92; Morton and, 264, 268; political views, 39–40, 122; and postwar expansion of AP, 261–62; retirement from AP, 262; Steinkopf and, 47; views on journalists as guests of host countries, 40, 122, 262; warnings to Lochner on controversial reporting, 248–49; and wartime photo exchange, 205, 208, 213–14

Counter Intelligence Corps, U.S. (CIC), 251–55, 258, 321n44

"Covering Tyranny: The AP and Nazi Germany: 1933–1945" (AP account), 8

Cowan, Howard, 237–38

Czechoslovakia: Hitler's annexation of Sudetenland, 12–13, 84, 131; and PK companies, 131; Roth in, 146
Częstochowa, 88–90, 158

Dachau concentration camp, 23, 29–30, 221, 237–38
Da Costa, Firmino Marques, 204, 206–8, 253
Daily Oklahoman, 36
Daily Telegraph, 224–25
d'Alquen, Guenther, 300n1
d'Alquen, Rolf, 300n1
Daniel, Leon, 65, 68, 289n15
Daniszewski, John, 6
Danzig, 2, 81–84, 94, 110, 133, 169
DDP (photo agency), 261
De Luce, Daniel, 93–94, 232–33, 249
Denmark, 3, 102–4
Des Moines Register, 228
De Terra, Hilde Steinberger. *See* Lochner, Hilde
Deuel, Wallace R., 20–22, 119, 177, 178
Deutsches Nachrichtenbüro. *See* DNB
Dewey, Thomas, 20
Dickson, John Paul, 179, 182
Diebow, Hans, 63
Dieckhoff, Hans-Heinrich, 19–20
Dietrich, Otto, 110, 133, 199, 294n50
Dietzel, Walter, 82
Dimbleby, Richard, 318n57
Dixon, Kenneth L., 227–28
DNB (official German news agency), 34, 174; absorption of foreign photo services, 72; AP reliance on, 111; and arrest of German reporters in America, 179; and invasion of Norway and Denmark, 102; and invasion of Poland, 83; news exchange agreement with AP, 49–50; photo agency Weltbild, 72, 198
Dodd, Martha, 43
Dodd, William E., 43
Drottningholm (Swedish refugee ship), 188, 189, 190, 192
Dulles, Allen, 127
Dunkirk, 104, 129

Editor's Law, 21, 55, 59
Eisenhower, Dwight D., 239
Eisenstaedt, Alfred, 65, 68, 289n15
Enderis, Guido, 118–20, 179, 182, 183
Erbelding, Rebecca, 227
Ernst, Mrs. (assistant at propaganda ministry), 14
ethics: and AP GmbH, 63, 65, 114–16; AP reporting standards and ethics, xv, 39, 123; and Associated Press's decision to remain in Nazi Germany, 25–40, 122, 269–71; and Büro Laux, 273; Cooper and, 39, 122, 123, 262; Lochner and, 119, 123–24; and press tours, 119–20; Shirer and, 119; and wartime photo exchange, 273. *See also* journalists, criticisms of; propaganda; Lochner, Louis
euthanasia program, 28
executions: execution of journalists, 4, 263, 266–68; and Holocaust.

INDEX 339

See also concentration camps, death camps, and execution sites

FBI, 179–80, 192–93
Final Solution, 223, 240, 273, 314n5. *See also* Holocaust
Finland, 3
First Casualty, The (Knightley), 131
Fischer, Ernest, 28–29, 32, 179; anti-Semitism of, 189–92; arrest and detention, 182, 188; and press tour of Kiev, 191, 192; and press tour of Krakow, 191; Schmidt and, 199
Fisher, Paul, 179, 187
Flannery, Harry W., 177, 178
Foe We Face, The (Huss), 178
Ford, Henry, 115
Foreign Office, German: Paul Schmidt as chief spokesman, 199; rivalry with propaganda ministry, 199; and struggle for control over AP GmbH, 198–99; and von Lewinski appointed as manager of AP GmbH, 198–99; and wartime photo exchange, 202, 204, 209, 211, 252. *See also* Büro Laux; Laux, Helmut; Ribbentrop, Joachim von; Schmidt, Paul
France, 104, 106–7
Franco, Francisco, 57, 143
Frank, Anne, 221
Frankfurter, Felix, 63
Franz Eher Nachfolger GmbH, 63
Froelich, Hans, 165
Fry, Varian, 34
Frye, William, 237

Gallagher, Wes, 102, 104, 249–50, 258, 260, 261
Gandhi, Mahatma, 142
Garai, Bert, 72
gatekeeping, xiv, xv, 37–38, 40
Geist, Raymond, 66
Germany: annexation of Sudetenland, 12–13, 84, 131; Bergen-Belsen concentration camp, 221, 222, 237–38, 318n57; Blitzkrieg style of warfare, 101–12; Buchenwald concentration camp, 23, 30, 221, 222, 235–36, 238–39; Dachau concentration camp, 23, 29–30, 221, 237–38; invasion of Poland, 81–99, 125; invasion of Soviet Union, 155–66; laws impacting journalists; Lochner's views on Nazis and Germany society, 44–45, 246–49; Oranienburg concentration camp, 30; Sachsenhausen concentration camp, 23; takeover of Austria, 12–13, 69–70, 144. *See also* AP Berlin news bureau; AP GmbH; Berlin; DNB; Editor's Law; Foreign Office, German; Hitler, Adolf; Holocaust; Jews; Nazis; PK companies; propaganda ministry; World War II
Germany Puts the Clock Back (Mowrer), 32
Gershkovich, Evan, 270
Gessen, Masha, 270
ghettos, 97–99, 135, 158, 162, 164, 191, 222, 228, 273
Gilbert, Adrian, 162

Gilmore, Eddy, 229–232
Goebbels, Joseph, 8; and constraints on German journalists, 21–22; diaries edited and translated by Lochner, 256; and food shortages, 169; and invasion of Soviet Union, 156, 161; and Kristallnacht, 17; and ousting of journalists from the profession, 49; personal characteristics, 22; and prewar reporting, 30; rivalry with Ribbentrop and Foreign Office, 199; Roth and, 139, 152, 153
Göring, Hermann, 25, 117; on Allied bombing, 170; and food shortages, 169; Lochner's reporting on, 247; newspaper columns commissioned from, 41; Steinkopf on, 47
Gould, Alan Jenks, 38–40, 205, 206
Graffis, Jean A., 179
Graubart, Arthur, 184
Great Britain: Atlantic Charter, 176–77; and beginning of WWII, 86; bombing of London, 167, 170; bombing raids on Berlin, 166–68, 170–73; German plans for attacks on, 106; liberation of concentration camps, 237
Gregg, Robert E., 253, 254
Grossman, Vasily, 221–22
Grynszpan, Herschel, 16

Hall, Harald, 301n4
Hanfstaegnl, Ernst, 46
Harsch, Joseph, 119–120, 177, 178
Hartford Courant, 228

Hauptmann, Bruno Richard, 49
Havas, 54
Heald, Morrell, 52, 245
Hearst, William Randolph, 20, 26, 41, 42, 179, 284n33. *See also* International News Service
Heimlich, William F., 258
Heinzerling, Agnes, 1, 2, 3
Heinzerling, Larry, xvi–xvii, 1–8
Heinzerling, Lynn, 1–2, 3–5; assessment of Lochner, 118; background and career summary, 47–48; in Copenhagen, 102–3; in Danzig, 81–83; and invasion of Soviet Union, 156–57, 166; and investigation of Joe Morton's fate, 263, 267–68; and life in wartime Berlin, 169; and radio broadcasts, 50; in Rotterdam, 111
Heinzerling, Lynn, Jr., 1, 4–5
Henry, Taylor, 108–9
Herschaft, Jacques and Jean, 6
Herschaft, Randy, xvi–xvii, 6–8
Hicks, Wilson, 41–42, 143
Himmler, Heinrich, 209, 243
Hitler, Adolf: annexation of Sudetenland, 12–13, 84, 131; assassination attempt, 127, 212, 247–48, 272; and Blitzkrieg style of warfare, 101; cabinet shakeup of February 1938, 51–52; declaration of war on U.S., 183–84; and eastern front, 166; and invasion of France, 107–10; and invasion of Poland, 83–85, 96, 125; Laux's iconic photo of, 257; Lochner's interview with

(1932), 123–24; Lochner's reporting on, 105–6, 189, 223, 247–48; Lochner's views on, 44–45; and Munich Pact, 12; newspaper columns commissioned from, 41–42; and Operation Barbarossa, 155, 156; prewar reporting on, 12–13, 30–31; takeover of Austria, 12–13, 69–70, 144; Thompson's interview with, 33; threats to annihilate Jewish population, 30–31, 223
Hitler, Alois Matzelsberger, Jr., 48
Hoffmann, Heinrich, 23, 68, 138, 144, 212
Holland, 95, 102–5, 111, 129–30
Hollander, Ron, 240, 273
Holocaust, 219–41; and Allied-liberated areas, 222, 235–40; difficulties of verifying and reporting on atrocities, xv–xvi, 223, 224, 226–27, 240, 241; evidence available from 1942, 220–21, 227–28, 240; execution methods, 220, 223–25, 314n5; Final Solution, 240, 273, 314n5; first reports and photos of gas chambers and crematoriums, 220, 224–25; ghettos, 97–99, 135, 158, 162, 164, 191, 222, 228, 273; photographs, 219–21, 224, 230–32, 235–36, 238, 240, 314n3; reports and photos downplayed, 225–28, 241; skepticism about Holocaust reports and photos, 221, 223, 226–27, 231, 239, 241; and Soviet Army–liberated areas, 219–21, 229–31, 233–35; U.S. public's knowledge about, 220–21, 227–28, 240–41, 273; victims not identified as Jews in early Soviet-made photos and reports, 220, 222, 224; and World Jewish Congress press conference (1942), 227. *See also* concentration camps, death camps, and execution sites
"Holocaust Papers, The" (AP series), 7
Hoover, Herbert, 20, 42
Hottelet, Richard, 33
Howard, N. R., 206
Hoylen, Paul J., 253, 254
Hugenberg, Alfred, 50
Hull, Cordell, 63
Hunt, Frazier, 30
Huss, Pierre, 108, 118–20, 167, 178

ICD. *See* Information Control Division
Ickes, Harold L., 114–17
Illustrierter Beobachter (Nazi Party magazine), 64, 139, 143, 151, 152
Information Control Division (ICD), 258–59
INS. *See* International News Service
International News Photo service, 26, 230
International News Service (INS), 14, 32, 103, 118, 119, 179, 284n33. *See also* Huss, Pierre; Speck, Hugo
Iran, 269–70

Jacobson, Willy, 65, 69, 70–71, 280n1
Jacobson-Sonnenfeld photo agency, 71

Japan, 175–76
Jenkins, Harry, 65
Jewish Telegraphic Agency (JTA), 223
Jews: and American anti-Semitism, 189–92; anti-Jewish photo captions, 63–64; AP assistance to Jewish staff, 65–66, 69; AP's reporting on threats to, 29–31, 222–23, 272–73; early official Nazi anti-Semitic actions, 29, 54–56; and Editor's Law, 55–56; fate of Jews in Austria, 70; fate of Jews in Lithuania, 164; fate of Jews in Poland, 97–99, 220–21, 225, 228, 231–35; fate of Jews in Soviet Union, 166, 220; fate of Jews in Ukraine, 162, 191–92, 219–20, 223–24, 229–30; and Fischer's anti-Semitism, 189–92; forced dismissal from AP GmbH, xiii, 54, 65, 69, 131; and Holocaust, 219–41; initial Holocaust atrocity photos by Soviets not identified as being of Jews, 220, 222, 224; Jewish employees of AP GmbH, 65–71; Lochner's warnings on hatred of Jews as a cardinal Nazi doctrine, 29; prewar arrest campaigns, 30; prewar Nazi threats to annihilate Jewish population, 30–31; and U.S. propaganda aimed at German population, 187–88; U.S. public's attitude toward Jews of Europe, 19, 240–41. *See also* concentration camps, death camps, and execution sites; Holocaust; Kristallnacht; Nürnberg Laws

Jordan, Lisa, 65, 68
Jordan, Max, 119
Josten, Rudolf, 49, 59–60, 181, 184
journalists: accounts following release from German detention, 188–89; and anti-Semitism, 189–92, 241; AP journalists' lack of prominence, 35, 36; and current world events, 269–70; detained American journalists exchanged for German journalists, 184, 185, 188–93; dual employment of photographers with PK companies and AP GmbH, 130–31, 137, 139–40, 143, 145–46, 149–50; embedded with the military, xvi, 2–3, 88, 246–47; fate of AP photographers present at Kristallnacht, 23; honest vs. favorable reporting, 119–20; inverted pyramid model of reporting, 271; journalists departing from Berlin, 174, 176–79; professional rivalries, 45; reputational benefits of being expelled from Germany, 32; as resource for U.S. Department of War, 187–88. *See also* journalists, and challenges in wartime; journalists, criticisms of; photographers; specific journalists, press agencies, and newspapers; criticisms of; Roth, Franz
journalists: battles with the Nazi hierarchy, 15, 20, 45–46, 57–60; constraints on German journalists, 21–22; difficulties of reporting in a

dictatorship, xvi, 13, 28–29; difficulties of verifying and reporting on atrocities, xv–xvi, 91–92, 223, 224, 226–27, 240, 241; and Editor's Law, 21, 55–56, 59; execution of journalists, 4, 263, 266–68; expulsion from Germany, 28, 32–35, 71–72; German manipulation of journalists, through trips or interviews used as rewards for favorable coverage, 119–20; importance of being "on the ground," 269–71; journalists killed or wounded in combat, 132–33, 139, 150–52; journalists ousted by Goebbels, 49; life in detention at Bad Nauheim, 185–88; life in wartime Berlin, 167–74; life in wartime Europe, 81–82, 85–86, 97; professional frustrations of wartime reporting, 97, 119, 174, 176–77; and protecting sources, 19, 31; reporting restricted to official German statements, 87–88, 111, 157–58, 170, 171, 172, 174. *See also* AP Berlin news bureau: and decision to maintain a presence in Nazi Germany; censorship; press tours; Kristallnacht

journalists, criticisms of: criticisms of journalists as duped by Nazis, 90–91, 104, 106, 113–17, 120–21, 165; criticisms of journalists as ignoring atrocities, 91; criticisms of journalists as incompetent adventurers, 142–43; criticisms of journalists participating in Nazi-escorted press tours, 104, 119–20; Harsch's memo, 119–21; Lochner accused of being a Nazi sympathizer, xii, 91, 102, 105, 108, 117, 124, 192, 248; Lochner's assessments of young AP journalists, 256; peers' assessments and criticisms of Lochner, 118–19, 247, 248; Roth's assessments of foreign journalists, 142–44

Joyce, William, 169–70
JTA. *See* Jewish Telegraphic Agency
Judenboykott, 29, 273
"Judenfrage" in Bild, Die (Scharnberg), 64
Juden in USA, Die (Nazi pamphlet), 63–64

Kalb, Marvin, 241
Kaltenbrunner, Ernst, 266, 268
Kansas City Star, 228
Katyn massacre, 314–15n6
Kelly, Hugh V., 204
Kelly, Mary Louise, 269–270
Kerch, 219–221
Keystone View Inc., 72, 131, 143
Kharkov, 230–31
Kherson, 191
Kidd, George, 82
Kiev, 166, 191, 192, 223–24, 228–29
Kirk, Alexander, 126
Knightley, Phillip, 131
Komor, Valerie, 6
Komsomolskaya Pravda (Soviet newspaper), 219

Krakow, 191, 294n50
Krasnaya Zvezda (Soviet Army newspaper), 221, 231
Kristallnacht, 11–23, 123, 280n1, 281n10; AP journalists' experiences during, 11–13, 15, 17, 20–21; and AP photographs and photographers, 13–18, 21–23; AP print stories on, 16–19; death and destruction caused by, 18, 23; Goebbels's radio address during, 17; Heinzerling family and, 2; Lochner and, 16–17, 20–21; and murder of Ernst vom Rath, 16–17; name origin, 19; photos approved for distribution, 15–18; and protecting sources, 19; restrictions on Jews following, 17; Roth and, 146; terror against people and property, 18; and U.S. public opinion, 19
Kuchuk/Kutschuk, Cecile, 65, 69
Kurzbein, Heiner: and agreement on AP GmbH's exclusive control of Roth's photographs, 137–38; Brandt and, 76, 198–99; as head of propaganda ministry photo department, 13–14; and Kristallnacht, 12, 15; personal characteristics, 14

La Guardia, Fiorello, 60, 63
Lange, Eitel, 67–68
Last Train from Berlin (Smith), 183
Latvia, 163
Laux, Claudia, 257
Laux, Helmut: and AP GmbH photo archive, 250; arrest, detention, and interrogation by U.S. military, 251–53; background and career summary, 200–1; and benefits of wartime photo exchange, 204; Brandt and, 200–2, 204–5, 214–15, 311n17, 313n9; and control over AP GmbH and its assets, 214–15; death of, 257; and end of the war, 243–45, 250–55; establishment of Büro Laux photo agency, 201; and financial difficulties, 214–15; health issues, 244; ICD assessment of, 258; and iconic Hitler photo, 257; internment at war's end, 257; Lochner and, 202–4, 211; military deferments arranged for Brandt and other AP GmbH employees, 210–11; postwar activities, 257, 259; and proposal for photo exchange, 200–5; as Ribbentrop's personal photographer at Foreign Office, 200; search for Lochner during final months of war, 250–52; and Waffen-SS affiliation, 210–11, 244, 250–52. *See also* Büro Laux
Leff, Laurel, 183, 240–41
Lehrbas, Lloyd, 85–87
Leibstandarte SS Adolf Hitler, 132, 148
Leningrad, 166
Lewinski, Karl von, 198–99, 310n5
Life magazine, 16, 257, 289n15
Lindbergh, Charles, 42, 115

INDEX 345

Lindbergh kidnapping and murder case, 49
Lippman, Walter, 63
Lipstadt, Deborah E., 19, 190, 223, 226–28
Lisbon, released journalists in, 188–89. *See also* AP Lisbon bureau
Lithuania, 163, 164
Lloyd, John, 107
Lochner, Frederick, 43
Lochner, Hilde (Hilde Steinberger De Terra), 44, 175, 178, 181, 184, 257
Lochner, Louis: accused of being a Nazi sympathizer, xii, 91, 102, 105, 108, 117, 124, 192, 248; accused of biased reporting, 113–24; and anticipating consequences of U.S. entry into war, 179–80, 182–83; as AP Berlin bureau chief and AP GmbH head, 42–46, 56–57, 65; and AP GmbH's agreement with Nazi government on exclusive photographs, 138; arrest and detention, 181–87; and avoiding expulsion from Germany, 26–27, 122; background and career summary, 42–44; battles with AP editors and executives over Berlin bureau's coverage, 36, 59; battles with propaganda ministry, 20–21, 45–46, 57–60, 65, 172; Brandt and, 73–74, 257–58; on constraints on German journalists, 22; contacts with underground German resistance, 125–27; controversial reporting, 246–49; Cooper and, 121–22, 256; Cooper's defenses of, xii, 38, 113–14, 121–23; Cooper's warnings to, 248–49; death of, 257; and decision not to purchase Sanden's photos of humiliated attorney Siegel, 26, 273; and determination to maintain a presence in Nazi Germany, xiii, 26–27, 31–32, 39, 59, 178–79, 270; dispatch following release from detention, 189; and Editor's Law, 55–56; effusive language in reporting on German military successes, 102, 105–6, 110–12, 124; and end of the war, 243–44, 246–49; family, 43–44, 175, 178, 184; and favoritism during press tours, 119–121; FBI investigation of, 192–93; gradual exit from reporting, 249–50; handling of wartime stories, 121–24; Heinzerling's assessment of, 118; and Hitler interview (1932), 123–24; on Hitler's plans to eliminate Jews, 223; and invasion of Poland, 82, 120–21, 125–27; and journalistic ethics, 119, 123–24; and Kristallnacht, 16–21; Laux and, 202–4, 211, 250–52; love of music, 118; motivations for staying in Berlin, 178–79; network of sources, 43, 178, 247; as news correspondent, 46, 65; as one of the last American correspondents in Berlin, 174; and passing on misinformation, 120–21; and Pearl Harbor attack, 175–76;

Lochner, Louis (*continued*)
  peers' assessments and criticisms of, 118–19, 247, 248; personal characteristics, 43, 52, 118; personal views of, 44–45, 124, 246–49, 256; and photo exchange with Nazi Germany, 193, 200–4, 243, 254; postwar career, 256; and postwar military investigation, 243, 254; and press tours, 88–90, 94, 96–97, 103, 105–8, 119, 158–166, 294n50; and professional rivalries, 45; and protecting AP GmbH, 31; and protecting sources, 31; public speeches after leaving Germany, 124; and Pulitzer Prize, 45, 52; reliance on propaganda ministry for access to news, 111; replaced by Gallagher at AP Berlin bureau, 249–250; reporting on Blitzkrieg, 101–3; reporting on Buchenwald, 238–39; reporting on final months of war, 246–49; reporting on Göring, 247; reporting on Hitler, 96, 109–10, 189, 247–48; reporting on interlude between hostilities (*Sitzkrieg*), 96–97; reporting on Nürnberg trials, 255; reporting on refugees and civilian impacts of battle, 89–90, 111–12, 124; and reporting restricted to official German statements, 172; retirement from AP, 255–56; return to U.S., 117, 192–93, 245; Roth and, 143, 144, 146; and Rust's order to boycott AP (1935), 34–35; and secret document about planned invasion of Poland, 125–27; and self-censorship, 27–28; Shirer on, 118–19; stories and photos passed up by, 26, 123, 273; story sent to Swiss bureau prior to arrest, 181; and suggestion for columns to be commissioned from Hitler, 41–42; support for Jewish employees of AP GmbH, 65–66, 69–70; and understaffing problems, 51; and U.S. propaganda aimed at German population, 188; as war correspondent embedded with military forces, 246–47; *What About Germany?* 126, 245

London, 167, 170. *See also* AP London bureau
Lorenz, Heinz, 198
Los Angeles Times, 225, 239
Lupi, Luiz, 193, 202, 203, 207, 253, 311n15
Luxembourg, 103, 104
Lwow (Lviv), 93–94, 160–64, 304n17

Majdanek death camp, 220–21, 231–33
Mariupol, 270
Matzhold, Louis, 71
Mauthausen concentration camp, 4, 263, 266, 268
Meixner, Gerhard, 116, 151
Meyer, Kurt, 148, 150, 151–52
Miami Herald, 228
military, German: journalists embedded with the military, 88,

131, 132; journalists traveling under military escort, 88–90. *See also* PK companies; press tours; Roth, Franz
military, U.S.: Allied occupation and non-fraternization order, 246–47; military investigation of AP photo exchange, 243, 251–55, 272; war correspondents embedding with military forces, 2, 246–47
Miller, Steve, 268–69, 310n1
Mills, James, 141, 142–43
Ministry of Public Enlightenment and Propaganda. *See* propaganda ministry
Minneapolis Star, 121, 213
misinformation, 91–92, 120–21, 136. *See also* propaganda
Molotov, Vyacheslav, 224
Molotov-Ribbentrop nonaggression pact, 83, 94, 156
Monte Cassino Abbey, 4
Morris, Leland, 188, 205
Morton, Joseph, 4, 263–69
Morton, Letty, 264, 268
Mowrer, Edgar, 31, 32–33
Münchner Neueste Nachrichten (newspaper), 58
Munich Pact, 12
Murrow, Edward R., 35, 167, 177, 240
Mussolini, Benito, 140, 201, 213, 225
Mutual Broadcasting Co., 179

Nazis: Blitzkrieg style of warfare, 101–12; Editor's Law, 55–56, 59;

euthanasia program, 28; favoritism in press tours, 119–21; and honest vs. favorable reporting, 119–20; increasingly poor relations with foreign press, 176–77; journalists' books on, 178; Molotov-Ribbentrop nonaggression pact, 83, 94, 156; Nazi Party control of German media, 49–50; Nürnberg Laws (1935), 12; Nürnberg trials, 83, 221, 255, 268; press tours and interviews as rewards for favorable coverage, 119; prewar attitudes toward, in the U.S., 41–42; and resistance movement, 125–27; and summer Olympics of 1936, 35. *See also* Brownshirts; DNB; Goebbels, Joseph; Hitler, Adolf; Holocaust; Jews PK companies; press tours; propaganda; propaganda ministry; Ribbentrop, Joachim von; Waffen-SS
NBC, 119, 179. *See also* Fisher, Paul
New Orleans Times Picayune, 228
news agencies and broadcasting companies. *See* ACME News Service; AP Berlin news bureau; Associated Press; CBS; DNB; International News Service; Jewish Telegraphic Agency; Mutual Broadcasting Co.; NBC; Overseas News Agency; Polish Telegraphic Agency; Reuters; TASS; Telegraphen-Union; Transocean; United Press; Wolff Telegraphic Bureau

"newshawks," 1, 8. *See also* journalists; photographers
Newspaper Enterprise Association, 30
newsreel films, 93, 235, 240
New York Daily News, 171
New York Herald Tribune, 33–34, 37–38, 114, 119, 120, 247, 248. *See also* Barnes, Ralph; Shirer, William
New York Post, 205
New York Times, 118; circulation in 1941, 35; Hitler's speeches printed by, 115; Holocaust reports downplayed, 225, 228; Morton and, 264; and photos of Jewish life in Poland, 98–99; picture service Wide World Photos, 72, 131; praise for reporters of, 114; staff at time of Pearl Harbor attack, 179; and variation in representation of AP reports, 38. *See also* Enderis, Guido; Tolischus, Otto
Night of the Long Knives (1934), 44, 49
nonfraternization order, 246–47
Norawski, Nawench, 91
Norgaard, Noland "Boots," 264, 265
North American Newspaper Alliance, 33
North Korea, 269
Norway, 102–4
Noyes, Frank, 114–16
Nürnberg Laws (1935), 12
Nürnberg trials, 83, 221, 255, 268

Odessa, 191, 192
Oechsner, Frederich, 108, 120, 173, 174, 179, 191

Office of Strategic Services (OSS), 263, 264–66
Olmsted, Kathryn S., 41
Olympics (1936), 35
ONA. *See* Overseas News Agency
Operation Barbarossa, 155–66
Operation Overlord, 308n28
Oranienburg concentration camp, 30
Orbis, 212
Ornstein, Wilhelm, 267
OSS. *See* Office of Strategic Services
Overseas News Agency (ONA), 223

Pacific & Atlantic (photo agency), 197
Parker, Robert B., 86
Parsons, Geoffrey, Jr., 248
Patterns of Conquest (Harsch), 178
Pearl Harbor attack, 175–76, 179
People Under Hitler (Deuel), 178
Peterson, Elmer W., 85–87
photo agencies: agencies exiting Germany, 131; competition among press agencies, 130, 134–35; Nazi assault on foreign photo services operating in Germany, 71–72. *See also* AP GmbH; Büro Laux; DDP; International News Photo service; Orbis; Pacific & Atlantic; PIX; Presse-Hoffmann; Pressens Bild; Sovfoto; United Features Syndicate; Weltbild GmbH; Wide World Photos
photo exchange between AP and Nazi Germany, 197–216; benefits to German Foreign Office and AP, 204–5, 209; Brandt and, 77, 200–5,

211, 212, 321n44; and Büro Laux photo agency, 200–5, 209–16; business prioritized over ethics, 273; and CIC investigation, 321n44; Cooper and, 205, 208, 213–14; Da Costa and, 205–8; denunciation of, 272; details of exchange obscured, 207–8, 213–14; diplomatic courier as transfer mechanism, 202, 203, 211, 253, 254; exchange scheme described, 203, 206–8, 211–12; Gould and, 205, 206, 207; and Laux's Waffen-SS affiliation, 210–11, 250; Lochner and, 200–4; Lupi and, 202, 203, 207, 253; origins of, 197–202; photo transmission technology, 212; Portugal as neutral intermediary, 200, 202, 203, 205; and postwar military investigation, 243, 251–55, 272; and propaganda, 209, 213, 253; Ribbentrop and, 204, 209; Schmidt and, 210; Sweden and, 211–12; and Trading with the Enemy Act, xiii, 254–55, 260, 272; U.S. and British censorship of photos, 205–6, 209; U.S. government knowledge about, 205–6; *See also* Laux, Helmut; Lupi, Luiz

photographers: dual employment of photographers with PK companies and AP GmbH, 130–31, 137, 139–40, 143, 145–46, 149–50; journalists embedded with the military, 157; and Kristallnacht, 13–18; photo monopoly of PK journalists, 93, 130–33. *See also* journalists; PK companies; propaganda; Roth, Franz

photographs, 129–38; AP GmbH photo archive, 197–98, 245, 250, 260–61; and beginning of WWII, 129–30; and Blitzkrieg, 129–130; caption issues, 54, 57–60, 64–65, 133–36, 149; and censorship, 130, 134, 205–6, 209; distribution of PK photos, 133–37; fake photographs, 214; and final months of WWII, 243; of German soldier and Polish prisoner, 91; of Hitler, 212, 257, 272; Holocaust photos, 219–21, 224, 230–32, 235, 236, 238, 240, 314n3; and invasion of Soviet Union, 157–66; "Jews-learning-to-work" photo series, 64; and Kristallnacht, 13–18; Nazi control over, 13–14, 54, 55, 130–33; news value of, 131, 157, 213, 216, 243, 272; photos sent and received through wartime photo exchange, 205, 209, 211–14, 243; photo transmission technology, 212; propaganda value of, xii–xiii, 5, 130, 131, 134–38, 149, 157, 213, 253; Roth's photo of Hitler's return to Berlin after defeat of the French, 109–10; Roth's photos of Soviet POWs, 148–49, 261; routes for sending out of Germany, 95; Sanden's photo of public humiliation of attorney Michael Siegel, 25–27; and Spanish Civil

photographs (*continued*)
  War, 57–58; statistics on photo transmissions, 303n10; Steinkopf's photos of carnage in Lwow, 161; Steinkopf's photos of Polish Jewish life, 98–99; U-boat photos distributed by AP, 115. *See also* photo exchange between AP and Nazi Germany; propaganda ministry
PIX (photo agency), 68–69, 99, 148, 289n15
PK companies (Propaganda Kompanien der Wehrmacht), 87–88, 130–33; distribution of photos from, 133–37; dual employment of photographers with PK companies and AP GmbH, 130–31, 137, 139–40, 143, 145–46, 149–50; journalists embedded with the military, 131, 132, 157; journalists killed or wounded in combat, 132–33, 150–52; and newsreels, 93; photo monopoly, 93, 130–33; propaganda as primary goal, 130, 131; recruited/drafted from all German media, 130–31; Roth and, 132, 148–51. *See also* Baatz, Gerhard; Borchert, Eric; Roth, Franz
Poland: Auschwitz, 6, 233–36, 238, 241; Baatz in, 132; Belzec death camp, 228, 233; Black Madonna of Częstochowa, 88–90; and caption issues in photos, 64, 136; document about planned invasion passed to Lochner, 125–27; fate of Jews in, 97–99, 220–21, 225, 228, 231–35; invasion of (1939), 28, 81–99, 120–21, 132; Majdanek death camp, 220–21, 231–33; and Molotov-Ribbentrop nonaggression pact, 83; press tours to, 88–90, 158, 191; Sobibor death camp, 228, 233; speedy distribution of photos from invasion, 133; Treblinka death camp, 99, 221–22, 228, 233
Polevoy, Boris, 234
Polish Telegraphic Agency, 91, 162
Pope, Arthur Upham, 116
Portugal, and wartime photo exchange, 200, 202, 203, 205
Pravda, 234
Presse-Hoffmann (photo agency), 23
Pressens Bild (photo agency), 211–12
Pressman, Joel, 64
press tours, 88–90; of cleaned-up bomb sites, 173–74; of concentration camps, death camps, and execution sites, 220, 229–33, 238–39; and criticisms of journalists, 104, 119–20; and difficulties of reporting in a dictatorship, 158; of eastern front, 158–66; and favoritism, 119–21; of occupied areas in Western Europe, 103–8; of occupied Poland, 88–90, 94–95, 191, 192, 294n50; press tours and interviews as rewards for favorable coverage, 119; and propaganda, 88–90, 104–6, 158, 173–74; tradeoffs of, 158

Price, Byron, 39–40, 91, 206, 312n29
prisoners of war, 148–49, 261
propaganda: AP photos turned into Nazi propaganda, xii–xiii, 5, 53, 60, 63–64, 134–38; criticisms of journalists as duped by Nazis, 90–91, 104, 106, 113–17, 120–21, 165; goals of, 88; and photographs, 130, 131, 134–38; and press tours, 88–90, 104–6, 158, 173–74; and pretext for invasion of Poland, 136; Roth as propaganda photographer, 146–49, 164; and skepticism about reports of atrocities, 221, 226, 239; Soviet Union and, 221; U.S. propaganda aimed at German population, 187–88; and wartime photo exchange, 209, 213, 253; and World War I, 226. *See also* censorship; PK companies; propaganda ministry
Propaganda Kompanien der Wehrmacht. *See* PK companies
propaganda ministry (Ministry of Public Enlightenment and Propaganda), 8; and anonymous critique of AP GmbH, 114–16; and AP GmbH, 53, 54, 57–61, 63, 68, 76–77, 116; and AP GmbH's agreement with Nazi government on exclusive photographs, 144–45, 151; and Brandt's takeover of AP GmbH, 76; and consequences of censorship transgressions, 59; and Editor's Law, 21, 55–56, 59; establishment of, 27; and Kristallnacht, 11–16; Kurzbein as head of photo department, 13–14; Lochner's battles with, 20–21, 45–46, 57–60, 65, 172; and Lochner's handling of wartime stories, 122; and Orbis photographs, 212; and photo captions, 54, 57–60; photos requiring ministry approval, 27, 54, 55; and PK companies, 130, 131; procedure for releasing/banning photographs, 13–14; and radio broadcasts, 27; and "responsibility censorship" of print media, 27; rivalry with Foreign Office, 199; and Roth's photographs, 147–49; and struggle for control over AP GmbH, 197–99. *See also* censorship; Kurzbein, Heiner; PK companies

Pulitzer, Joseph, 239–40
Pulitzer Prize, 311–12n29; and AP war correspondents, 3; De Luce and, 232; and Korean War atrocities, 6; Lehrbas and, 86; Lochner and, 45, 52; Mowrer and, 32–33

Radcliffe, Cyril, 134, 157
radio, 50; broadcasters in Berlin at time of Pearl Harbor attack, 179; and censorship, 174; fame of radio correspondents, 35; relative safety of radio correspondents, 32; smuggled radio at Bad Nauheim, 187
Radio Moscow, 166, 230, 234
Rado, Emmy, 127

Redkin, Mark, 219–20
refugees, 89–90, 162, 164, 189, 190
Reichenau, Walter von, 105
Reichssender Berlin (official German radio station), 50
Resch, Al, 134, 135, 136, 303n10
"responsibility censorship," 27, 54, 81, 166
Reuters, 14, 54, 287n3
Ribbentrop, Joachim von: and benefits of wartime photo exchange, 204, 209; and invasion of Soviet Union, 155, 156; and press tours of occupied areas, 103; rivalry with Goebbels and propaganda ministry, 199; and wartime photo exchange, 209, 252
Rising, David, 6
Roberts, Andrew, 177
Rollins, Byron H., 236
Romania, 264
Roosevelt, Franklin D., 127, 176, 177, 199, 209
Rosenberg, Alfred, 48
Rostov-on-Don, 220
Roth, Franz, 8, 76, 139–54, 301n4; as adventurer/daredevil, 141–42, 153–54; agreement on AP GmbH's exclusive control of Roth's photographs, 137–38, 163; and anonymous critique of AP GmbH, 116; archived papers, 152–54; arrangement with AP GmbH for right of first refusal of photographs, 144–45, 151; arrest in Austria, 140–41; in Austria at start of Anschluss, 144–46; background and career summary, 139–40; as committed Nazi, 23, 139, 143, 146, 153; in Czechoslovakia, 146; descendants' views on Roth and his work, 152–54; descriptions of other journalists, 142–44; dual employment with PK company and AP GmbH, 139–40, 143, 145–46, 149–50; and end of AP monopoly on distribution of photos within Germany, 151; in Ethiopia, 141; injuries and death in combat, 132–33, 139, 150–52; and Kristallnacht, 13, 146; medical service, 141; most photographs not distributed by AP, 147; photo of Hitler's return to Berlin (July 6, 1940), 109–10; photos of Lwow (Lviv), 163; photos of occupied Paris, 147–48; photos of Soviet POWs, 148–49, 261; as PK photographer, 132; prison cellar photo, 163; as propaganda photographer, 146–49, 164; publication of collected wartime photos (2008), 152; and Spanish Civil War, 143–44; unpublished memoir, 141–42, 150; and Waffen-SS affiliation, 23, 139, 148–51
Roth, Hans, 152–54
Roth, Tuya, 152–54
Rotterdam, 3, 111, 129
Rumors, 28, 92, 102, 117, 226–27, 231, 248, 255, 267

INDEX ❧ 353

Russia, invasion of Ukraine, 270
Rust, Bernhard, 34

Sachs, Solomon, 7
Sachsenhausen concentration camp, 23
Sanden, Heinrich, 25–27, 282n3
Schaleben, Joy, 28
Scharnberg, Harriet, 5, 6, 8, 53, 64, 68, 134, 140, 148, 149, 272
Schildbach, Robert, 49, 171, 172, 184
Schmidt, Paul, 180, 199, 210, 211, 244, 252
Schultze, Sigrid, 119, 178
Schuppler, Valentine, 141
Das Schwarze Korps (official SS publication), 30–31, 66–69, 72, 300n1
Scoop (Waugh), 142
Seidenstein, Berthold Leopold, 65, 66, 67
Seidler, Kurt, 224
Selassie, Haile, 141
Seymour, Gideon, 22, 58, 59, 61, 74
Shanke, Edwin, 179; arrest and detention, 182, 187; and arrest of German reporters in America, 179; background and career summary, 48; on Hitler's February 1938 internal shakeup, 51–52; and invasion of Poland, 83–84; on life in wartime Berlin, 168; and Pearl Harbor attack, 175–76; radio smuggled by, 187; reassigned to London, 192; on understaffing at AP Berlin bureau, 50–51
Shirer, William, 32, 108, 118; Berlin Diary, 118, 177, 178; departure from Berlin, 174, 177; integrity of, 119; on Lochner, 118–19, 247; on press tours of cleaned-up bomb sites, 173–74
Sibert, Edwin, 254–55
Siegel, Michael, 25, 123, 273, 282n2
Sitzkrieg, 96–97, 102
Slovakia, OSS operation in, 263
Small, Alex, 179, 182, 192
Smith, Charlie, 186
Smith, Howard K., 165, 177, 183, 199, 307n9
Smolensk, 164–65, 314n6
Snyder, Timothy, 222
Sobibor death camp, 228, 233
Sovfoto (Soviet photo agency), 232
Soviet Union: German invasion of, 155–66; Holocaust victims not identified as Jews in Soviet press, 220, 222, 224; invasion of Finland, 3; Katyn massacre, 314–15n6; liberation of concentration camps, 233–35; liberation of Kiev, 228–29; and press tours, 94–95, 158–66, 220, 229–31; and propaganda, 221; Redkin's photos of liberated Kerch, 219–20; Roth's photos of Lwow, 164; Roth's photos of Soviet POWs, 148–49, 261; Steinkopf's reporting and photos of German invasion, 158–66. *See also* Holocaust
Spanish Civil War, 57–58, 143–44
Speck, Hugo, 178, 182
SS-War Correspondent Company (SS-Kriegsberichter Kompanie), 131
Stalin, Joseph, 95, 155, 156, 165, 199, 249
Stalingrad, 272

La Stampa (Italian newspaper), 192
Stark, J. C., 86
Steinberger, Christian Hugo and Emma, 44
Steinkopf, Alvin, 69–71, 179, 256; arrest and detention, 182, 186; background and career summary, 47; and beginning of WWII, 86; reporting and photographs from eastern front, 158–65; reporting and photographs from occupied Poland, 97–98; reporting and photos of Buchenwald, 235–36; and U.S. propaganda aimed at German population, 187
Steinweis, Alan E., 281n10
St. Joseph News-Press, 268
St. Louis Post-Dispatch, 230, 239
Storm Troopers. *See* Brownshirts
Stratton, Lloyd, 99, 137, 145, 259, 303n10
Streicher, Julius, 48
Sulzberger, Arthur, 72
Sweden: Pressens Bild and wartime photo exchange, 211–12

Tampa Sunday Tribune, 93
Tanner, Väinö, 3
TASS (Soviet news agency), 219, 224
Telegraphen-Union, 49
Thompson, Dorothy, 33
Thompson, Milo, 45
Thompson, Stanley, 67, 68, 140–41
Thuermer, Angus, 50, 179; arrest and detention, 182, 186; background and career summary, 48–49; and

invasion of Poland, 82–83; and invasion of Soviet Union, 159–60, 166; and Pearl Harbor attack, 175; and Steinkopf's dictation on eastern front, 159–60; and wartime news downplayed during World Series, 95–96; "We leave for the jug" message to Swiss bureau, 181
Time magazine, 1, 22, 33, 166, 176, 248
Tolischus, Otto, 114
Trading with the Enemy Act, xiii, 254–55, 260, 272
Transocean, 33, 183, 212, 267, 308n28
Treblinka death camp, 99, 221–22, 228, 233

UFS. *See* United Features Syndicate
Uhlfelder, Max, 25
Ukraine: Babi Yar execution site, 191, 222, 229–31, 316n35; fate of Jews in, 162, 191–92, 219–20, 223–24, 229–231; and Operation Barbarossa, 161–63; Redkin's photos of liberated Kerch, 219–220; Russia's invasion of, 270
United Features Syndicate (UFS), 314n3
United Press (UP), 32, 38, 284n33; arrest of correspondent Richard Hottelet, 33; and British bombing raids, 171–72; as disfavored by Nazis compared to other news agencies, 120; and Holocaust, 225, 234; and Kristallnacht, 14; and press tours, 103, 120; rival agencies, 119; staff at time of Pearl Harbor

attack, 179. *See also* Oechsner, Frederich

United States: anti-Semitism in, 19, 189–92, 241; early reporting on and photos of Holocaust sites, 221; entry into war, 117, 176–77, 179–80; government's knowledge about wartime photo exchange, 205–6; Holocaust reports downplayed in, 225–28; journalists and congressional leaders summoned to witness Holocaust evidence, 239–40; liberation of concentration camps, 235–38; Pearl Harbor attack, 175–76, 179; public's attitude toward Jews of Europe, 19, 240–41; public's knowledge about the Holocaust, 220–21, 227–28, 240–41, 273; skepticism about Holocaust reports and photos, 221, 223, 227; Trading with the Enemy Act, xiii, 254–55, 260, 272; wavering neutrality, 176–77

Der Untermensch (SS indoctrination handbook), 149

UP. *See* United Press

Vilnius, 164
vom Rath, Ernst, 16–17
von Haugwitz, Maria, 43

Waffen-SS: Baatz and, 258; Brandt and, 210, 258; d'Alquen and, 300n1; Laux and, 210–11, 244, 250–52; Roth and, 23, 139, 148–51

Waffen SS: Hitler's Army at War (Gilbert), 162
Wallbaum, Jost, 98
Wall Street Journal, 270
Walters, Eugene P., 250–52
Warsaw, 93, 94, 96–99, 222, 228
Washington Post, 38, 228
Washington Times, 26
Waugh, Evelyn, 142
Welles, Sumner, 227
Weltbild GmbH, 72, 198
Werner, Wade, 45, 51
What About Germany? (Lochner), 126, 245
Whiteleather, Melvin, 70; arrests, 13; background and career summary, 46–47; and pitfalls of atrocity reporting, 92; reporting from Brest-Litovsk, 94–95; reporting from Warsaw, 94; return to U.S., 97; on working under a dictatorship, 28
Why Didn't the Press Shout? (collected studies and essays), 240, 241
Wide World Photos, 72, 131
Wise, Stephen, 37, 227–28
Wolff, Bernhard, 50
Wolff Telegraphic Bureau, 50, 54
World War I, 226
World War II: Allied war policy not prioritizing saving Jews, 241; beginning of, 86–87; Blitzkrieg style of warfare, 101–12; British bombing raids, 167–68, 170–73; Cooper's views on, 39–40; final months, 243–62;

World War II (*continued*)
   German invasion of Poland, 81–99; German invasion of Soviet Union, 155–66; Pearl Harbor attack, 175–76, 179; Sitzkrieg (interlude between hostilities), 96–97, 102; U.S. entry into war, 117, 176–77, 179–80. *See also* Germany; Holocaust; Nazis; photographs

Yad Vashem, 234

Zygielbojm, Szmul, 225, 315n17

GPSR Authorized Representative: Easy Access System Europe, Mustamäe tee 50, 10621 Tallinn, Estonia, gpsr.requests@easproject.com